Vital Statistics on Congress
2008

Vital Statistics on Congress 2008

Norman J. Ornstein
Thomas E. Mann
Michael J. Malbin

Brookings Institution Press
Washington, D.C.

ABOUT BROOKINGS

The Brookings Institution is a private nonprofit organization devoted to research, education, and publication on important issues of domestic and foreign policy. Its principal purpose is to bring the highest quality independent research and analysis to bear on current and emerging policy problems. Interpretations or conclusions in Brookings publications should be understood to be solely those of the authors.

THE BROOKINGS INSTITUTION
1775 Massachusetts Avenue, N.W., Washington, D.C. 20036
www.brookings.edu

ISBN 978-0-8157-6665-0 (pbk.: alk. paper)
ISSN 0896-9469
Library of Congress No. 87659232

9 8 7 6 5 4 3 2 1

The paper used in this publication meets minimum requirements of the American National Standard for Information Sciences—Permanence of Paper for Printed Library Materials: ANSI Z39.48-1992.

Typeset in Berkeley Book

Composition by Circle Graphics
Columbia, Maryland

Printed by Versa Press
East Peoria, Illinois

Contents

List of Figures and Tables

Maps

Figures

Tables

Preface

Vital Statistics on Congress began in 1980 as a slender volume of statistics on the post–World War II Congress. Our purpose was to provide some perspective on our national legislature after two decades of extraordinary change—in the recruitment, election, and composition of its membership as well as in its formal rules, informal norms, party structure, staff, and internal distribution of power. This is the twelfth edition, emerging nearly thirty years later.

The volume has become richer and bulkier over time, and the text expanded with the number of Congresses covered. We changed the format, some with the last edition. But our goal has remained the same: to make *Vital Statistics on Congress* a standard reference in newsrooms, libraries, and classrooms around the country.

Many colleagues have contributed to the collective effort that makes possible the publication of this biennial volume. In the early years, John Bibby, Allen Schick, and Richard Fenno helped build a solid foundation. Scores of scholars and journalists have offered suggestions, corrections, and assistance, most recently Gary Jacobson and Charles Stewart. As is evident in the footnotes to the statistical tables, we have drawn heavily on the outstanding work of Congressional Quarterly, the Congressional Research Service, the Federal Election Commission, and other public and private sources of data. Perhaps most important of all, we have been blessed by a succession of talented and dedicated research assistants, from Nina Kerstiens Fitzgerald on the first two editions to Chris Trendler, Matt Weil, Timothy Ryan, and Molly Reynolds on this one, who have labored mightily to keep *Vital Statistics* current and accurate. We also thank a slew of interns and researchers who helped out this time: Marissa Armanino, Daniel Baglieter, Zachary Baron, Austin Broussard, Max Corey, Dane Davis, Andy Duberstein, Devin Finn, Brian Haghighi, Jamie Hester, Blake Hulnick, Anna Kielbratowska, Emily McClintock, Toby Merrill, Ellen Michaels, Meghan Monaghan, Daniel O'Brien, Nicole Pszczolkowski, Seth Rokosky, Aaron Rosenthal, Steven Snell, Jamie Stephens, Amit Upadhyay, Matthew Warring, Micha Weinblatt, and Yifei Zhang.

Introduction

Congress is, and always has been, a curious mix of continuity and change. Some things about Congress have changed very little over more than two centuries. Consider the observation of Thomas Jefferson in his autobiography in 1820: "If the present Congress err in too much talking, how can it be otherwise, in a body to which the people send 150 lawyers, whose trade is to question everything, yield nothing, and talk by the hour?"[1]

Change the number of lawyers from 150 to its present 221 (162 of them in the House) and the number of members of the body (from 186 and 46 in the 1820 House and Senate, respectively, to 435 and 100 now), and this observation could easily apply to the 110th Congress—as could many of the enduring elements of every legislative body and of every Congress as opposed to a parliament.[2] But in many other respects, the 110th Congress is dramatically different from the 16th Congress, of which Jefferson wrote.

The 16th Congress was a tiny village, rarely in session in Washington, and with few staff, few committees, and modest activity when it was. The modern Congress is a huge enterprise unto itself, with nearly 23,000 employees and a budget of nearly $4 billion and with a myriad of buildings and entities spread over a space the size of a small city. Each member of Congress is an enterprise unto himself or herself, with personal staffs averaging nearly seventeen per House member and forty per senator. Today's senators from California have more staff than did the entire Congress in 1820.

Imagine Jefferson's reaction if he were to witness the simple physical arrangements on today's Jenkins Hill, where the Capitol is located. The building itself is more imposing than it was in 1820 (when it was still recovering from the damage wrought by British soldiers in 1812). But the site of the mammoth underground Capitol Visitors Center, not to mention the string of huge office buildings surrounding the Capitol, and the tens of thousands of people in and around the complex, would leave him openmouthed. In Jefferson's time there were a handful of committees, with most actions and decisions taking place in the full House and Senate. Today there are hundreds of panels and hundreds of members who chair them and hundreds of staff to support them. Congress works year-round, even when the members are away, and is a beehive of activity even when it is formally adjourned or in recess.

On the other hand, Jefferson (or perhaps more significantly Madison) would recognize the core elements that have been present from the creation, elements built into Article I of the Constitution: bargaining, logrolling, and floor debate. The word *congress* means "coming together," and the U.S. Congress is indeed the coming together of representatives from diverse areas of the country, geographically and politically. Still, the way the system works is far different today than in 1790, much less 1820 or even 1990.

Vital Statistics on Congress tracks in quantitative terms the important elements that define and describe Congress, focusing particularly on the post–World War II era. One way to survey the changes in Congress over that era is to consider for illustration three points in time spanning that era: 1951, 1975, and 2007.

The 82nd Congress, 1951

Congress in 1951 reflected the political unsettledness of the country that began in the aftermath of World War II. The House of Representatives had been in the hands of the Democrats for sixteen consecutive years, the Senate for fourteen consecutive years, before they both switched to the Republicans in 1946. They both promptly switched back two years later, when Harry Truman won his stunning election victory. But in the midterm contests of 1950, the president's party (fitting with historical patterns) lost seats in both houses, leaving the party barely in control in the Senate (48 to 47, with 1 independent) and, after a loss of 30 seats in the House, with a margin of only 234 to 199 (with 2 independents.)

The close divisions in Congress reflected a transition in the political balance that continued through the next two elections: the GOP gained back both houses in 1952 with the Eisenhower landslide, albeit with razor-thin margins, then lost both in the midterms of 1954, also by narrow margins. That Republican loss began a string of forty consecutive years of Democratic rule in the House and twenty-six in the Senate, a lead solidified by huge Democratic gains in Eisenhower's second midterm in 1958.

The transition actually began with the 1946 election, which brought into Congress a raft of newly returned war veterans, some of whom would have a profound impact on national politics over the next several decades—John F. Kennedy, Richard M. Nixon, and Carl Albert among them. In 1946 the House saw thirty-two members retire, eighteen more lose in primaries, and fifty-two lose in the general election, an extraordinary rate of turnover. The Senate's turnover was even more striking: nine retirees, six defeated in primaries, and seven defeated in the general election, for a total of twenty-two new senators and a reelection rate for incumbents of only 56.7 percent.

The desire for change continued with the 1948 election, which brought 112 new members to the House (with a modern high of 68 defeated in the general election) and 18 new members to the Senate, including Lyndon Johnson, Hubert Humphrey, Paul Douglas, Russell Long, Robert Kerr, Clinton Anderson, and Estes Kefauver.

The 1950 election that shaped the 82nd Congress brought some abatement in the high rates of turnover. Only thirty-eight incumbents were defeated in House elections, six of them in primaries; there were twenty-nine retirees. The Senate saw five of its incumbents beaten in the general election, five beaten in primaries, and four retirements. But among the general election losers was Majority Leader Scott Lucas of Illinois, beaten by Everett McKinley Dirksen. His whip, Pennsylvania's Francis Myers, also lost, opening up the top two Senate majority leadership positions. A notable winner was Richard M. Nixon, who after only two terms in the House was able to fend off Democratic Representative Helen Gahagan Douglas. In the new Congress the Democrats named Ernest McFarland of Arizona as leader and quite stunningly installed first-termer Lyndon B. Johnson as whip. (Two years later, upon McFarland's defeat, Johnson became his party's Senate leader, albeit in the minority—but notably in his first term in the Senate.)

The 82nd Congress was in some respects more placid than its two predecessors. The 80th—the famous Do-Nothing Congress, labeled as such by Harry Truman—and the 81st were both at regular loggerheads with the president. Truman employed seventy-five vetoes against actions by the 80th Congress (six were overridden). In the 81st Congress, despite the fact that it was controlled by his fellow Democrats, Truman actually vetoed more bills (seventy-nine). By the 82nd Congress, relations were somewhat improved, and the president only employed twenty-two vetoes. But sharp partisan and ideological battles were not unknown in this Congress; it saw President Truman's removal of General of the Army Douglas MacArthur (and congressional hearings blasting the president for his action); a continuation of Joseph McCarthy's crusades against communist infiltration in the U.S. government, including high officials in the Truman administration; contention over the Korean War; and controversy over the president's seizure of the nation's steel mills.

A visitor to the galleries of the House and Senate in 1951 would have looked down on a membership quite characteristic of the immediate postwar Congresses. It was virtually all white (2 African Americans in the House, 1 Hispanic each in the House and Senate) and all male (10 women in the House, 1 in the Senate). Nearly 60 percent of the members of both houses were lawyers. In the House, members from the eleven states of the Old South had a plurality of seats (106). The Mid-Atlantic region, dominated by New York, had 88. California, with 43 seats, tied with New York for the most seats for a state. Pennsylvania had 30 seats, the Midwest 87.

The South at the time was overwhelmingly Democratic (see map 1). Democrats held 98 percent of the House seats and 100 percent of those in the Senate. Southern and border states made up over half of the Democrats' representation in Congress and dominated the committee chairmanships as well. That fact led William S. White, in his definitive 1956 treatment of the Senate, *Citadel*, to describe it as follows: "The place is, to most peculiar degree, a *Southern* institution engrafted upon, or growing in at the heart of, this ostensibly national assembly of the sages."[3] Republicans countered the Democratic dominance of the South with their own superiority in New England, the Midwest, the Great Plains, and the Pacific Coast. More than half of their House members came from the Midwest and Mid-Atlantic regions.

Map 1 Apportionment of House Seats by Party and Region (1951)

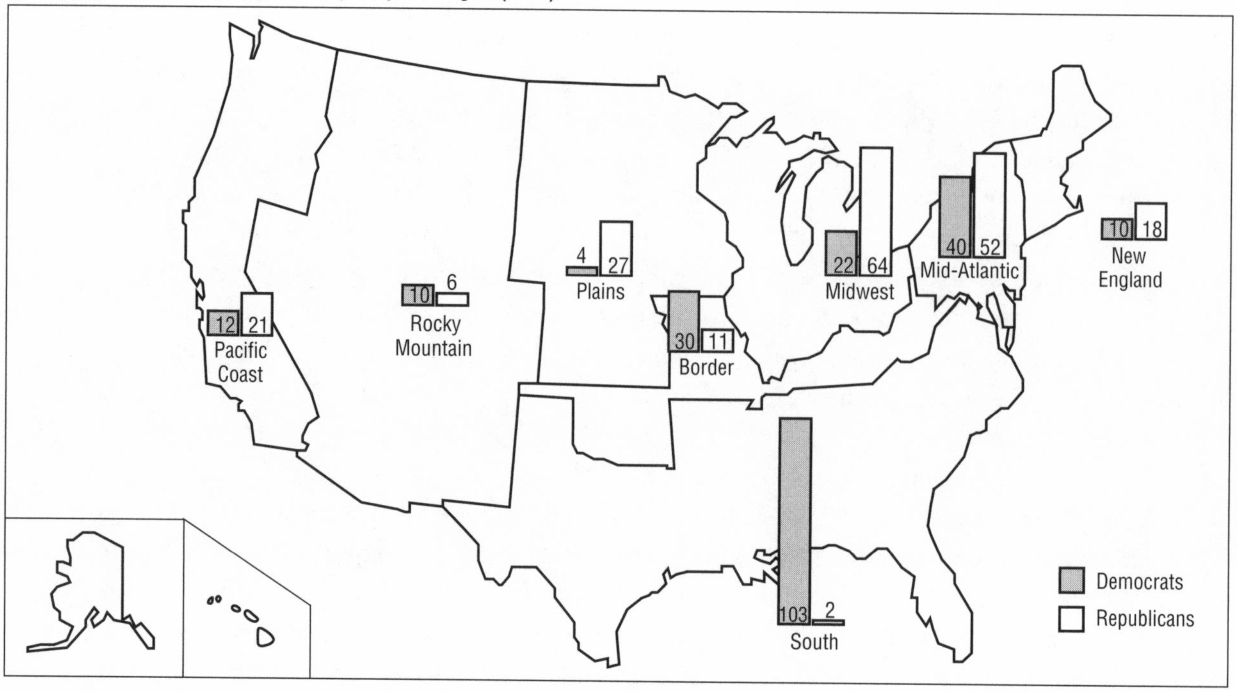

Due south of the Capitol were two office buildings, named for former Speakers Cannon (completed in 1908) and Longworth (begun in 1925 and completed in 1933), to accommodate members of the House of Representatives and their personal and committee staffs. The members each had about 3 or 4 staff members, for a total of around 1,600; the nineteen standing committees and their subcommittees had 246 employees (see figures 1 and 2). The Senate, on the north side of the Capitol, had one office building (occupied in 1909, enlarged three times, and named in 1972 for former Senator Richard Brevard Russell of Georgia) to house the ninety-six senators, their staffs (of about 700), and the employees (about 300) of the Senate's committees and subcommittees.

The dimensions of life in the 82nd Congress were described in a 1952 *Commentary* article by political scientist Stephen K. Bailey and Howard Samuel, "A Day in the Life of a Senator," describing the congressional office and activities of New York Senator Herbert H. Lehman on a day in mid-August 1951. Keep in mind that this is a description not of the average senator but of a senator from the largest state in the nation and, therefore, with more of everything—more staff, more visibility, more responsibilities:

> The offices of Senator Herbert H. Lehman of New York are located in seven rooms, in four buildings, in two cities. In New York City, at 41 East 57th Street, three people work for him full time, handling his relations with individual constituents. In Washington, D.C., a woman works for the Senator in an office in the Library of Congress, devoting most of her time to requests for private bills. In the Capitol, in a tiny, narrow room formed by a partition cutting off the end of a corridor, three research assistants prepare data, speeches, and testimony for him. Eleven people in the basement of the Senate Office Building process

Figure 1 Staff, House and Senate Members, 1891–2005

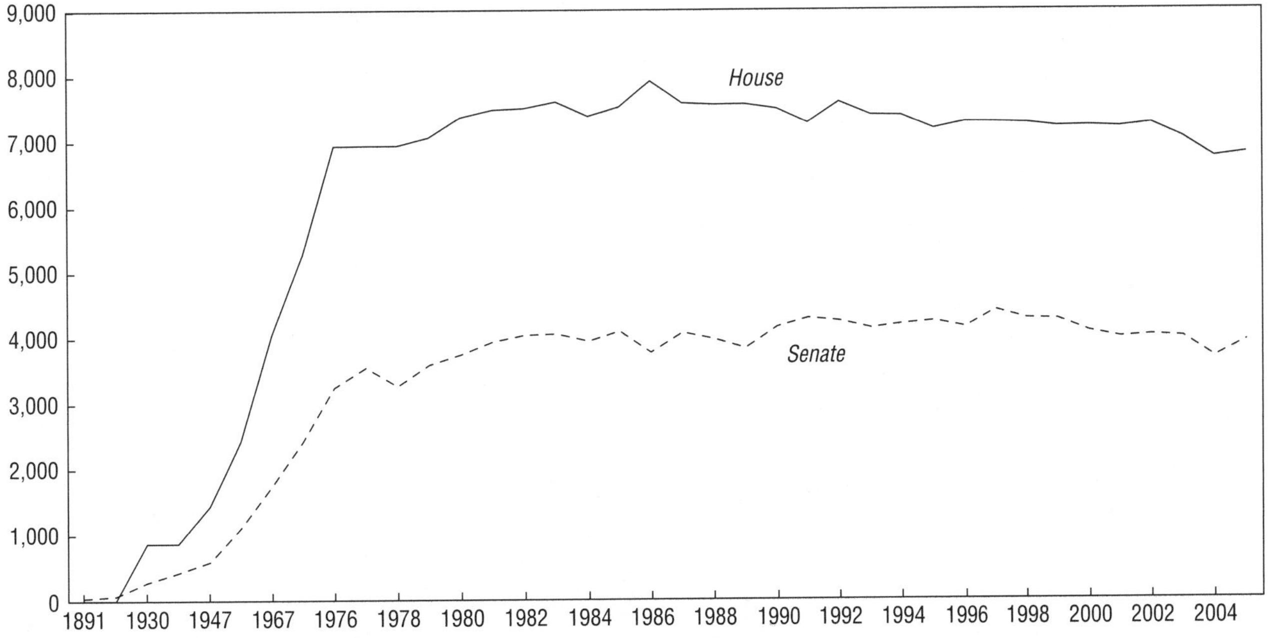

the Senator's mail and expedite requests from his constituents. And, on the fourth floor of the Senate Office Building, in a suite of three rooms, ten more staff assistants work for Mr. Lehman, including the executive secretary and administrative assistant—and the Senator himself.

To pay his staff assistants, Senator Lehman, whose own official salary is $12,500 annually plus a $2,500 tax-free, non-accountable expense fund, was allowed approximately $65,000 a year of federal funds . . . sufficient to pay for the services of about twelve assistants and secretaries, which is about the size of the staffs of most Senators. Senator Lehman, however, has found it necessary to hire sixteen more assistants and secretaries, whom he pays out of his own pocket, so that his total staff numbers twenty-eight people.[4]

Figure 2 Staff, House and Senate Standing Committees, 1891–2005

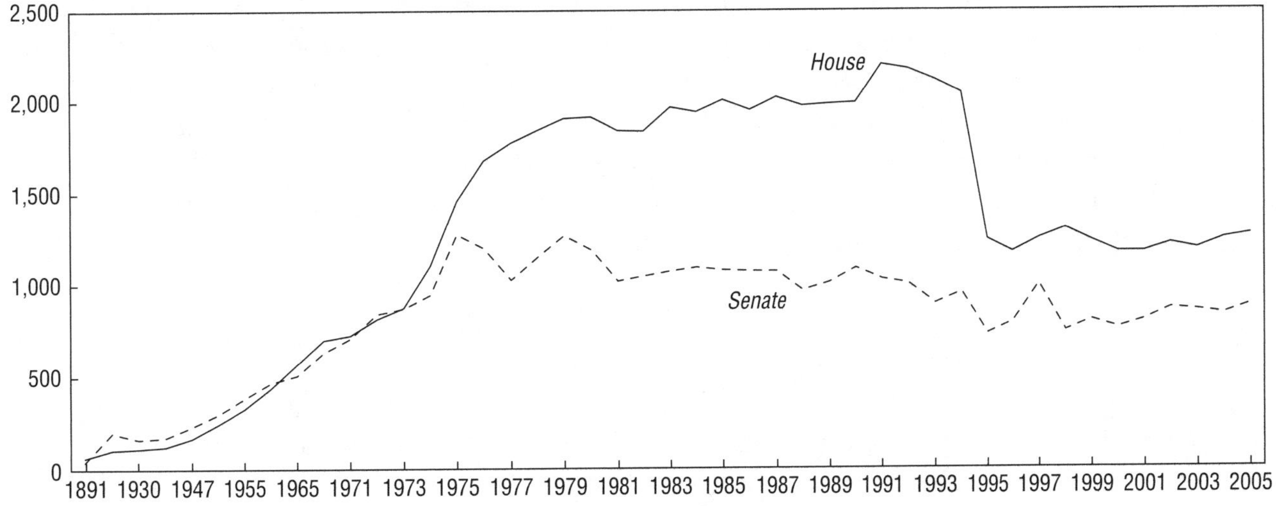

Figure 3 Bills Introduced and Passed, House and Senate, 1947–2006

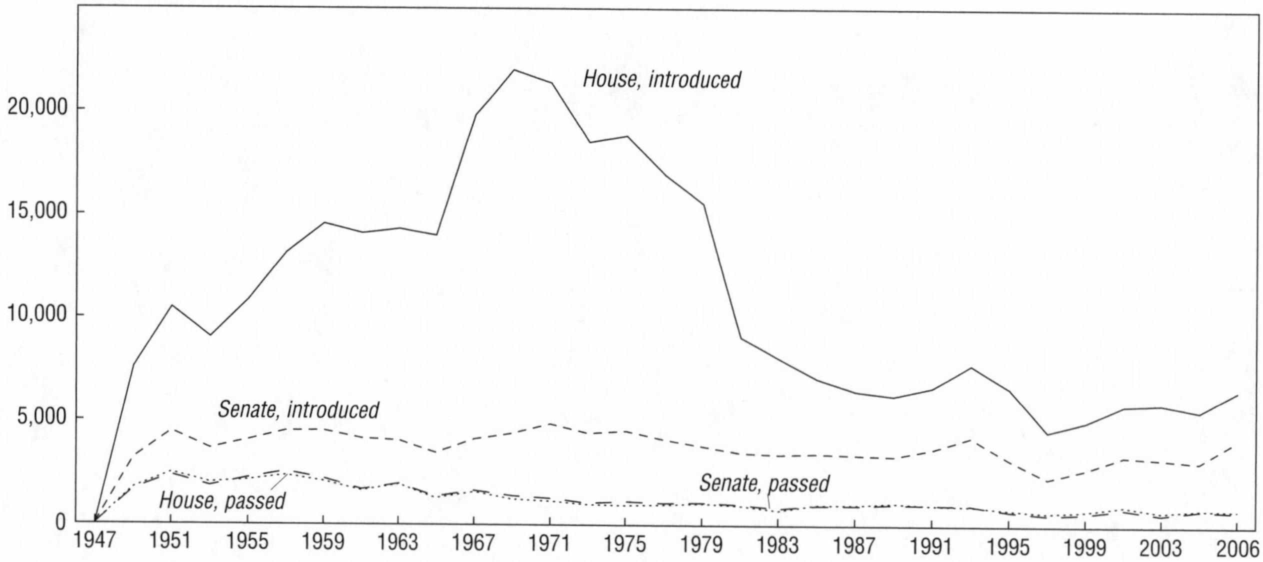

Harry McPherson, who came to the Senate a few years later to serve as the legislative assistant to Leader Lyndon Johnson, describes the committee staff culture in the Senate in his memoir *A Political Education*: "Senator Byrd of Virginia, whose ideas of economy reflected those of an eighteenth-century shopkeeper, allowed the Finance Committee a single professional staff member. Senator Russell had not many more on Armed Services, though they were competent and knowledgeable."[5] Not all committee staffs were so tiny: the Senate Judiciary Committee, for example, had a staff of close to a hundred, with professionals available to each chair of a subcommittee. Appropriations for Congress in 1951, nearly $72 million, were up 11.8 percent over those of the previous year. It took another six years for the legislative branch to hit the symbolic $100 million threshold.

With the notable exception of the televised Kefauver Senate hearings on organized crime, the 82nd Congress did not focus much on domestic affairs, instead concentrating on controversies in the international arena. In the House, 9,065 bills were introduced and 2,008 were passed (see figure 3)—fewer than its immediate predecessor (10,502 and 2,482, respectively) but more than the Do-Nothing 80th Congress (7,611 and 1,739). The House had 181 recorded votes, again fewer than the 81st, more than the 80th. The 82nd Senate saw 3,665 bills introduced, 1,849 bills passed, and 331 roll call votes, with similar patterns to the House in relationship to preceding congresses.

For the 82nd Congress as a whole, 594 public bills were enacted, with an average of 2.7 pages per statute, along with 1,023 private bills (see figure 4). The output was less than either of the preceding two congresses, which enacted 2,314 and 2,236 public bills, respectively. And in the era before civil rights battles, the 82nd Senate had no filibusters and consequently no cloture votes. Much of the legislative work of both bodies was done by consensus, in the Senate via a process termed a *Calendar Call*. As Harry McPherson describes it:

Figure 4 Public and Private Bills, Number Enacted and Total Pages, 1947–2006

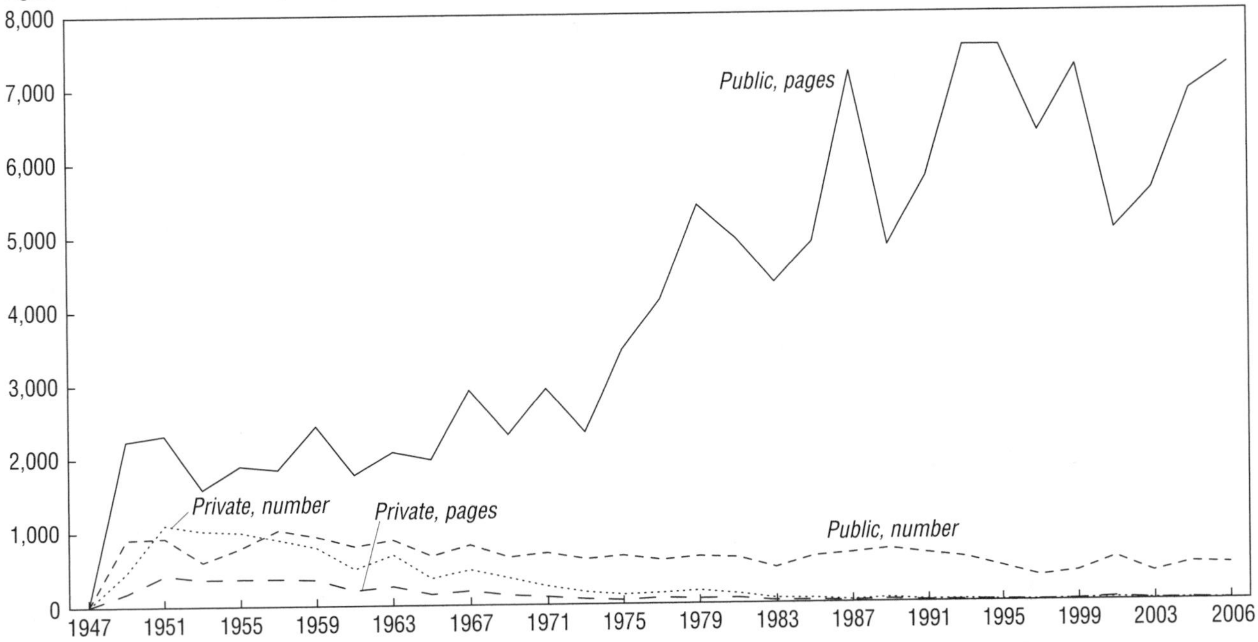

> A thin, dark-eyed clerk read off the number and title of every bill—there were sometimes hundreds of them—with a machine-gun rapidity that was interrupted occasionally by a senatorial shout of "Over!" If there was no interruption, the bill passed, by unanimous consent. "Over!" meant that the bill remained on the Calendar.
>
> In this way, the bulk of the Senate's work was done, at least in numbers of bills passed. Immigration bills, private claim bills, minor statutory amendments, and sometimes even significant legislation which, for one reason or another, senators did not choose to debate passed the Senate on Calendar Call and made their way to the House or the President.[6]

McPherson uses the calendar call process to reflect on a broader characteristic of the Senate of that era, namely, the cordiality and goodwill that permeated the Senate "club." He describes the easy working relationship between two ideological polar opposites, Senators Herman Talmadge and Joe Clark, noting that "understanding and accommodation in the ordinary course of the Senate day was essential to sanity."[7]

That kind of easy working relationship was less prevalent in the larger and more impersonal House of Representatives. Despite the junior status of the body—half the members of the House were in their first three terms—the House at the beginning of the 1950s operated with a clear hierarchy of privilege and initiative, with committee chairs, all determined through seniority, being the most dominant figures, along with the veteran and legendary Speaker of the House, Sam Rayburn. Rayburn met with the freshmen members at the beginning of each Congress and told them, "Don't try to go too fast. . . . Learn your job. Don't ever talk until you know what you are talking about. . . . If you want to get along, go along."[8]

That norm, called "apprenticeship" by political scientist Donald S. Matthews, also applied to the Senate, but its limits there were underscored by the rapid ascendance of Lyndon B. Johnson to a leadership post. As for the leaders in the Senate, the body was in transition. Ernest McFarland was in his first and only term as majority leader and was not particularly strong. Lyndon Johnson, as Senate whip, was hampered by his junior status but buoyed by his close relationship with Richard Russell. In this position he learned the techniques that made him a dominant leader in the Senate for the next eight years, starting in the minority in 1953 and moving to the majority two years hence.

In all, the system that operated in the 82nd Congress—and all the congresses of the 1950s—was a closed system, highly hierarchical, dominated (especially in the House) by seniority, and with most of the incentive structure focused on internal rewards and punishments.

Campaigns to elect Congress in the 1950s had just begun to use modern telecommunications like radio and television, adding to the costs of those campaigns. Some spending on campaigns was disclosed in reports filed with the House and Senate. In the 1950 campaign for Congress, *Congressional Quarterly* estimated total spending at about $10 million.[9] The number dropped to $5.6 million in 1952, as party committees channeled their money into the presidential contest. In the 1952 races, House candidates spent $1.9 million, an average of about $2,200 each. Senate candidates spent $723,000, or an average of about $11,000 each. The Republican House and Senate campaign committees spent an additional $2.5 million; the Democratic Party committees, an additional $103,000. Labor groups reported spending $352,000.

The five most expensive Senate races spent between $44,000 and $137,000, the latter being the Washington State race, with Democrat Henry M. Jackson taking on Republican Harry P. Cain. The most expensive House race was Maryland's Fifth District, with total spending of $33,000; the tenth most expensive, Montana's First District, reported totals of $13,756.74.

The 94th Congress, 1975

Imagine a modern-era Rip Van Winkle who visited the 82nd Congress in 1951, then went to sleep for a quarter of a century, awakening in Washington in 1975. As that visitor made his way around Capitol Hill, what would seem familiar, what alien, surprising, or incomprehensible? For one thing, Mr. Van Winkle would see few familiar faces. Only thirty members of the 94th House and eight members of the 94th Senate had been around during the 82nd sessions. In fact, the interim period had seen several waves of substantial turnover. In 1958, the sixth year of Dwight Eisenhower's presidency, Republicans lost forty-nine seats in the House and fifteen in the Senate. The following year seventy-three new members entered the House, including thirty-three who had defeated incumbents in the general election. That same year sixteen new members joined the Senate; ten of them had ousted incumbents. In 1964 President Lyndon Johnson's landslide election brought a net gain of thirty-seven Democrats to the House and one to the Senate. The following year eighty-six new members entered the House, forty-five having beaten incumbents in the fall; seven new senators joined them.

In 1966—LBJ's midterm election and the sixth year of Democratic presidents—Democrats lost forty-seven seats in the House and four in the Senate. There were seventy-one new House members and seven new senators, but Democrats held on to their majorities in both houses. In 1974, the election that brought in the 94th Congress, the Watergate scandal created a Democratic tide: Republicans lost forty-eight seats in the House and five in the Senate. Of the ninety-one new House members, seventy-four were Democrats (thirty-six of them defeated incumbent Republicans). The Senate had a freshman class of eleven.

The class of 1974 included a raft of political figures who helped shape American politics and policy for decades to follow. The House class included Max Baucus, Chris Dodd, Paul Simon, Paul Tsongas, Charles Grassley, and Tim Wirth, all of whom went on to distinguished careers in the Senate; James Florio, who subsequently became governor of New Jersey; Norm Mineta, whose productive House career was followed by stints as a cabinet member for two presidents; and Tom Downey, George Miller, Martin Russo, Phil Sharp, Henry Waxman, Bill Gradison, Henry Hyde, and Stephen Solarz, all of whom made a mark in the House and in public policy. The 1974 Senate class included John Glenn, Gary Hart, Dale Bumpers, and Patrick Leahy.

These new members were different in both their culture and their outlook from those who had gone before. More than a decade after their arrival on Capitol Hill, Chris Matthews characterizes the class of 1974 this way: "The American electorate sent a 'new breed' of legislator to Washington: young, brash, independent of its elders and their system. It was the year of Watergate." Matthews describes them as "a slate of fresh-faced candidates pledged to a new order of ethics and independence."[10] They also reflected some changes in demographics: the House now had nineteen women, still only 4.4 percent but enough of a change over a quarter of a century (from ten) to be noticed. Even more striking, after redistricting designed to create majority-minority districts, the number of African Americans rose from two to sixteen and the number of Hispanics from one to five.

In the 1950s and 1960s Congress had become more senior in experience than before. But with the several election waves discussed above, by 1975 Congress had returned to a pattern more like the immediate postwar years, with half of House members being in their first six years of service. Further, the average age of House members was younger. (The Senate's shift to more juniority lagged by a couple of Congresses, peaking in 1981, when fifty-five of its members were in their first term.)

The 94th Congress was characterized by two important elements: a major wave of congressional reform at its beginning and conflict from start to finish between the Democratic majorities in the House and Senate and the Republican president, Gerald R. Ford. Both the reform and the conflict were triggered in major part by Ford's pardon of Richard Nixon, which also accounted for the Democratic gains in Congress (a two-to-one advantage over Republicans in the House and a better than three-to-two margin in the Senate).

Reform in Congress had actually begun six years earlier. Spurred by growing tension among majority Democrats over America's role in Vietnam, a part of a broader tension between southern conservative Democrats and northern liberals, many of them products of the classes of 1958 and 1964, the reform movement tried to spread power and resources away

Map 2 Apportionment of House Seats by Party and Region (1976)

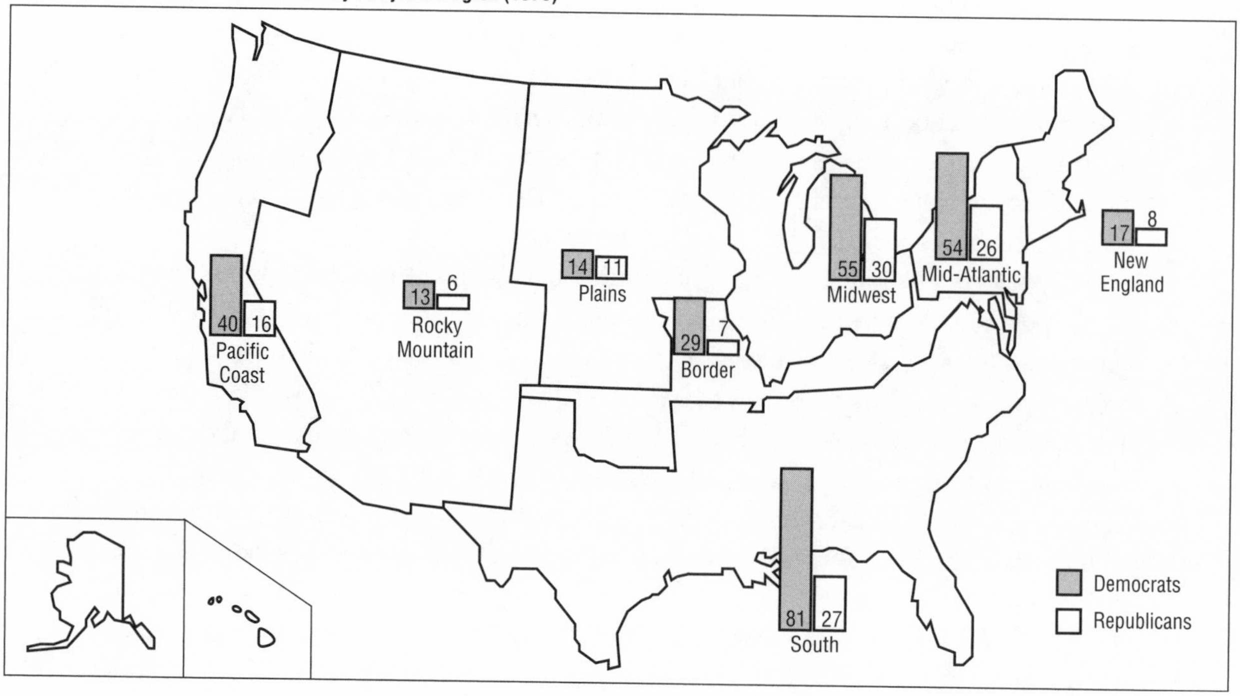

from committee chairs and party leaders toward rank-and-file members. The ideological differences between these groups of Democrats had been present for many decades, but they reached a critical mass in the late 1960s and early 1970s as membership in Congress changed.

Remember that throughout the 1950s southerners dominated the Democratic caucus, joining with border-state members to make up more than half the caucus while maintaining a near-stranglehold on committee chairmanships by virtue of their seniority. In 1955, for example, southerners made up 42 percent of the majority party and held 63 percent of committee chairmanships. From 1964 on, the Democratic dominance of the South declined—but a sizable number of very senior southerners stayed, continuing to dominate chairmanships. By 1967 the southern share of membership had declined to 35 percent (see map 2), while southerners constituted 50 percent of the chairmanships—and 100 percent of the chairs of the three exclusive (and most powerful) committees: Rules, Ways and Means, and Appropriations.

As nonsouthern members saw their proportions rise relative to the southerners, they became more frustrated by the disparities between their numbers and their power—a frustration exacerbated by the tendency among southern Democrats (particularly the most senior and powerful) to support America's involvement in Vietnam and the opposite tendency among nonsoutherners. These conflicts peaked when Richard Nixon became president in 1969, thus pitting nonsouthern Democrats against a Republican president and a coalition of Republicans and southern Democrats.

The reform movement had succeeded with small steps in early 1969 and 1971 in the organization of the 91st and 92nd Congresses, respectively, gaining individual secret ballot votes in the majority caucus on committee chairmanships, guarantees of separate committee caucus votes to select subcommittee chairs, staff resources and agenda-setting powers for subcommittee chairs, and recorded votes on amendments on the House floor.

Bolstered by the addition of seventy-five new members in 1974, the reformers were able to expand their gains sharply in early 1975. New reforms made separate, secret ballot votes on committee chairs not just available but also automatic—and three senior chairmen were then ousted and replaced by less senior members. The power to make committee assignments (and recommend chairmanships) was taken away from the Democratic members of the Ways and Means Committee and given to the party leaders. The best subcommittee slots were given to more junior members, and previously closed conference committees and other committee sessions were opened to the public. Democratization and decentralization were the order of the day.

The results of the reforms were reflected in the vital statistics of the 94th Congress. Power was decentralized, and power centers were expanded to bring in more of the junior members. The number of standing subcommittees in the House went up by 25 percent, to 151. (The number went up in the Senate as well, by more than 10 percent.) The average number of committee and subcommittee assignments for House members went from 5.1 in the 92nd Congress to 6.2 in the 94th. The number of House members chairing committees or subcommittees rose from 131 in 1972 to 150 in 1975. Chairs of the exclusive committees, held 100 percent by southern Democrats in the late 1960s and early 1970s, dropped to 33 percent in 1975. And the number of closed House and Senate meetings dropped from 707 in 1974 (15 percent of the total), to 449 in 1975 (7 percent of the total), to near zero in 1976.

The congressional establishment and bureaucracy also grew sharply. In 1947, the first postwar Congress, the House employed 1,441 staffers, or 3.3 per lawmaker; the Senate employed 590, just over 6 per member (figure 1). In the 94th Congress, the House members' staff totaled 6,939, or 16 per member; the Senate, 3,251, or 32.5 per member. In other words, there was a fivefold increase over thirty years, with a 30 percent increase over the four years between the 92nd and 94th Congresses.

Rip Van Winkle would have noted several new office buildings, built to accommodate some of these employees and panels. The Senate's second building, across the street from its first, is named the Dirksen Senate Office Building (for Everett McKinley Dirksen); it was completed in 1958. A third building, connected to Dirksen, was begun in 1975 during the 94th Congress and completed seven years later; it was named for Senator Philip Hart of Michigan. As for the House, a third office building, west of the other two and named for Sam Rayburn, was begun in 1962 and finished in 1965. At 2,375,000 square feet, it was more than twice the size of the other two House office buildings combined.

One of the elements of reform in the House was to extend committee resources from committee chairs to subcommittee leaders. As a result, committee staffs grew sharply (figure 2). In 1950 House committees employed 246 staff; Senate committees, 300. By 1970 staffs had grown to 702 and 635, respectively. In 1974 they numbered 1,107 and 948. One year later, after passage of the Subcommittee Bill of Rights in the majority caucus, the numbers grew to 1,460 and 1,277—again, a 30 percent increase in just one year.

Not surprisingly, Congress's workload also changed in reaction to these congressional dynamics. One reform in the House required recorded votes on amendments that previously had been tallied by voice vote or by tellers (representatives of the Speaker counting the votes of members in aggregate without recording the votes of individuals). This reform was implemented in the 92nd Congress. Recorded votes in the 1950s averaged about 175 per Congress. In the 1960s they grew to an average of around 300. For the 92nd Congress, in 1971–72, the number of roll calls was 649. That number ballooned to 1,078 in the 93rd and to 1,273 in the 94th. The number of committee and subcommittee meetings also grew sharply, from 5,114 in the 92nd Congress to 6,975 in the 94th. The increases were not simply reflections of reform; they were also a result of the increased legislative activism of members and the wider number of younger and more active lawmakers chairing committees and subcommittees. Thus the Senate, without comparable reforms, also saw increases in votes and meetings, even though not nearly as great as the House in percentage terms.

All of this additional activity might lead one to expect an equivalent increase in output—that is, in the number of bills and laws. Not so. In the 82nd Congress the House of Representatives passed 2,008 bills of 9,065 introduced (an average of 20.8 per member), with a ratio of bills passed to bills introduced of .222. (The 82nd Senate passed 1,849 bills of 3,665 introduced, a ratio of .505.) In the 94th House the number of bills passed was 968 of 16,982 introduced (figure 3). The number of bills introduced went up gradually from the mid-1950s on, peaking at just over 22,000 in 1967–68, then declining gradually to its 94th Congress level, which was still nearly double that of the 82nd.

But more bills introduced, along with more hearings held and more activity generally, combined with the decentralization in power and authority that characterized the reform era, made it harder to get the bills through the legislative labyrinth. So the House ratio of bills passed to bills introduced went down to .057, only one quarter of that in the earlier era. Even in the Senate, without the same array of reforms, the ratio of bills passed to bills introduced was cut in half over the twenty-five years, to .252.

Bills passed by one or the other house of Congress do not necessarily get any further. So another, and more significant, indicator of action is bills enacted into law. In the 1950s the average number of bills enacted by each Congress was 828; the 82nd Congress, characterized by a low level of legislative activity, saw 594 bills enacted, well below the average and the lowest number by far for the decade. In the 1970s the average number of bills enacted was 618; the number for the 94th "reform" Congress was 588 (figure 4). But as the number of bills enacted declined, the average length of each law, in pages, increased commensurately. In 1951–52 the average length of statutes was less than three pages. In 1975–76 the average length grew to seven pages. If the number of bills was not huge in comparison to the past, it did not stop President Ford from vetoing a large number of the bills that did get sent to him: Ford vetoed thirty-seven bills (eight of them were overridden). The House attempted to override seventeen of the vetoes, the Senate fifteen—many more attempts than any previous Congress, reflecting this Congress's tenacity and pugnacity.

A more active Congress passed fewer but longer laws and also built in far more regulatory requirements. In the 1950s the *Federal Register* ranged from 10,000 to 15,000 pages a year. In the 1970s its pages ranged from 25,000 to 77,000 a year, averaging over 50,000.

Congressional reforms of the early 1970s also affected the campaign finance system. Beginning with the 1972 elections, disclosure requirements opened up systematic information about congressional campaign funding and spending. In the election that brought in the 94th Congress, House candidates raised $45.7 million, 58 percent of it coming from individual contributions of less than $500. Senate candidates raised $28.2 million, 49 percent of it in individual contributions of less than $500. House candidates spent $44 million on their campaigns, an average of $54,384 per candidate. Senate candidates spent $28.4 million, an average of $437,000 per candidate. These numbers—up 15–20 percent from the 1972 congressional races—signaled a trend toward increased campaign fund-raising and spending, which continued throughout the decade.

The numbers for the 1974 congressional elections suggest several things about the dynamics of the elections. In general, incumbents spend much more than challengers. The 218 incumbent Democrats who ran for reelection spent an average of $38,743. The 161 Republican challengers to those incumbents (57 were uncontested) spent an average of little more than half that amount, or $20,644. The 163 incumbent Republicans who ran spent an average of $80,339; their Democratic challengers spent on average 25 percent less, or $59,266.

But in the races in which incumbents were defeated, the numbers are entirely different. Democratic incumbents spent an average of $64,191, much more than the overall average; the Republican challengers who beat them averaged $71,404, outspending them by a small margin. The figures for races in which Republican incumbents were defeated are just as striking. Incumbent spending averaged $105,203, while their successful challengers spent nearly the same, $103,661. The key difference appears to be the amount spent by the challengers, not that of the incumbents.

The 110th Congress, 2007

Rip van Winkle, awakening on Capitol Hill in 2007—after a sleep of thirty-two years—would not be especially amazed at its physical growth. The large complex of the Capitol itself, the House and Senate halves of the broader area called Capitol Hill, is different from 1975 but not dramatically so. The million-plus-square-foot Hart Senate Office Building, whose groundbreaking occurred during the 94th Congress, is open for business. Other buildings in the Capitol area have either been razed for parking lots (as with one hotel near the Senate) or converted for House office use (as with another hotel near the House).

Another element, though, would be striking to Rip: the extraordinary security surrounding the Capitol, which began after September 11, 2001. In 1975 a visitor could drive right up to the Capitol Building (though only members, staff, reporters, and some special visitors could park on the lot that filled much of the area off the East Front) and then walk straight inside. Now, concrete barriers, security devices inside and outside the building, and a much more robust and visible Capitol police force have changed the culture and appearance of Congress. Except for a few more braces to support the sagging parts of the Capitol, the majestic building itself is largely the same.

But a visitor to the gallery would see some significant changes in the membership of Congress. The 110th House has seventy-one women, about 16 percent of the body—still small compared to the 51 percent representation in the population but sharply higher from the nineteen women in 1975. Furthermore, the Speaker of the House is a woman, a historical first. The Senate is up to sixteen women, whereas there were none in 1975.

Representation of other minorities has also strikingly changed, but only in the House. The 82nd Congress had two African Americans in the House and none in the Senate; the 94th had sixteen in the House and one in the Senate. The 110th Congress has forty-one African Americans—with one, Barack Obama of Illinois, in the Senate. The 82nd Congress had one Hispanic American each in the House and Senate; the 94th had five in the House and one in the Senate. The 110th Congress has twenty-three Hispanics in the House and three in the Senate. Mr. Van Winkle would recognize few figures from his visit in 1975. Only seven senators remain from that era, along with only twelve representatives—in other words, 93 percent of the Senate and 97 percent of the House have changed over the thirty-two years.

Lawyers (as noted by Mr. Jefferson) remain important but much less so than in the 1950s or 1970s. Nearly 60 percent of the 83rd House (247 members) were lawyers; in the 94th, they were down to just over 50 percent (221). But when the 110th Congress convened, only 37 percent were lawyers. The Senate, however, remains a bastion of attorneys: 59 senators were lawyers in 1953, 67 in 1975, and again 59 in 2007.

Rip would also notice the continued decline of the South as a linchpin of the congressional Democratic Party—and would soon surmise that the dramatic regional changes in American politics that erased the Democrats' base and made it that of the Republicans contributed mightily to the change in majority in 1994. Democrats, who won 98 percent of southern House seats and 100 percent of southern Senate seats from the 1930s through the 1950s, had dropped to two-thirds of these seats by the early 1970s. After the 2006 elections, Democrats retained only 41.2 percent of southern House seats and 22.7 percent of southern Senate seats. In the 1950s Democrats from southern and border states made up over half the Democratic representation in both houses. By the 1970s such Democrats were only 40 percent of the congressional Democratic Party, and in 2007 were but 29 percent of House Democrats and only 20 percent of Senate Democrats (see map 3). Since these Democrats tend to be ideologically conservative, these changes also reflect the growing ideological homogenization (that is, liberalization) of the Democratic Party in Congress. The single largest growth area for congressional Democrats is the Pacific Coast, where their House representation grew from 5 percent or so in the 1950s to 14 percent in the early 1970s, to 20 percent in 2007.

Not surprisingly, the Republicans have a different history, in part the mirror opposite. In the 1950s the Mid-Atlantic and Midwest regions dominated the Republican Party in the House, representing 40–45 percent of the seats. In the Senate, New England and the Great Plains together held 40–45 percent of Republican seats. By the 1970s the Mid-Atlantic and the Midwest were down to 30–35 percent of the House GOP. New England and the Plains states were down to 25 percent of the Senate Republicans by the 1970s and to 20 percent by 2007. In the 1950s representation from southern and border states was minuscule for congressional Republicans. It was up to 20–30 percent in the early 1970s. These states were up

Map 3 Apportionment of House Seats by Party and Region (2001)

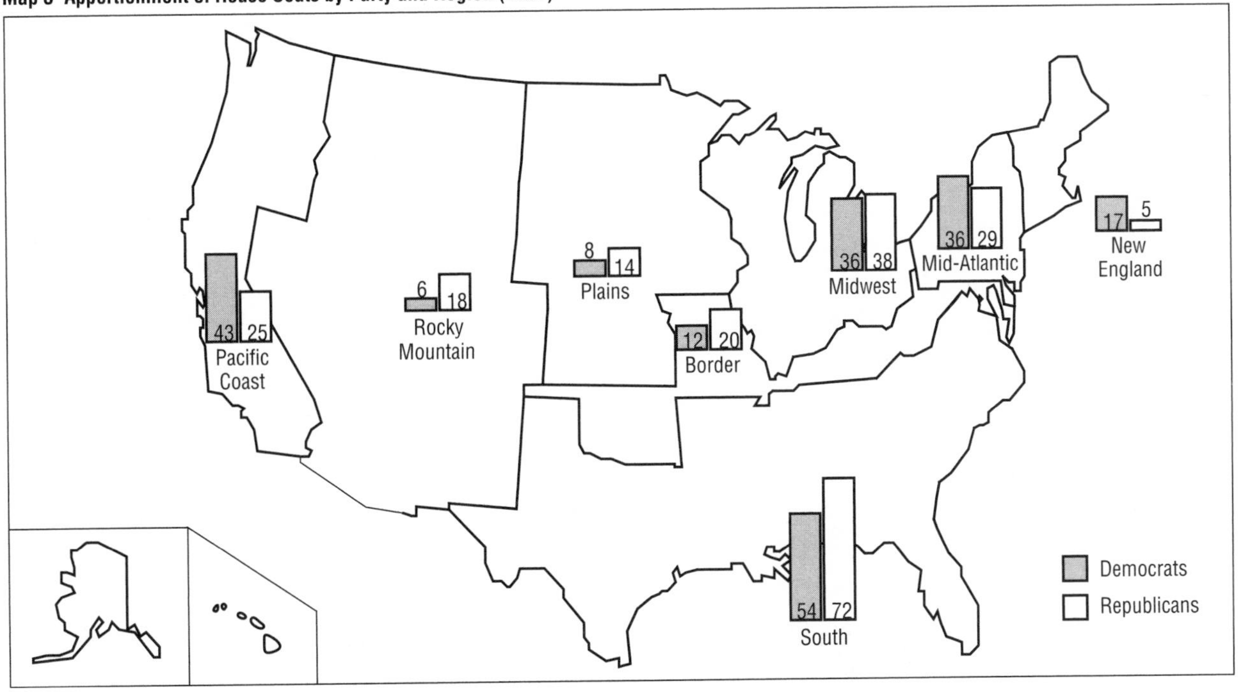

to roughly 45 percent of Republican representation in 2007, higher than any other region or combination of regions.

More generally, the 110th Congress is noteworthy because of the closeness of its partisan margin, a distinct contrast to the many years of lopsided Democratic majorities before the 1994 elections. For the first time in forty years, the Republicans took the House in a landslide, but their slender majority was reduced further in each of the three subsequent elections.

When the Republicans took the majority in 1994, not one Republican lawmaker had been in Congress the last time the GOP had been in charge, and not one had ever been in the majority in the House as a Republican. On the other side, only one Democrat, Sidney Yates of Illinois, had been in the minority in the House before. Extended, seemingly perpetual, minority status had led to growing frustration on the part of Republicans and growing complacency and insensitivity on the part of Democrats.

Frictions between the parties were not just related to majority or minority status, however; they also reflected long-term trends in ideology. From the mid-1960s on, the proportion of political moderates or centrists in each chamber of Congress began to decline, as those at both ideological ends increased in number (see figure 5). Democrats moved left, Republicans moved right, and any overlap between the parties shrank. Ideological polarization became the order of the day.[11]

In the first months of their majority, House Republicans made revolutionary changes in the House and in the way it operates. They passed a series of reforms as a part of their Contract with America, including centralizing the administration of the House under majority control, banning proxy voting in committee, and mandating that laws affecting the private

Figure 5 Ideological Positions, House Party Coalitions, 1947–2004[a]

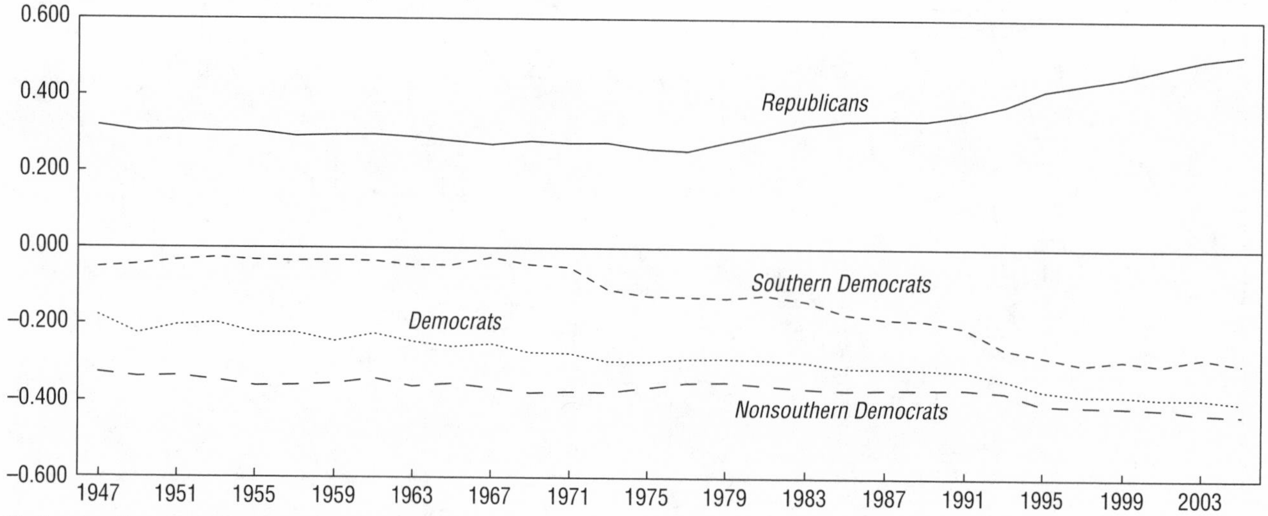

[a]Ideological position measured by mean DW-nominate score.

sector, such as worker safety requirements, would also apply to Congress. The new Speaker of the House, Newt Gingrich, accumulated power comparable to that of Speaker Cannon more than eight decades earlier, including command of committee assignments and chairmanships. Gingrich became the most visible congressional figure at least since Speaker Sam Rayburn.

After a remarkable initial flurry of legislative action, however, the 104th Congress settled into the more typical pattern of fits and starts, in part because of the slowness of the Senate; the Speaker's stranglehold over power and initiative in the House waned, even as criticism by his Republican colleagues increased. The criticism increased after the 1996 election, despite the Republicans' success in holding their House majority; in the summer of 1997 other House Republican leaders participated in an attempt to oust Gingrich—widely called a coup attempt—resulting in the departure from the leadership of at least one member. Gingrich stayed in his post, but after the 1998 election he announced his resignation at the conclusion of the 106th Congress, in the midst of a challenge from Louisiana Republican Representative Bob Livingston. But in December, as the 105th House considered the impeachment of President Clinton on the House floor, Livingston announced that he too would resign before assuming the speakership, amid rumors of extramarital affairs. Stunned Republican lawmakers chose Dennis Hastert of Illinois, the chief deputy whip, as their next Speaker.

The turmoil in Congress was exacerbated by congressional Republicans' impeachment and attempted removal of President Clinton. The president escaped removal after a trial in the Senate, and he finished out his term. As the 2000 elections approached the tension among political professionals was especially high, because the stakes were remarkably high—the open contest for the presidency was close, fluid, and unpredictable, and the majorities in both houses of Congress seemed clearly up for grabs.

The presidential contest ended up (thirty-six days late) with arguably the closest and most controversial outcome in American history. Republicans managed to hold on to their majorities in both houses in the 2000 elections, although losses in both houses left the GOP with a miniscule margin of five seats in the House and with a tie in the Senate, broken by the Republican Vice President Dick Cheney. Within weeks, the defection of one Republican senator, Jim Jeffords of Vermont, to independent status shifted the Senate majority, including its leadership and committee and subcommittee chairs, back to the Democrats. This only underscored the precariousness of majority status with two equally matched parties in Washington. The Republicans recaptured the majority in the Senate (by one) in the 2002 elections, while the House Republicans held on and even slightly extended their margins; the 2004 contests saw Republican majorities bolstered even more.

For the first time since 1954 Republicans held all the reins of power in Washington, and many elements of congressional behavior showed it. Republicans were remarkably unified, especially in the House, in support of the president. He returned the favor by going through his entire first term and more than a year into his second without vetoing a single bill, surpassing the record of President John Quincy Adams.

Inside the 110th Congress, Rip Van Winkle would see a number of both similarities and differences between it and the 94th Congress of thirty-two years earlier.

Consider committees. The number of committees and subcommittees peaked in both houses at the reform era apogee of 1975–76. Beginning with Senate reforms in 1976, these numbers began to decline. In the 94th Congress the Senate had 205 panels; the House, 204. By the 110th the Senate had only 96 and the House 126. The latter numbers are largely unchanged from the previous six Congresses. The decline came basically among subcommittees of standing committees, reflecting a step back from the rampant decentralization and democratization that characterized Congress in the mid-1970s, when every majority member clamored for a subcommittee chair and the staff and other resources that went along with it. In 1975, 142 House members had chairmanships; in 2007 there were 112.

Congressional committee staffs, which doubled in the 1960s and nearly tripled in the 1970s, stabilized in the 1980s and began to decline with the Republican takeover of Congress in 1995 (figure 2). House and Senate standing committees in 1976 had 2,881 employees. Fifteen years later, in 1991, they peaked at 3,231, rising in the House from 1,680 to 2,201, although dropping in the Senate from 1,201 to 1,030. But fourteen years later the number was 2,159, down by over 40 percent in the House and by 14 percent in the Senate.

Personal staffs grew rapidly in the 1950s and 1960s and continued to rise into the 1970s. At the height of the reform era, in 1976, House members had 6,939 employees and the Senate 3,251. By 1991 the numbers were 7,278 and 4,294, respectively. By 2005 the House had 6,804 personal staff members and the Senate 3,934 (figure 1). Put in other terms, House personal staffs went from an average of 4 per member in the early 1950s to 16 per member in the mid-1970s and to between 16 and 17 per member in the early 1990s and beyond. Senators went from an average of 17 per member in the early 1950s to 33 per member in the mid-1970s to 40 or so per senator in the 1990s and thereafter.

The changes in staff dynamics can be illustrated by describing New York Senator Charles Schumer's staff arrangements, compared to those of his 1952 counterpart Herbert

Lehman. Lehman, as mentioned above, had twenty-eight employees—twelve official and sixteen paid out of his own pocket. Three worked full time in his New York City office handling constituent relations; the rest were in Washington. Schumer, on the other hand, has (as of 2007) sixty-two official staff members, twenty-seven of whom work outside Washington in eight regional offices throughout New York State. Three of Lehman's staff did research on issues and wrote speeches; Schumer has four legal counsels, a policy director with two policy assistants, a legislative director, five legislative assistants, and six legislative correspondents. Lehman had a staff allowance of $65,000; Schumer has an allowance forty-eight times that, or $3,125,171.

If personal staffs did not show explosive growth in numbers in the postreform era, they did show one important and distinctive change: the number and proportion of staffers working at home in districts and states grew sharply throughout the period. In 1972 a count of House staff showed about 23 percent based in district offices, 28 percent in 1976, 42 percent in 1991, and 51 percent in 2005. The share in state offices was about 13 percent in 1972, 25 percent in the late 1970s, 32 percent in 1991, and 39 percent in 2005.

The growing staffing of home offices suggests a complementary trend—congressional members' efforts to spend more time at home (and more time fund-raising) and less time in Washington. That trend in turn has shaped the way Congress works. When the authors first came to Congress, we witnessed something called the Tuesday-to-Thursday Club, generally confined to members from the Northeast and Mid-Atlantic regions. Club members sped home after the last votes on Thursday evening and returned to Washington on Monday night or early Tuesday morning, before serious business began. Today the Tuesday-to-Thursday Club has nearly universal membership. In a typical week when Congress is in session, most members straggle in late Tuesday afternoon and leave for home early Thursday afternoon, staying in Washington only one full day and fragments of two others. In 2006 the legislative schedule had only seventy-one full days in session, with an additional twenty-six days with no votes before 6:30 p.m. (in many cases, with no votes at all). That is the lowest number by far in modern times, lower than the number in 1947, the famous Do-Nothing Congress criticized by President Harry Truman.

While we have no systematic data to prove it, we have observed Congresses in which most legislators lived in Washington with their families and socialized with other members and their families. For weeks at a time, legislating predominated. Now the atmosphere is frenetic. Today's House works many fewer days than it did in the past, so to make use of their time in Washington, members work longer days.

During the 1960s and 1970s the average Congress was in session 323 days. In the 1980s and 1990s the average number of days declined to 278 and has plummeted since; the average for each two-year Congress for the first six years of the Bush presidency was fewer than 250 days. Of course, days in session and days voting do not give a full picture of Congress and its work. Committees and subcommittees hold hearings, do oversight, and mark up bills. Still, the average Congress in the 1960s and 1970s had 5,372 committee and subcommittee meetings; in the 1980s and 1990s, the average was 4,793 meetings. In the last Congress, the 109th, the number of meetings was 2,492.

As days in session have shrunk, legislative output has changed as well. Congress is passing fewer bills and spending less time debating them, but the ones it passes are much longer. Omnibus bills, sometimes thousands of pages in length, have gone from rarity to commonplace. To be sure, this trend has been present for some time. The average length of a statute in the 1960s was just over three pages; in the 1970s, around seven pages, in the 1980s, around nine. But in the 1990s the length jumped sharply, to fifteen pages, with a comparable pattern in the years since.

Mr. Van Winkle would have seen one other element of congressional behavior different from what he had seen in 1975: an expansion of a three-decade-long trend toward individualism in the Senate. In the 94th Senate there were twenty-seven cloture votes, underscoring the frequency of filibusters and threatened filibusters in Senate life. (In the 82nd Congress of 1951–52 there were no cloture votes—meaning no filibusters.) Now filibusters are regular: in the first session of the 110th Congress there were sixty cloture votes. Any senator can threaten a filibuster or invoke one; many senators, at one time or another, have done so, both tying up the Senate and raising the bar for action from fifty votes to sixty votes.

As for campaign finance, the system in place for the 2006 election that swept the Democrats back into the majority would boggle Rip Van Winkle's mind, especially if he had seen campaign finance reform pass in 1974 (but had not been around to see it transformed by the Supreme Court's *Buckley* v. *Valeo* decision in 1976 or the ways the system changed in the three decades thereafter). The most important change was the explosion in money raised and money spent, both generally and in specific races. Despite the predictions of opponents of campaign reform, the first major reform bill enacted after the Buckley decision, the Bipartisan Campaign Reform Act of 2002 (BCRA), did not cause money to congressional candidates or political parties to shrink significantly. Rather, the money—now all "hard" money, with BCRA's abolition of federal "soft" money—increased again.

In the election that brought in the 110th Congress, House candidates spent almost $752 million, an average of nearly $995,669 per candidate. Recall that the average candidate expenditure in the 1974 election was $54,384. Thirty-two years is a long time, but an eighteenfold increase over that time period is still extraordinary and way beyond any inflation index. The situation was scarcely different in the Senate, in which candidate campaign expenditures for the 2006 cycle were almost $515 million, an average of $7,922,115 per candidate. In the 1974 cycle Senate candidate spending was $28.4 million, or $437,000 per candidate (see figure 6). One 2006 Senate candidate, Hillary Clinton of New York, spent $41 million to secure her relatively safe reelection!

Sources of funding for the campaigns changed sharply as well. In the 1974 cycle House candidates raised 73 percent of their money from individual contributions, 17 percent from nonparty political action committees (PACs), 4 percent from political parties, and 6 percent from themselves. In 2006 House candidates raised only 54 percent from individuals, got 35 percent from PACs, 1 percent from parties, and 5 percent from themselves. In the 1974 Senate contests, 76 percent of funds came from individual contributions, 11 percent from PACs, 6 percent from parties, and 1 percent from themselves. In 2006 Senate candidates got

Figure 6 Congressional Campaign Expenditures, 1980–2005
Millions of 2006 dollars

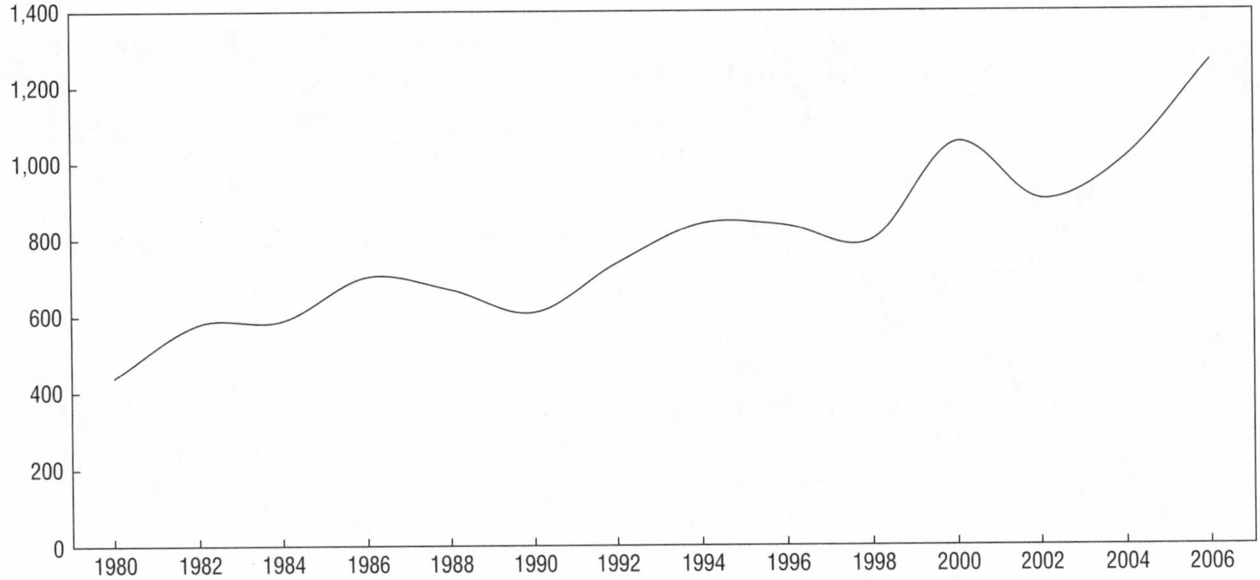

67 percent from individuals, 13 percent from PACs, 3 percent from parties, and 13 percent from themselves.

The role of parties changed as well. Direct contributions from parties to candidates stayed stable (and small). Coordinated expenditures by parties on behalf of candidates grew sharply. In 1976 Democratic Party expenditures on behalf of its House candidates were $500 and for Senate candidates, $4,359. The Republican Party was a big spender, comparatively: $329,583 for House candidates and $113,976 for Senate candidates. Consider the same category in 2006: the Democratic Party spent $2,409,914 on behalf of its House candidates and $5,769,005 for its Senate candidates; the GOP spent $4,519,856 on its House candidates and $8,784,685 for its Senate candidates. Unlimited independent expenditures by parties on behalf of their candidates have become the dominant form of party financing.

As in previous cycles, incumbents generally spent more than challengers (in the House, $1,261,559 on average, compared to $510,195 for challengers; in the Senate, $9.4 million, compared to $5.7 million for challengers). In House races in which incumbents won with more than 60 percent, they outspent challengers on average by more than nearly seven to one, or $975,047 to $147,072; in races in which incumbents won more narrowly, they outspent challengers by nearly two to one, with all candidates spending much more (incumbents on average, nearly $1.9 million; challengers, $1.0 million). And in races in which challengers beat incumbents, the incumbents still spent more on average, but all spent remarkable amounts, incumbents averaging more than $2.8 million and challengers $1.8 million.

Conclusion

These sketches of Congress in 1951, 1975, and 2007, informed by the statistical series that make up the bulk of this volume, illustrate the extraordinary changes that have swept through Washington over the last half century. By its very nature, Congress is a marvelous barometer of locally rooted national political trends. As a representative and institutionally powerful body, Congress registers, adapts to, and shapes the social, economic, and political forces in the country. And yet amid such constant change Congress also provides continuity and stability. The durability of American democracy is due in no small part to the capacity of its national legislature to accommodate and facilitate change within relatively stable constitutional and institutional arrangements.

In the broadest sense, those arrangements are defined by the separation-of-powers system, in which the president is elected independently of the Congress and for a fixed term, and by the checks and balances that flow from that separation. Other dominant features of the institutional environment include single-member constituencies with plurality elections, bicameralism, equal representation of the states in the Senate, federalism, and strong judicial review. Together these institutional arrangements facilitate such familiar patterns of American public life as a dominant two-party system, an independent and decentralized Congress, the pull of localism, the permeability of decisionmaking to outside interests, multiple veto points, limited party discipline, and a relatively weak bureaucracy, with substantial penetration by political appointees and congressional committees.

These prominent and largely durable features of the American political system make Congress the national political institution most worth watching. But it is the range and rapidity of change uncovered by examining Congress that render that exercise intriguing and productive. Over the course of American history the growth in the size and agenda of government, the professionalization of political careers, and the shifting modes of political communication have left enduring marks on the Congress and its immediate environment. In the period tracked most closely by *Vital Statistics on Congress*, the changes are more subtle but nonetheless important.

Demography is one such change. Shifts in population among and within the fifty states, and the social and economic status of those residing in growing and declining areas of the country, have altered the power of states, cities, and suburbs in the House but have had relatively little effect in the Senate. Changes in the geographical bases of the two major parties have shaped their ideological orientation and that of their leaders in party caucuses and on committees. The political mobilization of racial minorities and women, and the increasing percentage of foreign-born residents and citizens, have gradually left an imprint on the composition of the House and Senate.

Elections are the wellspring of change in Congress but often the source of stability and continuity as well. Over the past half-century both the House and Senate have experienced periods of membership stasis and bursts of turnover. The latter often presaged sharp departures in the dynamics and output of Congress. Incumbents have enormous electoral advantages and generally enjoy near perfect reelection success, yet strong national tides can leave their mark in the number of open and marginal seats. In spite of the advantages of incumbency, Republicans managed to end their decades-long minority status in the Senate (in 1980) and House (in 1994). Senate Republicans lost their majority in 1986 and regained it in 1994. And then majority control of both chambers reverted to Democrats in 2006. The parties today are evenly balanced in the Congress and in the country, with majority control of both chambers up for grabs in virtually every election. Yet the number of seats seriously contested has shrunk. An increasingly competitive struggle between the parties for control of Congress is waged on increasingly noncompetitive terrain.

Money has long played a prominent role in American elections, but only in recent decades has the public disclosure regime produced accurate statistics on contributions and expenditures. The time series since 1974 tells fascinating stories about the increasing costs of congressional elections; the rise of PACs and their shifting strategies; the increasing concentration of resources on incumbents and hotly contested races; the critical role of spending by challengers; the impact of redistricting; and the increased importance of political parties in campaign finance, with an attendant shift from hard (federal) to soft (nonfederal) funding strategies, a shift that was reversed with the enactment of BCRA. Before BCRA parties took full advantage of the Court's protection of issue advocacy, even when it was candidate specific and electioneering in content, to avoid the strictures of federal election law. Interest groups followed suit, leaving a growing component of campaign finance activity outside the statistics collected and reported by the Federal Election Commission. Parties today retain a critically important role in the financing of congressional campaigns, but they operate with exclusively hard dollars.

The internal organization of the House and Senate is built around parties, committees, and personal offices. Tracking how staff and other resources are budgeted over time and allocated among these components of congressional life provides insights into the place of Congress in the policy process and the structure of influence within the House and Senate. Additional insights along these lines emerge from a review of the allocation of committee and subcommittee chairmanships and the amount and forms of congressional activity.

Perhaps the most striking story to emerge from this volume of vital statistics on Congress is the decline and subsequent revival of political parties. The 1960s counterculture, the civil rights movement, and the Vietnam War all contributed to a fracturing of party coalitions in the electorate, a weakening of partisanship, and a rise of independents. Parties played a diminished role in fund-raising and campaigning, politicians took on a more independent and entrepreneurial cast, and congressional party leaders found it difficult to build coalitions. Some chroniclers of American politics wrote that the party was over.

That assessment has proved premature. The Voting Rights Act and the subsequent mobilization of black voters set in motion a regional realignment and an ideological sorting of citizens into the two parties. The rise of new issues—including the environment and abortion—diminished the Republican presence in the Northeast as it increased in the South. National party organizations adapted to the new electoral rules and became consequential campaign service and fund-raising entities. Members of Congress increasingly found themselves agreeing with their party colleagues on a broad range of issues and dissenting from those on the other side of the aisle.

Over time the statistics reveal growing unity among party members and increasing ideological polarization between parties in Congress. Congressional party leaders play a critical role in fund-raising and campaign strategy, and the congressional agenda is shaped importantly by strategic party considerations. This resurgence of parties is also evident in the mass public. Citizens who vote are remarkably faithful to their party identification: recent elections have witnessed a decline in partisan defection and split-ticket voting and a convergence in presidential and congressional voting. And those who participate more actively in politics have even stronger partisan ties.

That polarization has contributed to the highly contentious atmosphere in Washington and, more generally, to the demise of Congress as an independent and deliberative branch of government.[12] Whether the "broken branch" is able to overcome some of these structural and political impediments to a serious and bipartisan deliberative process and reassume its constitutional responsibility to check and balance the other branches will be the subject of scrutiny of future editions of *Vital Statistics on Congress*.

Notes

1. Quoted in Norris Cotton, *In the Senate* (N.Y.: Dodd, Mead, 1978), p. 31.
2. Congresses are numbered sequentially, every two years. For example, the 80th Congress was in session 1947–48, the 110th Congress in 2007–08.
3. William S. White, *Citadel* (New York: Harper & Brothers, 1956), p. 68.
4. Stephen K. Bailey and Howard D. Samuel, "A Day in the Life of a Senator: The Congressional Office, 1952," *Commentary,* May 1952, p. 434.
5. Harry McPherson, *A Political Education* (Boston: Little, Brown, 1972), p. 21.
6. Ibid., pp. 16–17.
7. Ibid., pp. 17–18.
8. As quoted in Neil MacNeil, *Forge of Democracy* (New York: David McKay, 1963), p. 129.
9. *Congressional Quarterly Almanac 1953,* p. 40.
10. Christopher J. Matthews, "The Old Breed Strikes Back," *New Republic,* March 2, 1987, p. 21.
11. See Sarah Binder, "The Disappearing Political Center," *Brookings Review* (Fall 1996): 36–39. Data have been updated by authors; also see tables 8-9 and 8-10, this volume.
12. Thomas E. Mann and Norman J. Ornstein, *The Broken Branch: How Congress Is Failing America and How to Get It Back on Track* (Oxford University Press, 2006).

1

Members of Congress

Table 1-1 Apportionment of Congressional Seats, by Region and State, 1910–2000 (435 seats)

Region and state	1910	1930	1940	1950	1960	1970	1980	1990	2000
South	104	102	105	106	106	108	116	125	131
Alabama	10	9	9	9	8	7	7	7	7
Arkansas	7	7	7	6	4	4	4	4	4
Florida	4	5	6	8	12	15	19	23	25
Georgia	12	10	10	10	10	10	10	11	13
Louisiana	8	8	8	8	8	8	8	7	7
Mississippi	8	7	7	6	5	5	5	5	4
North Carolina	10	11	12	12	11	11	11	12	13
South Carolina	7	6	6	6	6	6	6	6	6
Tennessee	10	9	10	9	9	8	9	9	9
Texas	18	21	21	22	23	24	27	30	32
Virginia	10	9	9	10	10	10	10	11	11
Border	47	43	42	38	36	35	34	32	31
Kentucky	11	9	9	8	7	7	7	6	6
Maryland	6	6	6	7	8	8	8	8	8
Missouri	16	13	13	11	10	10	9	9	9
Oklahoma	8	9	8	6	6	6	6	6	5
West Virginia	6	6	6	6	5	4	4	3	3
New England	32	29	28	28	25	25	24	23	22
Connecticut	5	6	6	6	6	6	6	6	5
Maine	4	3	3	3	2	2	2	2	2
Massachusetts	16	15	14	14	12	12	11	10	10
New Hampshire	2	2	2	2	2	2	2	2	2
Rhode Island	3	2	2	2	2	2	2	2	2
Vermont	2	1	1	1	1	1	1	1	1
Mid-Atlantic	92	94	93	88	84	80	72	66	62
Delaware	1	1	1	1	1	1	1	1	1
New Jersey	12	14	14	14	15	15	14	13	13
New York	43	45	45	43	41	39	34	31	29
Pennsylvania	36	34	33	30	27	25	23	21	19
Midwest	86	90	87	87	88	86	80	74	69
Illinois	27	27	26	25	24	24	22	20	19
Indiana	13	12	11	11	11	11	10	10	9
Michigan	13	17	17	18	19	19	18	16	15
Ohio	22	24	23	23	24	23	21	19	18
Wisconsin	11	10	10	10	10	9	9	9	8
Plains	41	34	31	31	27	25	24	22	22
Iowa	11	9	8	8	7	6	6	5	5
Kansas	8	7	6	6	5	5	5	4	4
Minnesota	10	9	9	9	8	8	8	8	8
Nebraska	6	5	4	4	3	3	3	3	3
North Dakota	3	2	2	2	2	1	1	1	1
South Dakota	3	2	2	2	2	2	1	1	1

Region and state	1910	1930	1940	1950	1960	1970	1980	1990	2000
Rocky Mountains	14	14	16	16	17	19	24	24	28
Arizona	1	1	2	2	3	4	5	6	8
Colorado	4	4	4	4	4	5	6	6	7
Idaho	2	2	2	2	2	2	2	2	2
Montana	2	2	2	2	2	2	2	1	1
Nevada	1	1	1	1	1	1	2	2	3
New Mexico	1[a]	1	2	2	2	2	3	3	3
Utah	2	2	2	2	2	2	3	3	3
Wyoming	1	1	1	1	1	1	1	1	1
Pacific Coast	19	29	33	43	52	57	61	69	70
Alaska	—	—	—	1[b]	1	1	1	1	1
California	11	20	23	30	38	43	45	52	53
Hawaii	—	—	—	1[c]	2	2	2	2	2
Oregon	3	3	4	4	4	4	5	5	5
Washington	5	6	6	7	7	7	8	9	9

a. New Mexico became a state in 1912; in 1910 it had a nonvoting delegate in Congress.

b. Alaska became a state on January 3, 1959. In 1950 Alaska had a nonvoting delegate in Congress, making the total for that year 437; subsequent reapportionment reduced the total to 435.

c. Hawaii became a state on August 21, 1959. In 1950 Hawaii had a nonvoting delegate in Congress, making the total for that year 437; subsequent reapportionment reduced the total to 435.

Sources: *Congressional Quarterly's Guide to U.S. Elections* (Washington, D.C.: Congressional Quarterly, various editions); *Congressional Quarterly Weekly Report,* various issues; U.S. Census data 2000, www.census.gov.

Table 1-2 Democratic Party Strength in the House, by Region, 69th–110th Congresses, 1925–2008

Congress	69th (1925–1926)	75th (1937–1938)	81st (1949–1950)	87th (1961–1962)	93rd (1973–1974)	96th (1979–1980)	97th (1981–1982)	98th (1983–1984)	100th (1987–1988)	101st (1989–1990)	102nd (1991–1992)	103rd (1993–1994)	104th (1995–1996)	105th (1997–1998)	106th (1999–2000)	107th (2001–2002)	108th (2003–2004)	109th (2005–2006)	110th (2007–2008)
Region																			
South																			
Percent	97.1	98.0	98.1	93.4	68.2	71.3	63.9	71.2	66.4	67.0	66.4	61.6	48.8	43.2	43.5	42.4	41.9	37.4	41.2
Seats	104	101	105	106	107[c]	108	108	116	116	115[h]	116	125	125	125	124[j]	125	131	131	131
Border																			
Percent	58.7	95.2	88.1	84.2	77.1	77.1	68.6	76.4	67.6	67.6	67.6	65.6	50.0	40.6	40.6	37.5	45.1	45.2	48.4
Seats	46	42	42	38	35	35	35	34	34	34	34	32	32	32	32	32	31	31	31
New England																			
Percent	12.5	44.8	39.3	50.0	60.0	72.0	64.0	66.6	62.5	58.3	66.7	60.9	60.9	78.3	78.3	73.9	68.2	72.7	95.5
Seats	32	29	28	28	25	25	25	24	24	24	24	23	23	23	23	23	22	22	22
Mid-Atlantic																			
Percent	26.4	68.0	48.4	48.9	53.8	63.8	53.8	58.3	56.9	58.3	56.9	54.5	50.0	53.0	54.5	54.5	53.2	54.8	66.1
Seats	91	94	93	88	80	80	80	72	72	72	72	66	66	66	66	66	62	62	62
Midwest																			
Percent	16.7	72.2	43.7	40.7	37.6	55.3	50.0	55.0	57.5	59.5	61.2	58.1	43.2	50.0	50.0	48.6	40.6	40.6	47.8
Seats	84	90	87	86[a]	85[d]	85[f]	86	80	80	79[i]	80	74	74	74	74	74	69	69	69
Plains																			
Percent	14.6	38.2	16.1	19.4	36.0	40.0	36.0	54.2	45.8	50.0	54.2	54.5	36.4	36.4	40.9	36.4	31.8	36.4	54.5
Seats	41	34	31	31	25	25	25	24	24	24	24	22	22	22	22	22	22	22	22
Rocky Mountains																			
Percent	28.6	93.3	75.0	68.8	42.1	47.4	36.8	33.3	37.5	37.5	45.8	45.8	25.0	20.8	20.8	25.0	25.0	28.6	39.3
Seats	14	15	16	16	19	19	19	24	24	24	24	24	24	24	24	24	28	28	28
Pacific Coast																			
Percent	19.0	80.0	36.4	51.2	58.9	66.1	56.1	62.3	59.0	59.0	60.6	63.8	49.3	55.1	56.5	63.2	64.3	63.8	65.7
Seats	21	30	33	43[b]	56[e]	56[g]	57	61	61	61	61	69	69	69	69	68[k]	70	69[L]	70

Note: Figures represent the makeup of Congress on the first day of the session.

a. J. Edward Roush (D-IN) was not sworn in until June 14, 1961 due to a disputed election result.
b. Alaska was admitted as a state in 1958 and Hawaii in 1959. There were 437 representatives elected in 1960, both included in the Pacific Coast row.
c. Hale Boggs (D-LA) was elected posthumously.
d. George Collins (D-IL) was elected in 1972 but died before being sworn into office.
e. Nicholas Begich (D-AK) was elected posthumously.
f. William Steiger (R-WI) was elected in 1978 but died before being sworn into office.
g. Leo Ryan (D-CA) was elected in 1978 but died before being sworn into office.
h. William Nichols (D-AL) was elected in 1988 but died before being sworn into office.
i. Daniel Coats (R-IN) won reelection in 1988 but was appointed to Dan Quayle's Senate seat on December 12, 1988.
j. Newt Gingrich (R-GA) was elected in 1998, but resigned from his seat before being sworn in.
k. Julian Dixon (D-CA) was elected in 2000 but died before being sworn into office.
L. Robert Matsui (D-CA) was elected in 2004 but died before being sworn into office.

Sources: *Congressional Directory*, various editions; *Congressional Quarterly Weekly Report*, various issues; Clerk of the U.S. House of Representatives, http://clerk.house.gov; *The Almanac of American Politics* (Washington, D.C.: National Journal Group, various editions).

Table 1-3 Democratic and Republican Seats in the House, by Region, 69th–110th Congresses, 1925–2008

	69th 1925–1926		75th 1937–1938		81st 1949–1950		87th 1961–1962		93rd 1973–1974		96th 1979–1980		97th 1981–1982		98th 1983–1984		101st 1989–1990	
Region	D	R	D	R	D	R	D	R	D	R	D	R	D	R	D	R	D	R
South																		
Percent	54.9	1.2	29.8	2.2	39.2	1.2	37.8	3.4	30.4	17.7	27.9	19.7	28.4	20.3	30.2	21.0	29.3	22.4
Seats	101	3	99	2	103	2	99	6	73	34	77	31	69	39	81	35	76	39
Border																		
Percent	14.7	7.8	12.0	2.2	14.1	2.9	12.2	3.4	11.3	4.2	9.8	5.1	9.9	5.7	9.7	4.8	8.9	6.3
Seats	27	19	40	2	37	5	32	6	27	8	27	8	24	11	26	8	23	11
New England																		
Percent	2.2	11.4	3.9	17.6	4.2	9.9	5.3	8.0	6.3	5.2	6.5	4.5	6.6	4.7	6.0	4.8	5.4	5.7
Seats	4	28	13	16	11	17	14	14	15	10	18	7	16	9	16	8	14	10
Mid-Atlantic																		
Percent	13.0	26.9	19.3	33.0	17.1	27.5	16.4	25.9	17.9	19.3	18.5	18.5	17.7	19.3	16.0	17.4	16.2	17.2
Seats	24	66	64	30	45	47	43	45	43	37	51	29	43	37	43	29	42	30
Midwest																		
Percent	7.6	28.2	19.6	19.8	14.4	28.7	13.4	29.3	13.3	27.6	17.0	24.2	17.7	22.4	16.4	21.6	18.1	18.4
Seats	14	69	65	18	38	49	35	51	32	53	47	38	43	43	44	36	47	32
Plains																		
Percent	3.3	13.5	3.9	17.6	1.9	15.2	2.3	14.4	3.8	8.3	3.6	9.6	3.7	8.3	4.5	7.2	4.6	6.9
Seats	6	33	13	16	5	26	6	25	9	16	10	15	9	16	12	12	12	12
Rocky Mountains																		
Percent	2.2	4.1	4.2	1.1	4.6	2.3	4.2	2.9	3.3	5.7	3.3	6.4	2.9	6.3	3.0	9.6	3.5	8.6
Seats	4	10	14	1	12	4	11	5	8	11	9	10	7	12	8	16	9	15
Pacific Coast																		
Percent	2.2	6.9	7.2	6.6	4.6	12.3	8.4	12.1	13.8	12.0	13.4	12.1	13.2	13.0	14.2	13.8	13.9	14.4
Seats	4	17	24	6	12	21	22	21	33	23	37	19	32	25	38	23	36	25
Total Seats	184	245	332	91	263	171	262	174	240	192	276	157	243	192	268	167	259	174

	102nd 1991–1992		103rd 1993–1994		104th 1995–1996		105th 1997–1998		106th 1999–2000		107th 2001–2002		108th 2003–2004		109th 2005–2007		110th 2007–2008	
Region	D	R	D	R	D	R	D	R	D	R	D	R	D	R	D	R	D	R
South																		
Percent	28.8	23.4	29.8	27.3	29.9	27.8	26.1	31.3	25.6	31.5	25.1	32.3	26.8	33.2	24.4	35.3	23.2	38.1
Seats	77	39	77	48	61	64	54	71	54	70	53	71	55	76	49	82	54	77
Border																		
Percent	8.6	6.6	8.1	6.3	7.8	7.0	6.3	8.4	6.2	8.6	5.7	9.1	6.8	7.4	7.0	7.3	6.4	7.9
Seats	23	11	21	11	16	16	13	19	13	19	12	20	14	17	14	17	15	16
New England																		
Percent	6.0	4.2	5.4	4.5	6.9	3.5	8.7	1.8	8.5	1.8	8.1	2.3	7.8	2.2	8.0	2.2	9.0	0.5
Seats	16	7	14	8	14	8	18	4	18	4	17	5	16	5	16	5	21	1
Mid-Atlantic																		
Percent	15.4	18.6	14.0	17.0	16.2	14.3	16.9	13.7	17.1	13.5	17.1	13.6	16.1	12.7	16.9	12.1	17.6	10.4
Seats	41	31	36	30	33	33	35	31	36	30	36	30	33	29	34	28	41	21
Midwest																		
Percent	18.4	18.6	16.7	17.6	15.7	18.3	17.9	16.3	17.5	16.7	17.5	16.8	13.7	17.9	13.9	17.7	14.2	17.8
Seats	49	31	43	31	32	42	37	37	37	37	37	37	28	41	28	41	33	36
Plains																		
Percent	4.9	6.6	4.7	5.7	3.9	6.1	3.9	6.2	4.3	5.9	3.8	6.4	3.4	6.6	4.0	6.0	5.2	5.0
Seats	13	11	12	10	8	14	8	14	9	13	8	14	7	15	8	14	12	10
Rocky Mountains																		
Percent	4.1	7.8	4.3	7.4	2.9	7.8	1.9	8.8	2.4	8.6	2.8	8.2	3.4	9.2	4.0	8.6	4.7	8.4
Seats	11	13	11	13	6	18	4	20	5	19	6	18	7	21	8	20	11	17
Pacific Coast																		
Percent	13.9	14.4	17.1	14.2	16.7	15.2	18.4	13.7	18.5	13.5	19.9	11.4	22.0	10.9	21.9	10.8	19.7	11.9
Seats	37	24	44	25	34	35	38	31	39	30	42	25	45	25	44	25	46	24
Total Seats	267	167	258	176	204	230	207	227	211	222	211	220	205	229	201	232	233	202

Note: D indicates Democrats; R indicates Republicans. Third parties are omitted. Figures represent the makeup of Congress on the first day of the session.

Sources: *Congressional Directory,* various editions; *Congressional Quarterly Weekly Report,* various issues; Clerk of the U.S. House of Representatives, http://clerk.house.gov; *The Almanac of American Politics* (Washington, D.C.: National Journal Group, various editions).

Table 1-4 Democratic Party Strength in the Senate, by Region, 69th–110th Congresses, 1925–2008

	69th (1925–1926)	75th (1937–1938)	81st (1949–1950)	87th (1961–1962)	93rd (1973–1974)	96th (1979–1980)	97th (1981–1982)	98th (1983–1984)	100th (1987–1988)	101st (1989–1990)	102nd (1991–1992)	103rd (1993–1994)	104th (1995–1996)	105th (1997–1998)	106th (1999–2000)	107th (2001–2002)	108th (2003–2004)	109th (2005–2006)	110th (2007–2008)
Region																			
South																			
Percent	100.0	100.0	100.0	100.0	63.6	50.0	54.4	50.0	72.7	68.2	68.2	59.1	36.4[a]	31.8	36.4	36.4	40.9	18.2	22.7
Seats	22	22	22	22	22	22	22	22	22	22	22	22	22	22	22	22	22	22	22
Border																			
Percent	50.0	100.0	80.0	60.0	50.0	70.0	70.0	70.0	60.0	60.0	60.0	60.0	50.0	50.0	40.0	50.0	40.0	40.0	50.0
Seats	10	10	10	10	10	10	10	10	10	10	10	10	10	10	10	10	10	10	10
New England																			
Percent	8.3	50.0	25.0	41.7	58.3	58.3	50.0	50.0	50.0	58.3	58.3	58.3	50.0	50.0	50.0	50.0	50.0	50.0	50.0
Seats	12	12	12	12	12	12	12	12	12	12	12	12	12	12	12	12	12	12	12
Mid-Atlantic																			
Percent	37.5	75.0	37.5	25.0	25.0	50.0	50.0	50.0	50.0	50.0	50.0	62.5	50.0	50.0	62.5	75.0	75.0	75.0	87.5
Seats	8	8	8	8	8	8	8	8	8	8	8	8	8	8	8	8	8	8	8
Midwest																			
Percent	10.0	80.0	20.0	70.0	60.0	80.0	60.0	60.0	70.0	70.0	70.0	80.0	60.0	60.0	50.0	60.0	60.0	70.0	80.0
Seats	10	10	10	10	10	10	10	10	10	10	10	10	10	10	10	10	10	10	10
Plains																			
Percent	0.0	50.0	16.7	25.0	58.3	41.7	25.0	25.0	50.0	50.0	58.3	58.3	58.3	58.3	58.3	66.7	58.3	50.0	50.0
Seats	12	12	12	12	12	12	12	12	12	12	12	12	12	12	12	12	12	12	12
Rocky Mountains																			
Percent	50.0	93.8	75.0	75.0	56.2	37.5	31.3	31.3	37.5	37.5	37.5	37.5	37.5	25.0	25.0	25.0	18.8	25.0	31.3
Seats	16	16	16	16	16	16	16	16	16	16	16	16	16	16	16	16	16	16	16
Pacific Coast																			
Percent	16.7	50.0	33.3	80.0	60.0	60.0	40.0	40.0	40.0	40.0	40.0	50.0	50.0	60.0	60.0	70.0	70.0	70.0	70.0
Seats	6	6	6	10	10	10	10	10	10	10	10	10	10	10	10	10	10	10	10

Note: Figures represent the makeup of Congress on the first day of the session.

a. Excludes Richard Shelby (AL) who switched from the Democratic to the Republican Party on the day following the election and before the beginning of the 104th Congress (1995).

Sources: *Congressional Directory*, various editions; *Congressional Quarterly Weekly Report*, various issues; US Senate, http://www.senate.gov; *The Almanac of American Politics* (Washington, D.C.: National Journal Group, various editions).

Table 1-5 Democratic and Republican Seats in the Senate, by Region, 69th–110th Congresses, 1925–2008

Congress	69th 1925–1926		75th 1937–1938		81st 1949–1950		87th 1961–1962		93rd 1973–1974		97th 1981–1982		101st 1989–1990		102nd 1991–1992	
Region	D	R	D	R	D	R	D	R	D	R	D	R	D	R	D	R
South																
Percent	53.7	0.0	28.9	0.0	40.7	0.0	33.8	0.0	25.0	16.7	23.9	18.9	27.3	15.6	26.8	15.9
Seats	22	0	22	0	22	0	22	0	14	7	11	10	15	7	15	7
Border																
Percent	12.2	9.3	13.2	0.0	14.8	4.8	9.2	11.4	8.9	11.9	15.2	5.7	10.9	8.9	10.7	9.1
Seats	5	5	10	0	8	2	6	4	5	5	7	3	6	4	6	4
New England																
Percent	2.4	20.4	7.9	37.5	5.6	21.4	7.7	20.0	12.5	11.9	13.0	11.3	12.7	11.1	12.5	11.4
Seats	1	11	6	6	3	9	5	7	7	5	6	6	7	5	7	5
Mid-Atlantic																
Percent	7.3	9.3	7.9	12.5	5.6	11.9	3.1	17.1	3.6	11.9	8.7	7.5	7.3	8.9	7.1	9.1
Seats	3	5	6	2	3	5	2	6	2	5	4	4	4	4	4	4
Midwest																
Percent	2.4	16.7	10.5	6.3	3.7	19.0	10.8	8.6	10.7	9.5	13.0	7.5	12.7	6.7	12.5	6.8
Seats	1	9	8	1	2	8	7	3	6	4	6	4	7	3	7	3
Plains																
Percent	0.0	20.4	7.9	18.8	3.7	23.8	4.6	25.7	12.5	11.9	6.5	17.0	10.9	13.3	12.5	11.4
Seats	0	11	6	3	2	10	3	9	7	5	3	9	6	6	7	5
Rocky Mountains																
Percent	19.5	14.8	19.7	6.3	22.2	9.5	18.5	11.4	16.1	16.7	10.9	20.8	10.9	22.2	10.7	22.7
Seats	8	8	15	1	12	4	12	4	9	7	5	11	6	10	6	10
Pacific Coast																
Percent	2.4	9.3	3.9	18.8	3.7	9.5	12.3	5.7	10.7	9.5	8.7	11.3	7.3	13.3	7.1	13.6
Seats	1	5	3	3	2	4	8	2	6	4	4	6	4	6	4	6
Total Seats	41	54	76	16	54	42	65	35	56	42	46	53	55	45	56	44

Congress	103rd 1993–1994		104th 1995–1996		105th 1997–1998		106th 1999–2000		107th 2001–2002		108th 2003–2004		109th 2005–2006		110th 2007–2008	
Region	D	R	D	R	D	R	D	R	D	R	D	R	D	R	D	R
South																
Percent	22.8	20.9	19.1	24.5	15.6	27.3	17.8	25.5	16.0	28.0	18.8	25.5	9.1	32.7	10.2	34.7
Seats	13	9	9	13[a]	7	15	8	14	8	14	9	13	4	18	5	17
Border																
Percent	10.5	9.3	10.6	9.4	11.1	9.1	8.9	10.9	10.0	10.0	8.3	11.8	9.1	10.9	10.2	10.2
Seats	6	4	5	5	5	5	4	6	5	5	4	6	4	6	5	5
New England																
Percent	12.3	11.6	12.8	11.3	13.3	10.9	13.3	10.9	12.0	12.0	12.5	9.8	13.6	9.1	12.2	8.2
Seats	7	5	6	6	6	6	6	6	6	6	6	5	6	5	6	4
Mid-Atlantic																
Percent	8.8	7.0	8.5	7.5	8.9	7.3	11.1	5.5	12.0	4.0	12.5	3.9	13.6	3.6	14.3	2.0
Seats	5	3	4	4	4	4	5	3	6	2	6	2	6	2	7	1
Midwest																
Percent	14.0	4.7	12.8	7.5	13.3	7.3	11.1	9.1	12.0	8.0	12.5	7.8	15.9	5.5	16.3	4.1
Seats	8	2	6	4	6	4	5	5	6	4	6	4	7	3	8	2
Plains																
Percent	12.3	11.6	14.9	9.4	15.6	9.1	15.6	9.1	16.0	8.0	14.6	9.8	13.6	10.9	12.2	12.2
Seats	7	5	7	5	7	5	7	5	8	4	7	5	6	6	6	6
Rocky Mountains																
Percent	10.5	23.3	10.6	20.8	8.9	21.8	8.9	21.8	8.0	24.0	6.3	25.5	9.1	21.8	10.2	22.4
Seats	6	10	5	11	4	12	4	12	4	12	3	13	4	12	5	11
Pacific Coast																
Percent	8.8	11.6	10.6	9.4	13.3	7.3	13.3	7.3	14.0	6.0	14.6	5.9	15.9	5.5	14.3	6.1
Seats	5	5	5	5	6	4	6	4	7	3	7	3	7	3	7	3
Total Seats	57	43	47	53	45	55	45	55	50	50	48	51	44	55	49	49

Note: D indicates Democrats; R indicates Republicans. Third parties are omitted. Figures represent the makeup of Congress on the first day of the session.

a. Includes Richard Shelby (AL) who switched from the Democratic to the Republican Party on the day following the election and before the beginning of the 104th Congress.

Sources: *Congressional Directory*, various editions; *Congressional Quarterly Weekly Report*, various issues; US Senate, http://www.senate.gov; *The Almanac of American Politics* (Washington, D.C.: National Journal Group, various editions).

Table 1-6 Seniority of Representatives, 1953–2007

Congress	Percentage of representatives serving									
Congress	1 term	2 terms	3 terms	1–3 terms	4–6 terms	7–9 terms	10+ terms	Total	Mean term	Median term
83rd (1953)										
Percent	18.7	16.9	14.8	50.3	27.0	13.4	9.2		4.5	3
Seats	81	73	64	218	117	58	40	433[a]		
84th (1955)										
Percent	13.1	16.8	14.5	44.4	27.4	16.8	11.5		5.0	4
Seats	57	73	63	193	119	73	50	435		
85th (1957)										
Percent	10.6	11.5	15.2	37.4	32.8	15.2	14.5		5.4	4
Seats	46	50	66	162	142	66	63	433[b]		
86th (1959)										
Percent	18.8	10.3	11.2	40.4	31.2	14.7	13.1		5.2	4
Seats	82	45	49	176	136	64	57	436[c]		
87th (1961)										
Percent	14.2	14.9	8.2	37.3	30.0	17.4	15.3		5.5	5
Seats	62	65	36	163	131	76	67	437[d]		
88th (1963)										
Percent	15.4	14.3	12.2	41.9	24.4	18.0	15.7		5.5	5
Seats	67	62	53	182	106	78	68	434[e]		
89th (1965)										
Percent	20.9	13.3	11.3	45.5	22.3	16.8	15.4		5.1	4
Seats	91	58	49	198	97	73	67	435		
90th (1967)										
Percent	16.6	14.8	10.9	42.3	24.9	15.9	16.9		5.3	4
Seats	72	64	47	183	108	69	73	433[f]		
91st (1969)										
Percent	9.2	17.2	12.9	39.3	29.0	14.9	16.8		5.6	5
Seats	40	75	56	171	126	65	73	435		
92nd (1971)										
Percent	12.9	9.7	14.7	37.2	28.0	15.6	19.1		5.8	5
Seats	56	42	64	162	122	68	83	435		
93rd (1973)										
Percent	16.0	12.7	8.8	37.5	29.6	15.3	17.6		5.5	5
Seats	69	55	38	162	128	66	76	432[g]		
94th (1975)										
Percent	21.1	14.7	9.2	45.1	23.0	17.9	14.0		5.2	4
Seats	92	64	40	196	100	78	61	435		
95th (1977)										
Percent	15.4	21.6	13.3	50.3	20.0	16.1	13.6		4.9	3
Seats	67	94	58	219	87	70	59	435		
96th (1979)										
Percent	17.8	14.8	18.0	50.6	21.9	15.0	12.5		4.8	3
Seats	77	64	78	219	95	65	54	433[h]		
97th (1981)										
Percent	17.0	17.5	13.6	48.0	27.8	12.9	11.3		4.7	4
Seats	74	76	59	209	121	56	49	435		
98th (1983)										
Percent	18.4	14.7	15.2	48.4	28.8	10.4	12.4		4.7	4
Seats	80	64	66	210	125	45	54	434[i]		
99th (1985)										
Percent	9.9	18.2	14.3	42.4	31.8	13.4	12.4		5.1	4
Seats	43	79	62	184	138	58	54	434[j]		

Congress	Percentage of representatives serving									
	1 term	2 terms	3 terms	1–3 terms	4–6 terms	7–9 terms	10+ terms	Total	Mean term	Median term
100th (1987)										
Percent	11.5	8.7	17.2	37.5	32.9	14.7	14.9		5.5	5
Seats	50	38	75	163	143	64	65	435		
101st (1989)										
Percent	7.6	12.5	7.6	27.7	38.6	19.9	13.9		5.8	5
Seats	33	54	33	120	167	86	60	433[k]		
102nd (1991)										
Percent	10.1	9.4	11.0	30.6	31.5	20.9	17.0		6.1	5
Seats	44	41	48	133	137	91	74	435		
103rd (1993)										
Percent	25.3	10.1	8.7	44.1	25.1	15.9	14.9		5.2	4
Seats	110	44	38	192	109	69	65	435		
104th (1995)										
Percent	19.8	22.3	8.5	50.6	17.9	17.9	13.6		4.9	3
Seats	86	97	37	220	78	78	59	435		
105th (1997)										
Percent	18.2	17.5	20.2	55.9	16.3	14.9	12.9		4.8	3
Seats	79	76	88	243	71	65	56	435		
106th (1999)										
Percent	9.4	17.2	15.9	42.5	29.2	13.3	14.9		4.8	4
Seats	41	75	69	185	127	58	65	435		
107th (2001)										
Percent	9.2	9.4	15.7	34.3	35.7	12.4	17.5		5.6	5
Seats	40	41	68	149	155	54	76	434[l]		
108th (2003)										
Percent	14.3	9.4	10.6	34.3	36.3	13.8	15.6		5.5	5
Seats	62	41	46	149	158	60	68	435		
109th (2005)										
Percent	9.9	11.5	10.1	31.6	29.5	22.4	16.6		5.9	5
Seats	43	50	44	137	128	97	72	434[m]		
110th (2007)										
Percent	13.1	9.9	11.3	34.3	26.7	22.8	16.3		6.0	5
Seats	57	43	49	149	116	99	71	435		

Note: Figures represent the makeup of Congress on the first day of the session.

a. E. E. Cox (D-GA) and Adolph Sabath (D-IL) were elected in 1952 but died before being sworn into office.

b. Antonio Fernandez (D-NM) and T. Millet Hand (R-NJ) were elected in 1956 but died before being sworn into office.

c. Alaska was admitted as a state in 1958. The total figure includes the addition of Alaska's representative.

d. Alaska was admitted as a state in 1958 and Hawaii in 1959. The total figure includes the addition of Alaska's and Hawaii's representatives. In 1963 the other states absorbed the proportionate loss in representatives necessary to give Alaska and Hawaii permanent representation under the 435-member figure established in 1911.

e. Clement Miller (D-CA) was elected posthumously.

f. John Fogarty (D-RI) was elected in 1966 but died before being sworn into office. Adam Powell (D-NY) was elected in 1966 but the results were contested and he was not sworn into office.

g. Nicholas Begich (D-AK) and Hale Boggs (D-LA) were elected posthumously. George Collins (D-IL) was elected in 1972 but died before being sworn into office.

h. Leo Ryan (D-CA) and William Steiger (R-WI) were elected in 1978 but died before being sworn into office.

i. Jack Swigert (R-CO) was elected in 1982 but died before being sworn into office.

j. Frank McCloskey's (D-IN) reelection in 1984 was disputed and he was not sworn into office until May 1, 1985.

k. William Nichols (D-AL) was elected in 1988 but died before being sworn into office. Daniel Coats (R-IN) won reelection in 1988 but was appointed to Dan Quayle's Senate seat on December 12, 1988.

l. Julian Dixon (D-CA) was elected in 2000 but died before being sworn into office.

m. Robert Matsui (D-CA) was elected in 2004 but died before being sworn into office.

Sources: *Congressional Quarterly Almanac* (Washington, D.C.: Congressional Quarterly, various editions); *Congressional Quarterly Weekly Report,* various issues; *Congressional Directory,* various editions; Clerk of the U.S. House of Representatives, http://clerk.house.gov; *The Almanac of American Politics* (Washington, D.C.: National Journal Group, various editions).

Table 1-7 Seniority of Senators, 1953–2007

Congress		Number of senators serving: 6 years or less	7–12 years	13–18 years	19 years or more	Total	Mean years service	Median years service
83rd	(1953)	46 (16)	29	14	7	96	8.5	7
84th	(1955)	42 (14)	37	8	9	96	8.4	7
85th	(1957)	37 (10)	36	13	10	96	9.6	9
86th	(1959)	42 (20)	30	14	12	98	9.4	8
87th	(1961)	42 (7)	25	22	11	100	9.7	9
88th	(1963)	42 (12)	26	18	14	100	9.9	7
89th	(1965)	29 (8)	36	16	19	100	11.1	9
90th	(1967)	28 (7)	34	19	19	100	11.6	9
91st	(1969)	32 (14)	32	17	19	100	11.2	11
92nd	(1971)	25 (10)	24	29	22	100	11.5	11
93rd	(1973)	40 (13)	20	20	20	100	11.2	9
94th	(1975)	36 (12)[a]	22	23	19	100	11.5	9
95th	(1977)	42 (17)	25	13	20	100	10.6	9
96th	(1979)	48 (20)	24	10	18	100	9.6	7
97th	(1981)	55 (18)	20	10	15	100	8.5	5
98th	(1983)	43 (5)	28	16	13	100	9.6	7
99th	(1985)	32 (7)	38	18	12	100	10.1	9
100th	(1987)	26 (13)	44	16	14	100	9.6	8
101st	(1989)	31 (10)	26	29	14	100	9.8	10
102nd	(1991)	30 (5)	23	28	19	100	11.1	11
103rd	(1993)	30 (13)	17	32	21	100	11.3	12
104th	(1995)	29 (11)	26	20	25	100	12.3	11
105th	(1997)	40 (15)	24	13	23	100	11.2	9
106th	(1999)	43 (8)	25	12	20	100	11.0	10
107th	(2001)	45 (11)	18	15	22	100	11.3	8
108th	(2003)	30 (10)	29	16	25	100	12.7	9.5
109th	(2005)	36 (9)	26	15	23	100	12.4	10
110th	(2007)	36 (10)	23	13	27	100	12.9	10

Note: Figures in parentheses are the number of freshmen senators. Senators who are currently in their first full term are listed under the "6 years or less" column. Figures represent the makeup of Congress on the first day of the session.

a. Total includes John Durkin (D-NH). After a contested election in 1974, the Senate declared the seat vacant as of August 8, 1975. He was then elected by special election, September 16, 1975, to fill the vacancy.

Sources: *Congressional Directory*, various editions; *Congressional Quarterly Almanac* (Washington, D.C.: Congressional Quarterly, various editions); *Congressional Quarterly Weekly Report*, various issues; *National Journal*, various issues; US Senate, http://www.senate.gov; *The Almanac of American Politics* (Washington, D.C.: National Journal Group, various editions).

Table 1-8 Prior Occupations of Representatives, 83rd–110th Congresses, 1953–2007

Occupation	83rd 1953	84th 1955	86th 1959	89th 1965	90th 1967	91st 1969	92nd 1971	93rd 1973	94th 1975	95th 1977	96th 1979	97th 1981	98th 1983
Acting/entertainer	—	—	—	—	—	—	—	—	—	—	—	—	—
Aeronautics	—	—	—	—	—	—	—	—	—	—	—	—	3
Agriculture	53	51	45	44	39	34	36	38	31	16	19	28	26
Business or banking	131	127	130	156	161	159	145	155	140	118	127	134	138
Clergy	—	—	—	3	3	2	2	4	5	6	6	3	2
Congressional aide	—	—	—	—	—	—	—	—	—	5	10	11	16
Education	46	47	41	68	57	59	61	59	64	70	57	59	43
Engineering	5	5	3	9	6	6	3	2	3	2	2	5	5
Journalism	36	33	35	43	39	39	30	23	24	27	11	21	22
Labor leader	—	—	—	3	2	3	3	3	3	6	4	5	2
Law	247	245	242	247	246	242	236	221	221	222	205	194	200
Law enforcement	—	—	—	—	—	2	1	2	2	7	5	5	5
Medicine	6	5	4	3	3	5	6	5	5	2	6	6	6
Military	—	—	—	—	—	—	—	—	—	—	—	—	1
Professional sports	—	—	—	—	—	—	—	—	—	—	—	—	3
Public service/politics	—	—	—	—	—	—	—	—	—	—	—	—	—
Real estate	—	—	—	—	—	—	—	—	—	—	—	—	—
Veteran	246	261	261	310	320	320	316	317	307	347	240	269	247
New Occupations Included													
Artistic/Creative	—	—	—	—	—	—	—	—	—	—	—	—	—
Healthcare	—	—	—	—	—	—	—	—	—	—	—	—	—
Homemaker/Domestic	—	—	—	—	—	—	—	—	—	—	—	—	—
Secretarial/clerical	—	—	—	—	—	—	—	—	—	—	—	—	—
Technical/Trade	—	—	—	—	—	—	—	—	—	—	—	—	—
Miscellaneous	—	—	—	—	—	—	—	—	—	—	—	—	—

Occupation	99th 1985	100th 1987	101st 1989	102nd 1991	103rd 1993	104th 1995	105th 1997	106th 1999	107th 2001	108th 2003	109th 2005	110th 2007
Acting/entertainer	—	1	2	2	1	1	1	1	1	2	3	3
Aeronautics	4	3	3	1	2	1	1	1	1	2	2	2
Agriculture	29	20	19	20	19	20	22	22	25	26	29	23
Business or banking	147	142	138	157	131	162	181	159	159	165	205	166
Clergy	2	2	2	2	2	2	1	1	2	2	3	3
Congressional aide	16	—	—	—	—	—	—	—	—	—	0	0
Education	37	38	42	57	66	75	74	84	92	88	91	88
Engineering	6	4	4	7	5	6	8	9	9	8	4	3
Journalism	20	20	17	25	24	15	12	9	9	11	11	7
Labor leader	2	2	2	3	2	2	1	1	2	7	9	13
Law	190	184	184	183	181	171	172	163	156	161	178	162
Law enforcement	8	7	8	5	10	11	10	10	10	9	9	10
Medicine	5	3	4	5	6	10	12	15	14	16	16	13
Military	1	0	0	1	0	0	1	1	2	3	3	4
Professional sports	3	5	4	3	1	2	3	2	3	1	2	1
Public service/politics	—	94	94	61	87	102	100	106	126	145	209	174
Real estate	—	—	—	—	—	—	—	20	24	30	31	36
Veteran	230	218	210	209	177	161	138	135	130	121	110	99
New Occupations Included												
Artistic/Creative	—	—	—	—	—	—	—	—	—	2	2	1
Healthcare	—	—	—	—	—	—	—	—	—	5	6	9
Homemaker/Domestic	—	—	—	—	—	—	—	—	—	4	4	7
Secretarial/clerical	—	—	—	—	—	—	—	—	—	2	4	9
Technical/Trade	—	—	—	—	—	—	—	—	—	4	3	2
Miscellaneous	—	—	—	—	—	—	—	—	—	4	3	2

Note: Blanks indicate years and occupations for which *Congressional Quarterly* did not compile data. Some members say they have more than one occupation.

Sources: *Congressional Quarterly Almanac* (Washington, D.C.: Congressional Quarterly, various editions); *Congressional Quarterly Weekly Report,* various issues; Clerk of the U.S. House of Representatives, http://clerk.house.gov; Military Officers Association of America; Veterans in Congress, The Veterans of Foreign Wars National Legislative Service, "Representatives with Military Service, 108th Congress;" Veterans' Information: Veterans in Congress, House Committee on Veterans' Affairs.

Table 1-9 Prior Occupations of Democratic Representatives, 83rd–110th Congresses, 1953–2007

Occupation	83rd 1953	84th 1955	86th 1959	89th 1965	90th 1967	91st 1969	92nd 1971	93rd 1973	94th 1975	95th 1977	96th 1979	97th 1981	98th 1983
Acting/entertainer	—	—	—	—	—	—	—	—	—	—	—	—	—
Aeronautics	—	—	—	—	—	—	—	—	—	—	—	—	0
Agriculture	21	22	28	26	17	14	19	14	13	6	10	11	13
Business or banking	55	59	71	98	82	76	70	72	84	69	71	58	73
Clergy	—	—	—	2	1	1	1	2	4	4	4	2	2
Congressional aide	—	—	—	—	—	—	—	—	—	3	7	9	10
Education	18	26	30	54	43	40	39	41	51	56	44	39	29
Engineering	3	3	2	6	4	3	2	1	1	0	0	2	2
Journalism	18	16	21	27	22	22	17	16	19	15	6	9	13
Labor leader	—	—	—	3	2	3	3	3	3	6	3	4	2
Law	130	136	168	171	150	150	150	137	158	154	135	121	132
Law enforcement	—	—	—	—	—	1	1	1	2	7	4	4	2
Medicine	2	2	2	1	1	2	4	3	3	1	1	2	2
Military	—	—	—	—	—	—	—	—	—	—	—	—	0
Professional sports	—	—	—	—	—	—	—	—	—	—	—	—	2
Public service/politics	—	—	—	—	—	—	—	—	—	—	—	—	—
Real estate	—	—	—	—	—	—	—	—	—	—	—	—	—
Veteran	118	131	175	210	183	181	185	175	198	—	—	—	—
New Occupations Included													
Artistic/Creative	—	—	—	—	—	—	—	—	—	—	—	—	—
Healthcare	—	—	—	—	—	—	—	—	—	—	—	—	—
Homemaker/Domestic	—	—	—	—	—	—	—	—	—	—	—	—	—
Secretarial/Clerical	—	—	—	—	—	—	—	—	—	—	—	—	—
Technical/Trade	—	—	—	—	—	—	—	—	—	—	—	—	—
Miscellaneous	—	—	—	—	—	—	—	—	—	—	—	—	—

Occupation	99th 1985	100th 1987	101st 1989	102nd 1991	103rd 1993	104th 1995	105th 1997	106th 1999	107th 2001	108th 2003	109th 2005	110th 2007
Acting/entertainer	—	0	1	1	0	0	0	0	0	0	1	3
Aeronautics	1	0	0	0	0	0	0	0	0	0	0	0
Agriculture	13	10	8	11	7	6	8	8	8	8	9	8
Business or banking	72	66	66	77	56	46	55	53	56	56	65	70
Clergy	2	2	2	2	1	1	1	0	1	1	2	1
Congressional aide	10	—	—	—	—	—	—	—	—	—	—	—
Education	24	24	25	37	45	39	40	49	53	50	51	55
Engineering	2	2	2	4	2	1	1	1	1	1	1	2
Journalism	10	11	9	14	11	4	4	2	1	3	2	3
Labor leader	2	2	2	3	2	1	1	1	1	5	4	7
Law	122	122	122	126	122	93	87	87	84	86	90	94
Law enforcement	6	6	6	4	8	7	8	8	7	6	6	7
Medicine	3	1	2	3	4	2	3	5	6	5	4	3
Military	0	0	0	0	0	0	0	0	0	0	0	2
Professional sports	2	3	3	2	0	0	0	0	0	0	0	1
Public service/politics	—	59	58	41	51	53	54	57	70	77	116	106
Real estate	—	—	—	—	—	—	—	3	2	3	3	4
Veteran	—	—	—	—	—	—	—	—	51	49	40	43
New Occupations Included												
Artistic/Creative	—	—	—	—	—	—	—	—	—	0	0	0
Healthcare	—	—	—	—	—	—	—	—	—	4	4	6
Homemaker/Domestic	—	—	—	—	—	—	—	—	—	2	2	3
Secretarial/Clerical	—	—	—	—	—	—	—	—	—	0	0	4
Technical/Trade	—	—	—	—	—	—	—	—	—	1	1	1
Miscellaneous	—	—	—	—	—	—	—	—	—	1	1	2

Note: Blanks indicate years and occupations or occupational fields for which *Congressional Quarterly* did not compile data. Some members say they have more than one occupation.

Sources: *Congressional Quarterly Almanac* (Washington, D.C.: Congressional Quarterly, various editions); *Congressional Quarterly Weekly Report*, various issues; Clerk of the U.S. House of Representatives, http://clerk.house.gov; Military Officers Association of America; Veterans in Congress, The Veterans of Foreign Wars National Legislative Service, "Representatives with Military Service, 108th Congress;" Veterans' Information: Veterans in Congress, House Committee on Veterans' Affairs.

Table 1-10 Prior Occupations of Republican Representatives, 83rd–110th Congresses, 1953–2007

Occupation	83rd 1953	84th 1955	86th 1959	89th 1965	90th 1967	91st 1969	92nd 1971	93rd 1973	94th 1975	95th 1977	96th 1979	97th 1981	98th 1983
Acting/entertainer	—	—	—	—	—	—	—	—	—	—	—	—	—
Aeronautics	—	—	—	—	—	—	—	—	—	—	—	—	3
Agriculture	32	29	17	18	22	20	17	24	18	10	9	17	13
Business or banking	76	68	59	58	79	83	75	83	56	49	56	76	65
Clergy	—	—	—	1	2	1	1	2	1	2	2	1	0
Congressional aide	—	—	—	—	—	—	—	—	—	2	3	2	6
Education	28	21	11	14	14	19	22	18	13	14	13	20	14
Engineering	2	2	1	3	2	3	1	1	2	2	2	3	3
Journalism	18	17	14	16	17	17	13	7	5	12	5	12	9
Labor leader	—	—	—	0	0	0	0	0	0	0	1	1	0
Law	117	109	74	76	96	92	86	84	63	68	70	73	68
Law enforcement	—	—	—	—	—	1	0	1	0	0	1	1	3
Medicine	4	3	2	2	2	3	2	2	2	1	5	4	4
Military	—	—	—	—	—	—	—	—	—	—	—	—	1
Professional sports	—	—	—	—	—	—	—	—	—	—	—	—	1
Public service/politics	—	—	—	—	—	—	—	—	—	—	—	—	—
Real estate	—	—	—	—	—	—	—	—	—	—	—	—	—
Veteran	128	130	86	100	137	139	131	142	109	—	—	—	—
New Occupations Included													
Artistic/Creative	—	—	—	—	—	—	—	—	—	—	—	—	—
Healthcare	—	—	—	—	—	—	—	—	—	—	—	—	—
Homemaker/Domestic	—	—	—	—	—	—	—	—	—	—	—	—	—
Secretarial/Clerical	—	—	—	—	—	—	—	—	—	—	—	—	—
Technical/Trade	—	—	—	—	—	—	—	—	—	—	—	—	—
Miscellaneous	—	—	—	—	—	—	—	—	—	—	—	—	—
Occupation	**99th 1985**	**100th 1987**	**101st 1989**	**102nd 1991**	**103rd 1993**	**104th 1995**	**105th 1997**	**106th 1999**	**107th 2001**	**108th 2003**	**109th 2005**	**110th 2007**	
Acting/entertainer	—	1	1	1	1	1	1	1	1	2	2	0	
Aeronautics	3	3	3	1	2	1	1	1	1	2	2	2	
Agriculture	16	10	11	9	12	14	14	14	17	18	20	15	
Business or banking	75	76	72	80	75	116	126	106	103	109	140	96	
Clergy	0	0	0	0	1	1	0	1	1	1	1	2	
Congressional aide	6	—	—	—	—	—	—	—	—	—	—	—	
Education	13	14	17	19	20	35	33	34	38	37	39	33	
Engineering	4	2	2	3	3	5	7	8	8	7	3	1	
Journalism	10	9	8	10	12	10	7	6	7	7	8	4	
Labor leader	0	0	0	0	0	1	0	0	1	2	5	6	
Law	68	62	62	57	59	78	85	76	71	75	88	68	
Law enforcement	2	1	2	1	2	4	2	2	3	3	3	3	
Medicine	2	2	2	2	2	8	9	10	8	11	12	10	
Military	1	0	0	1	0	0	1	1	2	3	3	2	
Professional sports	1	2	1	1	1	2	3	2	3	1	2	0	
Public service/politics	—	35	36	20	36	49	46	49	56	68	93	68	
Real estate	—	—	—	—	—	—	—	17	22	27	28	32	
Veteran	—	—	—	—	—	—	—	—	78	72	70	56	
New Occupations Included													
Artistic/Creative	—	—	—	—	—	—	—	—	—	1	1	1	
Healthcare	—	—	—	—	—	—	—	—	—	1	2	3	
Homemaker/Domestic	—	—	—	—	—	—	—	—	—	2	2	4	
Secretarial/Clerical	—	—	—	—	—	—	—	—	—	2	4	5	
Technical/Trade	—	—	—	—	—	—	—	—	—	3	2	1	
Miscellaneous	—	—	—	—	—	—	—	—	—	3	2	0	

Notes: Blanks indicate years and occupations or occupational fields for which *Congressional Quarterly* did not compile data. Some members say they have more than one occupation.

Sources: *Congressional Quarterly Almanac* (Washington, D.C.: Congressional Quarterly, various editions); *Congressional Quarterly Weekly Report*, various issues; Clerk of the U.S. House of Representatives, http://clerk.house.gov; Military Officers Association of America; Veterans in Congress, The Veterans of Foreign Wars National Legislative Service, "Representatives with Military Service, 108th Congress;" Veterans' Information: Veterans in Congress, House Committee on Veterans' Affairs.

Table 1-11 Prior Occupations of Senators, 83rd–110th Congresses, 1953–2007

Occupation	83rd 1953	84th 1955	86th 1959	89th 1965	90th 1967	91st 1969	92nd 1971	93rd 1973	94th 1975	95th 1977	96th 1979	97th 1981	98th 1983
Acting/entertainer	—	—	—	—	—	—	—	—	—	—	—	—	—
Aeronautics	—	—	—	—	—	—	—	—	—	—	—	—	2
Agriculture	22	21	17	18	18	16	13	11	10	9	6	9	9
Business or banking	28	28	28	25	23	25	27	22	22	24	29	28	29
Clergy	—	—	—	0	0	0	0	0	0	1	1	1	1
Congressional aide	—	—	—	—	—	—	—	—	—	0	0	0	0
Education	17	17	16	16	15	14	11	10	8	13	7	10	12
Engineering	5	2	2	2	2	2	2	2	2	0	0	2	0
Journalism	10	10	13	10	10	8	7	5	5	6	2	7	7
Labor leader	—	—	—	1	0	0	0	0	0	0	0	0	0
Law	59	60	61	67	68	68	65	68	67	68	65	59	61
Law enforcement	—	—	—	—	—	0	0	0	0	0	0	0	0
Medicine	1	2	1	1	1	0	1	1	1	1	1	1	1
Military	—	—	—	—	—	—	—	—	—	—	—	—	1
Professional sports	—	—	—	—	—	—	—	—	—	—	—	—	1
Public service/politics	—	—	—	—	—	—	—	—	—	—	—	—	—
Real estate	—	—	—	—	—	—	—	—	—	—	—	—	—
Veteran	63	62	61	63	65	69	73	73	73	65	58	73	76

Occupation	99th 1985	100th 1987	101st 1989	102nd 1991	103rd 1993	104th 1995	105th 1997	106th 1999	107th 2001	108th 2003	109th 2005	110th 2007
Acting/entertainer	—	0	0	0	0	1	1	1	1	0	0	1
Aeronautics	2	2	2	1	1	1	1	0	1	1	0	0
Agriculture	10	5	4	8	8	9	8	6	6	5	5	6
Business or banking	31	28	28	32	24	24	33	24	24	25	40	27
Clergy	1	1	1	1	1	0	1	1	1	0	0	0
Congressional aide	0	—	—	—	—	—	—	—	—	—	0	—
Education	12	12	11	10	11	10	13	13	16	12	13	14
Engineering	1	1	0	0	0	0	0	0	0	1	1	1
Journalism	8	8	8	10	9	8	9	8	7	6	7	8
Labor leader	0	0	0	0	0	0	0	0	1	2	3	3
Law	61	62	63	61	58	54	53	55	53	60	64	59
Law enforcement	0	0	0	0	0	0	0	0	0	0	1	0
Medicine	1	1	0	0	0	1	2	2	3	3	4	3
Military	1	1	1	1	1	1	1	1	1	1	1	1
Professional sports	1	1	1	1	1	1	0	1	1	1	1	1
Public service/politics	—	20	20	5	10	12	26	18	28	30	45	32
Real estate	—	—	—	—	—	—	—	4	4	3	3	3
Veteran	75	69	69	68	59	56	48	43	38	35	31	30

Note: Blanks indicate years and occupations or occupational fields for which *Congressional Quarterly* did not compile data. Some members say they have more than one occupation.

Sources: *Congressional Quarterly Almanac* (Washington, D.C.: Congressional Quarterly, various editions); *Congressional Quarterly Weekly Report,* various issues; US Senate, http://www.senate.gov; Military Officers Association of America; Veterans in Congress, The Veterans of Foreign Wars National Legislative Service, "Senators with Military Service, 108th Congress," Veterans' Information: Veterans in Congress.

Table 1-12 Prior Occupations of Democratic Senators, 83rd–110th Congresses, 1953–2007

Occupation	83rd 1953	84th 1955	86th 1959	89th 1965	90th 1967	91st 1969	92nd 1971	93rd 1973	94th 1975	95th 1977	96th 1979	97th 1981	98th 1983
Acting/entertainer	—	—	—	—	—	—	—	—	—	—	—	—	—
Aeronautics	—	—	—	—	—	—	—	—	—	—	—	—	1
Agriculture	8	7	7	10	9	7	5	4	5	3	2	2	2
Business or banking	11	10	14	14	12	12	15	12	12	14	15	13	14
Clergy				0	0	0	0	0	0	0	0	0	0
Congressional aide	—	—	—	—	—	—	—	—	—	0	0	0	0
Education	11	11	13	12	10	9	6	7	6	8	4	5	5
Engineering	2	0	2	2	2	2	2	2	2	0	0	1	0
Journalism	5	6	10	7	7	5	5	4	4	4	2	4	5
Labor leader	—	—	—	1	0	0	0	0	0	0	0	0	0
Law	34	27	43	48	48	42	41	42	45	46	43	33	32
Law enforcement	—	—	—	—	—	—	0	0	0	0	0	0	0
Medicine	1	2	1	1	1	0	1	1	1	1	1	1	1
Military	—	—	—	—	—	—	—	—	—	—	—	—	0
Professional sports	—	—	—	—	—	—	—	—	—	—	—	—	1
Public service/politics	—	—	—	—	—	—	—	—	—	—	—	—	—
Real estate	—	—	—	—	—	—	—	—	—	—	—	—	—
Veteran	31	32	40	44	43	41	41	42	45	—	—	—	—
Total number of Democratic members	46	48	64	68	64	58	54	56	60	61	58	46	46

Occupation	99th 1985	100th 1987	101st 1989	102nd 1991	103rd 1993	104th 1995	105th 1997	106th 1999	107th 2001	108th 2003	109th 2005	110th 2007
Acting/entertainer	—	0	0	0	0	0	0	0	0	0	0	1
Aeronautics	1	1	1	1	1	1	1	0	1	1	0	0
Agriculture	3	2	1	3	3	4	2	1	1	0	1	2
Business or banking	12	13	13	15	12	11	8	6	8	9	14	9
Clergy	0	0	0	0	0	0	0	0	0	0	0	0
Congressional aide	0	—	—	—	—	—	—	—	—	—	—	—
Education	4	6	6	6	6	5	5	5	8	7	6	7
Engineering	0	0	0	0	0	0	0	0	0	0	0	0
Journalism	6	6	5	8	7	5	2	2	1	1	2	3
Labor leader	0	0	0	0	0	0	0	0	0	0	1	—
Law	32	35	36	35	33	26	26	27	28	29	29	31
Law enforcement	0	0	0	0	0	0	0	0	0	0	1	0
Medicine	1	1	0	0	0	0	0	0	0	0	0	0
Military	1	0	0	0	0	0	0	0	0	0	0	0
Professional sports	0	1	1	1	1	1	0	0	0	0	0	0
Public service/politics	—	13	14	4	8	7	9	10	18	17	23	19
Real estate	—	—	—	—	—	—	—	2	2	2	2	1
Veteran	—	—	—	—	—	—	—	—	16	16	13	14
Total number of Democratic members	47	55	55	56	57	47	45	45	50	48	44	49

Note: Blanks indicate years and occupations or occupational fields for which *Congressional Quarterly* did not compile data. Some members say they have more than one occupation.

Sources: *Congressional Quarterly Almanac* (Washington, D.C.: Congressional Quarterly, various editions); *Congressional Quarterly Weekly Report*, various issues; US Senate, http://www.senate.gov; Military Officers Association of America; Veterans in Congress, The Veterans of Foreign Wars National Legislative Service, "Senators with Military Service, 108th Congress," Veterans' Information: Veterans in Congress.

Table 1-13 Prior Occupations of Republican Senators, 83rd–110th Congresses, 1953–2007

Occupation	83rd 1953	84th 1955	86th 1959	89th 1965	90th 1967	91st 1969	92nd 1971	93rd 1973	94th 1975	95th 1977	96th 1979	97th 1981	98th 1983
Acting/entertainer	—	—	—	—	—	—	—	—	—	—	—	—	—
Aeronautics	—	—	—	—	—	—	—	—	—	—	—	—	1
Agriculture	14	14	10	8	9	9	8	7	5	6	4	7	7
Business or banking	17	18	14	11	11	13	12	10	10	10	14	15	15
Clergy	—	—	—	0	0	0	0	0	0	1	1	1	1
Congressional aide	—	—	—	—	—	—	—	—	—	0	0	0	0
Education	6	6	3	4	5	5	5	3	2	5	3	5	7
Engineering	3	2	0	0	0	0	0	0	0	0	0	1	0
Journalism	5	4	3	3	3	3	2	1	1	2	0	3	2
Labor leader	—	—	—	0	0	0	0	0	0	0	0	0	0
Law	25	33	18	19	20	26	24	26	22	22	22	26	29
Law enforcement	—	—	—	—	0	0	0	0	0	0	0	0	0
Medicine	0	0	0	0	0	0	0	0	0	0	0	0	0
Military	—	—	—	—	—	—	—	—	—	—	—	—	1
Professional sports	—	—	—	—	—	—	—	—	—	—	—	—	0
Public service/politics	—	—	—	—	—	—	—	—	—	—	—	—	—
Real estate	—	—	—	—	—	—	—	—	—	—	—	—	—
Veteran	32	30	21	19	22	28	32	31	28	—	—	—	—
Total number of Republican members	48	47	34	32	36	42	44	42	37	38	41	53	54

Occupation	99th 1985	100th 1987	101st 1989	102nd 1991	103rd 1993	104th 1995	105th 1997	106th 1999	107th 2001	108th 2003	109th 2005	110th 2007
Acting/entertainer	—	0	0	0	0	1	1	1	1	0	0	0
Aeronautics	1	1	1	0	0	0	0	0	0	0	0	0
Agriculture	7	3	3	5	5	5	6	5	5	5	4	4
Business or banking	19	15	15	17	12	13	25	18	16	16	26	18
Clergy	1	1	1	1	1	0	1	1	1	0	0	0
Congressional aide	0	—	—	—	—	—	—	—	—	—	1	—
Education	8	6	5	4	5	5	8	8	8	5	7	6
Engineering	1	1	0	0	0	0	0	0	0	1	1	1
Journalism	2	2	3	2	2	3	7	6	6	5	5	4
Labor leader	0	0	0	0	0	0	0	0	1	2	2	1
Law	29	27	27	26	25	28	27	28	25	30	34	27
Law enforcement	0	0	0	0	0	0	0	0	0	0	0	0
Medicine	0	0	0	0	0	1	2	2	3	3	4	3
Military	1	1	1	1	1	1	1	1	1	1	1	1
Professional sports	0	0	0	0	0	0	0	1	1	1	1	1
Public service/politics	—	7	6	1	2	5	17	8	10	13	22	13
Real estate	—	—	—	—	—	—	—	2	2	1	2	2
Veteran	—	—	—	—	—	—	—	—	22	18	17	16
Total number of Republican members	53	45	45	44	43	53	55	55	50	51	55	49

Note: Blanks indicate years and occupations or occupational fields for which *Congressional Quarterly* did not compile data. Some members say they have more than one occupation.

Sources: *Congressional Quarterly Almanac* (Washington, D.C.: Congressional Quarterly, various editions); *Congressional Quarterly Weekly Report*, various issues; US Senate, http://www.senate.gov; Military Officers Association of America; Veterans in Congress, The Veterans of Foreign Wars National Legislative Service, "Senators with Military Service, 108th Congress," Veterans' Information: Veterans in Congress.

Table 1-14 Religious Affiliations of Representatives, 89th–110th Congresses, 1965–2007

	89th (1965)			90th (1967)			92nd (1971)			93rd (1973)			94th (1975)			95th (1977)			96th (1979)		
	D	R	Total	D	R	Total	D	R	Total	D	R	Total	D	R	Total	D	R	Total	D	R	Total
Catholic	81	13	94	73	22	95	77	24	101	67	30	97	88	22	110	95	24	119	92	23	115
Jewish	14	1	15	14	2	16	10	2	12	10	2	12	17	3	20	20	3	23	18	5	23
Protestant																					
Baptist	33	9	42	30	12	42	32	10	42	33	12	45	37	10	47	36	10	46	33	10	43
Episcopalian	29	25	54	25	25	50	27	22	49	25	25	50	29	21	50	26	22	48	29	21	50
Methodist	46	23	69	36	32	68	33	32	65	30	33	63	40	23	63	36	24	60	32	26	58
Presbyterian	30	26	56	26	37	63	26	41	67	25	35	60	25	25	50	23	22	45	25	27	52
All other	62	43	105	42	57	99	50	49	98	50	55	105	55	40	95	56	38	94	47	45	92
Total	295	140	435	249	184	433[a]	255	180	435	240	192	432[b]	291	144	435	292	143	435	276	157	433[c]

	97th (1981)			99th (1985)			101st (1989)			102nd (1991)			103rd (1993)			104th (1995)			105th (1997)		
	D	R	Total	D	R	Total	D	R	Total	D	R	Total	D	R	Total	D	R	Total	D	R	Total
Catholic	81	38	119	82	43	125	81	39	120	85	37	122	77	41	118	71	54	125	76	51	127
Jewish	21	6	27	24	6	30	26	5	31	26	6	33[e]	26	5	32[e]	20	4	25[e]	21	3	25[e]
Protestant																					
Baptist	28	13	41	27	9	36	33	10	43	35	12	47	38	13	51	30	27	57	31	27	58
Episcopalian	25	27	52	22	22	44	22	21	43	24	17	41	18	17	35	13	21	34	10	21	31
Methodist	26	30	56	35	27	62	37	25	62	38	24	62	31	23	54	21	29	50	17	29	46
Presbyterian	18	28	46	22	25	47	16	25	41	15	27	42	20	26	46	17	30	47	15	28	43
All other	4	50	94	41	50	91	44	49	93	44	44	88	49	50	99	32	65	97	37	68	105
Total	243	192	435	253	182	435	259	174	433[d]	267	167	435	258	176	435	204	230	435	207	227	435

	106th (1999)			107th (2001)			108th (2003)			109th (2005)			110th (2007)		
	D	R	Total	D	R	Total	D	R	Total	D	R	Total	D	R	Total
Catholic	76	50	126	76	49	125	71	53	124	72	57	129	87	41	128
Jewish	21	1	23[e]	24	2	27[e]	24	1	26[e]	24	1	26[e]	29	1	30
Protestant															
Baptist	34	28	62	33	30	64[f]	33	33	66	29	36	65	28	32	60
Episcopalian	9	21	30	7	23	30	10	24	34	9	23	32	8	20	28
Methodist	16	34	50	16	34	50	16	34	50	19	32	51	23	28	51
Presbyterian	15	26	41	15	23	38	11	26	37	11	25	36	13	21	34
All other	40	62	102	40	60	100	40	58	98	38	58	96	45	59	104
Total	211	222	435	211	221	434[g]	205	229	435	202	231	435	233	202	435

Notes: D indicates Democrats; R indicates Republicans. Third parties are omitted unless otherwise noted. Figures represent the makeup of Congress on the first day of the session.

a. John Fogarty (D-RI) was elected in 1966 but died before being sworn into office. Adam Powell (D-NY) was elected in 1966 but the results were contested and he was not sworn into office.

b. Nicholas Begich (D-AK) and Hale Boggs (D-LA) were elected posthumously. George Collins (D-IL) was elected in 1972 but died before being sworn into office.

c. Leo Ryan (D-CA) and William Steiger (R-WI) were elected in 1978 but died before being sworn into office.

d. William Nichols (D-AL) was elected in 1988 but died before being sworn into office. Daniel Coats (R-IN) won reelection in 1988 but was appointed to Dan Quayle's Senate seat on December 12, 1988.

e. Total includes Bernard Sanders (I-VT).

f. Total includes Virgil H. Goode, Jr. (I-VA).

g. Julian Dixon (D-CA) was elected in 2000 but died before being sworn into office.

Sources: *Congressional Quarterly Almanac* (Washington, D.C.: Congressional Quarterly, various editions); *Congressional Quarterly Weekly Report,* various issues.

Table 1-15 Religious Affiliations of Senators, 89th–110th Congresses, 1965–2007

	89th (1965)			90th (1967)			92nd (1971)			93rd (1973)			94th (1975)			95th (1977)			96th (1979)		
	D	R	Total	D	R	Total	D	R	Total	D	R	Total	D	R	Total	D	R	Total	D	R	Total
Catholic	12	2	14	11	2	13	9	3	12	10	4	14	12[a]	3	16[b]	10	3	13	9	4	13
Jewish	1	1	2	1	1	2	1	1	2	1	1	2	2	1	3	4	1	5	5	2	7
Protestant																					
Baptist	9	3	12	7	4	11	5	3	8	5	3	8	6	3	9	6	3	9	6	5	11
Episcopalian	8	7	15	8	7	15	4	13	17	6	11	17	5	9	15[c]	6	11	17	5	12	17
Methodist	15	7	22	15	8	23	13	7	20	13	5	18	11	5	16	13	7	20	13	6	19
Presbyterian	8	3	11	8	4	12	10	6	16	8	6	14	10	7	17	9	5	14	10	2	12
All other	15	9	24	14	10	24	13	12	25	15	12	27	15	9	24	14	8	22	11	10	21
Total	68	32	100	64	36	100	55	45	100	58	42	100	61	37	100	62	38	100	59	41	100

	97th (1981)			99th (1985)			101st (1989)			102nd (1991)			103rd (1993)			104th (1995)			105th (1997)		
	D	R	Total	D	R	Total	D	R	Total	D	R	Total	D	R	Total	D	R	Total	D	R	Total
Catholic	9	8	17	11	8	19	12	7	19	12	8	20	15	8	23	12	8	20	15	9	24
Jewish	3	3	6	4	4	8	5	3	8	6	2	8	9	1	10	8	1	9	9	1	10
Protestant																					
Baptist	3	6	9	4	7	11	4	8	12	4	8	12	4	7	11	3	7	10	2	7	9
Episcopalian	5	15	20	4	17	21	7	13	20	6	12	18	4	11	15	4	10	14	2	9	11
Methodist	9	9	18	9	7	16	9	4	13	9	4	13	7	5	12	5	6	11	5	8	13
Presbyterian	8	2	10	8	1	9	7	2	9	7	2	9	5	3	8	4	4	8	2	8	10
All other	10	10	20	7	9	16	11	8	19	11	9	20	13	8	21	11	17	28	10	13	23
Total	47	53	100	47	53	100	55	45	100	55	45	100	57	43	100	47	53	100	45	55	100

	106th (1999)			107th (2001)			108th (2003)			109th (2005)			110th (2007)		
	D	R	Total	D	R	Total	D	R	Total	D	R	Total	D	R	Total
Catholic	14	11	25	14	10	24	14	11	25	13	11	24	16	9	25
Jewish	10	1	11	9	1	10	9	2	11	9	2	11	11[e]	2	13
Protestant															
Baptist	1	7	8	2	7	9	1	5	6	1	6	7	1	6	7
Episcopalian	4	9	13	3	7	10	3	7	10	3	7	10	4	6	10
Methodist	5	7	12	10	6	16	7	5	12	5	7	12	5	7	12
Presbyterian	1	6	7	3	7	10	3	10	13	3	11	14	2	8	10
All other	10	14	24	9	12	21	12[d]	11	23	11[d]	11	22	12	11	23
Total	45	55	100	50	50	100	49	51	100	45	55	100	51	49	100

Notes: D indicates Democrats; R indicates Republicans. Third parties are omitted unless otherwise noted. Figures represent the makeup of Congress on the first day of the session.

a. Total includes John Durkin (D-NH) who was elected by special election to fill a disputed seat vacancy on September 16, 1975.
b. Total includes James Buckley (Conservative-NY).
c. Total includes Harry Byrd (I-VA).
d. Total includes James Jeffords (I-VT).
e. Total includes Bernie Sanders (I-VT) and Joseph Lieberman (I-CT).

Sources: *Congressional Quarterly Almanac* (Washington, D.C.: Congressional Quarterly, various years); *Congressional Quarterly Weekly Report*, various issues and January 31, 2005, 241. *The Almanac of American Politics 2004, 2006* (Washington, D.C.: National Journal Group, 2003, 2005).

Table 1-16 African Americans in Congress, 41st–110th Congresses, 1869–2007

	House		Senate			House		Senate	
Congress	D	R	D	R	Congress	D	R	D	R
41st (1869)	—	2	—	1	83rd (1953)	2	—	—	—
42nd (1871)	—	5	—	—	84th (1955)	3	—	—	—
43rd (1873)	—	7	—	—	85th (1957)	3	—	—	—
44th (1875)	—	7	—	1	86th (1959)	3	—	—	—
45th (1877)	—	3	—	1	87th (1961)	3	—	—	—
46th (1879)	—	—	—	1	88th (1963)	4	—	—	—
47th (1881)	—	2	—	—	89th (1965)	5	—	—	—
48th (1883)	—	2	—	—	90th (1967)	5	—	—	1
49th (1885)	—	2	—	—	91st (1969)	9	—	—	1
50th (1887)	—	—	—	—	92nd (1971)	13	—	—	1
51st (1889)	—	3	—	—	93rd (1973)	16	—	—	1
52nd (1891)	—	1	—	—	94th (1975)	16	—	—	1
53rd (1893)	—	1	—	—	95th (1977)	15	—	—	1
54th (1895)	—	1	—	—	96th (1979)	15	—	—	—
55th (1897)	—	1	—	—	97th (1981)	17	—	—	—
56th (1899)[a]	—	1	—	—	98th (1983)	20	—	—	—
71st (1929)	—	1	—	—	99th (1985)	20	—	—	—
72nd (1931)	—	1	—	—	100th (1987)	22	—	—	—
73rd (1933)	—	1	—	—	101st (1989)	23	—	—	—
74th (1935)	1	—	—	—	102nd (1991)	25	1	—	—
75th (1937)	1	—	—	—	103rd (1993)	38	1	1	—
76th (1939)	1	—	—	—	104th (1995)	37	2	1	—
77th (1941)	1	—	—	—	105th (1997)	36	1	1	—
78th (1943)	1	—	—	—	106th (1999)	36	1	—	—
79th (1945)	2	—	—	—	107th (2001)	35	1	—	—
80th (1947)	2	—	—	—	108th (2003)	37	—	—	—
81st (1949)	2	—	—	—	109th (2005)	40	—	1	—
82nd (1951)	2	—	—	—	110th (2007)	40	—	1	—

Notes: The data do not include nonvoting delegates or commissioners. Figures represent the makeup of Congress on the first day of the session.

a. After the 56th Congress, there were no African American members in either the House or Senate until the 71st Congress.

Sources: *Black Americans in Congress, 1870–1977,* H. Doc. 95-258, 95th Cong., 1st sess., 1977; *Congressional Quarterly Almanac* (Washington, D.C.: Congressional Quarterly, various editions); *Congressional Quarterly Weekly Report,* various issues; Clerk of the U.S. House of Representatives, http://clerk.house.gov.

Table 1-17 Hispanic Americans in Congress, 41st–110th Congresses, 1869–2007

Congress		House		Senate		Congress		House		Senate	
		D	R	D	R			D	R	D	R
41st	(1869)	—	1	—	—	86th	(1959)	1	—	1	—
42nd	(1871)	—	1	—	—	87th	(1961)	2	—	1	—
43rd	(1873)[a]	—	1	—	—	88th	(1963)	3	—	1	—
63rd	(1913)	1	—	—	—	89th	(1965)	3	—	1	—
64th	(1915)	1	1	—	—	90th	(1967)	3	—	1	—
65th	(1917)	1	—	—	—	91st	(1969)	3	1	1	—
66th	(1919)	1	1	—	—	92nd	(1971)	4	1	1	—
67th	(1921)	1	1	—	—	93rd	(1973)	4	1	1	—
68th	(1923)	1	—	—	—	94th	(1975)	4	1	1	—
69th	(1925)	1	—	—	—	95th	(1977)	4	1	—	—
70th	(1927)	1	—	—	1	96th	(1979)	5	1	—	—
71st	(1929)	—	—	—	—	97th	(1981)	6	1	—	—
72nd	(1931)	2	—	—	—	98th	(1983)	9	1	—	—
73rd	(1933)	2	—	—	—	99th	(1985)	10	1	—	—
74th	(1935)	1	—	1	—	100th	(1987)	10	1	—	—
75th	(1937)	1	—	1	—	101st	(1989)	9	1	—	—
76th	(1939)	1	—	1	—	102nd	(1991)	10	1	—	—
77th	(1941)	—	—	1	—	103rd	(1993)	14	3	—	—
78th	(1943)	1	—	1	—	104th	(1995)	14	3	—	—
79th	(1945)	1	—	1	—	105th	(1997)	14	3	—	—
80th	(1947)	1	—	1	—	106th	(1999)	16	3	—	—
81st	(1949)	1	—	1	—	107th	(2001)	16	3	—	—
82nd	(1951)	1	—	1	—	108th	(2003)	18	4	—	—
83rd	(1953)	1	—	1	—	109th	(2005)	19	4	1	1
84th	(1955)	1	—	1	—	110th	(2007)	20	3	2	1
85th	(1957)	1	—	1	—						

Notes: The data do not include nonvoting delegates or commissioners. Figures represent the makeup of Congress on the first day of the session.

a. After the 43rd Congress, there were no Hispanic members in either the House or Senate until the 63rd Congress.

Sources: *Biographical Directory of the United States Congress* 1774–1989; *Congressional Quarterly Almanac* (Washington, D.C.: Congressional Quarterly, various editions); *Congressional Quarterly Weekly Report*, various issues; Clerk of the U.S. House of Representatives, http://clerk.house.gov; http://www.senate.gov/galleries/daily/minority.htm.

Table 1-18 Women in Congress, 65th–110th Congresses, 1917–2007

Congress		House D	House R	Senate D	Senate R	Congress		House D	House R	Senate D	Senate R
65th	(1917)	—	1	—	—	88th	(1963)	6	6	1	1
66th	(1919)	—	—	—	—	89th	(1965)	7	4	1	1
67th	(1921)	—	2	—	1	90th	(1967)	5	5	—	1
68th	(1923)	—	1	—	—	91st	(1969)	6	4	—	1
69th	(1925)	1	2	—	—	92nd	(1971)	10	3	—	1
70th	(1927)	2	3	—	—	93rd	(1973)	14	2	1	—
71st	(1929)	4	5	—	—	94th	(1975)	14	5	—	—
72nd	(1931)	4	3	1	—	95th	(1977)	13	5	—	—
73rd	(1933)	4	3	1	—	96th	(1979)	11	5	1	1
74th	(1935)	4	2	2	—	97th	(1981)	10	9	—	2
75th	(1937)	4	1	2	—	98th	(1983)	13	9	—	2
76th	(1939)	4	4	1	—	99th	(1985)	13	9	—	2
77th	(1941)	4	5	1	—	100th	(1987)	12	11	1	1
78th	(1943)	2	6	1	—	101st	(1989)	14	11	1	1
79th	(1945)	6	5	—	—	102nd	(1991)	19	9	1	1
80th	(1947)	3	4	—	1	103rd	(1993)	36	12	5	1
81st	(1949)	5	4	—	1	104th	(1995)	31	17	5	3
82nd	(1951)	4	6	—	1	105th	(1997)	35	16	6	3
83rd	(1953)	5	7	—	1	106th	(1999)	40	16	6	3
84th	(1955)	10	7	—	1	107th	(2001)	41	18	10	3
85th	(1957)	9	6	—	1	108th	(2003)	38	21	9	5
86th	(1959)	9	8	—	1	109th	(2005)	42	23	9	5
87th	(1961)	11	7	1	1	110th	(2007)	50	21	11	5

Notes: The data include only women who were sworn in as members and served more than one day. Figures represent the makeup of Congress on the first day of the session.

Sources: *Women in Congress,* H. Rept. 94-1732, 94th Cong., 2nd sess., 1976; *Congressional Quarterly Almanac* (Washington, D.C.: Congressional Quarterly, various editions); *Congressional Quarterly Weekly Report,* various issues; Clerk of the U.S. House of Representatives, http://clerk.house.gov; US Senate, http://www.senate.gov.

Table 1-19 Political Parties of Senators and Representatives, 34th–110th Congresses, 1855–2007

	Senate					House of Representatives				
Congress	Number of senators	Democrats	Republicans	Other parties	Vacant	Number of representatives	Democrats	Republicans	Other parties	Vacant
34th (1855–1857)	62	42	15	5	—	234	83	108	43	—
35th (1857–1859)	64	39	20	5	—	237	131	92	14	—
36th (1859–1861)	66	38	26	2	—	237	101	113	23	—
37th (1861–1863)	50	11	31	7	1	178	42	106	28	2
38th (1863–1865)	51	12	39	—	—	183	80	103	—	—
39th (1865–1867)	52	10	42	—	—	191	46	145	—	—
40th (1867–1869)	53	11	42	—	—	193	49	143	—	1
41st (1869–1871)	74	11	61	—	2	243	73	170	—	—
42nd (1871–1873)	74	17	57	—	—	243	104	139	—	—
43rd (1873–1875)	74	19	54	—	1	293	88	203	—	2
44th (1875–1877)	76	29	46	—	1	293	181	107	3	2
45th (1877–1879)	76	36	39	1	—	293	156	137	—	—
46th (1879–1881)	76	43	33	—	—	293	150	128	14	1
47th (1881–1883)	76	37	37	2	—	293	130	152	11	—
48th (1883–1885)	76	36	40	—	—	325	200	119	6	—
49th (1885–1887)	76	34	41	—	1	325	182	140	2	1
50th (1887–1889)	76	37	39	—	—	325	170	151	4	—
51st (1889–1891)	84	37	47	—	—	330	156	173	1	—
52nd (1891–1893)	88	39	47	2	—	333	231	88	14	—
53rd (1893–1895)	88	44	38	3	3	356	220	126	10	—
54th (1895–1897)	88	39	44	5	—	357	104	246	7	—
55th (1897–1899)	90	34	46	10	—	357	134	206	16	1
56th (1899–1901)	90	26	53	11	—	357	163	185	9	—
57th (1901–1903)	90	29	56	3	2	357	153	198	5	1
58th (1903–1905)	90	32	58	—	—	386	178	207	—	1
59th (1905–1907)	90	32	58	—	—	386	136	250	—	—
60th (1907–1909)	92	29	61	—	2	386	164	222	—	—
61st (1909–1911)	92	32	59	—	1	391	172	219	—	—
62nd (1911–1913)	92	42	49	—	1	391	228	162	1	—
63rd (1913–1915)	96	51	44	1	—	435	290	127	18	—
64th (1915–1917)	96	56	39	1	—	435	231	193	8	3
65th (1917–1919)	96	53	42	1	—	435	210[a]	216	9	—
66th (1919–1921)	96	47	48	1	—	435	191	237	7	—
67th (1921–1923)	96	37	59	—	—	435	132	300	1	2
68th (1923–1925)	96	43	51	2	—	435	207	225	3	—
69th (1925–1927)	96	40	54	1	1	435	183	247	5	—
70th (1927–1929)	96	47	48	1	—	435	195	237	3	—
71st (1929–1931)	96	39	56	1	—	435	163	267	1	4
72nd (1931–1933)	96	47	48	1	—	435	216[b]	218	1	—
73rd (1933–1935)	96	59	36	1	—	435	313	117	5	—
74th (1935–1937)	96	69	25	2	—	435	322	103	10	—
75th (1937–1939)	96	75	17	4	—	435	333	89	13	—
76th (1939–1941)	96	69	23	4	—	435	262	169	4	—
77th (1941–1943)	96	66	28	2	—	435	267	162	6	—
78th (1943–1945)	96	57	38	1	—	435	222	209	4	—
79th (1945–1947)	96	57	38	1	—	435	243	190	2	—
80th (1947–1949)	96	45	51	—	—	435	188	246	1	—
81st (1949–1951)	96	54	42	—	—	435	263	171	1	—
82nd (1951–1953)	96	48	47	1	—	435	234	199	2	—
83rd (1953–1955)	96	46	48	2	—	435	213	221	1	—
84th (1955–1957)	96	48	47	1	—	435	232	203	—	—
85th (1957–1959)	96	49	47	—	—	435	234	201	—	—
86th (1959–1961)	98	64	34	—	—	436[c]	283	153	—	—
87th (1961–1963)	100	64	36	—	—	437[d]	262	175	—	—
88th (1963–1965)	100	67	33	—	—	435	258	176	—	1
89th (1965–1967)	100	68	32	—	—	435	295	140	—	—
90th (1967–1969)	100	64	36	—	—	435	246	187	—	2

Congress		Senate					House of Representatives				
		Number of senators	Democrats	Republicans	Other parties	Vacant	Number of representatives	Democrats	Republicans	Other parties	Vacant
91st	(1969–1971)	100	58	42	—	—	435	243	192	—	—
92nd	(1971–1973)	100	54	44	2	—	435	255	180	—	—
93rd	(1973–1975)	100	56	42	2	—	435	239	192	1	3
94th	(1975–1977)	100	61	37	2	—	435	291	144	—	—
95th	(1977–1979)	100	61	38	1	—	435	292	143	—	—
96th	(1979–1981)	100	58	41	1	—	435	276	157	—	2
97th	(1981–1983)	100	46	53	1	—	435	243	192	—	—
98th	(1983–1985)	100	46	54	—	—	435	268	166	—	1
99th	(1985–1987)	100	47	53	—	—	435	252	182	—	1
100th	(1987–1989)	100	55	45	—	—	435	258	177	—	—
101st	(1989–1991)	100	55	45	—	—	435	259	174	—	2
102nd	(1991–1993)	100	56	44	—	—	435	267	167	1	—
103rd	(1993–1995)	100	57	43	—	—	435	258	176	1	—
104th	(1995–1997)	100	47	53	—	—	435	204	230	1	—
105th	(1997–1999)	100	45	55	—	—	435	207	227	1	—
106th	(1999–2001)	100	45	55	—	—	435	211	223	1	—
107th	(2001–2003)	100	50	50	—	—	435	211	221	2	1
108th	(2003–2005)	100	48	51	1	—	435	205	229	1	—
109th	(2005–2007)	100	44	55	1	—	435	201	232	1	1
110th	(2007–2009)	100	49	49	2	—	435	233	202	—	—

Note: Figures represent the makeup of Congress on the first day of the session.

a. Democrats organized House with help of other parties.

b. Democrats organized House because of Republican deaths.

c. Alaska was admitted as a state in 1958. The total figure includes the addition of Alaska's representative.

d. Alaska was admitted as a state in 1958 and Hawaii in 1959. The total figure includes the addition of Alaska's and Hawaii's representatives.

Sources: *Congressional Directory,* various editions; *Congressional Quarterly Weekly Report,* various issues; Clerk of the U.S. House of Representatives, http://clerk.house.gov; US Senate, http://www.senate.gov; *The Almanac of American Politics* (Washington, D.C.: National Journal Group, various editions).

Map 4 Apportionment of Congressional Seats, by Region, 1910 and 2000 (435 seats)

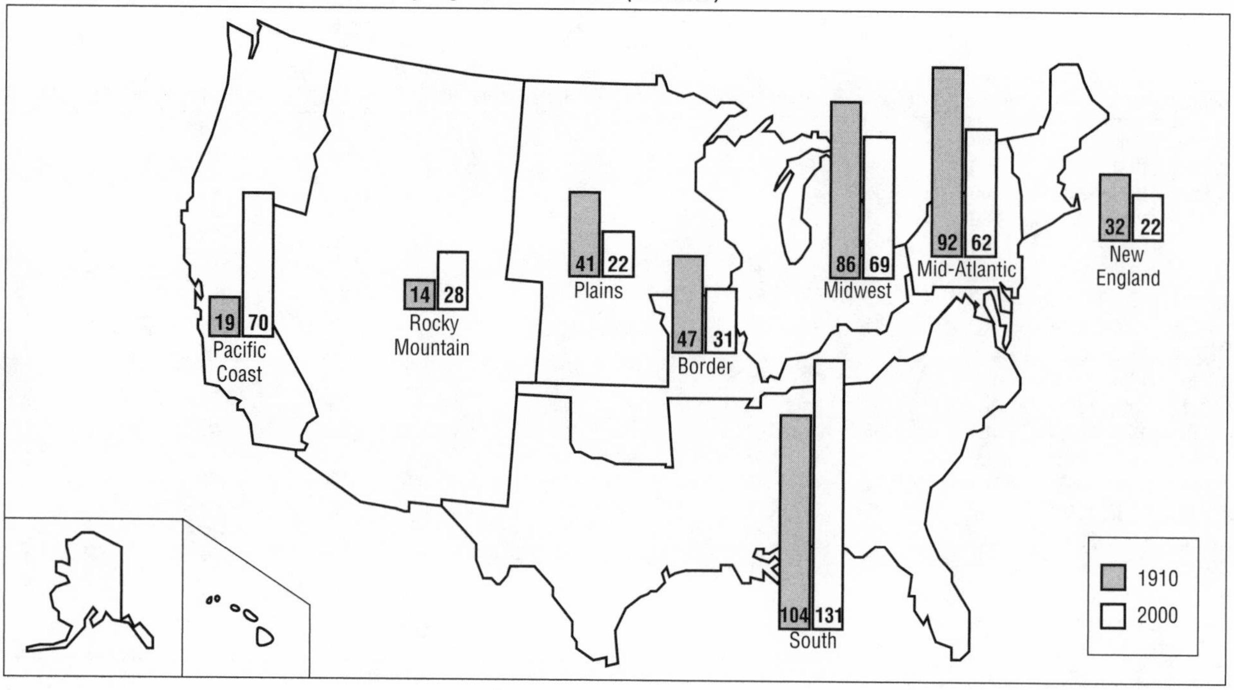

Source: Table 1-1.

Figure 1-1 Democratic Party Strength in Congress, by Region, 69th–110th Congresses, 1925–2008

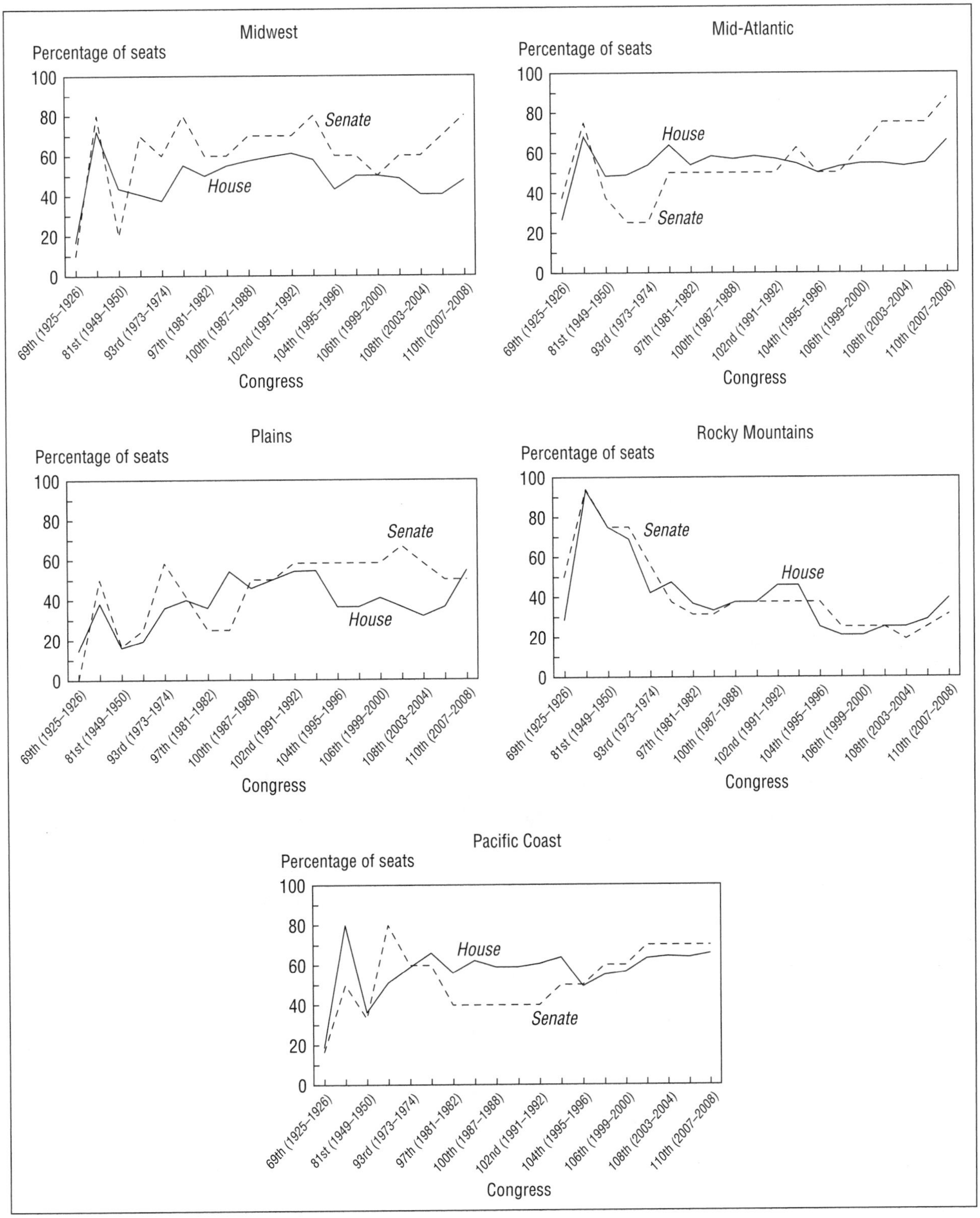

Source: Tables 1-2 and 1-4.

2

Elections

Table 2-1 Turnout in Presidential and House Elections, 1930–2006

Year	Presidential elections	House elections	Year	Presidential elections	House elections
1930	—	33.7	1970	—	48.4
1932	56.3	49.7	1972	56.6	51.4
1934	—	41.4	1974	—	40.0
1936	62.2	53.5	1976	55.1	50.3
1938	—	44.0	1978	—	39.5
1940	65.2	55.4	1980	54.7	49.3
1942	—	32.5	1982	—	42.2
1944	58.4	52.7	1984	56.0	50.2
1946	—	37.1	1986	—	38.2
1948	53.3	48.1	1988	53.1	47.6
1950	—	41.1	1990	—	38.1
1952	63.4	57.6	1992	58.1	53.6
1954	—	41.7	1994	—	40.5
1956	61.2	55.9	1996	51.5	48.2
1958	—	43.0	1998	—	37.6
1960	64.9	58.5	2000	54.3	50.2
1962	—	49.2	2002	—	37.2
1964	62.8	59.0	2004	60.7	55.3
1966	—	49.3	2006	—	40.4
1968	61.9	56.3			

Note: For all presidential elections and House elections 1962–2006, turnout is computed using the number of citizens eligible to vote in the United States. For House elections before 1962, it is computed using the voting age population (including non-citizens). The voting-eligible population is the population that is eligible to vote. Counted among the voting-age population are persons who are ineligible to vote, such as non-citizens, felons (depending on state law), and mentally incapacitated persons. Not counted are persons in the military or civilians living overseas.

Sources: For House elections 1930–60, U.S. Bureau of the Census, *Statistical Abstract of the United States* (Washington, D.C.: U.S. Government Printing Office); for all presidential elections and House elections 1962–2004, numbers were provided by Curtis Gans of the Center for the Study of the American Electorate at American University. For 2006, the VEP was calculated by Michael McDonald and can be found at http://elections.gmu.edu/Voter_Turnout_2006.htm.

Table 2-2 Popular Vote and House Seats Won by Party, 1946–2006

Year	Democratic candidates: Percentage of all votes[b]	Democratic candidates: Percentage of seats won[c]	Republican candidates: Percentage of all votes[b]	Republican candidates: Percentage of seats won[c]	Change from last election[a]: Percentage of major party votes	Change from last election[a]: Percentage of seats won[c]	Difference between Democratic percentage of seats and votes won
1946	44.3	43.3	53.5	56.7	6.4R	12.8R	–1.0
1948	51.6	60.6	45.4	39.4	7.9D	17.3D	9.0
1950	48.9	54.0	48.9	46.0	3.2R	6.6R	5.1
1952	49.2	49.1	49.3	50.9	0.1R	4.9R	–0.1
1954	52.1	53.3	47.0	46.7	2.6D	4.2D	1.2
1956	50.7	53.8	48.7	46.2	1.5R	0.5D	3.1
1958	55.5	64.9	43.6	35.1	5.0D	11.1D	9.4
1960	54.4	60.0	44.8	40.0	1.2R	4.9R	5.6
1962	52.1	59.4	47.1	40.6	2.3R	0.6R	7.3
1964	56.9	67.8	42.4	32.2	4.8D	8.4D	10.9
1966	50.5	57.0	48.0	43.0	6.0R	10.8R	6.5
1968	50.0	55.9	48.2	44.1	0.3R	1.1R	5.9
1970	53.0	58.6	44.5	41.4	3.4D	2.7D	5.6
1972	51.7	55.8	46.4	44.2	1.7R	2.8R	4.1
1974	57.1	66.9	40.5	33.1	5.8D	11.1D	9.8
1976	56.2	67.1	42.1	32.9	1.3R	0.2D	10.9
1978	53.4	63.7	44.7	36.3	2.8R	3.4R	10.3
1980	50.4	55.9	48.0	44.1	3.2R	7.8R	5.5
1982	55.2	61.8	43.3	38.2	5.2D	5.9D	6.6
1984	52.1	58.2	47.0	41.8	4.1R	3.6R	6.1
1986	54.5	59.3	44.6	40.7	2.4D	1.1D	4.8
1988	53.3	59.8	45.5	40.2	1.1R	0.5D	6.5
1990	52.9	61.4	45.0	38.4	0.1D	1.6D	8.5
1992	50.8	59.3	45.6	40.5	1.4R	2.1R	8.5
1994	45.4	46.9	52.4	52.9	6.3R	12.4R	1.5
1996	48.5	47.6	48.9	52.0	3.4D	0.7D	–0.9
1998	47.1	48.5	48.0	51.3	0.3R	0.9D	1.4
2000	47.0	48.7	47.3	50.8	0.3D	0.2D	1.7
2002	45.0	47.0	49.6	52.8	2.3R	2.0R	2.0
2004	46.6	46.4	49.2	53.4	1.1D	0.6R	–0.2
2006	52.0	53.6	45.6	46.4	5.4D	7.2D	1.6

a. The data show the percentage-point increase over previous election in votes or seats won by Republicans (R) or Democrats (D).

b. Republican and Democratic percentages of all votes excludes districts in which candidates ran unopposed and no vote was recorded.

c. Total percentage of seats won does not equal 100% due to the election of independents and/or rounding.

Sources: *Biographical Directory of the United States Congress 1774–1989* (Washington, D.C.: Government Printing Office, 1989); *Congressional Quarterly Almanac* (Washington, D.C.: Congressional Quarterly, various years); *National Journal,* various issues; *The Almanac of American Politics* (Washington, D.C.: National Journal Group, various years).

Table 2-3 Net Party Gains in House and Senate Seats, General and Special Elections, 1946–2006

	General elections[a]		Special elections[b]			General elections[a]		Special elections[b]	
Year	House	Senate	House	Senate	Year	House	Senate	House	Senate
			2R (13)	3R (8)				4R (6)	1R (2)
1946	56R	13R			1978	15R	3R		
			0 (16)	0 (3)				1R (6)	0 (0)
1948	75D	9D			1980	34R	12R		
			0 (10)	2R (6)				1D (8)	0 (0)
1950	28R	5R			1982	26D	1R		
			3R (13)	2R (4)				1R (7)	1R (1)
1952	22R	1R			1984	14R	2D		
			2D (8)	0 (9)				0 (4)	1D (1)
1954	19D	2D			1986	5D	8D		
			0 (2)	2R (3)				1R (6)	0 (0)
1956	2D	1D			1988	2D	0		
			0 (10)	1D (4)				1D (11)	0 (1)
1958	49D	15D			1990	9D	1D		
			1R (7)	1D (3)				1D (6)	2D (3)[c]
1960	22R	2R			1992	10R	0		
			0 (12)	0 (6)				2R (7)	1R (2)
1962	1R	3D			1994	52R	8R[d]		
			2R (9)	0 (2)				1R (5)	1D (1)
1964	37D	1D			1996	3D[e]	2R		
			0 (8)	1R (3)				0 (8)	0
1966	47R	4R			1998	5D	0		
			1R (5)	0 (0)				0 (3)	0
1968	5R	6R			2000	2D	4D		
			3D (9)	0 (2)				1R (9)[f]	0
1970	12D	2R			2002	8R	1R		
			0 (9)	0 (2)				1D (3)[g]	0
1972	12R	2D			2004	3R	4R		
			4D (10)	0 (0)				0 (3)	0
1974	49D	4D			2006	31D	6D		
			0 (6)	1D (1)				3 (11)[h]	0
1976	1D	0							

Note: D indicates Democrats; R indicates Republicans.

a. The general election figure is the difference between the number of seats won by the party gaining seats in that election and the number of seats won by that party in the preceding general election.

b. The special election figure is the net shift in seats held by the major parties as a result of special elections held between the two general elections. The figure does not include special elections held on the day of the general election. The number of special elections appears in parentheses.

c. The total number of special elections (3) includes the special election of Dianne Feinstein (D-CA) to fill the seat to which John Seymour was temporarily appointed. The special election was held at the same time as the generall election (November 3, 1992).

d. Sen. Richard Shelby (AL) switched from the Democratic to the Republican Party the day after the election and brought the total Republican gain to nine.

e. Between the two elections, six Representatives switched parties. When we consider those switches and special election Republican gains, the total 1996 Democratic gain was nine seats.

f. Includes Ed Case (D-HI) who was elected November 30, 2002 after sine die adjournment of the House of Representatives, to fill Patsy Mink's chair (D-HI) in the 107th Congress.

g. Includes Ed Case (D-HI) who was elected in a special election on January 4, 2003 to fill Patsy Mink's (D-HI) chair for the 108th Congress.

h. Through June 6, 2008.

Sources: *Congressional Quarterly Almanac* (Washington, D.C.: Congressional Quarterly, various years); *Congressional Quarterly Weekly Report*, various issues; *National Journal*, various issues.

Table 2-4 Losses by the President's Party in Midterm Elections, 1862–2006

Year	Party holding presidency	President's party gain/ loss of seats in House	President's party gain/ loss of seats in Senate
1862	R	–3	8
1866	R	–2	0
1870	R	–31	–4
1874	R	–96	–8
1878	R	–9	–6
1882	R	–33	3
1886	D	–15	3
1890	R	–85	0
1894	D	–125	–4
1898	R	–19	9
1902	R	9[a]	2
1906	R	–28	3
1910	R	–57	–8
1914	D	–61	5
1918	D	–22	–6
1922	R	–77	–6
1926	R	–9	–6
1930	R	–52	–8
1934	D	9	10
1938	D	–72	–7
1942	D	–44	–9
1946	D	–55	–12
1950	D	–28	–5
1954	R	–18	–1
1958	R	–48	–12
1962	D	–4	2
1966	D	–48	–4
1970	R	–12	1
1974	R	–48	–4
1978	D	–15	–3
1982	R	–26	1
1986	R	–5	–8
1990	R	–8	–1
1994	D	–54	–8[b]
1998	D	5	0
2002	R	8	1
2006	R	–30	–6

Notes: D indicates Democrats; R indicates Republicans.

Each entry is the difference between the number of seats won by the president's party in that midterm election and the number of seats won by that party in the preceding general election. Because of changes in the overall number of seats in the Senate and House, in the number of seats won by third parties, and in the number of vacancies, a Republican loss is not always matched precisely by a Democratic gain, or vice versa. Data reflect immediate election results.

a. Although the Republicans gained nine seats in the 1902 elections, they actually lost ground to the Democrats, who gained twenty-five seats after the increase in the overall number of Representatives after the 1900 census.

b. Sen. Richard Shelby (AL) switched from the Democratic to the Republican Party the day following the election, so that the total loss was nine seats.

Sources: *Biographical Directory of the United States Congress 1774–1989* (Washington, D.C.: Government Printing Office, 1989); *Congressional Quarterly Almanac* (Washington, D.C.: Congressional Quarterly, various years); *National Journal,* various issues; *The Almanac of American Politics* (Washington, D.C.: National Journal Group, various years).

Table 2-5 House Seats That Changed Party, 1954–2006

Year	Total changes	Incumbent defeated		Open seat	
		D → R	R → D	D → R	R → D
1954	26	3	18	2	3
1956	20	7	7	2	4
1958	49	1	34	0	14
1960	37	23	2	6	6
1962	19	9	5	2	3
1964	55	5	39	3	8
1966	47	38	2	5	2
1968	11	5	0	2	4
1970	25	2	9	6	8
1972	21	8	3	6	4
1974	55	4	36	2	13
1976	22	7	5	3	7
1978	32	15	5	7	5
1980	41	28	3	9	1
1982	31	1	23	3	4
1984	22	13	3	5	1
1986	22	2	7	7	6
1988	9	2	4	1	2
1990	20	6	8	0	6
1992	43	19	12	10	2
1994	60	35	0	21	4
1996	31	3	16	9	3
1998	18	1	5	5	7
2000	18	2	4	6	6
2002	15	2	2	6	5
2004	13	6	2	2	3
2006	31	0	22	0	9

Notes: D indicates Democrat; R indicates Republican.

This table reflects shifts in party control of seats from immediately before to immediately after the November elections. It does not include party gains resulting from the creation of new districts and does not account for situations in which two districts were reduced to one, thus forcing incumbents to run against each other.

Party gains that resulted from an incumbent being defeated in either a primary or general election are classified as incumbent defeats. In situations where the incumbent declined to run again, ran for another political office, or died or resigned before the end of the term are classified as open seats.

Sources: *Biographical Directory of the United States Congress 1774–1989* (Washington, D.C.: Government Printing Office, 1989); *Congressional Quarterly Almanac* (Washington, D.C.: Congressional Quarterly, various years); *National Journal,* various issues; *The Almanac of American Politics* (Washington, D.C.: National Journal Group, various years).

Table 2-6 Senate Seats That Changed Party, 1954–2006

Year	Total changes	Incumbent defeated		Open seat	
		D → R	R → D	D → R	R → D
1954	6	2	3	1	0
1956	8	1	3	3	1
1958	13	0	10	0	3
1960	3	1	1	1	0
1962	8	2	4	0	2
1964	4	1	3	0	0
1966	3	2	0	1	0
1968	9	5	1	2	1
1970	6	3	2	1	0
1972	10	2	4	2	2
1974	6	0	2	1[a]	3
1976	14	5	4	2	3
1978	13	5	3	3	2
1980	12	12	0	0	0
1982	3	1	1	0	1
1984	4	1	2	0	1
1986	10	0	7	1	2
1988	7	1	3	2	1
1990	1	0	1	0	0
1992	4	1	3	0	0
1994	8[b]	2	0	6	0
1996	3	0	1	2	0
1998	6	1	2	2	1
2000	8	1	5	1	1
2002	3	1	1	1[c]	0
2004	8	1	0	5	2
2006	6	0	6	0	0

Notes: D indicates Democrat; R indicates Republican.

This table reflects shifts in party control of seats from immediately before to immediately after the November election.

Party gains that resulted from an incumbent being defeated in either a primary or general election are classified as incumbent defeats. Situations where the incumbent declined to run again, ran for another political office, or died or resigned before the end of the term are classified as open seats.

a. Includes John Durkin (D-NH). After a contested election in which incumbent Sen. Norris Cotton did not run, the Senate declared the seat vacant as of August 8, 1975. Sen. Durkin was then elected by special election, September 16, 1975, to fill the vacancy.

b. Sen. Richard Shelby (AL) switched from the Democratic to the Republican Party the day after the election and brought the total change to nine.

c. Includes Norm Coleman (R-MN) who beat Walter Mondale (D-MN) after the death of Sen. Paul Wellstone (D-MN).

Sources: *Congressional Quarterly Almanac* (Washington, D.C.: Congressional Quarterly, various years); *Congressional Quarterly Weekly Report,* various issues; *National Journal,* various issues.

Table 2-7 House Incumbents Retired, Defeated, or Reelected, 1946–2006

Year	Retired[a]	Total seeking reelection	Defeated in primaries	Defeated in general election	Total reelected	Percentage of those seeking reelection	Reelected as percentage of House membership
1946	32	398	18	52	328	82.4	75.4
1948	29	400	15	68	317	79.3	72.9
1950	29	400	6	32	362	90.5	83.2
1952	42	389	9	26	354	91.0	81.4
1954	24	407	6	22	379	93.1	87.1
1956	21	411	6	16	389	94.6	89.4
1958	33	396	3	37	356	89.9	81.8
1960	26	405	5	25	375	92.6	86.2
1962	24	402	12	22	368	91.5	84.6
1964	33	397	8	45	344	86.6	79.1
1966	22	411	8	41	362	88.1	83.2
1968	23	409	4	9	396	96.8	91.0
1970	29	401	10	12	379	94.5	87.1
1972	40	393	11	13	365	93.6	83.9
1974	43	391	8	40	343	87.7	78.9
1976	47	384	3	13	368	95.8	84.6
1978	49	382	5	19	358	93.7	82.3
1980	34	398	6	31	361	90.7	83.0
1982	40	393	10	29	354	90.1	81.4
1984	22	411	3	16	392	95.4	90.1
1986	40	394	3	6	385	97.7	88.5
1988	23	409	1	6	402	98.3	92.4
1990	27	406	1	15	390	96.0	89.7
1992	65	368	19	24	325	88.3	74.7
1994	48	387	4	34	349	90.2	80.0
1996	49	384	2	21	361	94.0	83.0
1998	33	402	1	6	395	98.3	90.1
2000	30	403	3	6	394	97.8	90.1
2002	35	398[b]	8	8	383[c]	96.2	88.0
2004	29	404	2	7	395	92.9	90.8
2006	28	403	2	22	379	94.0	87.1

a. This entry does not include persons who died or resigned before the election.
b. Includes Jim Traficant (D- OH), who ran as an Independent in the election despite being expelled from the House of Representatives in July 2002.
c. Includes Patsy Mink (D-HI) who died shortly before the election yet remained on the ballot.
Sources: *Biographical Directory of the United States Congress 1774–1989* (Washington, D.C.: Government Printing Office, 1989); *Congressional Quarterly Almanac* (Washington, D.C.: Congressional Quarterly, various years); *National Journal,* various issues; *The Almanac of American Politics* (Washington, D.C.: National Journal Group, various years).

Table 2-8 Senate Incumbents Retired, Defeated, or Reelected, 1946–2006

Year	Not seeking reelection[a]	Total seeking reelection	Defeated in primaries	Defeated in general election	Total reelected	Reelected as percentage of those seeking reelection
1946	9	30	6	7	17	56.7
1948	8	25	2	8	15	60.0
1950	4	32	5	5	22	68.8
1952	4	29	1	10	18	62.1
1954	6	32	2	5	25	78.1
1956	5	30	0	4	26	86.7
1958	6	27	0	10	17	63.0
1960	5	29	0	2	27	93.1
1962	4	35	1	5	29	82.9
1964	3	32	0	4	28	87.5
1966	3	32	3	1	28	87.5
1968	7	27	4	4	19	70.4
1970	4	31	1	6	24	77.4
1972	6	27	2	5	20	74.1
1974	7	27	2	2	23	85.2
1976	8	25	0	9	16	64.0
1978	10	25	3	7	15	60.0
1980	5	29	4	9	16	55.2
1982	3	30	0	2	28	93.3
1984	4	29	0	3	26	89.7
1986	6	28	0	7	21	75.0
1988	6	27	0	4	23	85.2
1990	4	32	0	1	31	96.9
1992	9	28	1	4	23	82.1
1994	9	26	0	2	24	92.3
1996	13	21	1[b]	1	19	90.5
1998	5	29	0	3	26	89.7
2000	5	29	0	6	23	79.3
2002	7	27	1	2	24	88.9
2004	8	26	0	1	25	96.2
2006	5	28	1[c]	6	22	78.6

Note: Table includes all Senate contests in a given year, whether for full or partial terms.

a. This entry includes Senators who died or resigned before the election and those retiring at the end of their terms.

b. Sheila Frahm, appointed to fill Robert Dole's term, is counted as an incumbent in Kansas's "B" seat.

c. Sen. Joe Lieberman (CT) lost in the Democratic primary, but ran in the general election as an independent and won reelection.

Sources: *Congressional Quarterly Almanac* (Washington, D.C.: Congressional Quarterly, various years); *Congressional Quarterly Weekly Report,* various issues; *National Journal,* various issues.

Table 2-9 House and Senate Retirements by Party, 1930–2006

	House		Senate			House		Senate	
Year	D	R	D	R	Year	D	R	D	R
1930	8	15	2	5	1970	11	19	3	1
1932	16	23	1	1	1972	20	20	3	3
1934	29	9	3	1	1974	23	21	3	4
1936	29	3	4	2	1976	31	16	4	4
1938	21	5	3	1	1978	31	18	4	5
1940	16	6	1	2	1980	21	13	2	3
1942	20	12	0	0	1982	19	21	1	2
1944	17	5	3	2	1984	9	13	2	2
1946	17	15	4	3	1986	20	20	3	3
1948	17	12	3	4	1988	10	13	3	3
1950	12	17	3	1	1990	10	17	0	3
1952	25	17	2	1	1992	41	24	4	3
1954	11	13	1	1	1994	28	20	6	3
1956	7	13	4	1	1996	28	21	8	5
1958	6	27	0	6	1998	17	16	3	2
1960	11	15	3	1	2000	7	23	4	1
1962	10	14	2	2	2002	13	22	1	5[a]
1964	17	16	1	1	2004	12	17	5	3
1966	14	8	1	2	2006	9	17	2	1
1968	13	10	4	3					

Notes: D indicates Democrat; R indicates Republican.

These figures include members who did not run again for the office they held and members who sought other offices; the figures do not include members who died or resigned before the end of the particular Congress.

a. Includes Frank Murkowski (R-AK) who ran for governor, won and appointed Lisa Murkoswki to finish the last two years of his term.

Sources: Mildred L. Amer, "Information on the Number of House Retirees, 1930–1992" (Washington, D.C.: Congressional Research Service, Staff Report, May 19, 1992); *Congressional Quarterly Weekly Report,* various issues; *National Journal,* various issues.

Table 2-10 Defeated House Incumbents, 1946–2006

Election	Party	Incumbents lost	Average terms	Consecutive terms served						
				1	2	3	1–3	4–6	7–9	10+
1946	Democrat	62	2.7	35	5	4	44	11	5	2
	Republican	7	3.6	2	0	1	3	3	1	0
	Total	69	2.8	37	5	5	47	14	6	2
1948	Democrat[a]	9	2.7	4	1	1	6	3	0	0
	Republican	73	2.2	41	3	12	56	14	2	1
	Total	82	2.3	45	4	13	62	17	2	1
1958	Democrat[b]	6	5.0	1	1	0	2	2	1	1
	Republican	34	4.3	9	0	4	13	14	6	1
	Total	40	4.4	10	1	4	15	16	7	2
1966	Democrat	43	3.3	26	6	0	32	4	1	6
	Republican	2	11.0	1	0	0	1	0	0	1
	Total	45	3.6	27	6	0	33	4	1	7
1974	Democrat	9	4.7	1	1	1	3	3	2	1
	Republican	39	3.8	11	2	6	19	15	2	3
	Total	48	4.0	12	3	7	22	18	4	4
1978	Democrat	19	4.0	3	8	2	13	2	1	3
	Republican	5	5.4	2	0	0	2	2	0	1
	Total	24	4.3	5	8	2	15	4	1	4
1980	Democrat	32	5.2	5	2	10	17	5	4	6
	Republican	5	5.3	1	0	1	2	1	1	1
	Total	37	5.2	6	2	11	19	6	5	7
1982	Democrat	4	2.9	1	0	1	2	2	0	0
	Republican[c]	23	3.0	12	3	2	17	2	2	2
	Total	27	3.0	13	3	3	19	4	2	2
1984	Democrat	16	4.1	6	1	2	9	4	1	2
	Republican	3	3.7	0	0	2	2	1	0	0
	Total	19	4.0	6	1	4	11	5	1	2
1986	Democrat	3	1.8	2	0	0	2	1	0	0
	Republican	6	1.5	4	1	1	6	0	0	0
	Total	9	1.6	6	1	1	8	1	0	0
1988	Democrat	2	12.0	0	0	0	0	0	0	2
	Republican	5	1.6	2	3	0	5	0	0	0
	Total	7	4.6	2	3	0	5	0	0	2
1990	Democrat	6	6.3	0	1	0	1	3	1	1
	Republican[d]	10	3.6	2	3	0	5	4	1	0
	Total	16	4.6	2	4	0	6	7	2	1
1992	Democrat	30	5.6	2	1	4	7	12	10	1
	Republican	13	6.8	2	0	2	4	1	6	2
	Total	43	6.0	4	1	6	11	13	16	3
1994	Democrat	37	4.2	16	3	5	24	7	2	4
	Republican	0	0.0	0	0	0	0	0	0	0
	Total	37	4.2	16	3	5	24	7	2	4

Table 2-10 (continued)

Election	Party	Incumbents lost	Average terms	Consecutive terms served						
				1	2	3	1–3	4–6	7–9	10+
1996	Democrat	3	4.7	1	0	1	2	0	0	1
	Republican	18	1.8	12	4	1	17	0	1	0
	Total	21	2.2	13	4	2	19	0	1	1
1998	Democrat	1	1.0	1	0	0	1	0	0	0
	Republican	6	1.7	3	2	1	6	0	0	0
	Total	7	1.6	4	2	1	7	0	0	0
2000	Democrat	4	6.5	0	0	1	1	1	1	1
	Republican	5	2.4	1	2	1	4	1	0	0
	Total	9	4.2	1	2	2	5	1	1	1
2002	Democrat[e]	12	4.6	0	2	2	4	5	3	0
	Republican	5	4.8	2	0	0	2	1	1	1
	Total	17	4.7	2	2	2	6	6	4	1
2004	Democrat[f]	5	3	1	0	2	3	2	0	0
	Republican	2	9	1	0	0	1	0	0	1
	Total	7	4.7	2	0	2	4	2	0	1
2006	Democrat	0	0	0	0	0	0	0	0	0
	Republican	22	5.9	2	2	2	6	9	3	4
	Total	22	5.9	2	2	2	6	9	3	4

Note: The 1966 and 1982 numbers do not include races where incumbents ran against incumbents due to redistricting. We counted incumbents who lost in the primary as their party's incumbent but then ran in the general election as a write-in or third-party candidate as an incumbent loss.

a. This includes Leo Isacson (NY), who was a member of the American Labor Party.

b. This includes Vincent Dellay (NJ), who was elected as a Republican but switched to a Democrat. He ran for reelection as an Independent.

c. This includes Eugene Atkinson (PA), who began his House service January 3, 1979, as a Democrat. He became a Republican on October 14, 1981.

d. This includes Donald Lukens (OH) who was defeated in the primary and then resigned on October 24, 1990 and Bill Grant (FL) who began his House service January 6, 1987, as a Democrat, but later switched parties. The Republican Conference let his seniority count from 1987.

e. Includes Jim Traficant (OH) who ran as an Independent after being expelled from the House.

f. Excludes two 13-term representatives, Charles Stenholm (TX) and Martin Frost (TX), who ran against incumbents as a result of redistricting.

Sources: *Biographical Directory of the United States Congress 1774–1989* (Washington, D.C.: Government Printing Office, 1989); *Congressional Quarterly Almanac* (Washington, D.C.: Congressional Quarterly, various years); *National Journal*, various issues; *The Almanac of American Politics* (Washington, D.C.: National Journal Group, various years).

Table 2-11 Defeated Senate Incumbents, 1946–2006

Election	Party	Incumbents lost	Average terms	Consecutive terms served					
				1	2	3	4	5	6+
1946	Democrat	11	1.6	7	2	1	1	0	0
	Republican	2	4.0	0	0	0	2	0	0
	Total	13	2.0	7	2	1	3	0	0
1948	Democrat	2	1.5	1	1	0	0	0	0
	Republican	8	1.0	8	0	0	0	0	0
	Total	10	1.1	9	1	0	0	0	0
1958	Republican	10	1.4	6	4	0	0	0	0
	Total	10	1.4	6	4	0	0	0	0
1966	Democrat	4	2.0	2	0	2	0	0	0
	Total	4	2.0	2	0	2	0	0	0
1974	Democrat	2	3.0	1	0	0	0	1	0
	Republican	2	1.5	1	1	0	0	0	0
	Total	4	2.2	2	1	0	0	1	0
1978	Democrat	7	0.9	6	0	1	0	0	0
	Republican	3	2.7	0	2	0	1	0	0
	Total	10	1.4	6	2	1	1	0	0
1980	Democrat	12	2.4	5	1	3	2	0	1
	Republican	1	4.0	0	0	0	1	0	0
	Total	13	2.6	5	1	3	3	0	1
1982	Democrat	1	4.0	0	0	0	1	0	0
	Republican	1	1.0	1	0	0	0	0	0
	Total	2	2.5	1	0	0	1	0	0
1984	Democrat	1	2.0	0	1	0	0	0	0
	Republican	2	2.0	1	0	1	0	0	0
	Total	3	2.0	1	1	1	0	0	0
1986	Republican[a]	7	0.9	7	0	0	0	0	0
	Total	7	0.9	7	0	0	1	0	0
1988	Democrat	1	2.0	0	1	0	0	0	0
	Republican	3	1.4	2	0	1	0	0	0
	Total	4	1.6	2	1	1	0	0	0
1990	Republican	1	2.0	0	1	0	0	0	0
	Total	1	2.0	0	1	0	0	0	0
1992	Democrat	3	1.3	2	1	0	0	0	0
	Republican	2	1.2	1	1	0	0	0	0
	Total	5	1.3	3	2	0	0	0	0
1994	Democrat	2	1.8	1	0	1	0	0	0
	Total	2	1.8	1	0	1	0	0	0
1996	Republican	2	2.0	1	0	1	0	0	0
	Total	2	2.0	1	0	1	0	0	0
1998	Democrat	1	1.0	1	0	0	0	0	0
	Repbulican	2	2.0	1	1	0	0	0	0
	Total	3	1.7	2	1	0	0	0	0
2000	Democrat	1	2.0	0	1	0	0	0	0
	Republican	5	2.0	3	1	0	0	1	0
	Total	6	2.0	3	2	0	0	1	0
2002	Democrat[b]	2	1.0	2	0	0	0	0	0
	Republican	2	1.5	1	1	0	0	0	0
	Total	4	1.3	3	1	0	0	0	0
2004	Democrat	1	3.0	0	0	1	0	0	0
	Republican	0	0.0	0	0	0	0	0	0
	Total	1	3.0	0	0	1	0	0	0
2006	Democrat	0	0.0	0	0	0	0	0	0
	Republican	5	1.8	2	2	1	0	0	0
	Total	5	1.8	2	2	1	0	0	0

a. This includes James Broyhill (R-NC) who was appointed on July 14, 1986, until November 14, 1986. He lost to Terry Sanford (D-NC) who took over the seat on November 5, 1986.

b. Includes Jean Carnahan (D-MO) who was appointed to fill her husband's seat in 2001.

Sources: *Biographical Directory of the United States Congress 1774–1989* (Washington, D.C.: Government Printing Office, 1989); *Congressional Quarterly Almanac* (Washington, D.C.: Congressional Quarterly, various years); *National Journal*, various issues; *The Almanac of American Politics* (Washington, D.C.: National Journal Group, various years).

Table 2-12 House Elections Won with 60 Percent of Major Party Vote, 1956–2006

Year	Number of incumbents running in general election	Percentage of incumbents reelected with at least 60 percent of the major party vote
1956	403	59.1
1958	390	63.1
1960	400	58.9
1962	376	63.6
1964	388	58.5
1966	401	67.7
1968	397	72.2
1970	389	77.3
1972	373	77.8
1974	383	66.4
1976	381	71.9
1978	377	78.0
1980	392	72.9
1982	383	68.9
1984	406	74.6
1986	391	86.4
1988	407	88.5
1990	406	76.4
1992	349	65.6
1994	383	64.5
1996	383	73.6
1998	401	75.6
2000	400	77.3
2002	391[a]	85.4
2004	402	81.6
2006	403	80.9

a. Includes Jim Traficant (D-OH) who ran as an Independent after being expelled from the House of Representatives.

Sources: *Biographical Directory of the United States Congress 1774–1989* (Washington, D.C.: Government Printing Office, 1989); *Congressional Quarterly Almanac* (Washington, D.C.: Congressional Quarterly, various years); *National Journal,* various issues; *The Almanac of American Politics* (Washington, D.C.: National Journal Group, various years).

Table 2-13 Senate Elections Won with 60 Percent of Major Party Vote, 1944–2002

Election Period	Number of incumbents running in general election	Percentage of incumbents reelected with at least 60 percent of the major party vote[a]		
		South	North	Total U.S.
1944–1948	61	100.0	22.9	39.3
1950–1954	76	100.0	18.3	35.5
1956–1960	84	95.5	24.2	42.9
1962–1966	86	70.0	36.4	44.2
1968–1972	74	71.4	38.3	44.6
1974–1978	70	57.1	37.5	41.4
1980–1984[b]	84	63.3	51.9	54.1
1986–1990	87	68.2	53.9	57.5
1992–1996	72	50.0	32.1	36.6
1998–2002	85	51.5	62.3	57.6

a. For the purposes of this table, Senators appointed to the Senate are not considered incumbents in the elections just after appointment.
b. Includes two Democratic incumbents from Louisiana, who by winning more than 50 percent of the vote in that state's all-party primary, avoided a general election contest. In 1980, Russell Long won 59.8 percent of the vote, and in 1984, J. Bennett Johnston won 86 percent of the vote.

Sources: *Biographical Directory of the United States Congress 1774–1989* (Washington, D.C.: Government Printing Office, 1989); *Congressional Quarterly Almanac* (Washington, D.C.: Congressional Quarterly, various years); *National Journal*, various issues; *The Almanac of American Politics* (Washington, D.C.: National Journal Group, various years).

Table 2-14a Marginal Races among Members of the 109th Congress, 2005

Chamber	Members who ever won a congressional election with 60 percent of the vote or less		Members who ever won a congressional election with 55 percent of the vote or less	
	Number	Percentage	Number	Percentage
House	321	73.8	234	53.8
Senate	92	92.0	77	77.0

Table 2-14b Marginal Races among Members of the 110th Congress, 2007

Chamber	Members who won their last congressional election with 60 percent of the vote or less		Members who won their last congressional election with 55 percent of the vote or less	
	Number	Percentage	Number	Percentage
House	124	28.5	70	16.1
Senate	52	52.0	34	34.0

Sources: *Biographical Directory of the United States Congress 1774–1989* (Washington, D.C.: Government Printing Office, 1989); *Congressional Quarterly Almanac* (Washington, D.C.: Congressional Quarterly, various years); *National Journal*, various issues; *The Almanac of American Politics* (Washington, D.C.: National Journal Group, various years).

Table 2-15a Conditions of Initial Election for Members of the 109th Congress, 2005

	House				Senate		
Condition	Democrats	Republicans	Total	Percentage of entire house	Democrats	Republicans	Total
Defeated incumbent							
In primary	15	5	20	4.6	1	1	2
In general election	36	39	76[a]	17.5	17	11	28
Succeeded retiring incumbent							
Of same party	89	118	207	47.6	18	20	39[b]
Of other party	26	33	59	13.6	8	19	27
Succeeded deceased incumbent							
Of same party	13	11	24	5.5	1	1	2
Of other party	4	4	8	1.8	0	2	2
New districts	22	19	41	9.4	—	—	—
Total	205	229	435[a]	100.0	45	54	100[b]

a. Total includes Rep. Bernard Sanders (I-VT).

b. Total includes Sen. Jim Jeffords (I-VT) who succeeded retiring Sen. Robert Stafford (R-VT). At the time, Sen. Jeffords was a Republican.

Table 2-15b Conditions of Initial Election for Members of the 110th Congress, 2007

	House				Senate		
Condition	Democrats	Republicans	Total	Percentage of entire house	Democrats	Republicans	Total
Defeated incumbent							
In primary	16	7	23	5.3	1	2	3
In general election	56	24	80	18.4	20	8	29[c]
Succeeded retiring incumbent							
Of same party	83	93	176	40.5	19	20	40[d]
Of other party	43	41	84	19.3	8	17	25
Succeeded deceased incumbent							
Of same party	12	9	21	4.8	1	0	1
Of other party	3	4	7	1.6	0	2	2
New districts	20	24	44	10.1	—	—	—
Total	233	202	435	100.0	49	49	100

c. Total includes Sen. Joseph Lieberman (ID-CT).

d.Total includes Sen. Bernard Sanders (I-VT).

Note: Percentages of seats won does not equal 100% due to the election of independents and/or rounding.

Sources: *Biographical Directory of the United States Congress 1774–1989* (Washington, D.C.: Government Printing Office, 1989); *Congressional Quarterly Almanac* (Washington, D.C.: Congressional Quarterly, various years); *National Journal,* various issues; *The Almanac of American Politics* (Washington, D.C.: National Journal Group, various years).

Table 2-16 Ticket Splitting between Presidential and House Candidates, 1900–2004

		Districts with split results[a]	
Year	Districts[b]	Number	Percentage
1900	295	10	3.4
1904	310	5	1.6
1908	314	21	6.7
1912	333	84	25.2
1916	333	35	10.5
1920	344	11	3.2
1924	356	42	11.8
1928	359	68	18.9
1932	355	50	14.1
1936	361	51	14.1
1940	362	53	14.6
1944	367	41	11.2
1948	422	90	21.3
1952	435	84	19.3
1956	435	130	29.9
1960	437	114	26.1
1964	435	145	33.3
1968	435	139	32.0
1972	435	192	44.1
1976	435	124	28.5
1980	435	143	32.8
1984	435	190	43.7
1988	435	148	34.0
1992	435	100	23.0
1996	435	110	25.3
2000	435	86	19.8
2004	435	59	13.6

a. These are congressional districts carried by a presidential candidate of one party and a House candidate of another party.

b. Before 1952 complete data are not available on every congressional district.

Sources: *Congressional Quarterly Almanac* (Washington, D.C.: Congressional Quarterly, various years); *National Journal*, various issues; *The Almanac of American Politics* (Washington, D.C.: National Journal Group, various years).

Table 2-17 District Voting for President and Representative, 1952–2004

		President's vote compared with vote for his party's successful House candidates	
Year	Number of districts carried by president[a]	President ran ahead	President ran behind
1952	297	n.a.	n.a.
1956	329	155	43
1960	204	22	243
1964	375	134[b]	158[b]
1972	377	104	88
1976	220	22	270
1980	309	38[c]	150[c]
1984	372	59	123
1988	299	26	149
1992	257	4[b, d]	247[b, d]
1996	280	27[e]	174[e]
2000	228	26	195
2004	255	39	154

n.a. = not available.

a. This refers to the winning presidential candidate.

b. This does not include districts where the percentage of the total district vote won by House members equaled the percentage of the total district vote won by the president.

c. We computed this on the basis of the actual presidential vote with John Anderson and others included. If it is recomputed on the basis of President Reagan's percentage of the major party vote, the president ran ahead in 59 districts and behind in 129 districts.

d. We computed this on the basis of the actual presidential vote with Ross Perot included. If we recomputed this on the basis of President Clinton's percentage of the major party vote, the president ran ahead in 72 districts and behind in 179 districts.

e. We computed this on the basis of the actual presidential vote with Ross Perot included. If we recomputed this on the basis of President Clinton's percentage of the major party vote, the president ran ahead in 98 districts and behind in 97 districts.

Sources: *Congressional Quarterly Almanac* (Washington, D.C.: Congressional Quarterly, various years); *National Journal,* various issues; *The Almanac of American Politics* (Washington, D.C.: National Journal Group, various years). For 2000, Gregory Giroux, *Congressional Quarterly.*

Table 2-18 Shifts in Democratic Major Party Vote in Congressional Districts, 1956–2006

Period	Change in Democratic percentage nationally[a]	Change in Democratic percentage in congressional districts		
		Greatest loss	Greatest gain	Variance[b]
1956–58	5.0	–9.5	27.3	30.3
1958–60	–1.2	–22.1	14.4	31.4
1972–74	5.8	–18.8	36.2	92.2
1974–76	–1.3	–30.7	31.6	81.0
1976–78	–2.8	–37.6	39.6	106.1
1978–80	–3.2	–27.8	37.0	85.0
1982–84	–4.1	–40.6	16.5	68.8
1984–86	2.4	–46.1	22.5	63.6
1986–88	–1.1	–23.5	36.1	65.9
1988–90	0.1	–29.1	36.4	92.6
1992–94	–6.3	–38.0	28.0	67.2
1994–96	3.4	–31.2	21.5	51.1
1996–98	–0.3	–16.3	21.0	46.0
1998–2000	0.3	–28.7	27.0	41.2
2002–04	1.1	–28.0	22.8	36.7
2004–06	5.4	–22.2	34.4	41.3

Note: Includes only those districts in which two major party candidates competed in both elections and in which the boundaries remained unchanged for both elections. Because of massive redrawing of district lines after each decennial census, no figures are computed for 1970–1972, 1980–1982, 1990–1992, and 2000–2002.

a. See table 2-2, column 5.

b. Variance, the square of the standard deviation, measures the extent to which the changes in local returns differ from the change in national returns.

Source: For 2000–2004, computed by Gary Jacobson, University of California, San Diego. Data from Gregory Giroux, *Congressional Quarterly.*

Sources: Information for 1956–76 from Thomas E. Mann, *Unsafe at Any Margin* (Washington, D.C.: American Enterprise Institute, 1978). Calculations for subsequent years by Larry Bartels, Princeton University; Gary Jacobson, University of California, San Diego; and Molly Reynolds, Brookings Institution from official election returns.

Table 2-19 Party-Line Voting in Presidential and Congressional Elections, 1956–2004 (as a percentage of all voters)

Year	Presidential election			Senate elections			House elections		
	Party-line voters[a]	Defectors[b]	Pure independents[c]	Party-line voters[a]	Defectors[b]	Pure independents[c]	Party-line voters[a]	Defectors[b]	Pure independents[c]
1956	76	15	9	79	12	9	82	9	9
1958	—	—	—	85	9	5	84	11	5
1960	79	13	8	77	15	8	80	12	8
1962	—	—	—	n.a.	n.a.	n.a.	83	12	6
1964	79	15	5	78	16	6	79	15	5
1966	—	—	—	n.a.	n.a.	n.a.	76	16	8
1968	69	23	9	74	19	7	74	19	7
1970	—	—	—	78	12	10	76	16	8
1972	67	25	8	69	22	9	75	17	8
1974	—	—	—	73	19	8	74	18	8
1976	74	15	11	70	19	11	72	19	9
1978	—	—	—	71	20	9	69	22	9
1980	70	22	8	71	21	8	69	23	8
1982	—	—	—	77	17	6	76	17	6
1984	81	12	7	72	19	8	70	23	7
1986	—	—	—	76	20	4	72	22	6
1988	81	12	7	72	20	7	74	20	7
1990	—	—	—	75	20	5	72	22	5
1992	68	24	9	73	20	7	70	22	8
1994	—	—	—	76	18	5	77	17	6
1996	80	15	5	77	16	7	77	17	6
1998	—	—	—	77	15	8	74	20	6
2000	81	11	7	80	13	7	76	17	6
2002	—	—	—	82	14	4	78	18	4
2004	85	10	6	81	14	5	80	15	6

n.a. = not available

Note: Percentages may not add to 100 because of rounding.

a. These are party identifiers who voted for the candidate of their party.

b. These are party identifiers who voted for the candidate of the other party.

c. The SRC/CPS National Election Surveys use a seven-point scale to define party identification, including three categories of Independents—those who "lean" to one or the other party and those who are "pure" Independents. The "leaners" are included here among the party-line voters. Party identification here means self-identification as determined by surveys.

Sources: SRC/CPS *National Election Studies, 1956–2004.* Calculations for 1956–78 from Thomas E. Mann and Raymond E. Wolfinger, "Candidates and Parties in Congressional Elections," *American Political Science Review* (September 1980). Calculations for subsequent years by Peverill Squire, Michael Hagen, and Benjamin Highton, University of California State Data Program; Jon Krasno and Thomas E. Mann, Brookings Institution; Herb Asher, Ohio State University; and Gary Jacobson, University of California, San Diego.

Figure 2-1 House Seats That Changed Party, 1954–2006

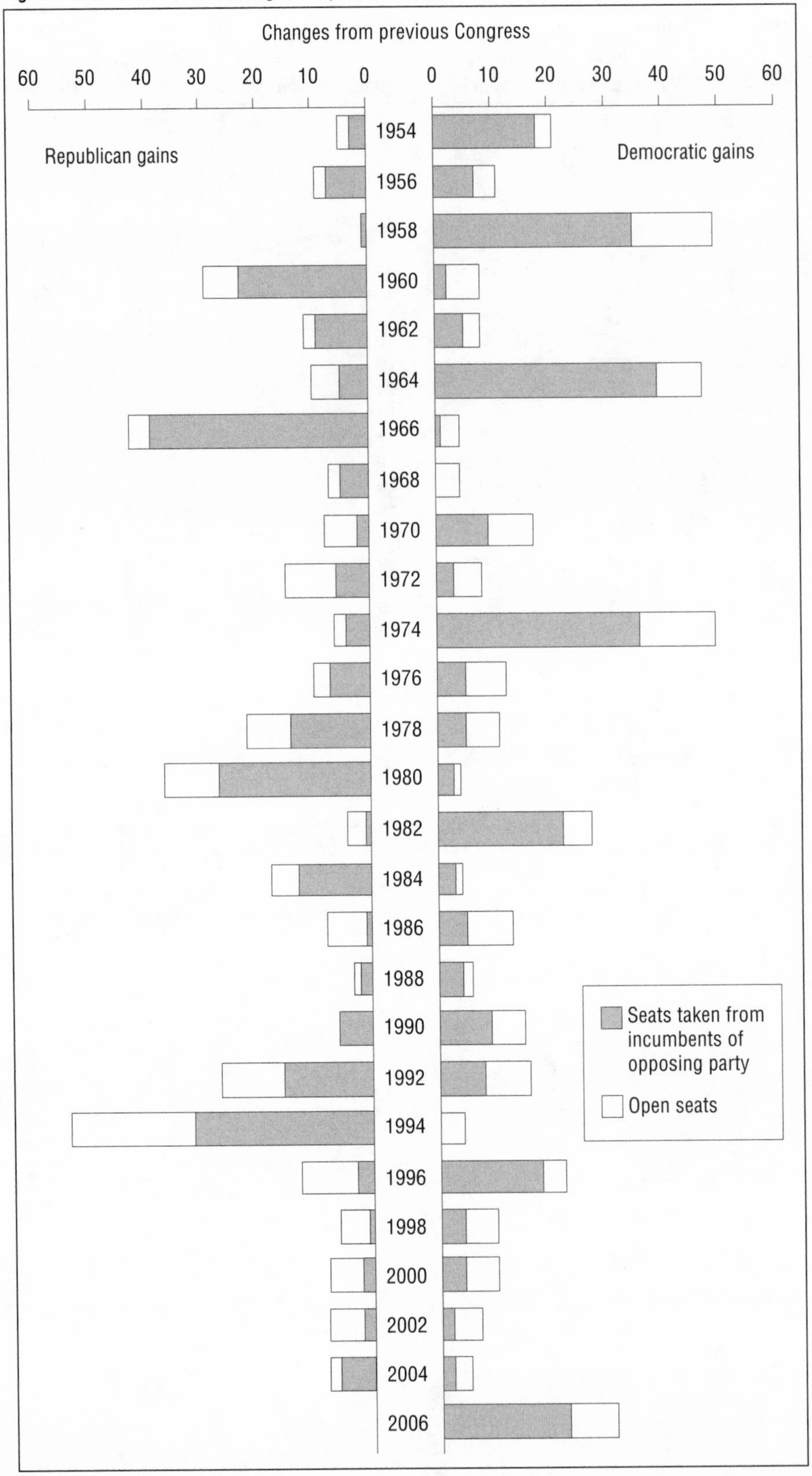

Source: Table 2-5.

Figure 2-2 Senate Seats That Changed Party, 1954–2006

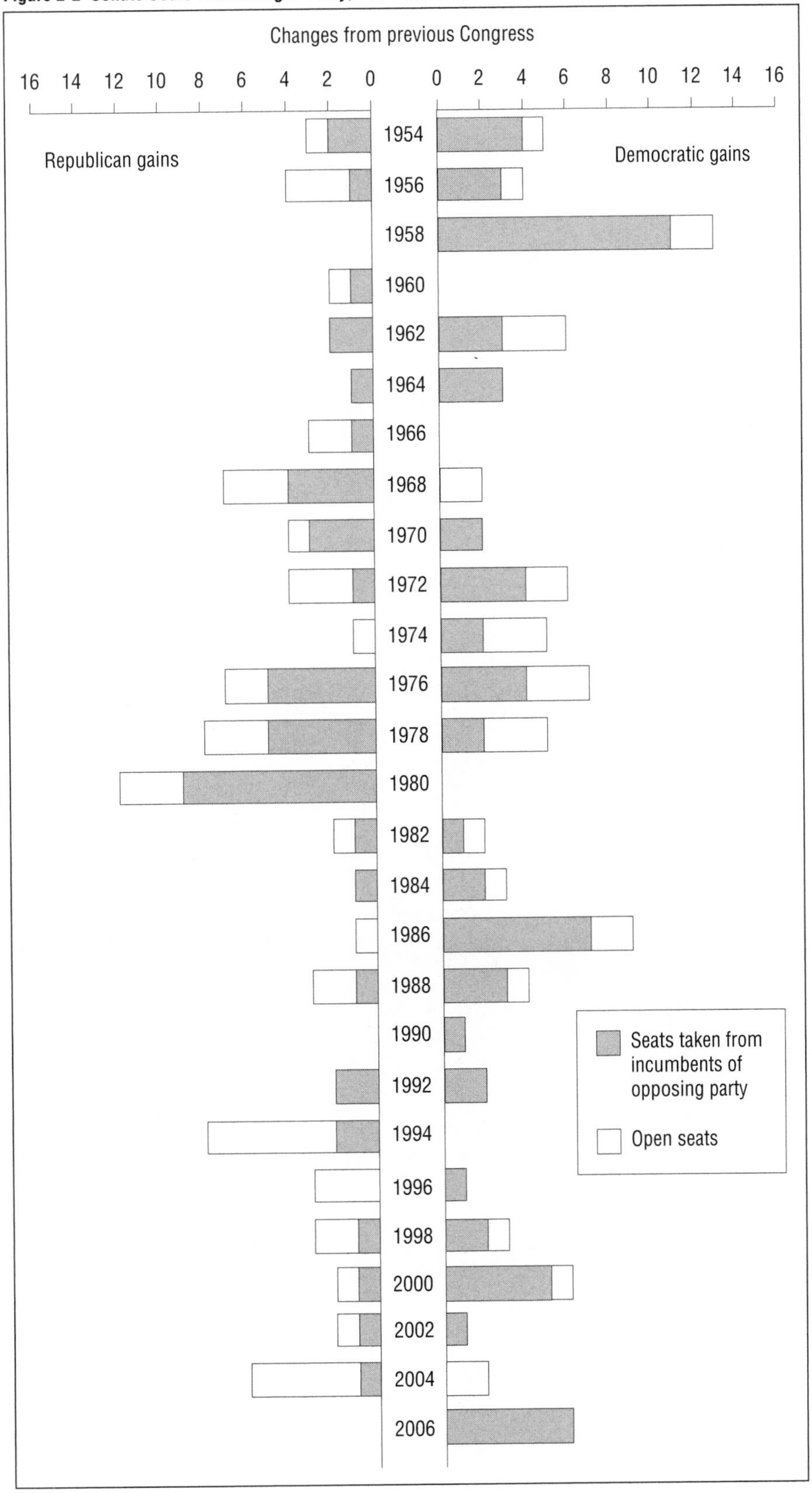

Source: Table 2-6.

3

Campaign Finance

Table 3-1 The Average Cost of Winning an Election, 1986–2006 (in nominal and 2006 dollars)

	House winners		Senate winners	
	Nominal dollars	2006 dollars	Nominal dollars	2006 dollars
2006	1,259,791	1,259,791	8,835,416	8,835,416
2004	1,038,391	1,115,883	7,183,825	7,719,931
2002	911,644	1,027,319	3,728,644	4,201,759
2000	845,907	998,448	7,198,423[a]	8,496,499
1998	677,807	838,318	4,655,806	5,758,347
1996	686,198	887,917	3,921,653	5,074,488
1994	541,121	741,101	4,488,195	6,146,876
1992	556,475	805,929	3,353,115	4,856,236
1990	423,245	662,985	3,298,324	5,166,605
1988	400,386	674,334	3,746,225	6,309,432
1986	359,577	658,408	3,067,559	5,616,893

a. Jon Corzine (D-N.J.) spent $63,209,506. Hillary Rodham Clinton (D-N.Y.) spent $29,941,194. The remaining Senate winners in 2000 spent an average of $4,737,365.

Source: Analysis of Federal Election Commission data.

Table 3-2 House Campaign Expenditures, 1974–2006 (net dollars)

	2006	2004	2002	2000	1998	1996	1994	1992	1990
All candidates									
Total	751,730,068	581,483,185[a]	525,986,157[a]	514,793,499[a]	397,221,879[a]	422,661,966[a]	346,189,285[a]	329,809,707[a]	235,130,542[a]
expenditures									
Mean	995,669	773,249	737,708	695,667	552,464	516,702	439,885	405,670	321,656
expenditure	(N=755)	(N=752)	(N=712)	(N=740)	(N=719)	(N=818)	(N=787)	(N=813)	(N=731)
Mean,	850,606	695,716	732,457	670,205	505,492	472,158	484,976	457,994	350,552
Democrats	(N=414)	(N=380)	(N=353)	(N=372)	(N=358)	(N=412)	(N=386)	(N=410)	(N=381)
Mean,	1,171,786	852,563	743,077	722,852	599,163	560,964	395,949	351,880	289,400
Republicans	(N=341)	(N=371)	(N=358)	(N=366)	(N=360)	(N=405)	(N=400)	(N=402)	(N=349)
Incumbents									
Mean,	1,261,559	1,026,589[a]	874,790[a]	829,132[a]	654,137[a]	675,506[a]	558,867[a]	590,405[a]	416,671
all incumbents	(N=402)	(N=401)	(N=387)	(N=400)	(N=400)	(N=382)	(N=382)	(N=349)	(N=405)
Mean,	983,625	956,127	836,982	755,411	590,935	587,005	619,389	615,920	419,417
Democrats	(N=191)	(N=190)	(N=188)	(N=201)	(N=189)	(N=168)	(N=224)	(N=211)	(N=247)
Mean,	1,513,148	1,091,373	911,755	908,131	711,613	744,057	472,199	551,212	412,377
Republicans	(N=211)	(N=210)	(N=198)	(N=197)	(N=210)	(N=213)	(N=157)	(N=137)	(N=158)
Challengers									
Mean,	510,195	322,061	340,135	377,334	332,092	290,038	240,008	166,406	134,415
all challengers	(N=289)	(N=284)	(N=226)	(N=272)	(N=254)	(N=331)	(N=302)	(N=290)	(N=270)
Mean,	590,557	313,126	414,364	442,963	325,759	322,272	176,747	142,414	131,269
Democrats	(N=190)	(N=158)	(N=115)	(N=136)	(N=136)	(N=191)	(N=110)	(N=111)	(N=104)
Mean,	355,966	333,264	264,591	311,704	339,391	246,061	276,251	181,283	133,759
Republicans	(N=99)	(N=126)	(N=111)	(N=136)	(N=118)	(N=140)	(N=192)	(N=179)	(N=165)
Open seats									
Mean,	1,517,764	1,169,486	1,126,482	1,183,910	787,932	653,487	584,657	433,912	537,266
all open-seat	(N=64)	(N=67)	(N=99)	(N=68)	(N=65)	(N=105)	(N=103)	(N=174)	(N=56)
candidates									
Mean,	1,577,958	1,038,566	1,075,836	1,063,873	756,855	648,268	557,992	477,393	543,737
Democrats	(N=33)	(N=32)	(N=50)	(N=35)	(N=33)	(N=53)	(N=52)	(N=88)	(N=30)
Mean,	1,453,687	1,289,184	1,179,284	1,311,221	819,980	658,807	611,846	389,420	529,799
Republicans	(N=31)	(N=35)	(N=49)	(N=33)	(N=32)	(N=52)	(N=51)	(N=86)	(N=26)

(continued)

Table 3-2 (continued)

	1988	1986	1984	1982	1980	1978	1976	1974
All candidates								
Total expenditures	225,114,380	217,562,967	176,882,849	174,921,844	115,222,222	86,129,169	60,046,006	44,051,125
Mean expenditure	303,389 (N=742)	295,602 (N=736)	241,313 (N=733)	228,060 (N=767)	153,221 (N=752)	109,440 (N=787)	73,316 (N=819)	53,384 (N=810)
Mean, Democrats	315,399 (N=397)	301,955 (N=397)	237,732 (N=399)	213,369 (N=411)	143,277 (N=396)	108,986 (N=416)	74,563 (N=429)	53,993 (N=434)
Mean, Republicans	289,447 (N=344)	290,092 (N=340)	245,591 (N=334)	245,020 (N=356)	164,282 (N=356)	109,995 (N=371)	71,945 (N=390)	54,835 (N=376)
Incumbents								
Mean, all incumbents	390,807 (N=408)	362,103 (N=389)	279,044 (N=408)	265,001 (N=383)	165,081 (N=391)	111,159 (N=377)	79,398 (N=382)	56,539 (N=382)
Mean, Democrats	374,603 (N=245)	349,918 (N=231)	279,203 (N=254)	247,573 (N=216)	158,010 (N=248)	103,519 (N=249)	73,322 (N=254)	38,743 (N=218)
Mean, Republicans	415,162 (N=163)	379,917 (N=158)	278,781 (N=154)	287,543 (N=167)	177,345 (N=143)	126,022 (N=128)	91,456 (N=128)	80,339 (N=163)
Challengers								
Mean, all challengers	136,884 (N=283)	155,607 (N=262)	161,994 (N=273)	151,717 (N=270)	121,751 (N=277)	74,802 (N=299)	50,795 (N=335)	40,015 (N=323)
Mean, Democrats	163,535 (N=126)	170,562 (N=123)	124,508 (N=119)	141,390 (N=137)	93,313 (N=105)	70,948 (N=109)	46,330 (N=122)	59,266 (N=162)
Mean, Republicans	115,494 (N=157)	141,356 (N=139)	190,960 (N=154)	162,354 (N=133)	139,111 (N=172)	77,012 (N=190)	53,352 (N=213)	20,644 (N=161)
Open seats								
Mean, all open-seat candidates	527,984 (N=51)	430,484 (N=86)	361,696 (N=52)	284,476 (N=114)	201,790 (N=84)	201,049 (N=111)	124,506 (N=102)	90,426 (N=106)
Mean, Democrats	493,467 (N=26)	420,138 (N=43)	350,804 (N=26)	256,004 (N=58)	180,312 (N=43)	211,871 (N=58)	145,497 (N=53)	99,743 (N=54)
Mean, Republicans	573,573 (N=24)	440,830 (N=43)	372,589 (N=26)	314,547 (N=56)	224,116 (N=41)	189,205 (N=53)	101,802 (N=49)	80,751 (N=52)

Note: The data include primary and general election expenditures for major party general election candidates only.

a. Includes one or more Independents. Independents are included only if they are incumbents or winning non-incumbents.

Source: Analysis of Federal Election Commission data.

Table 3-3 Expenditures of House Incumbents and Challengers, by Election Outcome, 1974–2006 (mean net dollars)

	2006	2004	2002	2000	1998	1996	1994	1992	1990	1988	1986	1984	1982	1980	1978	1976	1974
Incumbent won with 60% or more																	
Incumbents	975,047	869,368[a]	770,762[a]	654,887[a]	537,434[a]	521,946[a]	451,414	486,420[a]	357,798	345,037	291,876	232,853	200,170	125,912	92,696	63,628	40,925
	(N=300)	(N=343)	(N=336)	(N=326)	(N=309)	(N=262)	(N=263)	(N=234)	(N=313)	(N=359)	(N=330)	(N=318)	(N=264)	(N=284)	(N=287)	(N=272)	(N=251)
Democrats	913,487	835,267	749,196	605,512	447,989	474,059	449,710	489,450	367,388	336,606	293,484	219,506	206,670	117,773	85,424	56,937	35,146
	(N=180)	(N=166)	(N=159)	(N=167)	(N=144)	(N=124)	(N=120)	(N=138)	(N=197)	(N=220)	(N=209)	(N=183)	(N=178)	(N=170)	(N=184)	(N=185)	(N=194)
Republicans	1,067,388	901,868	790,850	709,989	616,019	562,219	452,844	481,074	341,512	358,381	289,099	250,945	186,717	138,050	105,687	77,855	60,593
	(N=120)	(N=176)	(N=176)	(N=157)	(N=164)	(N=137)	(N=143)	(N=95)	(N=116)	(N=139)	(N=121)	(N=135)	(N=86)	(N=114)	(N=103)	(N=87)	(N=57)
Challengers	147,072	184,172	195,274	152,739	133,148	104,440	113,943	86,726	60,277	79,000	92,436	71,922	82,373	47,525	34,132	25,492	16,372
	(N=188)	(N=230)	(N=179)	(N=198)	(N=161)	(N=212)	(N=183)	(N=187)	(N=180)	(N=234)	(N=202)	(N=184)	(N=163)	(N=170)	(N=209)	(N=225)	(N=193)
Democrats	115,477	164,672	221,500	166,982	112,388	97,926	132,598	76,022	43,057	87,361	72,769	73,835	36,628	44,120	36,040	26,606	25,891
	(N=99)	(N=126)	(N=95)	(N=96)	(N=89)	(N=115)	(N=96)	(N=76)	(N=65)	(N=102)	(N=85)	(N=99)	(N=62)	(N=75)	(N=84)	(N=81)	(N=56)
Republicans	182,217	207,796	146,045	139,334	158,811	112,162	93,358	94,055	70,009	72,540	106,724	69,693	110,454	50,213	32,850	24,865	12,481
	(N=89)	(N=104)	(N=86)	(N=102)	(N=72)	(N=96)	(N=87)	(N=111)	(N=115)	(N=132)	(N=117)	(N=85)	(N=101)	(N=95)	(N=125)	(N=144)	(N=137)
Incumbent won with 60% or less																	
Incumbents	1,910,840	1,884,901	1,477,582	1,447,392	1,029,650	992,563	718,490[a]	779,254	607,286	700,009	785,493	437,752	394,447	261,901	161,856	113,939	80,272
	(N=80)	(N=51)	(N=46)	(N=68)	(N=85)	(N=99)	(N=85)	(N=91)	(N=77)	(N=44)	(N=52)	(N=74)	(N=90)	(N=76)	(N=71)	(N=98)	(N=90)
Democrats	2,131,343	1,583,537	1,213,166	1,465,364	1,052,776	919,568	729,774	828,957	629,143	689,280	938,374	421,834	446,542	223,345	145,065	119,440	68,513
	(N=11)	(N=19)	(N=26)	(N=32)	(N=44)	(N=41)	(N=70)	(N=57)	(N=44)	(N=23)	(N=20)	(N=58)	(N=35)	(N=50)	(N=51)	(N=62)	(N=20)
Republicans	1,875,687	2,063,836	1,821,322	1,431,416	1,004,833	1,044,163	669,900	695,928	578,143	711,760	689,943	495,455	361,295	336,046	204,674	104,465	83,632
	(N=69)	(N=32)	(N=20)	(N=36)	(N=41)	(N=58)	(N=14)	(N=34)	(N=33)	(N=21)	(N=32)	(N=16)	(N=55)	(N=26)	(N=20)	(N=36)	(N=70)
Challengers	1,005,016	831,723	850,354	872,263	644,781	521,292	328,025	280,562	248,582	389,236	334,946	307,938	234,790	197,499	156,444	97,322	63,861
	(N=79)	(N=49)	(N=43)	(N=68)	(N=86)	(N=98)	(N=85)	(N=84)	(N=75)	(N=44)	(N=46)	(N=72)	(N=84)	(N=76)	(N=71)	(N=98)	(N=90)
Democrats	874,970	842,344	1,207,168	931,770	672,726	538,147	479,485	273,077	213,907	441,331	353,939	386,819	182,232	195,135	187,290	77,075	63,134
	(N=69)	(N=30)	(N=18)	(N=36)	(N=42)	(N=58)	(N=14)	(N=29)	(N=31)	(N=21)	(N=28)	(N=16)	(N=53)	(N=26)	(N=20)	(N=36)	(N=70)
Republicans	1,902,330	814,953	593,448	805,317	618,106	496,852	298,160	284,509	273,013	341,671	305,401	285,401	324,647	198,728	144,347	109,079	66,405
	(N=10)	(N=19)	(N=25)	(N=32)	(N=44)	(N=40)	(N=71)	(N=55)	(N=44)	(N=23)	(N=18)	(N=56)	(N=31)	(N=50)	(N=51)	(N=62)	(N=20)
Incumbent was defeated																	
Incumbents	2,807,512	2,477,049	1,848,559	2,529,571	1,344,603	1,096,655	990,992	888,204	666,647	956,081	582,647	463,070	453,459	286,559	200,607	154,774	101,102
	(N=22)	(N=7)[b]	(N=8)[b]	(N=6)	(N=6)	(N=21)	(N=34)	(N=24)[b]	(N=15)	(N=5)	(N=6)	(N=16)	(N=29)	(N=31)	(N=19)	(N=12)	(N=40)
Democrats	—	2,584,509	1,793,020	1,332,829	854,227	710,406	990,992	947,775	589,707	935,494	528,101	483,204	353,201	285,636	189,994	97,874	64,191
	(N=0)	(N=5)	(N=5)	(N=2)	(N=1)	(N=3)	(N=34)	(N=16)	(N=6)	(N=2)	(N=1)	(N=13)	(N=3)	(N=28)	(N=14)	(N=7)	(N=4)
Republicans	2,807,512	2,208,400	1,941,124	3,127,942	1,442,678	1,170,502	—	769,062	717,941	969,806	593,556	375,824	465,027	295,170	230,323	234,435	105,203
	(N=22)	(N=2)	(N=3)	(N=4)	(N=5)	(N=18)	(N=0)	(N=8)	(N=9)	(N=3)	(N=5)	(N=3)	(N=26)	(N=3)	(N=5)	(N=5)	(N=36)
Challengers	1,836,394	1,670,261	1,603,226	1,980,195	1,148,979	1,088,275	698,489	445,930	453,241[a]	625,120	455,071	515,622	296,273	343,093	217,083	144,720	100,435
	(N=22)	(N=5)	(N=4)	(N=6)	(N=6)	(N=21)	(N=34)	(N=19)	(N=15)	(N=5)	(N=11)	(N=16)	(N=23)	(N=31)	(N=19)	(N=12)	(N=40)
Democrats	1,836,394	1,727,446	1,977,279	2,479,356	1,209,237	1,064,852	—	351,847	527,773	808,908	504,673	249,462	292,781	353,855	192,037	144,491	103,661
	(N=22)	(N=2)	(N=2)	(N=4)	(N=5)	(N=18)	(N=0)	(N=6)	(N=8)	(N=3)	(N=9)	(N=3)	(N=22)	(N=4)	(N=5)	(N=5)	(N=36)
Republicans	—	1,632,138	1,229,173	981,874	847,692	1,231,615	698,489	489,353	334,444	349,438	231,864	577,044	373,093	341,499	226,028	144,883	71,404
	(N=0)	(N=3)	(N=2)	(N=2)	(N=1)	(N=3)	(N=34)	(N=13)	(N=6)	(N=2)	(N=2)	(N=13)	(N=1)	(N=27)	(N=14)	(N=7)	(N=4)

Note: The data include primary and general election expenditures for major party general election candidates only.

a. Includes one or more Independents. Independents are included only if they are incumbents or winning non-incumbents.

b. The N for incumbents in "Incumbent was defeated" is greater than that of challengers because some races were incumbent v. incumbent races resulting from redistricting.

Source: Analysis of Federal Election Commission data.

Table 3-4 Expenditures for Open House Seats, by Election Outcome, 1984–2006 (mean net dollars)

	2006	2004	2002	2000	1998	1996	1994	1992	1990	1988	1986	1984
All winners	1,885,671 (N=33)	1,503,719 (N=36)	1,290,443 (N=49)	1,364,737 (N=36)	993,978 (N=34)	768,069 (N=53)	602,009 (N=52)	536,918 (N=91)	618,705 (N=30)	606,434 (N=27)	523,759 (N=46)	440,912 (N=26)
Democrats	1,765,031 (N=20)	1,455,906 (N=15)	1,237,139 (N=18)	1,303,041 (N=10)	949,685 (N=18)	749,246 (N=24)	676,437 (N=14)	505,550 (N=57)	587,804 (N=18)	551,275 (N=13)	515,570 (N=22)	428,416 (N=8)
Republicans	2,071,270 (N=13)	1,537,870 (N=21)	1,321,394 (N=31)	1,388,466 (N=26)	1,043,808 (N=16)	783,646 (N=29)	574,588 (N=38)	589,505 (N=34)	665,058 (N=12)	657,654 (N=14)	531,266 (N=24)	446,467 (N=18)
Winners with 60% or more	1,170,543 (N=15)	1,293,878 (N=20)	1,143,757 (N=24)	1,076,754 (N=14)	754,860 (N=11)	651,225 (N=18)	618,153 (N=21)	516,055 (N=44)	618,152 (N=14)	543,935 (N=11)	543,382 (N=19)	372,989 (N=8)
Democrats	1,216,683 (N=11)	956,768 (N=8)	1,299,407 (N=8)	968,414 (N=4)	657,743 (N=8)	593,421 (N=8)	587,314 (N=3)	395,193 (N=33)	523,728 (N=9)	391,885 (N=7)	537,552 (N=7)	290,693 (N=3)
Republicans	1,043,660 (N=4)	1,518,618 (N=12)	1,065,932 (N=16)	1,120,090 (N=10)	1,013,839 (N=3)	697,469 (N=10)	623,293 (N=18)	878,644 (N=11)	788,116 (N=5)	810,023 (N=4)	546,783 (N=12)	422,366 (N=5)
Winners with 60% or less	2,481,610 (N=18)	1,766,019 (N=16)	1,431,263 (N=25)	1,547,998 (N=22)	1,108,339 (N=23)	828,160 (N=35)	591,072 (N=31)	556,449 (N=47)	619,189 (N=16)	649,402 (N=16)	509,950 (N=27)	471,100 (N=18)
Democrats	2,435,235 (N=9)	2,026,350 (N=7)	1,187,325 (N=10)	1,526,125 (N=6)	1,183,239 (N=10)	827,158 (N=16)	700,743 (N=11)	657,293 (N=24)	651,880 (N=9)	737,230 (N=6)	505,312 (N=15)	511,049 (N=5)
Republicans	2,527,985 (N=9)	1,563,540 (N=9)	1,593,888 (N=15)	1,556,201 (N=16)	1,050,724 (N=13)	829,003 (N=19)	530,754 (N=20)	451,221 (N=23)	577,159 (N=7)	596,706 (N=10)	515,749 (N=12)	455,736 (N=13)
All losers	1,126,122 (N=31)	781,345 (N=31)	955,544 (N=47)	980,479 (N=32)	561,945 (N=31)	536,703 (N=52)	566,966 (N=51)	320,997 (N=83)	443,297 (N=26)	439,728 (N=24)	323,718 (N=40)	282,480 (N=26)
Democrats	1,290,154 (N=13)	670,325 (N=17)	982,176 (N=31)	968,206 (N=25)	525,458 (N=15)	564,701 (N=29)	514,354 (N=38)	425,618 (N=31)	477,638 (N=12)	435,660 (N=13)	320,161 (N=21)	316,309 (N=18)
Republicans	1,007,655 (N=18)	916,156 (N=14)	903,944 (N=16)	1,024,312 (N=7)	596,152 (N=16)	501,401 (N=23)	720,753 (N=13)	258,595 (N=52)	413,862 (N=14)	455,860 (N=10)	326,596 (N=19)	206,363 (N=8)
Losers with 40% or more	1,684,233 (N=18)	1,373,472 (N=16)	1,221,532 (N=25)	1,470,378 (N=20)	762,097 (N=22)	652,323 (N=35)	683,257 (N=31)	449,666 (N=47)	465,767 (N=16)	565,182 (N=16)	360,978 (N=23)	352,961 (N=18)
Democrats	1,792,526 (N=9)	1,063,167 (N=9)	1,121,145 (N=15)	1,545,889 (N=15)	620,288 (N=12)	657,299 (N=19)	596,359 (N=20)	472,034 (N=23)	435,365 (N=8)	505,609 (N=9)	294,362 (N=10)	393,262 (N=13)
Republicans	1,575,940 (N=9)	1,772,435 (N=7)	1,372,113 (N=10)	1,243,844 (N=5)	932,269 (N=10)	646,414 (N=16)	841,253 (N=11)	428,230 (N=24)	496,168 (N=8)	693,525 (N=6)	412,220 (N=13)	248,180 (N=5)
Losers with 40% or less	353,353 (N=13)	149,744 (N=15)	625,350 (N=22)	163,982 (N=12)	72,685 (N=9)	298,660 (N=17)	386,715 (N=20)	152,967 (N=36)	407,346 (N=10)	188,819 (N=8)	193,794 (N=15)	123,896 (N=8)
Democrats	159,815 (N=4)	228,378 (N=8)	851,892 (N=16)	101,682 (N=10)	146,137 (N=3)	388,764 (N=10)	423,239 (N=18)	292,173 (N=8)	562,183 (N=4)	278,276 (N=4)	228,939 (N=9)	116,232 (N=5)
Republicans	439,370 (N=9)	59,876 (N=7)	123,663 (N=6)	475,481 (N=2)	35,959 (N=6)	169,941 (N=7)	58,005 (N=2)	113,194 (N=28)	304,122 (N=6)	99,363 (N=4)	141,077 (N=6)	136,668 (N=3)

Note: The data include primary and general election expenditures for major party general election candidates only.

Source: Analysis of Federal Election Commission data.

Table 3-5 Senate Campaign Expenditures, 1974–2006 (net dollars)

	2006	2004	2002	2000	1998	1996	1994	1992	1990
All candidates									
Total expenditures	514,937,502[a]	367,514,648	281,529,788	384,591,165	249,184,622	230,420,000	279,483,211	194,322,039	173,370,282
Mean expenditure	7,922,115 (N=65)	5,404,627 (N=68)	4,540,803 (N=62)	5,827,139 (N=66)	3,775,525 (N=66)	3,544,918 (N=65)	3,992,617 (N=70)	2,816,261 (N=69)	2,587,616 (N=67)
Mean, Democrats	8,609,875 (N=31)	5,625,326 (N=34)	4,602,810 (N=30)	6,095,450 (N=33)	3,481,733 (N=34)	3,385,904 (N=32)	3,394,769 (N=35)	2,813,701 (N=35)	2,465,285 (N=34)
Mean, Republicans	7,035,429 (N=32)	5,183,929 (N=34)	4,482,671 (N=32)	5,558,828 (N=33)	4,087,678 (N=32)	3,699,114 (N=33)	4,590,465 (N=35)	2,818,898 (N=34)	2,713,654 (N=33)
Incumbents									
Mean, all incumbents	9,426,175 (N=29)	6,566,787 (N=26)	4,535,740 (N=27)	4,530,693 (N=29)	4,728,639 (N=29)	4,233,304 (N=20)	7,672,755 (N=26)	3,708,456 (N=27)	3,577,980 (N=32)
Mean, Democrats	9,560,029 (N=14)	7,418,068 (N=14)	6,142,399 (N=12)	3,672,975 (N=11)	4,560,721 (N=15)	5,207,602 (N=7)	5,152,998 (N=16)	2,849,946 (N=15)	3,616,906 (N=17)
Mean, Republicans	8,758,947 (N=14)	5,573,627 (N=12)	3,250,414 (N=15)	5,054,855 (N=18)	4,908,551 (N=14)	3,708,682 (N=13)	3,904,368 (N=10)	4,781,593 (N=12)	3,533,864 (N=15)
Challengers									
Mean, all challengers	5,659,763 (N=28)	2,425,098 (N=26)	2,885,335 (N=21)	3,153,464 (N=27)	3,144,244 (N=27)	3,109,930 (N=17)	3,997,011 (N=26)	1,824,993 (N=26)	1,699,247 (N=29)
Mean, Democrats	7,129,691 (N=14)	1,554,631 (N=12)	2,182,146 (N=11)	3,281,655 (N=17)	2,615,103 (N=14)	2,920,075 (N=11)	1,226,228 (N=10)	2,550,724 (N=12)	1,395,011 (N=14)
Mean, Republicans	4,189,836[b] (N=14)	3,171,212 (N=14)	3,658,843 (N=10)	2,935,540 (N=10)	3,714,088 (N=13)	3,457,997 (N=6)	5,703,750 (N=16)	1,202,034 (N=14)	1,983,202 (N=15)
Open seats									
Mean, all Open	10,388,132[a] (N=8)	8,357,852 (N=16)	7,033,769 (N=14)	16,805,752 (N=10)	2,715,951 (N=10)	3,317,314 (N=28)	3,003,850 (N=18)	2,922,286 (N=16)	1,599,459 (N=6)
Mean, Democrats	11,083,353 (N=3)	8,594,068 (N=8)	5,767,416 (N=7)	20,991,796 (N=5)	2,671,336 (N=5)	2,841,062 (N=14)	2,634,075 (N=9)	3,140,205 (N=8)	934,046 (N=3)
Mean, Republicans	10,962,693 (N=4)	8,121,636 (N=8)	8,300,122 (N=7)	12,619,707 (N=5)	2,760,565 (N=5)	3,793,565 (N=14)	3,373,624 (N=9)	2,704,366 (N=8)	2,264,872 (N=3)

(continued)

Table 3-5 (continued)

	1988	1986	1984	1982	1980	1978	1976	1974
All candidates								
Total expenditures	184,695,501	183,432,489	141,962,276	114,036,379	74,163,669	64,695,510	38,108,745	28,436,308
Mean expenditure	2,798,417 (N=66)	2,737,798 (N=67)	2,327,250 (N=61)	1,781,815 (N=64)	1,106,920 (N=67)	951,405 (N=68)	595,499 (N=64)	437,482 (N=65)
Mean, Democrats	2,930,305 (N=33)	2,260,415 (N=33)	2,160,637 (N=31)	1,881,379 (N=32)	1,170,580 (N=34)	762,831 (N=35)	569,902 (N=33)	487,775 (N=34)
Mean, Republicans	2,666,529 (N=33)	3,201,141 (N=34)	2,499,417 (N=30)	1,682,252 (N=32)	1,041,332 (N=33)	1,151,407 (N=33)	616,635 (N=30)	382,343 (N=31)
Incumbents								
Mean, all incumbents	3,748,132 (N=27)	3,374,602 (N=28)	2,539,929 (N=28)	1,858,140 (N=29)	1,301,692 (N=25)	1,341,942 (N=22)	623,809 (N=25)	555,714 (N=25)
Mean, Democrats	3,457,144 (N=15)	2,712,796 (N=9)	1,755,004 (N=12)	1,696,226 (N=18)	1,355,660 (N=19)	618,211 (N=11)	503,111 (N=17)	525,766 (N=15)
Mean, Republicans	4,111,866 (N=12)	3,688,089 (N=19)	3,128,622 (N=16)	2,123,089 (N=11)	1,130,792 (N=6)	2,065,674 (N=11)	891,342 (N=7)	600,636 (N=10)
Challengers								
Mean, all challengers	1,817,161 (N=27)	1,899,417 (N=27)	1,241,434 (N=25)	1,217,034 (N=29)	842,547 (N=24)	697,766 (N=21)	452,275 (N=23)	332,579 (N=22)
Mean, Democrats	2,154,283 (N=12)	1,911,693 (N=18)	1,515,412 (N=15)	1,516,015 (N=11)	557,006 (N=6)	830,282 (N=11)	645,441 (N=8)	390,297 (N=10)
Mean, Republicans	1,547,464 (N=15)	1,874,864 (N=9)	830,466 (N=10)	1,034,324 (N=18)	937,727 (N=18)	551,999 (N=10)	349,253 (N=15)	284,480 (N=12)
Open seats								
Mean, all Open	2,869,383 (N=12)	3,138,282 (N=12)	4,976,051 (N=8)	4,142,687 (N=6)	1,132,560 (N=18)	820,787 (N=25)	756,951 (N=16)	401,484 (N=18)
Mean, Democrats	3,165,250 (N=6)	2,628,009 (N=6)	5,797,131 (N=4)	4,331,959 (N=3)	1,188,903 (N=9)	828,127 (N=13)	636,295 (N=8)	532,691 (N=9)
Mean, Republicans	2,573,516 (N=6)	3,648,555 (N=6)	4,154,971 (N=4)	3,953,415 (N=3)	1,076,218 (N=9)	812,835 (N=12)	877,606 (N=8)	270,277 (N=9)

Note: The data include primary and general election expenditures for major party general election candidates only.

a. Includes one or more Independents. Independents are included only if they are incumbents or winning non-incumbents.

b. Alan Schlesinger (R-CT) is not included in the data. He raised $221,019 and was third in the voting.

Source: Analysis of Federal Election Commission data.

Table 3-6 Expenditures of Senate Incumbents and Challengers, by Election Outcome, 1974–2006 (mean net dollars)

	2006	2004	2002	2000	1998	1996	1994	1992	1990
Incumbent won with 60% or more									
Incumbents	6,681,589	4,710,449	3,287,355	3,421,925	2,640,723	2,418,451	3,610,535	2,695,624	2,314,689
	(N=17)	(N=18)	(N=16)	(N=20)	(N=19)	(N=6)	(N=10)	(N=13)	(N=19)
Democrats	8,661,938	5,741,981	4,779,508	3,359,248	3,131,344	2,266,951	1,735,768	2,661,397	2,439,405
	(N=11)	(N=10)	(N=6)	(N=10)	(N=9)	(N=2)	(N=3)	(N=9)	(N=10)
Republicans	3,050,950	3,421,034	2,392,063	3,484,603	2,199,165	2,494,201	4,414,006	2,772,633	2,176,116
	(N=6)	(N=8)	(N=10)	(N=10)	(N=10)	(N=4)	(N=7)	(N=4)	(N=9)
Challengers	2,255,831	1,001,610	849,543	764,569	447,843	762,003	1,002,306	701,442	844,346
	(N=16)	(N=18)	(N=10)	(N=18)	(N=17)	(N=3)	(N=10)	(N=12)	(N=16)
Democrats	398,864	211,821	909,843	486,019	292,748	479,791	1,365,651	595,192	438,732
	(N=5)	(N=8)	(N=6)	(N=9)	(N=10)	(N=2)	(N=7)	(N=4)	(N=8)
Republicans	3,099,908	1,633,441	759,091	1,043,118	669,406	1,326,427	154,500	754,568	1,249,961
	(N=11)	(N=10)	(N=4)	(N=9)	(N=7)	(N=1)	(N=3)	(N=8)	(N=8)
Incumbent won with 60% or less									
Incumbents	12,579,501[a]	9,424,745	5,424,130	5,738,301	6,609,358	5,052,842	5,312,041	4,550,595	5,273,925
	(N=6)	(N=7)	(N=8)	(N=3)	(N=7)	(N=13)	(N=14)	(N=10)	(N=12)
Democrats	12,853,029	8,819,323	5,905,346	—	6,619,822	6,383,863	6,020,368	2,841,405	5,299,049
	(N=3)	(N=3)	(N=4)	(N=0)	(N=5)	(N=5)	(N=11)	(N=4)	(N=7)
Republicans	10,012,253	9,878,811	4,942,914	5,738,301	6,583,197	4,220,954	2,715,212	5,690,055	5,238,751
	(N=2)	(N=4)	(N=4)	(N=3)	(N=2)	(N=8)	(N=3)	(N=6)	(N=5)
Challengers	10,356,810[b]	4,337,629	2,570,080	2,757,598	4,932,471	3,660,942	5,546,353	2,283,708	2,865,673
	(N=6)	(N=7)	(N=8)	(N=3)	(N=7)	(N=13)	(N=14)	(N=10)	(N=12)
Democrats	12,527,378	4,240,253	2,466,826	2,757,598	4,304,098	3,521,336	1,034,241	3,032,533	2,927,948
	(N=3)	(N=4)	(N=4)	(N=3)	(N=2)	(N=8)	(N=3)	(N=6)	(N=5)
Republicans	8,186,241	4,467,463	2,673,335	—	5,183,821	3,884,311	6,776,929	1,160,471	2,821,191
	(N=3)	(N=3)	(N=4)	(N=0)	(N=5)	(N=5)	(N=11)	(N=4)	(N=7)
Incumbent was defeated									
Incumbents	14,049,176	19,975,170	8,824,759	7,622,785	13,563,761	4,468,434	5,508,854	4,894,814	7,229,154
	(N=6)	(N=1)	(N=3)	(N=6)	(N=3)	(N=1)	(N=2)	(N=4)	(N=1)
Democrats	—	19,975,170	10,705,177	6,810,252	7,129,612	—	5,508,854	3,751,500	—
	(N=0)	(N=1)	(N=2)	(N=1)	(N=1)	(N=0)	(N=2)	(N=2)	(N=0)
Republicans	14,049,176	—	5,063,923	7,785,291	16,780,836	4,468,434	—	6,074,128	7,229,154
	(N=6)	(N=0)	(N=1)	(N=5)	(N=2)	(N=1)	(N=0)	(N=2)	(N=1)
Challengers	10,039,869	14,660,167	4,698,340	10,518,085	14,251,319	2,990,554	8,125,137	4,045,732	1,380,560
	(N=6)	(N=1)	(N=3)	(N=6)	(N=3)	(N=1)	(N=2)	(N=4)	(N=1)
Democrats	10,039,869	—	3,629,022	8,628,233	12,537,880	2,990,554	—	5,016,438	1,380,560
	(N=6)	(N=0)	(N=1)	(N=5)	(N=2)	(N=1)	(N=0)	(N=2)	(N=1)
Republicans	—	14,660,167	5,232,999	19,967,341	17,678,198	—	8,125,137	3,075,026	—
	(N=0)	(N=1)	(N=2)	(N=1)	(N=1)	(N=0)	(N=2)	(N=2)	(N=0)

(continued)

Table 3-6 (continued)

	1988	1986	1984	1982	1980	1978	1976	1974
Incumbent won with 60% or more								
Incumbents	2,733,348 (N=15)	1,963,140 (N=14)	1,612,152 (N=18)	1,494,578 (N=13)	1,162,385 (N=10)	456,062 (N=7)	340,362 (N=11)	447,234 (N=11)
Democrats	2,320,232 (N=10)	1,672,182 (N=8)	1,620,869 (N=7)	1,401,794 (N=12)	1,220,616 (N=6)	559,046 (N=4)	340,362 (N=11)	447,234 (N=11)
Republicans	3,559,581 (N=5)	2,351,083 (N=6)	1,606,604 (N=11)	2,607,983 (N=1)	1,075,038 (N=4)	318,749 (N=3)	— (N=0)	— (N=0)
Challengers	581,494 (N=15)	451,671 (N=13)	384,263 (N=15)	777,830 (N=13)	302,812 (N=9)	47,346 (N=6)	171,997 (N=9)	222,955 (N=8)
Democrats	805,077 (N=5)	155,853 (N=5)	322,263 (N=10)	424,507 (N=1)	265,822 (N=4)	38,458 (N=3)	— (N=0)	— (N=0)
Republicans	469,702 (N=10)	636,557 (N=8)	508,264 (N=5)	807,276 (N=12)	332,404 (N=5)	56,233 (N=3)	171,997 (N=9)	222,955 (N=8)
Incumbent won with 60% or less								
Incumbents	6,235,198 (N=8)	5,213,789 (N=7)	4,505,574 (N=7)	2,224,235 (N=14)	945,423 (N=6)	2,496,483 (N=8)	503,773 (N=5)	567,597 (N=14)
Democrats	6,829,055 (N=4)	11,037,707 (N=1)	1,833,432 (N=4)	2,417,100 (N=5)	796,984 (N=4)	586,055 (N=2)	1,237,910 (N=1)	741,729 (N=4)
Republicans	5,641,341 (N=4)	4,243,136 (N=6)	8,068,429 (N=3)	2,117,088 (N=9)	1,242,300 (N=2)	3,133,293 (N=6)	320,239 (N=4)	497,945 (N=10)
Challengers	3,784,451 (N=8)	3,389,477 (N=7)	2,296,194 (N=7)	1,615,338 (N=14)	864,870 (N=6)	1,075,965 (N=8)	358,964 (N=5)	298,133 (N=14)
Democrats	3,209,075 (N=4)	1,990,836 (N=6)	4,028,715 (N=3)	1,629,490 (N=9)	1,139,376 (N=2)	1,212,929 (N=6)	282,441 (N=4)	254,374 (N=10)
Republicans	4,359,826 (N=4)	11,781,316 (N=1)	996,804 (N=4)	1,589,864 (N=5)	727,617 (N=4)	332,537 (N=2)	665,058 (N=1)	407,531 (N=4)
Incumbent was defeated								
Incumbents	2,579,437 (N=4)	4,358,340 (N=7)	3,520,088 (N=3)	1,658,623 (N=2)	1,693,991 (N=9)	908,348 (N=7)	983,196 (N=9)	513,456 (N=2)
Democrats	1,338,622 (N=1)	— (N=0)	2,380,239 (N=1)	1,625,042 (N=1)	1,693,991 (N=9)	678,4—6 (N=5)	714,201 (N=5)	— (N=0)
Republicans	2,993,042 (N=3)	4,358,340 (N=7)	4,090,013 (N=2)	1,692,204 (N=1)	— (N=0)	1,483,203 (N=2)	1,319,440 (N=4)	513,456 (N=2)
Challengers	2,516,337 (N=4)	3,098,027 (N=7)	3,066,175 (N=3)	793,123 (N=2)	1,367,400 (N=9)	918,054 (N=7)	784,392 (N=9)	679,614 (N=2)
Democrats	2,996,572 (N=3)	3,098,027 (N=7)	3,711,199 (N=2)	1,586,245 (N=1)	— (N=0)	870,079 (N=2)	1,008,440 (N=4)	679,614 (N=2)
Republicans	1,075,631 (N=1)	— (N=0)	1,776,128 (N=1)	981,197 (N=1)	1,367,400 (N=9)	937,244 (N=5)	605,153 (N=5)	— (N=0)

Note: The Federal Election Commission included the following disclaimer along with its 1986 data, and *Vital Statistics* considers it appropriate for all years: "The small N's and unique nature of some Senate campaigns make all measures of central tendency like averages or medians problematic and, as a result, the Commission would not include tables such as these in its regular release of information."

a. Includes one or more Independents. Independents are included only if they are incumbents or winning non-incumbents.

b. Alan Schlesinger (R-CT) is not included in the data. He raised $221,019 and was third in the voting.

Source: Analysis of Federal Election Commission data.

Table 3-7 Expenditures for Open Senate Seats, by Election Outcome, 1986–2006 (mean net dollars)

	2006	2004	2002	2000	1998	1996	1994	1992	1990	1988	1986
All winners	10,566,377[a]	9,853,572	7,202,893	21,625,081[b]	3,820,837	3,582,000	3,378,624	3,338,507	2,264,872	3,779,715	3,827,158
	(N=4)	(N=8)	(N=7)	(N=5)	(N=5)	(N=14)	(N=9)	(N=8)	(N=3)	(N=6)	(N=7)
Democrats	8,847,675	12,129,704	2,926,239	25,627,472[b]	3,518,576	4,532,955	—	4,177,040	—	5,186,633	2,714,673
	(N=2)	(N=2)	(N=1)	(N=4)	(N=2)	(N=5)	(N=0)	(N=5)	(N=0)	(N=2)	(N=4)
Republicans	18,565,935	9,094,861	7,915,668	5,615,514	4,022,354	3,053,692	3,378,624	1,940,951	2,264,872	3,076,256	5,310,471
	(N=1)	(N=6)	(N=6)	(N=1)	(N=3)	(N=9)	(N=9)	(N=3)	(N=3)	(N=4)	(N=3)
Winners with 60% or more	7,512,141	10,789,785	—	—	2,739,093	2,518,955	2,754,664	1,191,005	1,535,352	1,879,272	2,216,412
	(N=2)	(N=2)	(N=0)	(N=0)	(N=2)	(N=2)	(N=4)	(N=1)	(N=2)	(N=2)	(N=2)
Democrats	9,020,059	14,372,856	—	—	3,914,375	2,732,011	—	1,191,005	—	2,881,666	2,057,422
	(N=1)	(N=1)	(N=0)	(N=0)	(N=1)	(N=1)	(N=0)	(N=1)	(N=0)	(N=1)	(N=1)
Republicans	—	7,206,714	—	—	1,563,811	2,305,898	2,754,644	0	1,535,352	876,877	2,375,402
	(N=0)	(N=1)	(N=0)	(N=0)	(N=1)	(N=1)	(N=4)	(N=0)	(N=2)	(N=1)	(N=1)
Winners with 60% or less	13,620,613	9,541,501	7,202,893	21,625,081[b]	4,542,000	3,759,175	3,868,793	3,645,293	3,723,911	4,729,937	4,471,457
	(N=2)	(N=6)	(N=7)	(N=5)	(N=3)	(N=12)	(N=5)	(N=7)	(N=1)	(N=4)	(N=5)
Democrats	8,675,291	9,886,551	2,926,239	25,627,472[b]	3,122,776	4,983,191	—	4,923,549	—	7,491,600	2,933,757
	(N=1)	(N=1)	(N=1)	(N=4)	(N=1)	(N=4)	(N=0)	(N=4)	(N=0)	(N=1)	(N=3)
Republicans	18,565,935	9,472,491	7,915,668	5,615,514	5,251,613	3,147,166	3,868,793	1,940,951	3,723,911	3,809,383	6,778,006
	(N=1)	(N=5)	(N=6)	(N=1)	(N=2)	(N=8)	(N=5)	(N=3)	(N=1)	(N=3)	(N=2)
All losers	10,209,886	6,862,133	6,864,645	11,986,423[c]	1,611,064	3,052,627	2,634,075	2,506,064	934,046	1,959,051	2,952,009
	(N=4)	(N=8)	(N=7)	(N=5)	(N=5)	(N=14)	(N=9)	(N=8)	(N=3)	(N=6)	(N=7)
Democrats	15,554,709	7,415,523	6,240,945	2,449,093	2,106,510	1,901,122	2,634,075	1,412,146	934,046	2,154,558	2,181,463
	(N=1)	(N=6)	(N=6)	(N=1)	(N=3)	(N=9)	(N=9)	(N=3)	(N=3)	(N=4)	(N=3)
Republicans	8,428,279	5,201,962	10,606,843	14,370,756[c]	867,896	5,125,336	—	3,162,415	—	1,568,036	3,529,919
	(N=3)	(N=2)	(N=1)	(N=4)	(N=2)	(N=5)	(N=0)	(N=5)	(N=0)	(N=2)	(N=4)
Losers with 40% or more	11,885,985	7,913,929	6,862,710	11,986,423[c]	2,390,365	3,439,376	2,802,500	2,792,915	1,936,914	2,730,542	3,686,638
	(N=2)	(N=6)	(N=7)	(N=5)	(N=3)	(N=12)	(N=5)	(N=7)	(N=1)	(N=4)	(N=5)
Democrats	15,554,709	7,924,995	6,240,945	2,449,093	3,039,044	2,051,827	2,802,500	1,412,146	1,936,914	2,689,441	3,006,346
	(N=1)	(N=5)	(N=6)	(N=1)	(N=2)	(N=8)	(N=5)	(N=3)	(N=1)	(N=3)	(N=2)
Republicans	8,217,260	7,858,598	10,606,843	14,370,756[c]	1,093,007	6,214,473	—	3,828,492	—	2,853,842	4,140,166
	(N=1)	(N=1)	(N=1)	(N=4)	(N=1)	(N=4)	(N=0)	(N=4)	(N=0)	(N=1)	(N=3)
Losers with 40% or less	8,533,788	3,706,745	—	—	442,114	732,136	2,423,544	498,107	432,613	416,069	1,115,437
	(N=2)	(N=2)	(N=0)	(N=0)	(N=2)	(N=2)	(N=4)	(N=1)	(N=2)	(N=2)	(N=2)
Democrats	—	4,868,165	—	—	241,443	695,482	2,423,544	0	432,613	549,908	531,698
	(N=0)	(N=1)	(N=0)	(N=0)	(N=1)	(N=1)	(N=4)	(N=0)	(N=2)	(N=1)	(N=1)
Republicans	8,533,788	2,545,325	—	—	642,784	768,789	0	498,107	0	282,229	1,699,175
	(N=2)	(N=1)	(N=0)	(N=0)	(N=1)	(N=1)	(N=0)	(N=1)	(N=0)	(N=1)	(N=1)

Notes: The data include primary and general election expenditures for major party general election candidates only. The Federal Election Commission included the following disclaimer along with its 1986 data, and *Vital Statistics* considers it appropriate for all years: "The small N's and unique nature of some Senate campaigns make all measures of central tendency like averages or medians problematic, and, as a result, the commission would not include tables such as these in regular release of information.

a. Includes one or more Independents. Independents are included only if they are incumbents or winning non-incumbents.

b. Jon Corzine (D-NJ) spent $63,209,506. Hillary Rodham Clinton (D-NY) spent $29,871,577. Excluding these candidates, the remaining winners (N=3) in open Senate seats spent an average of $5,014,773. For Democrats the average would be $4,714,403 (N=2). The average for Republicans would be unchanged.

c. Rick Lazio spent $40,576,273. Excluding him from the candidates who lost with more than 40%, the average for all candidates would be $4,838,961 (N=4). The average for Republican candidates would be $5,635,583 (N=3). The average for Democrats would be unchanged.

Source: Analysis of Federal Election Commission data.

Table 3-8 Campaign Funding Sources for House and Senate Candidates, 1984–2006

Party and candidate status	Number of candidates	Contributions plus party coordinated expenditures on behalf of candidates ($ millions)	Percentage of funding from				
			Individuals	PAC's	Party (contributions plus coordinated expenditures)	Candidate to self (contributions plus loans)	Other
House, 2006							
All candidates	815	777.8	54	35	1	5	5
Democrats	427	375.5	58	33	1	4	4
Incumbents	191	205.9	49	45	1	1	5
Challengers	203	115.3	70	16	2	9	3
Open Seats	33	54.3	66	20	1	8	5
Republicans	388	402.3	51	38	1	5	5
Incumbents	211	318.4	50	43	1	1	5
Challengers	144	36.2	56	10	2	27	5
Open Seats	33	47.7	52	23	3	16	6
Senate, 2006							
All candidates	65	530.9	67	13	3	13	5
Democrats	31	275.5	70	11	2	13	3
Incumbents	14	141.3	76	15	2	4	3
Challengers	14	101.7	59	6	3	29	3
Open Seats	3	32.5	82	11	1	0	6
Republicans	32	230.2	60	16	4	15	6
Incumbents	14	125.4	65	23	4	1	7
Challengers	14	61.2	54	5	4	34	3
Open Seats	4	43.6	55	10	3	26	5
House, 2004							
All candidates	812	609.5	55	35	2	4	4
Democrats	403	274.1	56	34	2	5	3
Incumbents	193	190.5	55	41	1	0	4
Challengers	177	50.4	69	15	2	20	4
Open Seats	33	33.2	63	26	4	7	0
Republicans	409	335.4	54	36	2	4	4
Incumbents	210	246.5	53	42	1	1	4
Challengers	163	41.5	67	13	6	11	4
Open Seats	36	47.4	50	25	6	14	5
Senate, 2004							
All candidates	69	367.0	69	16	5	3	7
Democrats	35	194.7	73	14	5	2	5
Incumbents	14	103.3	73	18	5	0	5
Challengers	12	18.6	77	10	4	4	5
Open Seats	9	72.8	73	9	7	6	6
Republicans	34	172.3	64	18	6	4	9
Incumbents	12	65.6	63	29	3	0	5
Challengers	14	45.3	69	7	5	14	5
Open Seats	8	61.4	61	14	8	2	14
House, 2002							
All candidates	807	556.7	49	36	2	9	4
Democrats	400	273.2	46	36	2	12	5
Incumbents	193	170.1	48	45	1	0	5
Challengers	161	53.7	41	16	2	38	3
Open Seats	46	49.5	45	24	2	25	4
Republicans	407	283.5	51	35	3	6	5
Incumbents	199	192.4	50	43	1	1	5
Challengers	162	33.1	58	12	7	20	3
Open Seats	46	58.1	49	25	5	17	4

Party and candidate status	Number of candidates	Contributions plus party coordinated expenditures on behalf of candidates ($ millions)	Percentage of funding from				
			Individuals	PAC's	Party (contributions plus coordinated expenditures)	Candidate to self (contributions plus loans)	Other
Senate, 2002							
All candidates	69	300.5	63	19	5	8	6
Democrats	33	139.9	68	17	2	8	6
Incumbents	12	72.8	71	22	1	<1	6
Challengers	17	36.3	69	13	2	11	5
Open Seats	4	30.8	59	8	3	24	7
Republicans	36	160.6	58	21	7	7	7
Incumbents	15	51.8	55	36	4	0	5
Challengers	17	68.5	55	13	8	15	9
Open Seats	4	40.3	68	14	10	3	6
House, 2000							
All candidates	820	550.0	51	34	2	7	5
Democrats	416	271.6	50	36	2	8	6
Incumbents	206	170.5	48	45	1	<1	7
Challengers	176	66.1	56	19	2	18	4
Open Seats	32	34.9	47	23	4	22	5
Republicans	404	278.4	54	33	2	6	5
Incumbents	197	190.7	54	39	1	1	5
Challengers	175	45.9	58	15	5	18	4
Open Seats	32	76.9	49	29	4	14	3
Senate, 2000							
All candidates	70	387.3	53	13	4	24[a]	6
Democrats	34	210.2	40	9	3	43[a]	6
Incumbents	11	46.5	56	20	6	12	5
Challengers	18	56.4	43	8	1	41	8
Open Seats	5	107.3	32	4	2	57[a]	5
Republicans	36	177.1	68	18	6	1	6
Incumbents	18	90.7	60	27	5	2	7
Challengers	13	20.9	70	9	8	3	10
Open Seats	5	65.5	79	10	8	0	3
House, 1998							
All candidates	782	436.1	51	35	3	6	4
Democrats	390	199.6	49	38	3	6	4
Incumbents	194	130.6	47	46	2	0	5
Challengers	162	41.6	52	19	4	21	3
Open Seats	34	27.4	59	27	4	6	3
Republicans	392	236.5	53	33	3	6	4
Incumbents	211	166.6	54	39	2	1	5
Challengers	149	42.3	54	15	8	17	5
Open Seats	32	27.6	45	28	5	18	3
Senate, 1998							
All candidates	70	265.9	58	18	7	11	7
Democrats	35	126.1	58	16	8	9	9
Incumbents	15	71.9	65	22	7	0	6
Challengers	15	39.4	45	4	10	27	15
Open Seats	5	14.7	59	2	9	4	26
Republicans	35	139.8	57	19	7	12	4
Incumbents	14	72.7	60	26	6	3	5
Challengers	16	52.7	52	9	8	29	3
Open Seats	5	14.3	59	25	8	0	8

(continued)

Table 3-8 (continued)

Party and candidate status	Number of candidates	Contributions plus party coordinated expenditures on behalf of candidates ($ millions)	Percentage of funding from: Individuals	PAC's	Party (contributions plus coordinated expenditures)	Candidate to self (contributions plus loans)	Other
House, 1996							
All candidates	873	460.8	53	33	4	6	4
Democrats	435	211.6	48	35	4	9	4
Incumbents	171	108.8	47	46	2	1	5
Challengers	211	67.3	50	24	6	17	3
Open Seats	53	35.5	48	26	5	18	3
Republicans	438	249.2	57	30	4	4	4
Incumbents	213	171.3	58	37	2	1	2
Challengers	174	40.0	64	11	9	13	3
Open Seats	51	35.0	53	23	8	12	3
Senate, 1996							
All candidates	68	242.1	58	17	9	12	4
Democrats	34	116.2	59	13	8	16	4
Incumbents	7	36.4	74	13	4	5	4
Challengers	14	36.5	50	6	8	34	2
Open Seats	13	43.3	55	18	11	9	7
Republicans	34	125.9	57	21	9	8	4
Incumbents	13	50.0	57	29	9	2	4
Challengers	8	25.6	70	14	10	3	3
Open Seats	13	50.3	50	18	9	18	5
House, 1994							
All candidates	824	371.3	49	34	5	8	4
Democrats	403	196.7	43	43	5	5	4
Incumbents	226	142.4	34	50	3	1	12
Challengers	130	23.6	45	23	11	17	4
Open Seats	47	30.7	47	27	8	15	3
Republicans	421	174.6	56	24	6	11	3
Incumbents	157	82.9	58	36	2	1	3
Challengers	217	58.6	56	10	10	20	4
Open Seats	47	33.1	50	19	8	19	4
Senate, 1994							
All candidates	70	291.7	54	15	8	19	4
Democrats	35	124.9	55	18	10	12	5
Incumbents	16	86.4	54	18	8	14	6
Challengers	10	11.7	46	16	13	21	4
Open Seats	9	26.9	60	16	14	3	7
Republicans	35	166.7	53	13	6	24	4
Incumbents	10	35.4	60	30	6	<1	4
Challengers	16	96.1	47	3	5	41	4
Open Seats	9	35.2	61	21	11	1	6
House, 1992							
All candidates	851	331.5	47	36	5	9	3
Democrats	427	184.7	43	43	4	6	4
Incumbents	213	122.1	40	50	2	1	7
Challengers	140	25.1	48	26	10	13	3
Open Seats	74	37.5	49	30	4	17	<1
Republicans	424	146.9	51	26	6	13	4
Incumbents	138	74.8	52	39	3	1	5
Challengers	216	44.5	47	9	10	22	12
Open Seats	70	27.5	57	21	7	14	1

Party and candidate status	Number of candidates	Contributions plus party coordinated expenditures on behalf of candidates ($ millions)	Percentage of funding from				
			Individuals	PAC's	Party (contributions plus coordinated expenditures)	Candidate to self (contributions plus loans)	Other
Senate, 1992							
All candidates	71	214.2	58	21	13	5	3
Democrats	35	108.5	60	23	11	2	4
Incumbents	15	43.9	52	35	6	2	5
Challengers	13	43.1	68	12	14	3	3
Open Seats	7	21.5	61	19	13	3	4
Republicans	36	106.9	55	19	15	7	4
Incumbents	12	59.4	58	25	13	<1	4
Challengers	17	24.0	55	9	20	14	2
Open Seats	7	23.5	48	16	16	18	2
House, 1990							
All candidates	807	257.5	44	40	3	6	7
Democrats	413	146.5	39	47	3	5	6
Incumbents	249	113.2	37	52	1	2	8
Challengers	132	16.0	44	27	9	16	4
Open Seats	32	17.3	42	33	4	17	4
Republicans	394	108.8	51	32	4	7	6
Incumbents	159	70.7	50	41	2	1	6
Challengers	206	23.9	54	10	7	24	5
Open Seats	29	14.1	50	24	10	12	4
Senate, 1990							
All candidates	67	191.0	61	21	7	5	6
Democrats	34	90.8	63	22	6	4	5
Incumbents	17	66.7	65	25	5	0	5
Challengers	14	21.0	58	12	9	15	6
Open Seats	3	3.1	50	18	11	21	<1
Republicans	33	100.2	59	21	9	5	6
Incumbents	15	58.9	65	22	7	0	6
Challengers	15	33.4	51	16	12	15	6
Open Seats	3	7.9	43	36	7	0	14
House, 1988							
All candidates	813	249.0	46	40	4	5	5
Democrats	429	140.0	40	47	3	5	5
Incumbents	238	103.8	39	51	2	1	7
Challengers	154	23.5	46	31	7	13	3
Open Seats	27	12.7	39	36	7	14	4
Republicans	384	109.0	52	31	6	6	5
Incumbents	164	73.7	51	39	3	1	6
Challengers	194	21.6	55	10	13	19	3
Open Seats	26	13.7	54	21	13	12	<1
Senate, 1988							
All candidates	66	199.4	59	22	9	5	5
Democrats	33	103.0	58	23	7	8	4
Incumbents	15	53.0	61	29	4	1	5
Challengers	12	29.1	66	16	11	3	4
Open Seats	6	20.9	37	16	8	35	4
Republicans	33	96.3	61	22	11	2	4
Incumbents	12	50.8	62	26	8	<1	4
Challengers	15	27.7	63	11	18	6	2
Open Seats	6	17.8	54	26	13	1	6

(continued)

Table 3-8 (continued)

Party and candidate status	Number of candidates	Contributions plus party coordinated expenditures on behalf of candidates ($ millions)	Percentage of funding from				
			Individuals	PAC's	Party (contributions plus coordinated expenditures)	Candidate to self (contributions plus loans)	Other
House, 1986							
All candidates	810	234.2	48	36	4	6	6
Democrats	427	125.7	44	42	2	6	6
Incumbents	235	84.1	42	49	1	2	6
Challengers	147	22.1	49	29	6	13	3
Open Seats	45	19.5	47	31	3	15	4
Republicans	383	108.5	53	29	6	7	5
Incumbents	160	67.3	53	37	4	1	5
Challengers	182	21.4	54	11	10	22	3
Open Seats	41	19.8	53	24	10	10	3
Senate, 1986							
All candidates	68	208.6	60	21	9	6	4
Democrats	34	90.2	56	22	8	9	5
Incumbents	9	28.2	62	26	7	2	3
Challengers	18	40.3	51	19	9	16	5
Open Seats	7	21.7	60	22	8	5	5
Republicans	34	118.5	63	21	9	2	5
Incumbents	18	68.9	63	24	8	<1	5
Challengers	9	20.4	64	9	18	6	3
Open Seats	7	29.1	61	22	6	2	9
House, 1984							
All candidates	816	203.8	47	36	7	6	5
Democrats	434	107.2	44	41	3	6	6
Incumbents	258	81.8	39	46	2	2	11
Challengers	152	16.3	43	29	6	18	5
Open Seats	24	9.1	45	22	6	24	3
Republicans	382	96.6	49	30	11	6	5
Incumbents	154	52.1	51	37	6	1	5
Challengers	204	33.8	48	18	17	13	4
Open Seats	24	10.7	47	31	13	7	2
Senate, 1984							
All candidates	68	157.7	61	18	6	10	4
Democrats	33	73.1	56	18	6	16	4
Incumbents	12	22.8	61	28	3	<1	8
Challengers	17	25.5	69	17	9	2	3
Open Seats	4	24.8	39	9	6	44	2
Republicans	35	84.6	65	18	6	5	4
Incumbents	17	55.7	68	21	6	1	5
Challengers	13	10.0	55	15	20	8	2
Open Seats	5	19.0	60	10	9	17	8

Note: The data include primary and general election receipts for major party general election candidates and for independents who are incumbents or non-incumbent winners.

a. In 2000, without Jon Corzine (D-NJ), the self-funding percentage for open seat Democrats would be only 2%, for all Democrats it would be 20%, and for all candidates it would be 10%.

Source: Federal Election Commission.

Table 3-9 Number of Active Political Action Committees, 1976–2006

Committee type	2006	2004	2002	2000	1998	1996	1994	1992	1990	1988	1986	1984	1982	1980	1978	1976[a]
Corporate	1,463	1,402	1,359	1,365	1,425	1,470	1,468	1,514	1,540	1,616	1,584	1,584	1,317	1,037	704	433
Labor	202	206	215	236	232	236	255	255	233	256	261	261	293	225	215	224
Trade/membership/health	734	722	697	662	664	650	633	633	609	633	598	598	407	463	122	489
Nonconnected	870	819	700	670	560	529	509	534	511	630	576	576	204	201	400	—
Cooperative	35	34	36	37	41	41	50	48	51	51	51	51	46	27	11	—
Corporation without stock	89	75	86	94	102	109	112	114	114	122	117	117	78	44	22	—
Total	3,393	3,258	3,093	3,064	3,024	3,035	3,027	3,098	3,058	3,308	3,187	3,187	2,345	1,997	1,474	1,146

Note: Active PACs in this and subsequent tables include all registered non-party political committees giving one or more contributions to a federal candidate during the cycle.

a. For 1976, number of registered PACs is listed.

Source: Federal Election Commission.

Table 3-10 PAC Contributions to Congressional Candidates, 1978–2006 (in millions of dollars)

Type of PAC	2006	2004	2002	2000	1998	1996	1994	1992	1990	1988	1986	1984	1982	1980	1978
Labor	56.9	50.3	51.9	50.2	43.4	46.5	40.7	39.7	33.6	33.9	29.9	24.8	20.3	13.2	9.9
Corporate	128.4	104.3	91.6	84.2	71.1	69.7	64.1	64.3	53.5	50.4	46.2	35.5	27.5	19.2	9.5
Trade/membership/health	98.4	78.2	71.5	68.3	59.0	56.2	50.1	51.4	42.5	38.9	32.9	26.7	21.9	15.9	11.2
Nonconnected	70.9	49.8	44.6	35.6	27.1	22.0	17.3	17.5	14.3	19.2	18.8	14.5	10.7	4.9	2.5
Other	8.7	6.5	6.5	7.1	6.2	6.8	6.6	6.6	5.9	5.4	4.9	3.8	3.2	2.0	1.0
Total	363.3	289.1	266.1	245.4	206.8	201.2	178.8	179.4	149.7	147.8	132.7	105.3	83.6	55.2	34.1

Note: The data are for contributions to all candidates for election in the year indicated that were made during the two-year cycle.

Source: Federal Election Commission.

Table 3-11 How PACs Distributed Contributions to Congressional Candidates, 1978–2006

	Percentage distribution								Percentage distribution									
	Incumbent		Challenger		Open seat		Percent to Chamber	Dollars to chamber (in millions)	Incumbent		Challenger		Open seat		Percent to Chamber	Dollars to chamber (in millions)	Total percent	Total dollars (in millions)
	D	R	D	R	D	R			D	R	D	R	D	R				
	House, 2006								Senate, 2006									
Corporate	25	49	<1	<1	1	2	78	99.9	7	11	1	1	1	2	22	29	100	128.4
Association	28	46	2	1	2	3	83	81.3	5	8	1	1	1	1	17	17	100	98.3
Labor	51	10	18	<1	8	<1	87	49.4	6	1	4	<1	2	1	13	8	100	56.9
Nonconnected	14	36	10	4	4	6	75	52.9	6	9	4	2	2	3	25	18	100	70.9
Other PACs	31	39	2	1	2	3	77	7.1	6	7	1	1	2	7	23	2	100	9.3
All PACs	28	39	6	1	3	3	80	290.7	6	8	2	1	1	2	20	73	100	363.8
	House, 2004								Senate, 2004									
Corporate	23	47	<1	1	1	3	76	79	7	10	<1	1	2	5	24	25	100	104.3
Association	26	45	1	2	2	5	81	63	6	7	<1	1	1	4	19	15	100	78.2
Labor	56	10	10	<1	8	1	85	43	7	1	2	<1	5	<1	15	8	100	50.3
Nonconnected	14	30	5	7	4	11	71	35	7	7	2	3	4	7	29	15	100	49.8
Other PACs	29	42	1	2	3	3	79	5	8	6	<1	1	2	3	21	1	100	6.5
All PACs	28	37	3	2	3	5	78	225	7	7	1	1	3	4	22	64	100	289.1
	House, 2002								Senate, 2002									
Corporate	24	41	1	1	2	6	74	68.2	7	10	<1	4	<1	3	26	23.4	100	91.6
Association	27	39	1	2	3	8	80	57.2	6	8	1	4	<1	2	20	14.3	100	71.5
Labor	53	8	10	<1	14	1	85	44.4	7	1	5	<1	2	<1	15	7.5	100	51.9
Nonconnected	18	23	6	5	8	12	72	32.2	8	7	3	6	2	2	28	12.5	100	44.6
Other PACs	29	38	<1	1	2	6	76	4.9	9	8	<1	4	<1	2	24	1.5	100	6.5
All PACs	30	31	3	2	6	7	78	206.9	7	7	2	3	1	2	22	59.2	100	266.1
	House, 2000								Senate, 2000									
Corporate	25	40	1	2	1	5	74	61.3	4	15	1	1	1	4	26	21.6	100	83
Association	29	39	2	3	2	6	81	54.1	3	10	1	1	1	3	19	13.0	100	67.1
Labor	55	7	16	<1	9	<1	87	42.6	4	1	5	<1	3	<1	13	6.1	100	48.7
Nonconnected	19	24	8	8	6	11	76	26.3	4	10	3	1	2	4	24	8.3	100	34.6
Other PACs	33	36	3	2	1	5	80	5.5	5	10	1	1	1	3	20	1.4	100	6.9
All PACs	32	31	5	3	3	5	79	189.9	4	10	2	1	2	3	21	50.5	100	240.3
	House, 1998								Senate, 1998									
Corporate	21	41	0	2	1	5	70	50.3	8	14	0	3	2	3	29	20.9	100	71.1
Association	25	40	2	3	3	6	79	46.5	6	9	0	2	2	2	21	12.5	100	59.0
Labor	54	7	12	<1	13	<1	86	37.3	8	1	2	<1	2	<1	14	6.0	100	43.4
Nonconnected	18	24	5	11	5	11	74	20.0	9	9	1	3	2	2	26	7.1	100	27.1
Other PACs	31	35	1	3	2	3	76	4.7	10	9	1	2	1	1	24	1.5	100	6.2
All PACs	29	31	4	3	5	5	77	158.7	8	9	1	2	2	2	23	48.1	100	206.8

					House, 1996								**Senate, 1996**						
Corporate	20	44	<1	2	2	5	74	51.3	2	11	<1	3	3	7	26	18.3	100	69.6
Association	21	40	3	3	4	6	79	44.0	2	8	1	2	3	6	22	12.0	100	56.0
Labor	41	5	25	<1	13	<1	85	39.4	3	1	3	<1	8	<1	15	6.9	100	46.3
Nonconnected	16	26	10	6	4	7	69	15.1	4	9	2	4	5	7	31	6.9	100	22.0
Other PACs	27	36	3	3	3	5	76	5.2	3	7	2	3	4	5	24	1.5	100	6.7
All PACs	25	30	8	3	5	5	76	155.0	3	7	2	2	5	5	24	45.6	100	200.6
					House, 1994								**Senate, 1994**						
Corporate	34	22	1	4	2	5	68	43.4	9	9	<1	3	2	9	32	20.6	100	64.1
Association	37	22	2	5	5	6	77	38.6	7	6	1	2	2	5	23	11.3	100	50.0
Labor	55	3	10	<1	14	<1	82	33.3	9	<1	4	<1	5	<1	18	7.2	100	40.4
Nonconnected	31	11	4	7	7	6	66	11.6	11	7	1	3	5	5	33	5.6	100	17.3
Other PACs	43	18	2	4	4	4	74	4.0	11	5	1	1	3	4	26	1.8	100	6.6
All PACs	40	15	4	4	6	4	74	138.8	9	5	1	2	3	5	26	46.5	100	178.4
					House, 1992								**Senate, 1992**						
Corporate	32	23	1	3	1	5	67	42.9	10	13	2	2	2	5	33	21.2	100	64.1
Association	35	22	3	3	7	6	76	38.7	8	8	2	1	2	2	24	12.4	100	51.1
Labor	48	3	11	<1	16	1	78	30.5	9	1	7	<1	5	<1	22	8.6	100	39.1
Nonconnected	25	11	5	5	9	1	60	10.3	12	10	6	2	6	3	40	6.9	100	17.2
Other PACs	43	19	1	2	4	3	72	4.2	11	9	2	<1	4	1	28	1.6	100	5.7
All PACs	36	17	4	2	8	4	71	127.0	9	8	3	1	3	3	29	51.1	100	178.1
					House, 1990								**Senate, 1990**						
Corporate	32	25	1	2	2	4	66	35.4	13	11	<1	6	<1	3	34	18.0	100	53.5
Association	40	25	2	2	5	5	77	32.5	9	8	1	3	<1	2	33	10.0	100	42.5
Labor	54	5	9	<1	13	<1	82	27.6	11	1	5	<1	1	<1	18	6.0	100	33.6
Nonconnected	26	13	4	4	8	5	60	8.5	20	10	2	5	1	2	40	5.7	100	14.3
Other PACs	46	21	1	2	2	2	74	4.3	13	8	1	2	<1	2	26	1.5	100	5.8
All PACs	39	19	3	1	6	4	72	108.5	11	9	2	3	1	2	28	41.2	100	149.7
					House, 1988								**Senate, 1988**						
Corporate	31	26	1	2	1	3	63	31.6	11	14	1	4	3	5	37	18.8	100	50.4
Association	37	26	2	1	3	4	73	28.6	9	9	1	2	2	3	27	10.4	100	38.9
Labor	50	6	15	<1	9	<1	79	26.8	9	1	6	<1	4	<1	21	7.1	100	33.9
Nonconnected	25	12	8	4	6	4	59	11.4	13	9	7	3	4	4	41	7.8	100	19.2
Other PACs	41	23	1	2	2	2	72	3.8	12	9	2	1	2	2	28	1.5	100	5.3
All PACs	36	19	6	1	4	3	69	102.2	10	9	3	2	3	3	31	45.7	100	147.8
					House, 1986								**Senate, 1986**						
Corporate	26	24	1	2	1	4	58	26.4	5	20	3	3	2	9	42	19.0	100	45.3
Association	33	27	2	2	3	5	71	23.0	6	12	4	1	2	4	29	9.4	100	32.4
Labor	45	5	14	<1	10	<1	75	21.9	6	2	11	<1	6	<1	25	7.1	100	29.1
Nonconnected	21	12	8	5	7	6	59	10.7	6	11	10	2	7	5	41	7.5	100	18.2
Other PACs	36	23	1	2	2	2	67	3.2	6	15	6	1	2	3	33	1.6	100	4.8
All PACs	32	19	5	2	5	4	66	85.2	5	13	6	1	4	5	34	44.6	100	129.8

(continued)

Table 3-11 (continued)

	Percentage distribution						Percent to Chamber	Dollars to chamber (in millions)	Percentage distribution						Percent to Chamber	Dollars to chamber (in millions)	Total percent	Total dollars (in millions)
	Incumbent		Challenger		Open seat				Incumbent		Challenger		Open seat					
	D	R	D	R	D	R			D	R	D	R	D	R				
				House, 1984								Senate, 1984						
Corporate	29	26	<1	7	<1	4	67	22.9	7	19	1	2	1	4	33	11.4	100	34.3
Association	36	28	2	5	2	4	77	19.8	6	11	2	1	1	1	23	6.0	100	25.8
Labor	57	4	14	<1	5	<1	80	18.7	6	1	9	<1	4	<1	20	4.6	100	23.3
Nonconnected	26	9	5	15	3	6	63	8.6	7	10	10	4	3	2	37	5.1	100	13.7
Other PACs	48	23	2	2	1	2	78	2.9	7	10	2	1	2	1	22	0.8	100	3.7
All PACs	38	18	4	6	2	3	72	72.9	6	11	4	2	2	2	28	27.9	100	100.8
				House, 1982								Senate, 1982						
Corporate	22	31	1	6	2	6	69	18.1	8	13	<1	5	<1	4	31	8.3	100	26.4
Association	26	32	3	6	3	6	77	15.9	9	9	1	2	<1	2	23	4.9	100	20.8
Labor	40	3	21	<1	11	1	75	14.6	14	2	7	<1	2	<1	25	4.8	100	19.4
Nonconnected	20	13	11	12	5	7	69	6.9	9	6	5	7	2	2	31	3.2	100	10.0
Other PACs	40	25	3	1	4	3	78	2.4	11	5	2	<1	<1	3	22	0.7	100	3.1
All PACs	28	22	8	5	5	5	73	57.9	9	6	5	7	2	2	27	21.8	100	79.7
				House, 1980								Senate, 1980						
Corporate	23	21	1	13	1	6	64	11.7	9	5	<1	17	1	4	36	6.4	100	18.1
Association	29	24	1	13	2	6	75	11.2	9	4	1	8	1	2	25	3.8	100	15.0
Labor	50	3	12	<1	7	<1	72	8.9	18	3	4	<1	3	<1	28	3.4	100	12.3
Nonconnected	13	9	3	26	2	8	62	2.8	8	2	<1	20	<1	5	37	1.7	100	4.5
Other PACs	40	19	2	2	3	4	72	1.4	16	4	1	5	2	2	28	0.5	100	1.9
All PACs	31	17	3	10	3	5	69	36.0	11	4	1	10	2	2	31	15.9	100	51.9
				House, 1978								Senate, 1978						
Corporate	22	18	1	10	4	8	63	6.2	6	14	2	7	3	6	37	3.6	100	9.8
Association	27	20	2	11	7	9	76	8.6	5	8	2	4	2	3	24	2.8	100	11.3
Labor	43	2	12	<1	14	<1	72	7.5	10	2	9	<1	5	<1	28	2.8	100	10.3
Nonconnected	9	10	3	29	4	18	74	2.1	3	5	3	10	1	5	26	0.7	100	2.8
Other PACs	49	12	2	1	8	5	77	0.8	5	5	3	2	4	3	23	0.2	100	1.0
All PACs	30	14	5	9	8	7	71	25.0	6	8	4	4	3	3	29	10.2	100	35.2

Notes: The data are for general election candidates only. D indicates Democrat; R indicates Republican.
Percentages may not add up to 100 because of rounding.
Source: Federal Election Commission.

Table 3-12 Political Party Contributions, Coordinated and Independent Expenditures for Congressional Candidates, 1976–2006 (in dollars)

	Senate			House			
		Expenditures			Expenditures		
	Contributions	Coordinated	Independent	Contributions	Coordinated	Independent	Total
2006							
Democrats	596,800	5,796,005	42,627,472	2,429,919	2,409,914	64,141,253	118,001,363
Republicans	386,782	8,784,685	32,156,053	785,435	4,519,856	83,085,694	129,718,505
2004							
Democrats	1,082,388	10,154,423	21,710,954	806,115	2,880,867	32,036,890	68,671,637
Republicans	1,875,740	9,277,459	11,500,079	1,156,771	3,220,419	43,440,699	70,471,167
2002							
Democrats	493,852	2,085,319	413	891,626	2,730,563	250,262	6,452,035
Republicans	2,027,001	10,378,872	501,208	2,131,531	5,388,717	1,362,431	21,789,760
2000							
Democrats	356,618	5,149,704	257,920	977,690	3,325,207	2,031,421	12,098,560
Republicans	519,110	10,823,862	395,190	1,747,012	4,394,759	1,161,612	19,041,545
1998							
Democrats	302,478	9,349,948	1,460,149	1,542,312	4,596,380	29,558	17,280,825
Republicans	514,657	9,334,065	219,074	2,098,276	6,310,120	46,286	18,522,478
1996							
Democrats	637,734	8,611,897	1,452,507	1,387,952	6,786,959	31,914	18,908,963
Republicans	772,244	10,751,093	9,438,331	2,462,999	7,998,844	35,812	31,459,323
1994							
Democrats	638,618	13,204,309	—	1,501,220	8,455,070	—	23,799,217
Republicans	748,011	11,561,866	—	2,036,712	8,851,871	—	23,198,460
1992							
Democrats	689,953	11,915,878	—	1,234,553	5,883,678	—	19,724,062
Republicans	807,397	16,509,940	—	2,197,611	6,906,729	—	26,421,677
1990							
Democrats	515,332	5,210,002	—	943,135	3,401,579	—	10,070,048
Republicans	862,621	7,725,853	—	2,019,279	3,012,313	—	13,620,066
1988							
Democrats	501,777	6,592,264	—	1,258,952	2,891,152	—	11,244,145
Republicans	719,006	10,260,600	—	2,657,069	4,162,207	—	17,798,882
1986							
Democrats	620,832	6,656,286	—	968,913	1,836,213	—	10,082,244
Republicans	729,522	10,077,902	—	2,520,278	4,111,474	—	17,439,176
1984							
Democrats	441,467	3,947,731	—	1,280,672	1,774,452	—	7,444,322
Republicans	590,922	6,518,415	—	4,060,120	6,190,309	—	17,359,766
1982							
Democrats	579,337	2,265,197	—	1,052,286	694,321	—	4,591,141
Republicans	600,221	8,715,761	—	4,720,959	5,293,260	—	19,330,201
1980							
Democrats	480,464	1,132,912	—	1,025,989	256,346	—	2,895,711
Republicans	677,004	5,434,758	—	3,498,323	2,203,748	—	11,813,833

(continued)

Table 3-12 (continued)

	Senate			House			
		Expenditures			Expenditures		
	Contributions	Coordinated	Independent	Contributions	Coordinated	Independent	Total
1978							
Democrats	466,683	229,218	—	1,262,298	72,892	—	2,031,091
Republicans	703,204	2,723,880	—	3,621,104	1,297,079	—	8,345,267
1976							
Democrats	468,795	4,359	—	1,465,629	500	—	1,939,283
Republicans	930,034	113,976	—	3,658,310	329,583	—	5,031,903

Note: The table includes three different kinds of party support for candidates: direct contributions, coordinated expenditures and independent spending.

Direct contributions: A House candidate may receive a maximum of $40,000 in a primary and general election combined from national and state party committees. A Senate candidate may receive $39,900 from national party committees and another $10,000 from state parties. Since 2004, these limits have been adjusted for inflation.

Coordinated expenditures: For most House candidates, party committees may spend an inflation adjusted amount that in 2007 came to $81,800. The limit is doubled (to $163,600 in 2007) for states with only one congressional district. For Senate candidates, the limit goes up with a state's population as well as inflation. In the smallest states, this was $163,600 in 2007. In the largest states (California) it was more than $4.4 million. The median states (Kentucky and Louisiana) had party-coordinated spending limits of $523,800 in 2007.

Independent spending by the parties cannot be limited since the Supreme Court's decision in *Colorado Republican Federal Campaign Committee* v. *Federal Election Commission* 518 U.S. 604 (1996). Despite this ruling, the parties did not do a great deal of independent spending between 1996 and 2002 because such spending has to be funded entirely with money raised under federal contribution limits. The parties preferred to use "soft" money (no contribution limits) to help pay for communications that were designed to get around these restraints. After the Bipartisan Campaign Reform Act of 2002 prohibited national party soft money, the parties shifted more money into independent expenditures. Unfortunately, it is not possible to know how much soft money was spent to help congressional candidates in the elections through 2002. In 2004, party independent spending in House contests focused on about thirty districts, with a maximum of $6.1 million spent in one. Senate independent spending focused on twelve races, with $8 million spent in Florida.

Source: Federal Election Commission.

Table 3-13 Hard and Soft Money Raised by National Party Committees, 1992–2006 (in millions of dollars)

	2006	2004	2002			2000			1998			1996			1994			1992		
	Hard	Hard	Hard	Soft	Total	Hard	Soft	Total	Hard	Soft	Total	Hard	Soft	Total	Hard	Soft	Total	Hard	Soft	Total
Democratic																				
National Committee	130.8	394.4	67.5	97.0	164.5	124.0	135.3	259.3	64.8	57.4	122.2	108.4	100.5	208.9	41.8	45.1	86.9	65.8	28.4	94.2
Senatorial	121.4	88.7	48.4	96.9	145.3	40.5	63.3	103.8	35.7	25.9	61.5	30.8	14.1	44.9	26.4	0.4	26.9	25.5	0.5	26.0
Congressional	139.9	93.2	46.4	56.8	103.2	48.4	58.0	106.4	25.2	16.6	41.8	26.6	11.8	38.4	19.4	5.1	24.6	12.8	4.0	16.8
Total	392.1	576.2	162.3	250.7	413.0	212.9	256.6	469.5	125.6	99.9	225.5	165.8	126.4	292.2	87.7	50.7	138.4	104.1	32.9	137.0
Republican																				
National Committee	243.0	392.4	170.1	118.7	288.8	212.8	163.5	376.3	104.1	74.3	178.4	193.0	114.4	307.4	87.4	42.4	129.8	85.5	33.6	119.1
Senatorial	88.8	79.0	59.2	66.9	126.1	51.5	44.6	96.1	53.4	37.3	90.7	64.5	29.4	93.9	65.3	6.5	71.9	73.8	7.7	81.5
Congressional	179.5	185.7	123.6	73.3	196.9	97.3	52.9	150.2	72.7	24.1	96.8	74.2	28.8	103.0	26.7	4.8	31.5	35.3	6.2	41.5
Total	511.3	657.1	352.9	258.9	611.8	361.6	261.1	622.7	230.2	135.7	365.9	331.8	172.5	504.3	179.4	53.7	233.1	194.5	47.5	242.0

Notes: The data are as reported to the Federal Election Commission for each full two-year cycle. The national party committees were prohibited from raising soft money by the Bipartisan Campaign Reform Act of 2002.

Source: Federal Election Commission.

Table 3-14 Non-Party Independent Expenditures in House and Senate Elections, 1978–2006 (in dollars)

	For Democrats	Against Democrats	For Republicans	Against Republicans	Total
2006					
House	6,441,484	771,557	6,382,708	12,084,897	25,680,646
Senate	2,924,466	305,268	5,700,633	1,474,496	10,404,863
2004					
House	1,346,007	66,693	3,898,440	545,190	5,856,330
Senate	415,371	311,123	7,740,022	364,568	8,831,084
2002					
House	2,664,722	261,922	2,522,441	538,808	5,987,893
Senate	5,275,291	181,233	3,547,488	1,173,796	10,177,808
2000					
House	4,112,071	234,237	2,893,836	1,665,755	8,905,899
Senate	1,481,901	607,809	4,378,023	2,729,069	9,196,802
1998					
House	1,787,439	258,276	3,778,331	601,976	6,426,022
Senate	869,191	146,564	1,440,075	1,011,575	3,467,405
1996					
House	679,312	127,706	2,624,887	1,401,101	4,833,006
Senate	291,109	832,161	2,872,325	833,208	4,828,803
1994					
House	502,621	488,479	1,088,356	50,815	2,130,271
Senate	204,212	433,947	1,309,572	537,531	2,485,262
1992					
House	1,485,768	430,902	1,586,017	452,942	3,955,629
Senate	1,137,321	164,358	864,493	210,490	2,376,662
1990					
House	709,292	130,695	669,726	74,444	1,584,157
Senate	780,832	266,230	1,436,553	584,429	3,068,044
1988					
House	1,465,554	278,723	919,929	148,705	2,812,911
Senate	831,064	617,066	2,809,517	143,441	4,401,088
1986					
House	2,385,685	227,286	1,313,578	120,032	4,046,581
Senate	988,382	632,412	3,342,790	348,006	5,311,590
1984					
House	560,727	118,171	633,646	26,847	1,339,391
Senate	326,031	410,428	1,807,981	2,082,207	4,626,647
1982					
House	241,442	862,654	492,404	66,296	1,662,796
Senate	127,451	3,182,986	298,410	483,750	4,092,597
1980					
House	190,615	38,023	410,478	45,132	684,248
Senate	127,381	1,282,613	261,678	12,430	1,684,102
1978					
House	28,725	31,034	70,701	5,298	135,758
Senate	102,508	36,717	26,065	1,985	167,275

Note: An independent expenditure is defined as an "expenditure by a person for a communication expressly advocating the election or defeat of a clearly identified candidate that is not made with the cooperation or with the prior consent of, or in consultation with, or at the request or suggestion of, a candidate or any agent or authorized committee of such candidate" (11 C.F.R. 109.1 [a]).

Source: Federal Election Commission.

Figure 3-1 Mean Expenditures of House Challengers Who Beat Incumbents, 1984–2006

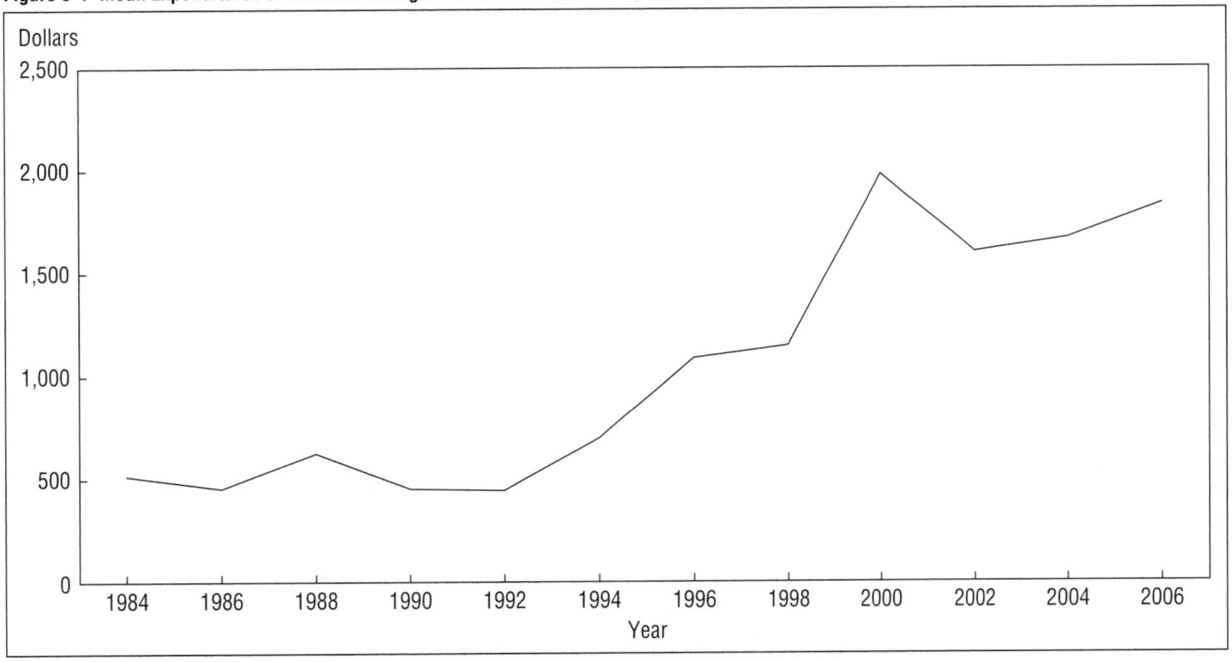

Source: Table 3-3.

Figure 3-2 Percentage of Incumbents' Campaign Funds That Came from PACs, House and Senate, 1984–2006

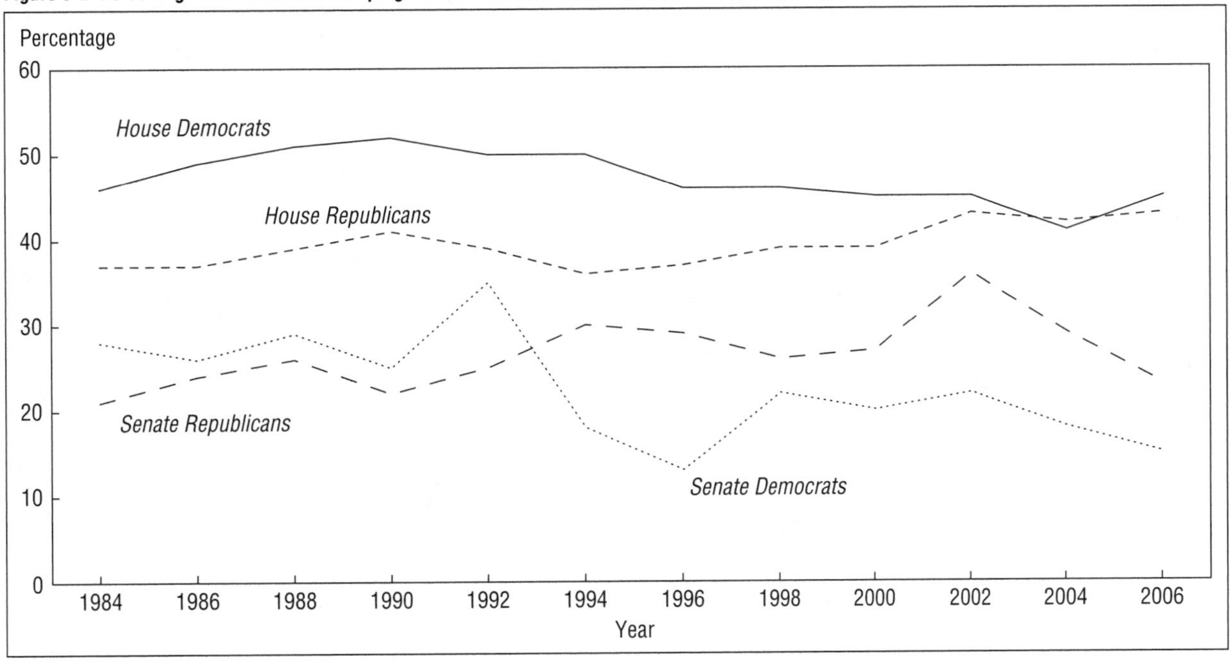

Source: Table 3-8.

Figure 3-3 Percentage of PAC Support for Nonincumbents, 1978–2006

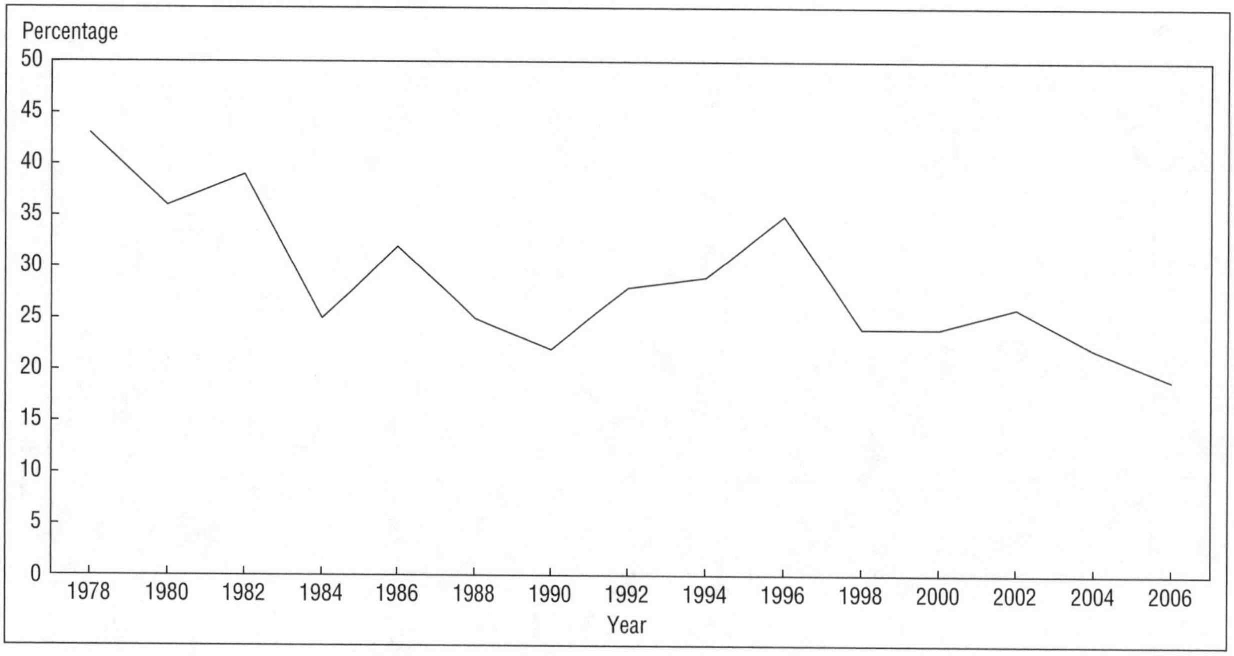

Source: Table 3-11.

Figure 3-4 Political Party Contributions and Coordinated Expenditures for Congress, 1976–2006 (in thousands of dollars)

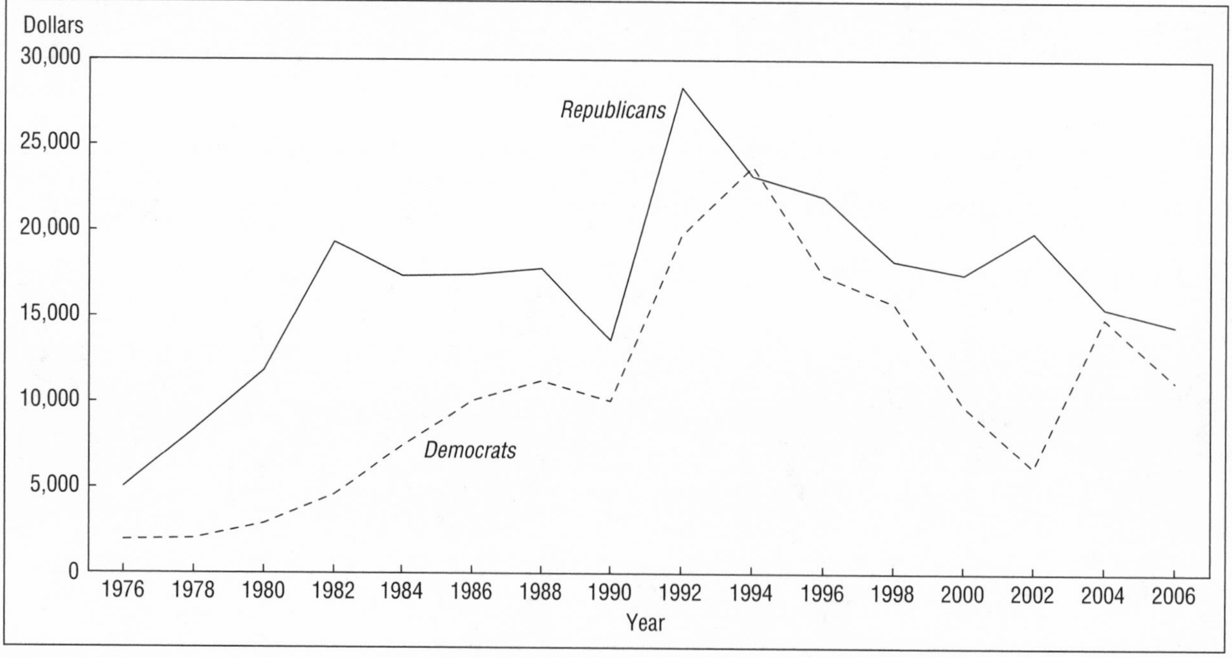

Source: Table 3-12.

Figure 3-5 Independent Expenditures in Senate and House Elections by the Political Parties, 1996–2006 (in thousands of dollars)

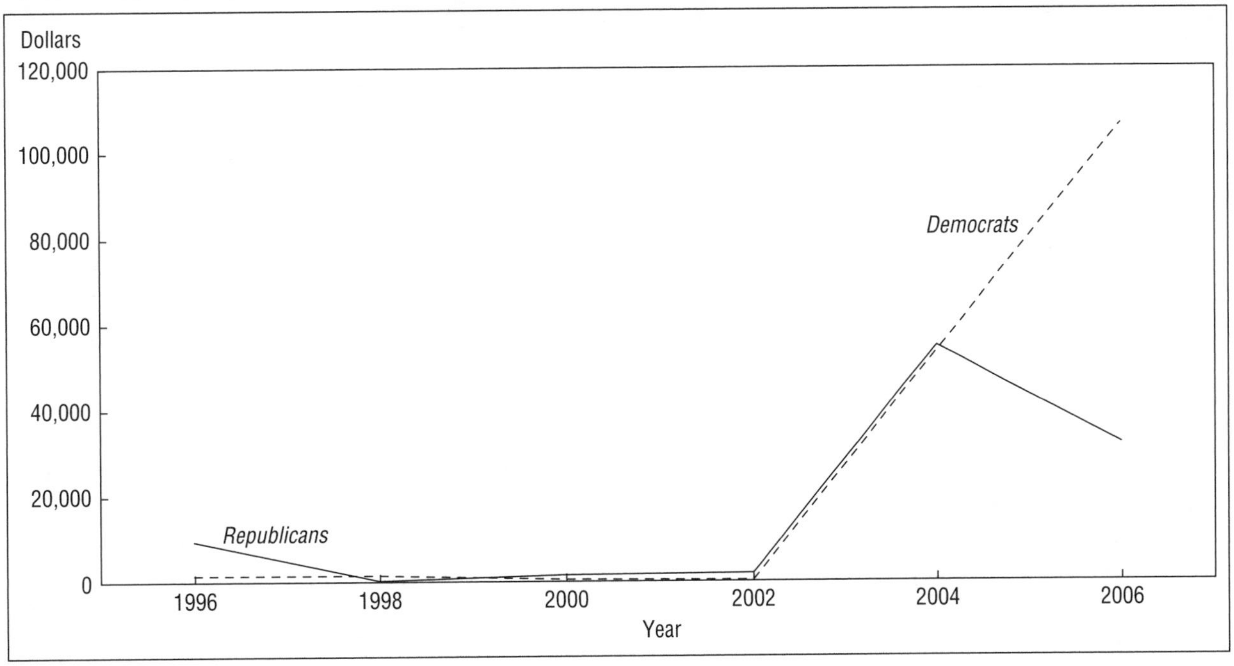

Source: Table 3-12.

4

Committees

Table 4-1 Number of Committees in the Senate and House, 84th–110th Congresses, 1955–2008

Congress	Senate	House	Total[a]
84th (1955–1956)	133	130	242
90th (1967–1968)	155	185	315
92nd (1971–1972)	181	175	333
94th (1975–1976)	205	204	385
96th (1979–1980)	130	193	314
97th (1981–1982)	136	174	300
98th (1983–1984)	137	172	299
99th (1985–1986)	120	191	301
100th (1987–1988)	118	192	298
101st (1989–1990)	118	189	295
102nd (1991–1992)	119	185	284
103rd (1993–1994)	111	146	252
104th (1995–1996)	92	110	198
105th (1997–1998)	92	112	200
106th (1999–2000)	94	111	201
107th (2001–2002)	91	116	203
108th (2003–2004)	92	122	210
109th (2005–2006)	92	120	212
110th (2007–2008)	96	126	218

Note: "Committees" include standing committees, subcommittees of standing committees, select and special committees, subcommittees of select and special committees, joint committees, and subcommittees of joint committees.

a. The total is less than for the Senate and House combined because joint panels count only once.

Sources: *The Almanac of American Politics* (Washington, D.C.: National Journal Group, various editions); U.S. House of Representatives, http://www.house.gov; U.S. Senate, http://www.senate.gov.

Table 4-2 Number and Type of House Committees, 84th–110th Congresses, 1955–2008

Congress	Standing committees	Subcommittees of standing committees	Select and special committees	Subcommittees of select and special committees	Joint committees	Subcommittees of joint committees
84th (1955–1956)	19	83	2	5	10	11
90th (1967–1968)	20	133	1	6	10	15
92nd (1971–1972)	21	120	3	8	8	15
94th (1975–1976)	22	151	3	4	7	17
96th (1979–1980)	22	149[a]	5	8	4	5
97th (1981–1982)	22	132	3	7	4	6
98th (1983–1984)	22	130	3	7	4	6
99th (1985–1986)	22	142	5	12	4	6
100th (1987–1988)	22	140[b]	6	12	4	8
101st (1989–1990)	22	138[b]	5	12	4	8
102nd (1991–1992)	22	135[b]	5	11	4	8
103rd (1993–1994)	22	115	1	3	5	0
104th (1995–1996)	19	84	1	2	4	0
105th (1997–1998)	19	86	1	2	4	0
106th (1999–2000)	19	85	1	2	4	0
107th (2001–2002)	19	89	1	3	4	0
108th (2003–2004)	19	88	2	9	4	0
109th (2005–2006)	20	92	1	4	4	0
110th (2007–2008)	20	97	1	4	4	0

a. This number includes nine budget task forces and the Welfare and Pension Plans Task Force (of the Subcommittee on Labor Management Relations of the Education and Labor Committee).

b. This number includes panels and task forces only if the committee has no subcommittees.

Sources: Garrison Nelson, *Committees in the U.S. Congress 1947–1992, Committee Jurisdictions and Member Rosters* (Washington, D.C.: Congressional Quarterly, 1993); Congressional Quarterly Committee Guide, *Congressional Quarterly Weekly Report,* various issues; U.S. House of Representatives, http://www.house.gov.

Table 4-3 Number and Type of Senate Committees, 84th–110th Congresses, 1955–2008

Congress	Standing committees	Subcommittees of standing committees	Select and special committees	Subcommittees of select and special committees	Joint committees	Subcommittees of joint committees
84th (1955–1956)	15	88	3	6	10	11
90th (1967–1968)	16	99	3	12	10	15
92nd (1971–1972)	17	123	5	13	8	15
94th (1975–1976)	18	140	6	17	7	17
96th (1979–1980)	15	91	5	10	4	5
97th (1981–1982)	15	94	5	12	4	6
98th (1983–1984)	16	103	4	4	4	6
99th (1985–1986)	16	90	4	0	4	6
100th (1987–1988)	16	85	5	0	4	8
101st (1989–1990)	16	86	4	0	4	8
102nd (1991–1992)	16	87	4	0	4	8
103rd (1993–1994)	17	86	3	0	5	0
104th (1995–1996)	17	68	3	0	4	0
105th (1997–1998)	17	68	3	0	4	0
106th (1999–2000)	17	68	4	0	4	0
107th (2001–2002)	16	68	4	0	3	0
108th (2003–2004)	17	68	3	0	4	0
109th (2005–2006)	17	72	3	0	4	0
110th (2007–2008)	17	72	3	0	4	0

Sources: Garrison Nelson, *Committees in the U.S. Congress 1947–1992, Committee Jurisdictions and Member Rosters* (Washington, D.C.: Congressional Quarterly, 1993); Congressional Quarterly Committee Guide, *Congressional Quarterly Weekly Report,* various issues; U.S. Senate, http://www.senate.gov.

Table 4-4 Committee Assignments for Representatives, 84th–110th Congresses, 1955–2008

Congress	Mean no. of standing committee assignments	Mean no. of subcommittees of standing committee assignments	Mean no. of other committee assignments[a]	Total
84th (1955–1956)	1.2	1.6	0.2	3.0
92nd (1971–1972)	1.5	3.2	0.4	5.1
94th (1975–1976)	1.8	4.0	0.4	6.2
96th (1979–1980)	1.7	3.6	0.5	5.8
97th (1981–1982)	1.7	3.4	0.4	5.5
98th (1983–1984)	1.7	3.6	0.5	5.8
99th (1985–1986)	1.8	4.0	0.8	6.6
100th (1987–1988)	1.7	3.8	1.0[b]	6.5
101st (1989–1990)	1.8	3.9	1.1[b]	6.8
102nd (1991–1992)	1.9	4.0	0.9[b]	6.8
103rd (1993–1994)	2.0	3.7	0.2	5.9
104th (1995–1996)	1.8	2.9	0.1	4.8
105th (1997–1998)	1.8	3.2	0.1	5.1
106th (1999–2000)	1.9	3.2	0.1	5.2
107th (2001–2002)	1.9	3.6	0.1	5.6
108th (2003–2004)	1.9	3.5	0.2	5.6
109th (2005–2006)	2	2.9	0.2	5.1
110th (2007–2008)	1.9	2.8	0.2	4.9

a. Other committees include select and special committees, subcommittees of select and special committees, joint committees, and subcommittees of joint committees.

b. This number includes task forces when the committee has no other subcommittees.

Sources: Garrison Nelson, *Committees in the U.S. Congress 1947–1992, Committee Jurisdictions and Member Rosters* (Washington, D.C.: Congressional Quarterly, 1993); Congressional Quarterly Committee Guide, *Congressional Quarterly Weekly Report,* various issues; U.S. House of Representatives, http://www.house.gov.

Table 4-5 Committee Assignments for Senators, 84th–110th Congresses, 1955–2008

Congress	Mean no. of standing committee assignments	Mean no. of subcommittees of standing committee assignments	Mean no. of other committee assignments[a]	Total
84th (1955–1956)	2.2	4.8	0.9	7.9
92nd (1971–1972)	2.5	9.5	3.3	15.3
94th (1975–1976)	2.5	11.0	4.1	17.6
96th (1979–1980)	2.3	6.6	1.5	10.4
97th (1981–1982)	2.5	6.7	1.5	10.7
98th (1983–1984)	2.9	7.5	1.2	11.6
99th (1985–1986)	2.8	6.9	0.9	10.6
100th (1987–1988)	2.9	7.0	1.2	11.1
101st (1989–1990)	3.0	7.0	1.1	11.1
102nd (1991–1992)	2.9	7.4	1.1	11.4
103rd (1993–1994)	3.2	7.8	0.8	11.8
104th (1995–1996)	3.1	6.2	0.7	10.0
105th (1997–1998)	3.1	6.5	0.7	10.3
106th (1999–2000)	3.2	6.8	0.7	10.7
107th (2001–2002)[b]	3.2	8.5	0.7	12.4
108th (2003–2004)	3.5	8	0.7	12.2
109th (2005–2006)	3.3	9.3	0.7	13.3
110th (2007–2008)	3.4	7.7	0.6	11.7

a. Other committees include select and special committees, subcommittees of select and special committees, joint committees, and subcommittees of joint committees.

b. These numbers are correct as of the start of the 107th Congress and do not reflect changes in committee assignments that occurred after Jim Jeffords (VT) left the Republican Party to become an Independent, shifting control of the Senate to the Democrats.

Sources: Garrison Nelson, *Committees in the U.S. Congress 1947–1992, Committee Jurisdictions and Member Rosters* (Washington, D.C.: Congressional Quarterly, 1993); Congressional Quarterly Committee Guide, *Congressional Quarterly Weekly Report,* various issues; U.S. Senate, http://www.senate.gov.

Table 4-6 Majority Party Chairmanships of House Committees and Subcommittees, 84th–110th Congresses, 1955–2008

Congress	Party in majority	No. of majority party members in the House	No. chairing standing committees and subcommittees	No. with two or more chairmanships	% chairing standing committees and subcommittees	No. chairing all committees and subcommittees[a]	No. with two or more chairmanships	% chairing all committees and subcommittees[a]
84th (1955–1956)	D	232	63	18	27.2	75	22	32.3
90th (1967–1968)	D	247	111	32	44.9	117	38	47.4
92nd (1971–1972)	D	254	120	25	47.2	131	31	51.6
94th (1975–1976)	D	289	142	24	49.1	150	28	51.9
96th (1979–1980)	D	276	144	19	52.2	149	28	54.0
97th (1981–1982)	D	243	121	16	49.8	125	26	51.4
98th (1983–1984)	D	267	124	23	46.4	127	33	47.6
99th (1985–1986)	D	253	129	27	51.0	131	37	51.8
100th (1987–1988)	D	258	128	28	49.6	132[b]	42	51.2
101st (1989–1990)	D	260	134	26	51.5	137	38	52.7
102nd (1991–1992)	D	267	130	25	48.7	135[b]	37	50.6
103rd (1993–1994)	D	258	113	19	43.8	116	22	45.0
104th (1995–1996)	R	230	102	1	44.3	103	4	44.8
105th (1997–1998)	R	227	101	4	44.5	102	9	44.9
106th (1999–2000)	R	223	100	2	44.8	101	6	45.3
107th (2001–2002)	R	221	108	1	48.4	111	2	49.3
108th (2003–2004)	R	229	104	2	45.4	112	6	48.9
109th (2005–2006)	R	231	109	3	47.2	114	6	49.4
110th (2007–2008)	D	233	112	4	48.1	117	7	50.2

a. This number includes standing committees, subcommittees of standing committees, select and special committees, subcommittees of select and special committees, joint committees, and subcommittees of joint committees.

b. This number includes task forces when the committee has no other subcommittees.

Sources: Garrison Nelson, *Committees in the U.S. Congress 1947–1992, Committee Jurisdictions and Member Rosters* (Washington, D.C.: Congressional Quarterly, 1993); Congressional Quarterly Committee Guide, *Congressional Quarterly Weekly Report,* various issues; U.S. House of Representatives, http://www.house.gov.

Table 4-7 Majority Party Chairmanships of Senate Committees and Subcommittees, 84th–110th Congresses, 1955–2008

Congress	Party in majority	No. of majority party members in Senate	No. chairing standing committees and subcommittees	% chairing standing committees and subcommittees	Average no. of standing committees and subcommittees chaired by majority members	No. chairing all committees and subcommittees[a]	% chairing all committees and subcommittees[a]	Average no. of all committees and subcommittees chaired by majority members
84th (1955–1956)	D	48	42	87.5	1.8	42	87.5	2.0
90th (1967–1968)	D	64	55	85.9	1.8	58	90.6	2.1
92nd (1971–1972)	D	55[b]	51	92.7	2.6	52	94.5	2.9
94th (1975–1976)	D	62[b]	57	91.9	2.4	57	91.9	2.9
96th (1979–1980)	D	59[b]	58	98.3	1.8	58	98.3	2.1
97th (1981–1982)	R	53	51	96.2	1.9	52	98.1	2.3
98th (1983–1984)	R	54	52	96.3	1.9	52	96.3	2.5
99th (1985–1986)	R	53	49	92.5	1.9	49	92.5	2.0
100th (1987–1988)	D	54	47	87.0	1.8	47	87.0	2.0
101st (1989–1990)	D	55	46	83.6	1.9	46	83.6	1.9
102nd (1991–1992)	D	56	50	89.3	1.8	50	89.3	2.0
103rd (1993–1994)	D	57	46	80.7	1.8	46	80.7	1.9
104th (1995–1996)	R	54	44	81.5	1.8	44	81.5	1.9
105th (1997–1998)	R	55	48	87.3	1.7	48	87.3	1.9
106th (1999–2000)	R	55	53	96.4	1.6	53	96.4	1.7
107th (2001–2002)[c]	R	50	49	98.0	1.7	49	98.0	1.8
108th (2003–2004)	R	51	51	100.0	1.7	51	100.0	1.8
109th (2005–2006)	R	55	52	94.5	1.6	53	96.4	1.7
110th (2007–2008)	D	51[d]	40	78.4	1.6	40	78.4	1.7

a. This number includes standing committees, subcommittees of standing committees, select and special committees, subcommittees of select and special committees, joint committees, and subcommittees of joint committees.
b. This number includes Harry Byrd, Jr., who was elected as an Independent.
c. These numbers are correct as of the start of the 107th Congress and do not reflect changes in committee assignments that occurred after Jim Jeffords (VT) left the Republican Party to become an Independent, shifting control of the Senate to the Democrats.
d. This number includes Joe Lieberman and Bernard Sanders, who were elected as Independents.

Sources: Garrison Nelson, *Committees in the U.S. Congress 1947–1992, Committee Jurisdictions and Member Rosters* (Washington, D.C.: Congressional Quarterly, 1993); Congressional Quarterly Committee Guide, *Congressional Quarterly Weekly Report,* various issues; U.S. Senate, http://www.senate.gov.

Table 4-8 Southern Chairmanships of House and Senate Standing Committees, 84th–110th Congresses, 1955–2008

	House					Senate				
Year	Party control	Number of southern chairmen	% of chairmanships held by southerners	% of exclusive committees chaired by southerners[a]	% of majority party from the South	Party control	Number of southern chairmen	% of chairmanships held by southerners	% of exclusive committees chaired by southerners[a]	% of majority party from the South
84th (1955–1956)	D	12	63	67	43	D	8	53	50	46
90th (1967–1968)	D	10	50	100	35	D	9	56	100	28
92nd (1971–1972)	D	8	38	100	31	D	9	53	100	30
94th (1975–1976)	D	9	41	33	28	D	6	33	100	27
96th (1979–1980)	D	5	23	33	28	D	4	27	50	28
97th (1981–1982)	D	6	27	33	29	R	3	20	25	19
98th (1983–1984)	D	7	32	67	30	R	3	19	25	20
99th (1985–1986)	D	8	36	67	29	R	2	13	0	19
100th (1987–1988)	D	7	31	67	29	D	7	44	75	30
101st (1989–1990)	D	8	36	67	29	D	6	38	50	27
102nd (1991–1992)	D	8	36	33	29	D	6	38	50	27
103rd (1993–1994)	D	6	27	33	33	D	6	35	25	26
104th (1995–1996)	R	4	21	67	25	R	2	12	50	25
105th (1997–1998)	R	3	17	67	31	R	4	24	50	29
106th (1999–2000)	R	6	32	67	32	R	4	24	50	25
107th (2001–2002)	R	3	16	33	32	R[b]	4	25	50	26
108th (2003–2004)	R	4	21	33	33	R	4	24	25	26
109th (2005–2006)	R	4	21	0	33	R	4	24	50	26
110th (2007–2008)	D	3	15	0	26	D	0	0	0	8

a. In the House these include Ways and Means, Rules, and Appropriations; in the Senate these include Appropriations, Finance, Foreign Relations, and Armed Services.

b. These numbers are correct as of the start of the 107th Congress and do not reflect changes in committee assignments that occurred after Jim Jeffords (VT) left the Republican Party to become an Independent, shifting control of the Senate to the Democrats.

Sources: Garrison Nelson, *Committees in the U.S. Congress 1947–1992, Committee Jurisdictions and Member Rosters* (Washington, D.C.: Congressional Quarterly, 1993); Congressional Quarterly Committee Guide, *Congressional Quarterly Weekly Report,* various issues; U.S. House of Representatives, http://www.house.gov; U.S. Senate, http://www.senate.gov.

5

Congressional Staff and Operating Expenses

Table 5-1 Congressional Staff, 1979–2005

	1979	1981	1985	1987	1989	1991	1993	1995	1997	1999	2001	2002	2003	2004	2005
House															
Committee staff[a]	2,027	1,917	2,146	2,136	2,267	2,321	2,147[b]	1,266	1,276	1,267	1,201	1,255	1,231	1,280	1,272
Personal staff	7,067	7,487	7,528	7,584	7,569	7,278	7,400	7,186	7,282	7,216	7,209	7,263	7,048	6,742	6,804
Leadership staff[c]	162	127	144	138	133	149	132	134	126	179	166	158	160	161	176
Officers of the House, staff[d]	1,487	1,686	1,818	1,845	1,215	1,293	1,194	1,327	1,146	974	892	1,023	1,099	453	490
Subtotal, House	10,743	11,217	11,636	11,703	11,184	11,041	10,873	9,913	9,830	9,636	9,468	9,699	9,538	8,636	8,742
Senate															
Committee staff[a]	1,410	1,150	1,178	1,207	1,116	1,154	994	796	1,216	910	889	961	924	903	957
Personal staff	3,593	3,945	4,097	4,075	3,837	4,294	4,138	4,247	4,410	4,272	3,994	4,024	3,998	3,687	3,934
Leadership staff[c]	91	106	118	103	105	125	132	126	148	219	221	201	227	245	189
Officers of the Senate, staff[d]	828	878	976	904	926	1,092	1,165	994	958	990	950	940	940	995	1,114
Subtotal, Senate	5,922	6,079	6,369	6,289	5,984	6,665	6,429	6,163	6,732	6,391	6,054	6,126	6,089	5,830	6,194
Joint committee staffs	138	126	131	132	138	145	145	108	120	104	94	104	103	107	98
Support agencies															
Government Accountability Office	5,303	5,182	5,042	5,016	5,063	5,054	4,958	4,342	3,500	3,275	3,155	3,275	3,269	3,252	3,215
Congressional Research Service	847	849	860	860	860	831	835	746	726	703	722	681	692	729	700
Congressional Budget Office	204	218	222	226	226	226	230	214	232	232	228	232	236	236	235
Office of Technology Assessment	145	130	143	143	143	143	143	n.a.[f]	n.a.	n.a.	n.a.	n.a.	n.a.	n.a	n.a
Subtotal, Support agencies	6,499	6,379	6,267	6,245	6,292	6,254	6,166	5,302	4,458	4,210	4,105	4,188	4,197	4,217	4,150
Miscellaneous															
Architect	2,296	1,986	2,073	2,412	2,088	2,099	2,060	2,151	1,854	2,012	2,012	2,081	2,133	2,183	1,533
Capitol Police[g]	1,167	1,163	1,227	1,250	1,259	1,265	1,159	1,076	1,076	1,251	1,215	1,570	1,771	1,592	1,730
Subtotal, Miscellaneous	3,463	3,149	3,300	3,662	3,347	3,364	3,219	3,227	2,930	3,263	3,227	3,651	3,904	3,775	3,263
Total	26,765	26,950	27,703	28,031	26,945	27,469	26,832	24,713	24,070	23,604	22,948	23,768	23,831	22,565	22,447

n.a. = not available

Note: The totals reflect the number of full-time paid employees.

a. This includes select and special committee staffs. Therefore, the figures do not agree with those in table 5-5.

b. In addition to the staffs of the Permanent Select Committee on Intelligence and the Joint Committee on the Organization of Congress, which each retained twenty-nine staff members, three other select committees were in operation in 1993: the Select Committee on Aging, the Select Committee on Children, Youth, and Families, and the Special and Select Committee on Funerals. The 104th Congress did not reauthorize those committees, but the committees stayed on for a few months to complete previous business. Although the committees did little business in 1993, they did retain small staffs during that time.

c. This includes legislative counsels' offices.

d. These include doorkeepers, parliamentarians, sergeants-at-arms, the clerk of the House, Senate majority and minority secretaries, and postmasters.

e. This does not include the Joint Committee on the Library.

f. The Office of Technology Assessment was eliminated in 1995.

g. This includes sworn officers only.

Sources: *Report of the Secretary of the Senate,* various editions; *Statement of Disbursements of the House,* various editions; Legislative Branch Appropriations, various years.

Table 5-2 Staffs of Members of the House and Senate, 1891–2005

Year	Employees in House	Employees in Senate	Year	Employees in House	Employees in Senate
1891	n.a.	39	1987	7,584	4,075
1914	n.a.	72	1988	7,564	3,977
1930	870	280	1989	7,569	3,837
1935	870	424	1990	7,496	4,162
1947	1,440	590	1991	7,278	4,294
1957	2,441	1,115	1992	7,597	4,249
1967	4,055	1,749	1993	7,400	4,138
1972	5,280	2,426	1994	7,390	4,200
1976	6,939	3,251	1995	7,186	4,247
1977	6,942	3,554	1996	7,288	4,151
1978	6,944	3,268	1997	7,282	4,410
1979	7,067	3,593	1998	7,269	4,281
1980	7,371	3,746	1999	7,216	4,272
1981	7,487	3,945	2000	7,226	4,087
1982	7,511	4,041	2001	7,209	3,994
1983	7,606	4,059	2002	7,263	4,024
1984	7,385	3,949	2003	7,048	3,998
1985	7,528	4,097	2004	6,742	3,687
1986	7,920	3,774	2005	6,804	3,934

n.a. = not available

Note: The totals reflect the number of full-time paid employees.

Sources: *Report of the Secretary of the Senate,* various editions; *Statement of Disbursements of the House,* various editions.

Table 5-3 House Staff Based in District Offices, 1970–2005

Year	Employees	Percentage of total personal staffs in district offices	Year	Employees	Percentage of total personal staffs in district offices
1970	1,035	n.a.	1988	2,954	39.6
1971	1,121	n.a.	1989	2,916	38.5
1972	1,189	22.5	1990	3,027	40.4
1973	1,347	n.a.	1991	3,022	41.5
1974	1,519	n.a.	1992	3,128	41.2
1975	1,732	n.a.	1993	3,130	42.3
1976	1,943	28.0	1994	3,335	45.1
1977	2,058	29.6	1995	3,459	48.1
1978	2,317	33.4	1996	3,144	43.1
1979	2,445	34.6	1997	3,209	44.1
1980	2,534	34.4	1998	3,214	44.2
1981	2,702	36.1	1999	3,192	44.2
1982	2,694	35.8	2000	3,216	44.5
1983	2,785	36.6	2001	3,004	41.7
1984	2,872	38.9	2002	3,302	45.5
1985	2,871	38.1	2003	3,241	45.9
1986	2,940	43.6	2004	3,392	50.3
1987	2,503	33.0	2005	3,450	50.7

n.a. = not available

Note: The totals reflect the number of full-time paid employees.

Sources: *Congressional Staff Directory; Statement of Disbursements of the House,* various editions.

Table 5-4 Senate Staff Based in State Offices, 1972–2005

Year	Employees	Percentage of total personal staffs in district offices	Year	Employees	Percentage of total personal staffs in district offices
1972	303	12.5	1992	1,368	32.2
1978	816	25.0	1993	1,335	32.3
1979	879	24.4	1994	1,345	32.0
1980	953	25.4	1995	1,278	30.1
1981	937	25.8	1996	1,290	31.1
1982	1,053	26.1	1997	1,366	31.0
1983	1,132	27.9	1998	1,381	32.3
1984	1,140	28.9	1999	1,414	33.2
1985	1,180	28.8	2000	1,405	34.4
1986	1,249	33.1	2001	1,228	30.7
1987	1,152	28.3	2002	1,456	36.2
1988	1,217	30.6	2003	1,440	36.0
1989	1,200	31.3	2004	1,468	39.8
1990	1,293	31.1	2005	1,534	39.0
1991	1,316	30.6			

Note: The totals reflect the number of full-time paid employees.

Sources: *Congressional Staff Directory; Report of the Secretary of the Senate,* various editions.

Table 5-5 Staffs of House and Senate Standing Committees, 1891–2005

Year	Employees in House	Employees in Senate	Year	Employees in House	Employees in Senate
1891	62	41	1984	1,944	1,095
1914	105	198	1985	2,009	1,080
1930	112	163	1986	1,954	1,075
1935	122	172	1987	2,024	1,074
1947	167	232	1988	1,976	970
1950	246	300	1989	1,986	1,013
1955	329	386	1990	1,993	1,090
1960	440	470	1991	2,201	1,030
1965	571	509	1992	2,178	1,008
1970	702	635	1993	2,118	897
1971	729	711	1994	2,046	958
1972	817	844	1995	1,246	732
1973	878	873	1996	1,177	793
1974	1,107	948	1997	1,250	1,002
1975	1,460	1,277	1998	1,305	747
1976	1,680	1,201	1999	1,238	805
1977	1,776	1,028	2000	1,176	762
1978	1,844	1,151	2001	1,177	805
1979	1,909	1,269	2002	1,222	869
1980	1,917	1,191	2003	1,193	857
1981	1,843	1,022	2004	1,249	838
1982	1,839	1,047	2005	1,272	887
1983	1,970	1,075			

Notes: The totals reflect the number of full-time paid employees.

Figures for 1947–1986 are for the statutory and investigative staffs of standing committees. They do not include select committee staffs, which varied between 31 and 238 in the House and between 62 and 172 in the Senate during the 1970s. For that reason, the numbers do not agree with those in table 5-1. In an attempt to provide further accuracy, we have counted certain individuals as .5 of a staff member on the basis of the length of employment and salary received. Rounding of those numbers then means that figures in this table do not necessarily equal those of the individual committees in tables 5-6 and 5-7.

Source: *Statement of Disbursements of the House,* various editions.

Table 5-6 Staffs of House Standing Committees, 1947–2005

Committee	1947	1960	1970	1975	1981	1985	1987	1989	1991	1993	1994	1995	1996	1997	1998	1999	2000	2001	2002	2003	2004	2005
Appropriations	29	59	71	98	127	182	188	196	218	227	202	126	143	156	152	158	147	148	158	156	162	164
Government Reform and Oversight (Government Operations)	9	54	60	68	84	86	80	82	90	86	82	75	100	120	161	129	116	107	111	96	111	108
Commerce (Energy and Commerce)	10	45	42	112	151	162	153	138	155	140	139	67	93	94	91	90	87	87	97	96	90	94
Education and the Workforce	10	25	77	114	121	119	127	114	117	112	114	66	75	77	94	74	75	78	80	71	72	73
Ways and Means	12	22	24	63	91	99	108	94	94	142	122	60	67	65	67	66	67	69	73	73	71	73
International Relations (Foreign Affairs)	10	14	21	54	84	97	101	98	104	96	98	62	69	73	66	68	64	68	68	73	72	75
Transportation and Infrastructure (Public Works)	6	32	40	88	86	84	83	83	97	89	87	70	74	84	75	80	70	80	75	70	72	65
Judiciary	7	27	35	69	75	81	81	80	71	75	74	47	61	85	74	70	73	73	75	69	73	73
Resources (Natural Resources)[b]	4	10	14	57	70	73	71	67	85	71	66	56	62	71	66	69	64	57	68	67	68	64
Banking and Financial Services (Banking)	4	14	50	85	87	90	78	108	112	100	98	46	56	64	52	59	54	57	66	63	64	62
Science (Science, Space and Technology)	—[a]	17	26	47	74	78	70	79	84	87	86	48	56	63	57	59	58	62	65	59	61	60
National Security (Armed Services)	10	15	37	38	49	64	69	66	82	76	78	44	70	60	58	57	55	53	46	54	54	58
Budget	—[a]	—[a]	—[a]	67	93	109	124	96	101	98	98	61	67	61	67	68	60	50	57	47	45	43
Agriculture	9	10	17	48	62	67	228	69	69	70	66	48	50	62	53	48	44	47	49	46	46	42
House Oversight (House Administration)[c]	7	4	25	217	252	275	43	275	317	317	316	270	33	36	41	35	34	40	40	43	42	41
Rules	4	2	7	18	43	45	62	41	49	48	47	37	36	41	36	35	35	37	33	35	33	34
Veterans' Affairs	7	18	18	26	34	32	11	41	44	46	45	28	28	27	25	30	30	26	30	32	28	28
Small Business	—[a]	—[a]	—[a]	27	54	53	44	54	53	45	40	24	28	40	32	30	30	27	26	31	28	31
Standards of Official Conduct	—[a]	—[a]	5	5	9	9	85	8	11	9	9	10	9	11	12	13	13	11	12	13	11	12
Post Office and Civil Service[d]	6	9	46	61	74	83	77	83	87	76	70	6	—	—	—	—	—	—	—	—	—	—
Merchant Marine and Fisheries[d]	6	9	21	28	82	79	42	74	76	75	75	6	—	—	—	—	—	—	—	—	—	—
District of Columbia[d]	7	8	15	43	41	42	42	39	40	34	36	6	—	—	—	—	—	—	—	—	—	—
Homeland Security	—	—	—	—	—	—	—	—	—	—	—	—	—	—	—	—	—	—	—	—	46	41

Notes: The totals reflect the number of full-time paid employees. Many of the committee names and jurisdictions changed in the 104th Congress. For continuity, we have included the old committee names in parentheses. The committees are ranked in order of their staff size in 2001.

a. Not a standing committee

b. In 1993, the Natural Resources Committee was created out of the old Interior Committee. The staff figures for 1947–1991 are actually those of the Interior Committee.

c. After 1972, the figures include employees of House Informations Systems, the House of Representatives' central computer facility.

d. These three committees were eliminated in the first few weeks of the 104th Congress. The juridictions of the Post Office and Civil Service Committee and the District of Columbia Committee became part of the Government Reform and Oversight Committee. The jurisdiction of the Merchant Marine and Fisheries Committee was divided among several other committees.

Source: *Statement of Disbursements of the House,* various editions.

Table 5-7 Staffs of Senate Standing Committees, 1947–2005

Committee	1947	1960	1970	1975	1979	1981	1985	1989	1993	1994	1995	1996	1997	1998	1999	2000	2001	2002	2003	2004	2005
Appropriations	23	31	42	72	80	79	82	80	72	70	60	59	76	70	79	80	91	96	105	112	111
Judiciary	19	137	190	251	223	134	141	127	108	110	74	100	141	90	122	86	89	99	98	76	91
Governmental Affairs (and Homeland Security)	29	47	55	144	179	153	131	111	96	95	66	63	147	70	75	73	73	83	81	77	79
Labor and Human Resources	9	28	69	150	155	119	127	122	108	117	80	83	94	76	73	74	78	93	64	81	70
Finance	6	6	16	26	67	50	54	55	46	54	46	49	51	41	44	43	65	59	62	55	50
Environment and Public Works	10	11	34	70	74	56	56	50	40	44	37	34	39	35	36	41	50	44	50	45	43
Commerce, Science, and Transportation	8	52	53	111	96	78	93	76	68	70	56	65	68	53	56	54	49	56	62	57	58
Armed Services	10	23	19	30	31	36	48	51	50	45	43	49	49	45	48	49	49	53	52	46	53
Budget	—[a]	—[a]	—[a]	90	91	82	81	66	58	66	46	46	48	41	42	46	46	40	50	39	50
Foreign Relations	8	25	31	62	75	59	61	58	54	58	42	50	54	47	50	46	49	50	49	58	58
Energy and Natural Resources (Interior)	7	26	22	53	55	50	57	50	46	47	39	37	39	36	41	39	38	44	40	39	44
Banking, Housing, and Urban Affairs	9	22	23	55	48	39	38	51	51	58	44	47	51	45	29	43	43	49	39	44	50
Agriculture	3	10	7	22	34	34	34	42	29	35	28	33	47	27	28	33	28	36	33	31	32
Small Business	—[a]	—[a]	—[a]	—[a]	—[a]	—[a]	24	22	24	26	20	20	27	21	22	19	24	26	25	25	27
Indian Affairs	—[a]	—[a]	—[a]	—[a]	—[a]	—[a]	—[a]	—[a]	—[a]	22	15	16	23	12	16	16	20	17	17	17	16
Rules and Administration	41	15	13	29	37	31	28	27	24	24	20	25	27	16	23	19	17	19	16	16	17
Veterans' Affairs	—[a]	—[a]	—[a]	32	24	22	25	25	24	14	14	17	21	22	21	17	16	22	17	20	34

Notes: The totals reflect the number of full-time paid employees. Committees are ranked in the order of their staff size in 2001.

a. The committee did not yet exist or it existed only as a special committee.

Source: *Report of the Secretary of the Senate,* various editions.

Table 5-8 Staffs of Congressional Support Agencies, FY1946–FY2005

Year	Library of Congress	Congressional Research Service only	Government Accountability Office	Congressional Budget Office	Office of Technology Assessment
1946			14,219	—	—
1947	1,898	160	10,695	—	—
1950	1,973	161	7,876	—	—
1955	2,459	166	5,776	—	—
1960	2,779	183	5,074	—	—
1965	3,390	231	4,278	—	—
1970	3,848	332	4,704	—	—
1971	3,963	386	4,718	—	—
1972	4,135	479	4,742	—	—
1973	4,375	596	4,908	—	—
1974	4,504	687	5,270	—	10
1975	4,649	741	4,905	193	54
1976	4,880	806	5,391	203	103
1977	5,075	789	5,315	201	139
1978	5,231	818	5,476	203	164
1979	5,390	847	5,303	207	145
1980	5,047	868	5,196	218	122
1981	4,799	849	5,182	218	130
1982	4,803	849	5,027	218	130
1983	4,815	853	4,960	211	130
1984	4,802	858	4,985	210	139
1985	4,809	860	5,042	222	143
1986	4,806	860	5,019	222	143
1987	4,983	860	5,016	226	143
1988	4,874	825	5,042	211	143
1989	4,793	860	5,063	226	143
1990	4,659	797	5,066	226	143
1991	5,043	831	5,054	226	143
1992	5,050	838	5,062	218	143
1993	5,033	835	4,958	230	143
1994	4,701	835	4,572	218	143
1995	4,572	746	4,572	214	143
1996	4,399	729	3,677	232	—
1997	4,299	726	3,341	232	—
1998	4,275	708	3,245	219	—
1999	4,317	703	3,275	232	—
2000	3,920	696	3,192	223	—
2001	4,099	722	3,155	228	—
2002	4,251	681	3,275	232	—
2003	4,200	692	3,269	236	—
2004	4,334	729	3,252	236	—
2005	4,292	700	3,215	235	—

Note: The totals reflect the number of full-time paid employees.

Sources: *Legislative Branch Appropriations,* various years. *Employment and Trends* (Washington, D.C.: Office of Personnel Management, November 2002, 2003, and 2004).

Table 5-9 Legislative Branch Appropriations and the Consumer Price Index, 1946–2005

Year	Appropriation (dollars)	Increase (percent)	Consumer price index	Increase (percent)
1946	54,065,614	n.a.	19.5	8.3
1947	61,825,020	14.4	22.3	14.4
1948	62,119,714	0.5	24.1	8.1
1949	62,057,678	–0.1	23.8	–1.2
1950	64,313,460	3.6	24.1	1.3
1951	71,888,244	11.8	26.0	7.9
1952	75,673,896	5.3	26.5	1.9
1953	77,670,076	2.6	26.7	0.8
1954	70,925,361	–8.7	26.9	0.7
1955	86,304,923	21.7	26.8	–0.4
1956	94,827,986	9.9	27.2	1.5
1957	120,775,798	27.4	28.1	3.3
1958	107,785,560	–10.8	28.9	2.8
1959	136,153,580	26.3	29.1	0.7
1960	131,055,385	–3.7	29.6	1.7
1961	140,930,781	7.5	29.9	1.0
1962	136,686,715	–3.0	30.2	1.0
1963	150,426,185	10.1	30.6	1.3
1964	168,467,869	12.0	31.0	1.3
1965	221,904,318	31.7	31.5	1.6
1966	197,965,307	–10.8	32.4	2.9
1967	221,715,643	12.0	33.4	3.1
1968	282,003,322	27.2	34.8	4.2
1969	311,542,399	10.5	36.7	5.5
1970	361,024,327	15.9	38.8	5.7
1971	443,104,319	22.7	40.5	4.4
1972	564,107,992	27.3	41.8	3.2
1973	645,127,365	14.4	44.4	6.2
1974	662,180,668	2.6	49.3	11.0
1975	785,618,833	18.6	53.8	9.1
1976	947,185,778	20.6	56.9	5.8
1977	963,921,185	1.8	60.6	6.5
1978	1,009,225,350	4.7	65.2	7.6

Year	Appropriation (dollars)	Increase (percent)	Consumer price index	Increase (percent)
1979	1,124,766,400	11.4	72.6	11.3
1980	1,199,061,463	6.6	82.4	13.5
1981	1,285,943,826	7.2	90.9	10.3
1982	1,365,272,433	6.2	96.5	6.2
1983	1,467,318,263	7.5	99.6	3.2
1984	1,644,160,600	12.0	103.9	4.3
1985	1,599,977,138	–2.7	107.6	3.6
1986	1,783,255,000	11.4	109.6	1.9
1987	1,635,190,214	–8.3	113.6	3.6
1988	1,745,201,500	6.7	118.3	4.1
1989	1,804,624,000	3.4	124.0	4.8
1990	1,968,441,000	9.1	130.7	5.4
1991	2,161,367,000	9.8	136.2	4.2
1992	2,303,844,000	6.6	140.3	3.0
1993	2,302,924,000	–0.1	144.5	3.0
1994	2,269,558,000	–1.4	148.2	2.6
1995	2,390,600,000	5.3	152.4	2.8
1996	2,125,000,000	–11.1	156.9	3.0
1997	2,165,400,000	1.9	160.5	2.3
1998	2,288,000,000	5.7	163.0	1.6
1999	2,581,000,000	12.8	166.6	2.2
2000	2,486,000,000	–3.7	172.2	3.4
2001	2,730,000,000	9.8	177.1	2.8
2002	3,227,000,000	18.2	179.9	1.6
2003	3,461,000,000	7.3	184.0	2.3
2004	3,570,000,000	3.2	189.0	2.7
2005	3,768,000,000	5.5	194.4	2.8
1946–2005	—	6,301.5	—	843.6

Notes: Appropriations include supplementals, except for 1986. Appropriations are for fiscal years, but the consumer price index is the year average for calendar years.

Sources: Paul E. Dwyer, *Congressional Research Service Report for Congress, RL30512: Appropriations for FY2001: Legislative Branch;* Legislative Branch Appropriations Bills, various years; U.S. Department of Labor, Bureau of Labor Statistics.

Table 5-10 Legislative Branch Appropriations, by Category, FY1984–FY2005 (in thousands)

	1984	1985	1986[a]	1987	1988	1989	1990	1991	1992	1993
Senate	255,856	285,930	308,834	307,658	337,314	340,677	373,761	437,223	449,568	451,451
House of Representatives	419,784	439,398	455,431	463,907	513,786	506,068	537,207	647,675	693,970	699,109
Joint Items[b]	128,933	96,415	155,804	103,136	94,981	120,983	170,454	114,187	80,716	80,476
Architect of the Capitol[d]	82,021	85,181	112,191	101,633	107,306	103,640	116,221	139,806	151,633	149,613
Botanic Garden	2,158	2,080	2,197	2,062	2,221	2,521	2,638	3,519	2,862	4,906
Congressional Budget Office	16,723	17,541	18,455	17,251	17,886	18,361	19,580	21,183	22,542	22,542
Congressional Research Service	36,700	39,833	38,963	39,602	43,022	44,684	46,895	52,743	56,583	57,291
Copyright Royalty Commission[f]	210	217	227	123	129	123	101	127	130	130
General Accountability Office	271,710	299,704	339,639	304,910	329,847	347,339	364,720	419,130	442,647	435,167
Government Printing Office[d]	125,700	122,704	122,268	94,956	89,521	85,731	98,018	79,615	91,591	89,591
Library of Congress	228,715	228,242	242,829	183,670	191,998	199,650	211,100	239,924	248,308	252,808
Office of Technology Assessment	14,831	15,692	17,000	15,532	16,901	17,937	18,900	19,557	21,025	21,025
Office of Compliance										

	1994	1995	1996	1997	1998	1999	2000	2003	2004	2005
Senate	443,315	460,600	426,900	441,200	461,100	474,891	487,370	663,404	726,067	720,194
House of Representatives	684,696	728,700	671,600	684,000	708,700	740,481	757,993	960,871	1,048,581	1,079,516
Joint Items[b]	78,750	86,200	86,800	85,300	86,700	204,916[c]	100,854	257,505	18,974	260,356
Architect of the Capitol[d]	150,223	159,700	143,000	139,800	164,700	289,746[e]	213,474	456,782	308,042	362,200
Botanic Garden	3,008	3,200	3,100	2,900	3,000	3,052	3,438	6,063	5,932	6,275
Congressional Budget Office	22,317	23,200	24,300	24,500	24,800	25,671	26,121	31,892	34,790	34,640
Congressional Research Service	56,718	60,100	60,100	62,600	64,600	67,124	70,973	88,250	96,385	96,118
Copyright Royalty Commission[f]	128	—	—	—	—	—	—	—	—	53,518
General Accountability Office	430,815	449,400	374,000	332,500	339,500	359,268	377,561	453,051	473,500	467,205
Government Printing Office[d]	29,082	32,200	30,307	29,077	29,077	29,264	29,872	119,025	88,800	119,787
Library of Congress	250,813	263,100	264,600	269,100	281,800	296,516	323,380	414,925	544,092	545,362
Office of Technology Assessment	21,315	22,000	—	—	—	—	—	—	—	10,470
Office of Compliance	—	—	—	2,600	2,500	2,086	1,992	2,157	2,421	2,402

Notes: The figures include supplemental appropriations, except for 1986. Appropriations for legislative operations only.

a. The figures for 1986 are before Gramm-Rudman-Hollings sequestration.

b. This category includes such items as joint committees and the Capitol Police. Before 1991, official mail costs were also included in this category.

c. This includes $106,782,000 for emergency security enhancements funded under the Capitol Police Board's general expenses account, as well as $2 million for the Trade Deficit Review Commission.

d. The figures for the Architect of the Capitol and the Government Printing Office include appropriations for legislative activities only.

e. This includes $100 million for construction of a Capitol Visitor Center.

f. The commission was abolished after fiscal year 1994. Its duties have been taken over by a Copyright Office panel; therefore, there is no further appropriation.

Sources: Paul E. Dwyer, *Congressional Research Service Report for Congress, RL30512: Appropriations for FY2001: Legislative Branch;* Legislative Branch Appropriations Bills, various years.

Table 5-11 Allowances for Representatives, 1977–2005

Category	1977	1981	1983	1985	1987	1989	1991	1993
Clerk-hire	$238,580	$336,384	$366,648	$394,680	$406,560	$431,760[a]	$475,000[a]	$557,400[a]
Postage	$211	—[c]	—[c]	—[c]	—[c]	—[c]	—[c]	—[c]
Stationery	$6,500	—[c]	—[c]	—[c]	—[c]	—[c]	—[c]	—[c]
Travel (round trips)	33	—[c]	—[c]	—[c]	—[c]	—[c]	—[c]	—[c]
Telephone/telegraph	$5,200 for equipment; 15000 long-distance minutes	—[c]	—[c]	—[c]	—[c]	—[c]	—[c]	—[c]
District and state offices rental	2500 sq. ft.	—[c]	—[c]	—[c]	—[c]	—[c]	—[c]	—[c]
Furnishings (one-time)	$27,000	—[c]	—[c]	—[c]	—[c]	—[c]	—[c]	—[c]
Official expenses	$7,000	$66,200–248,601	$279,470–588,850	$105,513–306,509	$105,513–306,509	$108,400–306,500	$135,000–317,000	$152,128–302,008
Constituent communications (begun in 1975)	$5,000	—[c]	—[c]	—[c]	—[c]	—[c]	—[c]	—[c]
Equipment lease	$9,000	—[c]	—[c]	—[c]	—[c]	—[c]	—[c]	—[c]
Members' representational allowance	—[b]	—[b]	—[b]	—[b]	—[b]	—[b]	—[b]	—[b]

Category	1995	1997	1999	2001	2003	2004	2005
Clerk-hire	$568,560[a]	—[b]	—[b]	—[b]	—[b]	—[b]	—[b]
Postage	—[c]	—[b]	—[b]	—[b]	—[b]	—[b]	—[b]
Stationery	—[c]	—[b]	—[b]	—[b]	—[b]	—[b]	—[b]
Travel (round trips)	—[c]	—[b]	—[b]	—[b]	—[b]	—[b]	—[b]
Telephone/telegraph	—[c]	—[b]	—[b]	—[b]	—[b]	—[b]	—[b]
District and state offices rental	—[c]	—[b]	—[b]	—[b]	—[b]	—[b]	—[b]
Furnishings (one-time)	—[c]	—[b]	—[b]	—[b]	—[b]	—[b]	—[b]
Official expenses	$152,128–334,629	—[b]	—[b]	—[b]	—[b]	—[b]	—[b]
Constituent communications (begun in 1975)	—[c]	—[b]	—[b]	—[b]	—[b]	—[b]	—[b]
Equipment lease	—[c]	—[b]	—[b]	—[b]	—[b]	—[b]	—[b]
Members' representational allowance	—[b] —	$814,090–1,233,780	$858,707–1,311,594	$980,699–1,469,930	$1,087,407–1,636,750	$1,198,149 —	$1,246,228 —

a. Each member is entitled to an annual clerk-hire allowance of the designated amount for a staff not to exceed twenty-two employees, four of whom must fit into five categories: (1) shared payroll—employees, such as computer experts, who are shared by members; (2) interns; (3) employees on leave without pay; (4) part-time employees; (5) temporary employees—employees hired for a specific purpose for not more than ninety days.

b. On September 1, 1995, members' three former expense allowances (clerk-hire, official expenses, and official mail allowances) were consolidated into one members' representational allowance (MRA). Although the MRA is calculated on the basis of those three components, members may spend the MRA as they see fit. Within the MRA, each member's expenditures for franked mail may not exceed the total amount allocated by the Committee on House Oversight for official mail expenses, plus an additional $25,000, transferable within the MRA at the member's discretion according to the procedures under the previous allowance structure. The 2008 mean MRA was $1,335,632.

c. As of January 3, 1978, previous individual allowances for travel, office equipment lease, district office lease, stationery, telecommunications, mass mailings, postage, computer services, and other official expenses were consolidated in a single allowance category—the official expenses allowance. Members may budget funds for each category as they see fit. The average allowance for 1995 was $193,000. After 1995 this was incorporated into the MRA.

Sources: Committee on House Administration, House of Representatives; Legislative Branch Appropriations Bills, various years.

Table 5-12 Allowances for Senators, 1977–2005

Category	1977	1979	1981	1983	1985	1987	1989	1991
Clerk-hire[a]	$311,577–588,145	$508,221–1,021,167	$592,608–1,190,724	$645,897–1,297,795	$695,244–1,396,947	$716,102–1,438,856	$754,000–1,636,000	$814,000–1,760,000
Legislative assistance[b]	n.a.	$157,626	$183,801	$200,328	$215,634	$243,543	$248,000	$269,000
Postage	$1215–1520	—	—[c]	—[c]	—[c]	—[c]	—[c]	—[c]
Stationery	3600–5000	—	—[c]	—[c]	—[c]	—[c]	—[c]	—[c]
Travel (round trips)	20–22	—	—[c]	—[c]	—[c]	—[c]	—[c]	—[c]
District and state offices rental[d]	n.a. —	4,800–8,000 sq. ft.	4,800–8,000 sq. ft.	4,800–8,000 sq. ft.	4,800–8,000 sq. ft.	4,800–8,000 sq. ft.	4,800–8,000 sq. ft.	4,800–8,000 sq. ft.
Furnishings, state offices[e]	n.a. —	$22,550–31,350	$22,550–31,350	$22,550–31,350	$22,550–31,350	$30,000–41,744	$30,000–41,744	$30,000–41,744
Official office expense account[f]	n.a. —	$33,000–143,000	$33,000–143,000	$36,000–156,000	$36,000–156,000	$36,000–156,000	$33,000–156,000	$47,000–122,000

Category	1993	1995	1997	1999	2001	2003	2004	2005
Clerk-hire[a]	$1,540,000–1,914,000	$1,660,000–1,935,000	$1,087,597–1,974,051	$1,210,467–2,157,222	$1,347,851–2,360,512	$1,568,333–2,669,720	$1,809,792–3,008,969	$1,926,936–3,170,602
Legislative assistance[b]	$374,000	$377,400	$385,050	$396,477	$410,277	$436,377	$460,677	$472,677
Postage	—[c]	—[c]	—[c]	—[c]	—[c]	—[c]	$300,000	$300,000
Stationery	—[c]	—[c]	—[c]	—[c]	—[c]	—[c]	—	—
Travel (round trips)	—[c]	—[c]	—[c]	—[c]	—[c]	—[c]	—	—
District and state offices rental[d]	4,800–8,000 sq. ft.	4,800–8,000 sq. ft.	4,800–8,000 sq. ft.	4,800–8,000 sq. ft.	5,000–8,200 sq. ft.	5,000–8,200 sq. ft.	5,000–8,200 sq. ft.	5,000–8,200 sq. ft.
Furnishings, state offices[e]	$30,000–41,744	$30,000–41,744	$30,000–41,744	$30,000–41,744	$40,000–56,000	$40,000–56,000	— —	— —
Official office expense account[f]	$44,000–200,000	$90,000–250,000	$95,825–245,000	$127,384–470,272	$128,178–474,282	$128,525–468,377	$128,553–466,908	$128,580–468,102

n.a. = not available

a. There is no limit on the number of employees a senator may hire. He or she must, however, use only the clerk-hire or legislative assistance allowance to pay staff salaries. The clerk-hire allowance varies according to state population.

b. In addition to clerk-hire, each senator has a legislative assistance allowance worth $472,677 in 2005. That allowance is reduced for any committee chairman or ranking minority member of a committee. It is also reduced for any other senator authorized by a committee chairman to recommend or approve any individuals for appointment to the committee staff who will assist that senator "solely and directly" in his duties as a member of the committee. The reduction requirements were waived for the 99th and 100th Congresses.

c. This allowance is one of the allocations of the consolidated office expense allowance. Before January 1, 1973, senators were authorized individually controlled allowances for six expense categories as follows: transportation expenses for the senator and his staff; stationery; air mail and special delivery postage; long-distance telephone calls; telegram charges; and home state expenses, which include home state office expenses; telephone service charges incurred outside Washington, DC; subscriptions to newspapers, magazines, periodicals, and clipping or similar services; and home state office rent (repealed effective July 1, 1974). Effective January 1, 1973, the Supplemental Appropriations Act, 1973, provided for the consolidation of those same allowances to give senators flexibility in the management of the same dollars allocated for their expense allowances. That authorization imposed no limit on any expense category. The allowance was designated as the consolidated office expense allowance. Effective January 1, 1977, the Legislative Branch Appropriation Act redesignated the consolidated office expense allowance as the official office expense account.

d. Effective July 1, 1974, the Legislative Branch Appropriations Act, 1975, provided a formula for the allowable aggregate square feet of office space in the home state of a senator. There is no limit on the number of offices that a senator may establish in his home state, but the designated square footage may not be exceeded. The cost of office space in the home state is not chargeable to the official office expense account.

e. An aggregate furniture and furnishings allowance is provided through the General Services Administration for one or more state offices in either federal or privately owned buildings. Before 1987, the $22,550 minimum allowance for office space not greater than 4,800 square feet was increased by $550 for each authorized increase of 200 square feet of space. From 1987 through 1999, the $30,000 minimum allowance for office space not greater than 4,800 square feet was increased by $734 for each authorized increase of 200 square feet of space. In 2001, the $40,000 minimum allowance for office space not greater than 5,000 square feet is increased by $1,000 for each authorized increase of 200 square feet of space. The FY 2000 Appropriations Act indexed this figure for inflation at the beginning of each Congress.

f. The expense account may be used for the following expenses (2 U.S.C. 58[a], as amended):

(1) official telegrams and long-distance phone calls and related services;

(2) stationery and other office supplies purchased through the stationery room for official business;

(3) costs incurred in the mailing or delivery of matters relating to official business;

(4) official office expenses in home state, other than equipment or furniture (purchase of office equipment beyond stated allocations may be made through 10 percent of the funds listed under item 9 below);

(5) official telephone charges incurred outside Washington, D.C.;

(6) subscriptions to newspapers, magazines, periodicals, or clipping or similar services;

(7) travel expenses incurred by a senator or staff member, subject to certain limitations;

(8) expenses incurred by individuals selected by a senator to serve on panels or other bodies making recommendations for nominees to service academies or federal judgeships; and

(9) other official expenses as the senator determines are necessary, including (a) additional office equipment for Washington, D.C., or state offices; (b) actual transportation expenses incurred by the senator and employees for official business in the Washington metropolitan area (this is also allowed to employees assigned to a state office for actual transportation expenses in the general vicinity of the office to which assigned but is not available for a change of assignment within the state or for commuting between home and office).

The total reimbursement expense for the calendar year may not exceed 10 percent of the total official office expense account.

Beginning with FY1981, each senator was also allowed to transfer funds from the administrative, clerical, and legislative assistance allowances to the official office expense account.

Sources: Paul E. Dwyer, *Congressional Research Service Report for Congress, RL30512: Appropriations for FY2001: Legislative Branch;* Legislative Branch Appropriations Bills, various years.

Figure 5-1 Staffs of Members and of Committees of Congress, 1891–2005

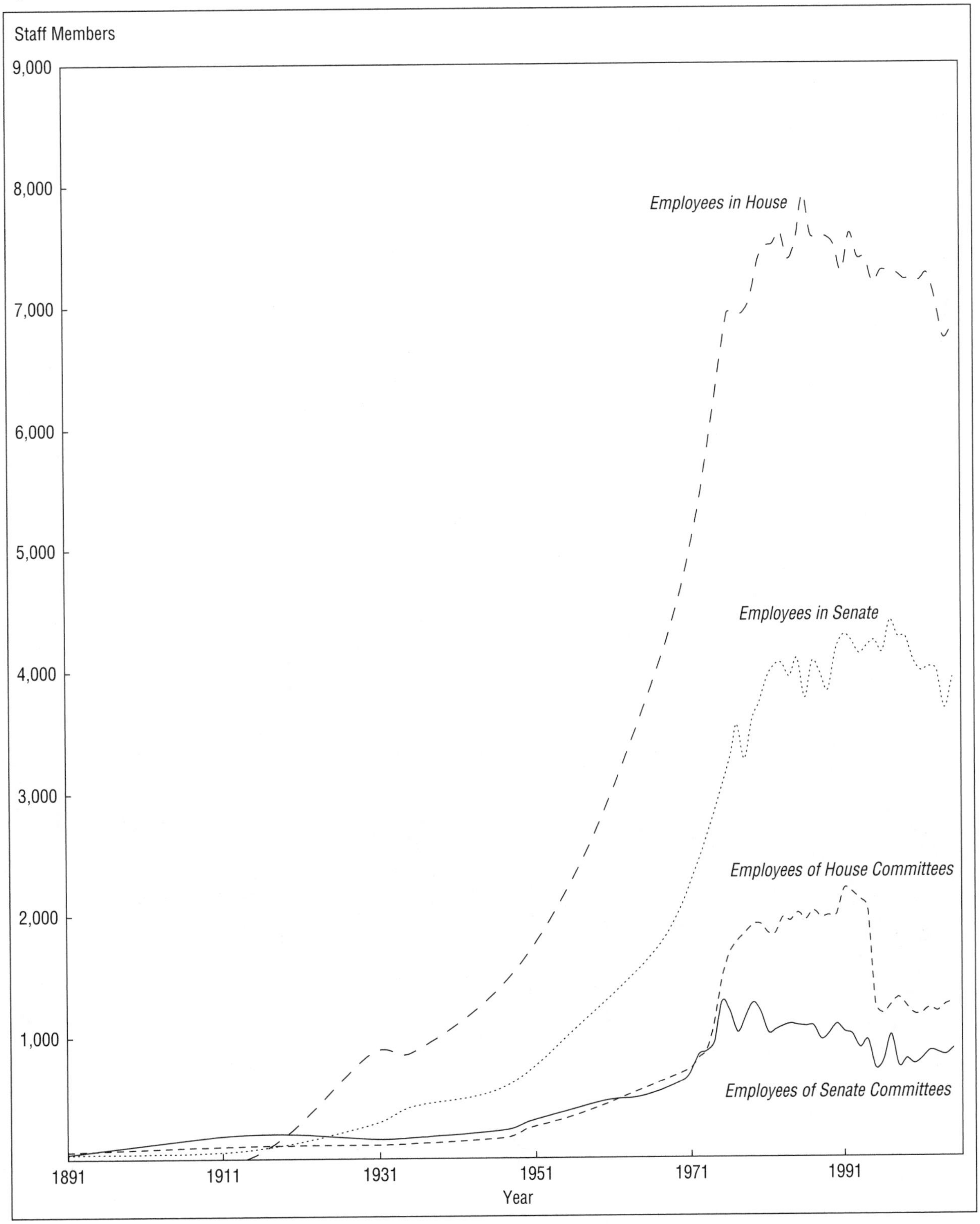

Source: Tables 5-2 and 5-5.

6

Workload

Table 6-1 House Workload, 80th–109th Congresses, 1947–2006

Congress	Bills introduced[a]	Average no. of bills introduced per member	Bills passed	Ratio of bills passed to bills introduced	Recorded votes[b]	Time in session: days	Time in session: hours	Hours per day in session	Committee, subcommittee meetings[c]
80th (1947–1948)	7,611	17.5	1,739	0.228	285	254	1,224	4.8	n.a.
81st (1949–1950)	10,502	24.1	2,482	0.236	543	345	1,501	4.4	n.a.
82nd (1951–1952)	9,065	20.8	2,008	0.222	364	274	1,163	4.2	n.a.
83rd (1953–1954)	10,875	25.0	2,129	0.196	271	240	1,033	4.3	n.a.
84th (1955–1956)	13,169	30.3	2,360	0.179	279	230	937	4.1	3,210
85th (1957–1958)	14,580	33.5	2,064	0.142	415	276	1,148	4.2	3,750
86th (1959–1960)[d]	14,112	32.3	1,636	0.116	382	265	1,039	3.9	3,059
87th (1961–1962)[d]	14,328	32.8	1,927	0.134	524	304	1,227	4.0	3,402
88th (1963–1964)	14,022	32.2	1,267	0.090	528	334	1,251	3.7	3,596
89th (1965–1966)	19,874	45.7	1,565	0.079	782	336	1,548	4.6	4,367
90th (1967–1968)	22,060	50.7	1,213	0.055	875	328	1,595	4.9	4,386
91st (1969–1971)	21,436	49.3	1,130	0.053	812	350	1,613	4.6	5,066
92nd (1971–1972)	18,561	42.7	970	0.052	934	298	1,429	4.8	5,114
93rd (1973–1974)	18,872	43.4	923	0.049	1,453	334	1,603	4.8	5,888
94th (1975–1976)	16,982	39.0	968	0.057	1,692	311	1,788	5.7	6,975
95th (1977–1978)	15,587	35.8	1,027	0.066	1,724	323	1,898	5.9	7,896
96th (1979–1980)	9,103	20.9	929	0.102	1,439	326	1,876	5.8	7,033
97th (1981–1982)	8,094	18.6	704	0.087	859	303	1,420	4.7	6,078
98th (1983–1984)	7,105	16.3	978	0.138	996	266	1,705	6.4	5,661
99th (1985–1986)	6,499	14.9	973	0.150	970	281	1,794	6.4	5,272
100th (1987–1988)	6,263	14.4	1,061	0.169	976	298	1,659	5.6	5,388
101st (1989–1990)	6,664	15.3	968	0.145	915	281	1,688	6.0	5,305
102nd (1991–1992)	6,775	15.6	932	0.138	932	277	1,796	6.5	5,152
103rd (1993–1994)	5,739	13.2	749	0.131	1,122	265	1,887	7.1	4,304
104th (1995–1996)	4,542	10.4	611	0.135	1,340	290	2,445	8.4	3,796
105th (1997–1998)	5,014	11.5	710	0.142	1,187	251	2,002	8.0	3,624
106th (1999–2000)	5,815	13.4	957	0.165	1,214	272	2,179	8.0	3,347
107th (2001–2002)	5,892	13.5	677	0.115	996	265	1,694	6.4	2,254
108th (2003–2004)	5,547	12.8	801	0.144	1,221	243	1,894	7.8	2,135
109th (2005–2006)	6,540	15.0	770	0.118	1,212	241	1,918	8.0	2,492

n.a. = not available

a. This number includes all bills and joint resolutions introduced.

b. This number includes all quorum calls, yea and nay votes, and recorded votes.

c. Figures do not include the House Appropriations Committee for the 84th to 88th Congresses. House Appropriations Committee meetings included in subsequent Congresses numbered 584 in the 89th Congress, 705 in the 90th Congress, 709 in the 91st Congress, 854 in the 92nd Congress, and 892 in the 93rd Congress.

d. The House of Representatives included 437 members to reflect the addition of Alaska and Hawaii.

Sources: *Congressional Record* (thomas.loc.gov); Office of the Clerk, U.S. House of Representatives; "Resume of Congressional Activity," Congressional Record, 80th Congress–109th Congress; End of Session Committee Reports; Committee Websites.

Table 6-2 Senate Workload, 80th–109th Congresses, 1947–2006

Congress	Bills introduced[a]	Average no. of bills introduced per member	Bills passed	Ratio of bills passed to bills introduced	Recorded votes[b]	Time in session: days	Time in session: hours	Hours per day in session	Committee, subcommittee meetings[c]
80th (1947–1948)	3,186	33.2	1,670	0.524	248	257	1,462	5.7	n.a.
81st (1949–1950)	4,486	46.7	2,362	0.527	455	389	2,410	6.2	n.a.
82nd (1951–1952)	3,665	38.2	1,849	0.505	331	287	1,648	5.7	n.a.
83rd (1953–1954)	4,077	42.5	2,231	0.547	270	294	1,962	6.7	n.a.
84th (1955–1956)	4,518	47.1	2,550	0.564	224	224	1,362	6.1	2,607
85th (1957–1958)	4,532	47.2	2,202	0.486	313	271	1,876	6.9	2,748
86th (1959–1960)	4,149	41.5	1,680	0.405	422	280	2,199	7.9	2,271
87th (1961–1962)	4,048	40.5	1,953	0.482	434	323	2,164	6.7	2,532
88th (1963–1964)	3,457	34.6	1,341	0.388	541	375	2,395	6.4	2,493
89th (1965–1966)	4,129	41.3	1,636	0.396	497	345	1,814	5.3	2,889
90th (1967–1968)	4,400	44.0	1,376	0.313	595[d]	358	1,961	5.5	2,892
91st (1969–1971)	4,867	48.7	1,271	0.261	667	384	2,352	6.1	3,264
92nd (1971–1972)	4,408	44.1	1,035	0.235	955	348	2,295	6.6	3,559
93rd (1973–1974)	4,524	45.2	1,115	0.246	1,138	352	2,152	6.1	4,067
94th (1975–1976)	4,115	41.2	1,038	0.252	1,311	320	2,210	6.9	4,265
95th (1977–1978)	3,800	38.0	1,070	0.282	1,156	337	2,510	7.4	3,960
96th (1979–1980)	3,480	34.8	976	0.280	1,055	333	2,324	7.0	3,790
97th (1981–1982)	3,396	34.0	786	0.231	966	312	2,160	6.9	3,236
98th (1983–1984)	3,454	34.5	936	0.271	673	281	1,951	6.9	2,471
99th (1985–1986)	3,386	33.9	940	0.278	740	313	2,531	8.1	2,373
100th (1987–1988)	3,325	33.3	1,002	0.301	799	307	2,342	7.6	2,493
101st (1989–1990)	3,669	36.7	980	0.267	638	274	2,254	8.2	2,340[e]
102nd (1991–1992)	3,738	37.4	947	0.253	550	287	2,292	8.0	2,039
103rd (1993–1994)	2,805	28.1	682	0.243	724	291	2,514	8.6	2,043
104th (1995–1996)	2,266	22.7	518	0.229	919	343	2,876	8.4	1,601
105th (1997–1998)	2,718	27.2	586	0.216	612	296	2,188	7.4	1,954
106th (1999–2000)	3,343	33.4	819	0.245	672	303	2,202	7.3	1,862
107th (2001–2002)	3,242	32.4	554	0.171	633	322	2,280	7.1	1,605
108th (2003–2004)	3,078	30.8	759	0.247	675	300	2,486	8.3	1,506
109th (2005–2006)	4,163	41.6	684	0.164	645	297	2,250	7.6	1,513

n.a. = not available

a. This number includes all bills and joint resolutions introduced.

b. This number includes all yea and nay votes.

c. Figure includes all hearings and business meetings.

d. This number does not include one yea and nay vote that was ruled invalid for lack of a quorum.

e. Where final legislative calendars were not available, we compiled figures from Congressional Information Service Abstracts and the Congressional Record.

Sources: *Congressional Record* (thomas.loc.gov); Office of the Secretary, U.S. Senate; Senate Daily Digest; "Resume of Congressional Activity," Congressional Record, 80th Congress–109th Congress; End of Session Committee Reports; Committee Websites.

Table 6-3 Recorded Votes in the House and the Senate, 80th–109th Congresses, 1947–2006

Year	House	Senate	Year	House	Senate
1947	153	138	1977	782	636
1948	132	110	1978	942	520
1949	236	226	1979	758	509
1950	307	229	1980	681	546
1951	217	202	1981	371	497
1952	147	129	1982	488	469
1953	123	89	1983	533	381
1954	148	181	1984	463	292
1955	147	88	1985	482	381
1956	132	136	1986	488	359
1957	220	111	1987	511	420
1958	195	202	1988	465	379
1959	176	215	1989	379	312
1960	206	207	1990	536	326
1961	231	207	1991	444	280
1962	293	227	1992	488	270
1963	256	229	1993	615	395
1964	272	312	1994	507	329
1965	383	259	1995	885	613
1966	399	238	1996	455	306
1967	447	315	1997	640	298
1968	428	280[a]	1998	547	314
1969	353	245	1999	611	374
1970	459	422	2000	603	298
1971	472	423	2001	512	380
1972	462	532	2002	484	253
1973	726	594	2003	677	459
1974	727	544	2004	544	216
1975	828	611	2005	671	366
1976	864	700	2006	541	279

Note: House figures include the total number of quorum calls, yea and nay votes, and recorded votes, while Senate figures include only yea and nay votes.

a. This figure does not include one yea and nay vote that was ruled invalid for lack of a quorum.

Sources: "Resume of Congressional Activity," Congressional Record, 80th Congress–109th Congress.

Table 6-4 Congressional Workload, 80th–109th Congresses, 1947–2006

	Public bills			Private bills		
Congress	No. of bills enacted	Total pages of statutes	Average pages per statute	No. of bills enacted	Total pages of statutes	Average pages per statute
80th (1947–1948)	906	2,236	2.5	458	182	0.40
81st (1949–1950)	921	2,314	2.5	1,103	417	0.38
82nd (1951–1952)	594	1,585	2.7	1,023	360	0.35
83rd (1953–1954)	781	1,899	2.4	1,002	365	0.36
84th (1955–1956)	1,028	1,848	1.8	893	364	0.41
85th (1957–1958)	936	2,435	2.6	784	349	0.45
86th (1959–1960)	800	1,774	2.2	492	201	0.41
87th (1961–1962)	885	2,078	2.3	684	255	0.37
88th (1963–1964)	666	1,975	3.0	360	144	0.40
89th (1965–1966)	810	2,912	3.6	473	188	0.40
90th (1967–1968)	640	2,304	3.6	362	128	0.35
91st (1969–1971)	695	2,927	4.2	246	104	0.42
92nd (1971–1972)	607	2,330	3.8	161	67	0.42
93rd (1973–1974)	649	3,443	5.3	123	48	0.39
94th (1975–1976)	588	4,121	7.0	141	75	0.53
95th (1977–1978)	634	5,403	8.5	170	60	0.35
96th (1979–1980)	613	4,947	8.1	123	63	0.51
97th (1981–1982)	473	4,343	9.2	56	25	0.45
98th (1983–1984)	623	4,893	7.9	52	26	0.50
99th (1985–1986)	664	7,198	10.8	24	13	0.54
100th (1987–1988)	713	4,839	6.8	48	29	0.60
101st (1989–1990)	650	5,767	8.9	16	9	0.56
102nd (1991–1992)	590	7,544	12.8	20	11	0.55
103rd (1993–1994)	465	7,553	16.2	8	9	1.13
104th (1995–1996)	333	6,369	19.1	4	4	1.00
105th (1997–1998)	394	7,269	18.4	10	11	1.10
106th (1999–2000)	580	5,045	8.7	24	35	1.46
107th (2001–2002)	377	5,584	14.8	6	8	1.33
108th (2003–2004)	498	6,923	13.9	6	11	1.83
109th (2005–2006)	482	7,323	15.2	1	1	1.00

Sources: *Federal Register,* Statutes Branch; The Library of Congress—*THOMAS,* (http://thomas.loc.gov).

Table 6-5 Pages in the *Federal Register,* 1936–2006

Year	Pages	Year	Pages	Year	Pages
1936	2,355	1980	87,012	1994	68,107
1946	14,736	1981	63,554	1995	68,108
1956	10,528	1982	58,493	1996	69,368
1966	16,850	1983	57,703	1997	68,530
1969	20,464	1984	50,997	1998	72,356
1971	25,442	1985	53,479	1999	73,880
1972	28,920	1986	47,418	2000	83,093[a]
1973	35,586	1987	49,654	2001	67,703
1974	45,422	1988	53,376	2002	80,333
1975	60,221	1989	53,821	2003	75,796
1976	57,072	1990	53,618	2004	78,852
1977	63,629	1991	67,715	2005	77,752
1978	61,261	1992	62,919	2006	78,724
1979	77,497	1993	69,684		

a. Although the number of pages is correctly given as 83,093, a page-numbering error on May 22, 2000 resulted in a 201-page "jump." Thus, the pages are (incorrectly) numbered up to 83,294.

Source: *Federal Register.*

Table 6-6 Vetoes and Overrides, 80th–109th Congresses, 1947–2006

Congress	Total no. of presidential vetoes	No. of regular vetoes	No. of pocket vetoes	Vetoes overridden		House attempts to override vetoes	Senate attempts to override vetoes
				Total	Percentage of regular vetoes		
80th (1947–1948)	75	42	33	6	14.3	8	8
81st (1949–1950)	79	70	9	3	4.3	5	5
82nd (1951–1952)	22	14	8	3	21.4	4	4
83rd (1953–1954)	52	21	31	0	0.0	0	0
84th (1955–1956)	34	12	22	0	0.0	1	1
85th (1957–1958)	51	18	33	0	0.0	1	1
86th (1959–1960)	44	22	22	2	9.1	5	6
87th (1961–1962)	20	11	9	0	0.0	0	0
88th (1963–1964)	9	5	4	0	0.0	0	0
89th (1965–1966)	14	10	4	0	0.0	0	0
90th (1967–1968)	8	2	6	0	0.0	0	0
91st (1969–1971)	11	7	4	2	28.6	4	4
92nd (1971–1972)	20	6	14	2	33.3	3	4
93rd (1973–1974)	39	27	12	5	18.5	12	10
94th (1975–1976)	37	32	5	8	25.0	17	15
95th (1977–1978)	19	6	13	0	0.0	2	0
96th (1979–1980)	12	7	5	2	28.6	2	2
97th (1981–1982)	15	9	6	2	22.2	4	3
98th (1983–1984)	24	9	15	2	22.2	2	2
99th (1985–1986)	20	13	7	2	15.4	3	3
100th (1987–1988)	19	8	11	3	37.5	5	4
101st (1989–1990)	21	16	5	0	0.0	9	5
102nd (1991–1992)	25	15	10[a]	1	6.7	3	3
103rd (1993–1994)	0	0	0	0	0.0	0	0
104th (1995–1996)	17	17	0	1	5.9	6	1
105th (1997–1998)	8	8	0	0	0.0	1	1
106th (1999–2000)	12	11	1	0	0.0	3	1
107th (2000–2002)	0	0	0	0	0.0	0	0
108th (2003–2004)	0	0	0	0	0.0	0	0
109th (2005–2006)	1	1	0	0	0.0	1	0

Note: This table does not include line-item vetoes. After President Clinton excised several Pentagon programs from the 1998 budget, both houses of Congress, under the line-item veto law, passed legislation restoring some of the programs (H.R. 2631). President Clinton subsequently vetoed that bill, and both houses of Congress passed legislation overriding his veto. Subsequently, the Supreme Court declared the line-item veto unconstitutional.

a. President George H. W. Bush asserted that he had pocket-vetoed S. 1176, although some members in Congress dispute that assertion on the grounds that bills can be pocket-vetoed only after Congress had adjourned, not during a recess.

Sources: "Resume of Congressional Activity," Congressional Record, 80th Congress–109th Congress.

Table 6-7 Attempted and Successful Cloture Votes, 66th–109th Congresses, 1919–2006

	1st session		2nd session		Total	
Congress	Attempted	Successful	Attempted	Successful	Attempted	Successful
66th (1919–1920)	1	1	0	0	1	1
67th (1921–1922)	1	0	1	0	2	0
68th (1923–1924)	0	0	0	0	0	0
69th (1925–1926)	0	0	2	1	2	1
70th (1927–1928)	5	2	0	0	5	2
71st (1929–1930)	0	0	0	0	0	0
72nd (1931–1932)	0	0	0	0	0	0
73rd (1933–1934)	1	0	0	0	1	0
74th (1935–1936)	0	0	0	0	0	0
75th (1937–1938)	0	0	2	0	2	0
76th (1939–1940)	0	0	0	0	0	0
77th (1941–1942)	0	0	1	1	1	1
78th (1943–1944)	0	0	1	1	1	1
79th (1945–1946)	0	0	4	0	4	0
80th (1947–1948)	0	0	0	0	0	0
81st (1949–1950)	0	0	2	0	2	0
82nd (1951–1952)	0	0	0	0	0	0
83rd (1953–1954)	0	0	1	0	1	0
84th (1955–1956)	0	0	0	0	0	0
85th (1957–1958)	0	0	0	0	0	0
86th (1959–1960)	0	0	1	0	1	0
87th (1961–1962)	1	0	3	1	4	1
88th (1963–1964)	1	0	2	1	3	1
89th (1965–1966)	2	1	5	0	7	1
90th (1967–1968)	1	0	5	1	6	1
91st (1969–1971)	2	0	4	0	6	0
92nd (1971–1972)	10	2	10	2	20	4
93rd (1973–1974)	10	2	21	7	31	9
94th (1975–1976)	23	13	4	4	27	17
95th (1977–1978)	5	1	8	2	13	3
96th (1979–1980)	4	1	17	9	21	10
97th (1981–1982)	7	2	20	7	27	9
98th (1983–1984)	7	2	12	9	19	11
99th (1985–1986)	9	1	14	9	23	10
100th (1987–1988)	23	5	20	6	43	11
101st (1989–1990)	9	6	15	5	24	11
102nd (1991–1992)	20	9	27	13	47	22
103rd (1993–1994)	24[a]	4	22	10	46	14
104th (1995–1996)	21	4	29	5	50	9
105th (1997–1998)	24	7	29	11	53	18
106th (1999–2000)	36	11	22	17	58	28
107th (2001–2002)	22	12	39	22	61	34
108th (2003–2004)	23	1	26	11	49	12
109th (2005–2006)	20	13	34	21	54	34

Note: The number of votes required to invoke cloture was changed on March 7, 1975, from two-thirds of those present and voting to three-fifths of the total Senate membership, as Rule XXII of the standing rules of the Senate was amended.

a. On November 3, 1993, one vote was taken to break filibusters on five separate presidential nominees. *Vital Statistics* counts this as five attempted cloture votes.

Sources: "Indicators of Congressional Workload and Activity," Congressional Research Service; U.S. Senate website (www.senate.gov).

Figure 6-1 Ratio of Bills Passed to Bills Introduced, 80th–109th Congresses, 1947–2006

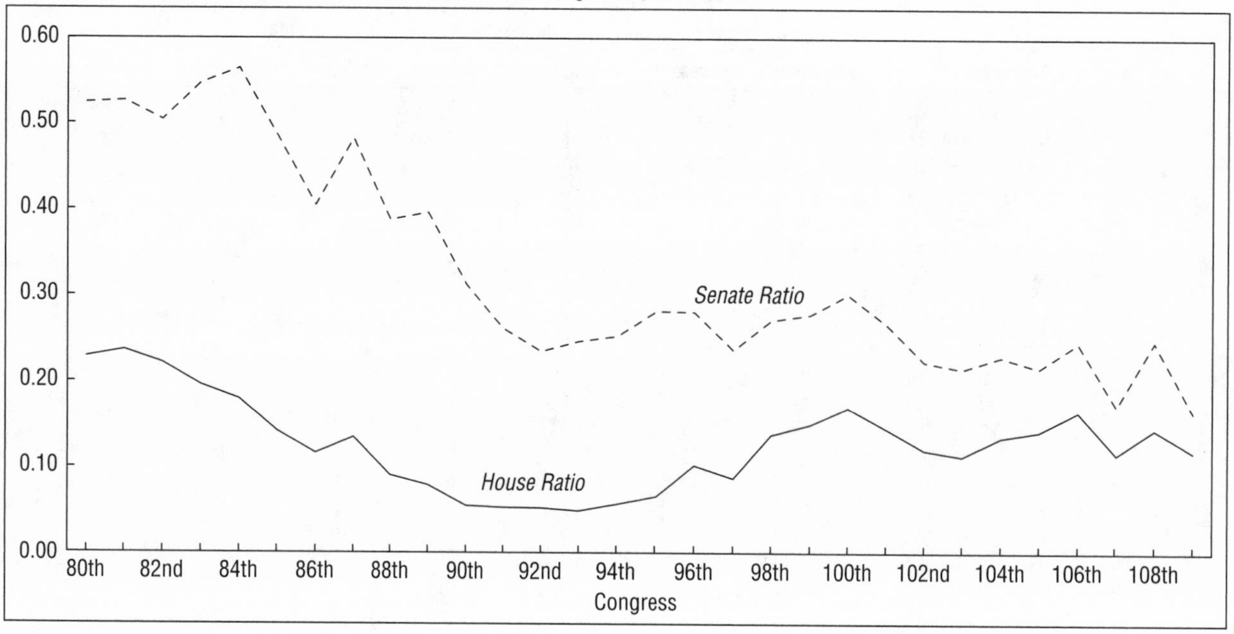

Source: Tables 6-1 and 6-2.

Figure 6-2 Recorded Votes in the House and Senate, 80th–109th Congress, 1947–2006

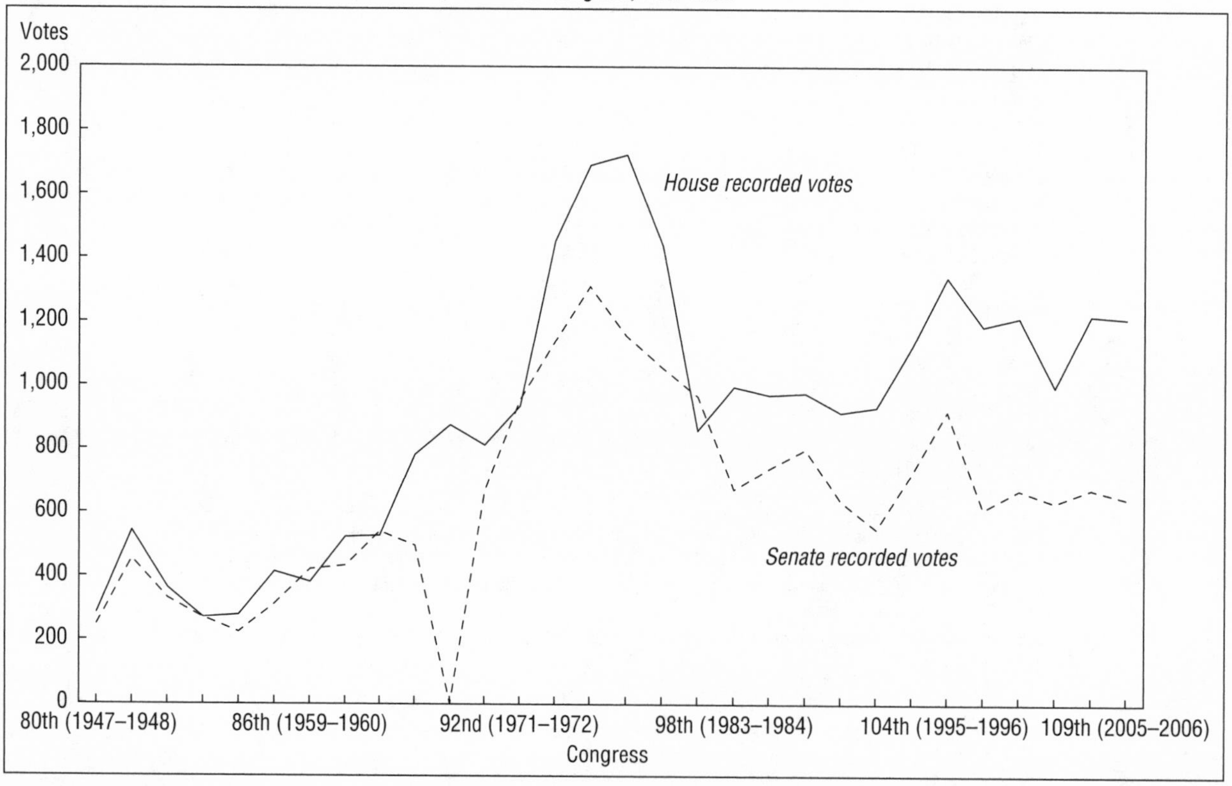

Source: Tables 6-1 and 6-2.

Figure 6-3 Public Bills in the Congressional Workload, 80th–109th Congresses, 1947–2006

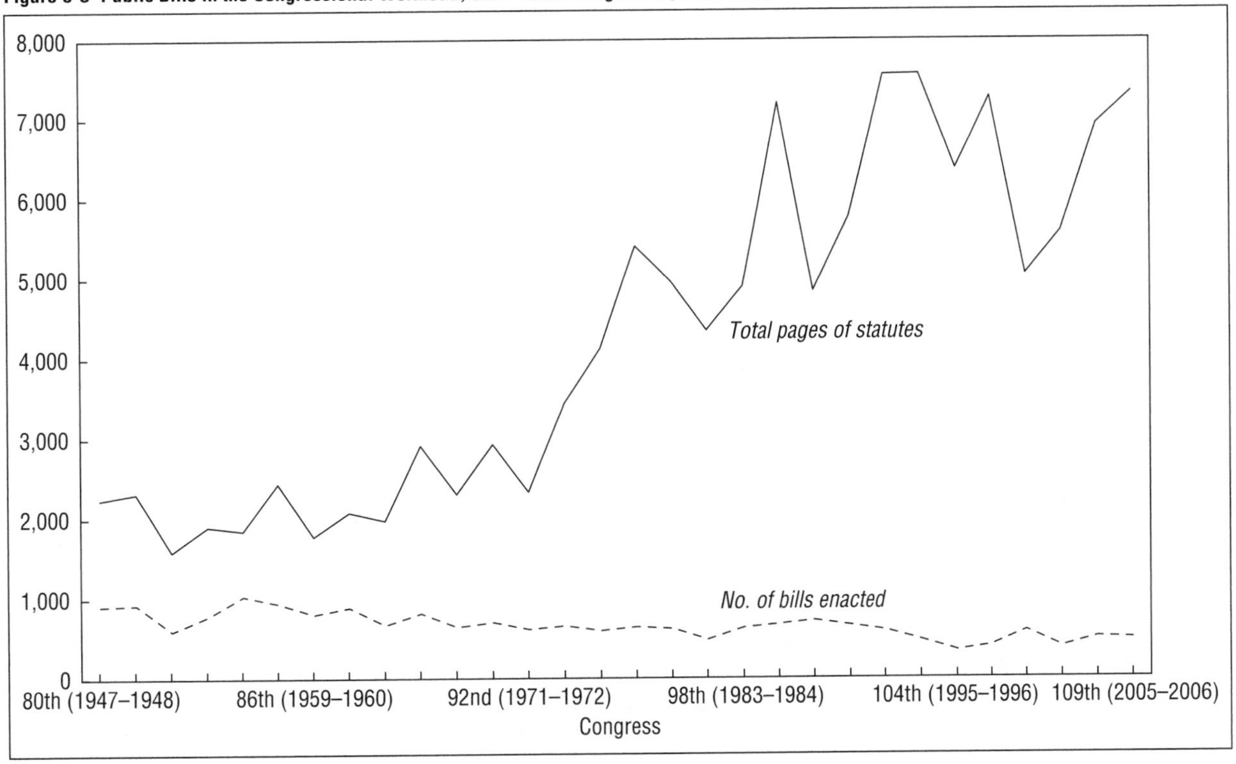

Source: Table 6-4.

7

Budgeting

Table 7-1 House Votes on Adoption of Budget Resolutions, by Party, FY1976–FY2007

		Total		Democrats		Republicans	
Fiscal year	Resolution	Yes	No	Yes	No	Yes	No
1976	First	200	196	197	68	3	128
	Second	225	191	214	67	11	124
1977	First	221	155	208	44	13	111
	Second	227	151	215	38	12	113
	Third	239	169	225	50	14	119
1978	First (first round)	84	320	82	185	2	135
	First (second round)	213	179	206	58	7	121
	Second	199	188	195	59	4	129
1979	First	201	197	198	61	3	136
	Second	217	178	215	42	2	136
1980	First	220	184	211	50	9	134
	Second (first round)	192	213	188	67	4	146
	Second (second round)	212	206	212	52	0	154
	Third[a]	241	174	218	45	23	129
1981	First	225	193	203	62	22	131
	Second	203	191	201	45	2	146
1982	First	270	154	84	153	186	1
	Second	206	200	70	150	136	50
1983	First	219	206	63	174	156	32
1984	First	229	196	225	36	4	160
1985	First	250	168	229	29	21	139
1986	First	258	170	234	15	24	155
1987	First	245	179	228	19	17	160
1988	First	215	201	212	34	3	167
1989	First	319	102	227	24	92	78
1990	First	263	157	157	96	106	61
1991	First	218	208	218	34	0	174
1992	First	239	181	231	25	8	155
1993	First	209	207	209	47	0	159
1994	First	243	183	242	11	0	172
1995	First	223	175	222	11	0	164
1996	First	238	194	8	191	230	1
1997	First	216	211	4	191	212	19
1998	First	333	99	132	72	201	26
1999	First[b]	216	204	3	194	213	9
2000	First	221	205	3	204	218	0
2001	First	220	208	6	202	213	5
2002	First	222	205	3	202	218	2
2003	First	221	209	1	206	219	2
2004	First	215	212	1	199	214	12
2005	First	215	212	0	201	215	10
2006	First	218	214	0	201	218	12
2007	First	218	210	0	197	218	12

Note: These votes are on passage of the resolutions in the House, not on adoption of the conference report. Beginning with the FY1983, Congress has adopted only one budget resolution each year, rather than the two originally prescribed by the Congressional Budget Act.

a. The third resolution for FY1980 was part of the first resolution for the FY1981, but it was voted on separately in the House.

b. Although both chambers passed a FY1999 budget resolution, the two different versions were so far apart that Congress never seriously attempted to reconcile the two bills, so that FY1999 was the first year under the Congressional Budget Act that Congress did not pass a budget resolution.

Sources: *Congressional Quarterly Almanac* (Washington, D.C.: Congressional Quarterly, various years); *Congressional Quarterly Weekly Report,* various issues.

Table 7-2 Senate Votes on Adoption of Budget Resolutions, by Party, FY1976–FY2007

		Total		Democrats		Republicans	
Fiscal year	Resolution	Yes	No	Yes	No	Yes	No
1976	First	69	22	50	4	19	18
	Second	69	23	50	8	19	15
1977	First	62	22	45	6	17	16
	Second	55	23	41	5	14	18
	Third	72	20	55	3	17	17
1978	First	56	31	41	14	15	17
	Second	63	21	46	8	17	13
1979	First	64	27	48	8	16	19
	Second	56	18	42	6	14	12
1980	First	64	20	44	5	20	15
	Second	62	36	45	14	17	22
1981	First	68	28	49	6	19	22
	Second	48	46	33	21	15	25
1982	First	78	20	28	18	50	2
	Second	49	48	2	44	47	4
1983	First	49	43	3	41	46	2
1984	First	50	49	29	17	21	32
1985	First	41	34	1	31	40	3
1986	First	50	49	1	45	49[a]	4
1987	First	70	25	38	6	32	19
1988	First	53	46	50	3	3	43
1989	First	69	26	44	6	25	20
1990	First	68	31	38	17	30	14
1991	First[b]	—	—	—	—	—	—
1992	First	57	41	49	7	8	34
1993	First	52	41	36	16	16	25
1994	First	54	45	54	2	0	43
1995	First	57	40	55	0	2	40
1996	First	57	42	3	42	54	0
1997	First	53	46	0	46	53	0
1998	First	78	22	37	8	41	14
1999	First[c]	57	41	3	44	54	0
2000	First	54	44	0	44	54	0
2001	First	50	48	0	44	50	4
2001	First	50	48	0	44	50	4
2002	First	65	35	15	35	50	0
2003[d]	—	—	—	—	—	—	—
2004	First	56	44	6	42	50	1
2005	First	51	45	1	43	50	1
2006	First	51	49	0	44	51	4
2007	First	51	49	1	43	50	5

Note: These votes are on passage of the resolutions in the Senate, not on adoption of the conference report. Beginning with the FY1983, Congress has adopted only one budget resolution each year, rather than the two originally prescribed by the Congressional Budget Act.

a. Vice President George Bush cast the deciding vote for the Republicans.

b. The Senate Budget Resolution (S. Con. Res. 110) was approved by voice vote on June 14, 1990.

c. Although both chambers passed a FY1999 budget resolution, the two different versions were so far apart that Congress never seriously attempted to reconcile the two bills, so that FY1999 was the first year under the Congressional Budget Act that Congress did not pass a budget resolution.

d. The Senate did not pass a FY2003 budget resolution.

Sources: *Congressional Quarterly Almanac* (Washington, D.C.: Congressional Quarterly, various years); *Congressional Quarterly Weekly Report,* various issues.

Table 7-3 Budgeted and Actual Revenues, Budget Authority, Outlays, and Deficits, FY1976–FY2007 (billions of dollars)

Fiscal year	Revenues	Budget authority	Budget outlays	Budget deficit/surplus
1976				
President's budget	297.7	385.8	349.4	–51.7
First budget resolution	298.2	395.8	367.0	–68.8
Second budget resolution	300.8	408.0	374.9	–74.1
Actual	300.0	415.3	366.4	–66.4
1977				
President's budget	351.3	433.4	394.2	–42.9
First budget resolution	362.5	454.2	413.3	–50.8
Second budget resolution	362.5	451.6	413.1	–50.6
Third budget resolution	347.7	472.9	417.5	–69.8
Fourth budget resolution	356.6	470.2	409.2	–52.6
Actual	357.8	464.4	402.7	–44.9
1978				
Ford budget	393.0	480.4	440.0	–47.0
Carter budget	401.6	507.3	459.4	–57.8
First budget resolution	396.3	503.5	461.0	–64.7
Second budget resolution	397.0	500.1	458.3	–61.3
Actual	402.0	500.4	450.8	–48.8
1979				
President's budget	439.6	568.2	500.2	–60.6
First budget resolution	447.9	568.9	498.8	–50.9
Second budget resolution	448.7	555.7	487.5	–38.8
Third budget resolution	461.0	559.2	494.5	–33.5
Actual	465.9	556.7	493.6	–27.7
1980				
President's budget	502.6	615.5	531.6	–29.0
First budget resolution	509.0	604.4	532.0	–23.0
Second budget resolution	517.8	638.0	547.6	–29.8
Third budget resolution	525.7	658.9	572.7	–47.0
Actual	520.0	658.8	579.6	–59.6
1981				
President's budget	600.0	696.1	615.8	–15.8
Revised budget	628.0	691.3	611.5	16.5
First budget resolution	613.8	697.2	613.6	0.2
Second budget resolution	605.0	694.6	632.4	–27.4
Third budget resolution	603.3	717.5	661.4	–58.1
Actual	599.3	718.4	657.2	–57.9
1982				
Carter budget	711.8	809.8	739.3	–27.5
Reagan budget	650.3	772.4	695.3	–45.0
Budget resolution	657.8	770.9	695.5	–37.7
Revised resolution	628.4	777.7	734.1	–105.7
Actual	617.8	779.9	728.4	–110.6
1983				
President's budget	666.1	801.9	757.6	–91.5
Budget resolution	665.9	822.4	769.8	–103.9
Actual	600.6	866.7	796.0	–195.4
1984				
President's budget	659.7	900.1	848.5	–188.8
Budget resolution[a]	679.6	919.5	849.5	–169.9
		928.7	858.9	–858.9
Revised resolution	672.9	918.9	845.6	–172.7
Actual	666.5	949.8	851.8	–185.3

Fiscal year	Revenues	Budget authority	Budget outlays	Budget deficit/surplus
1985				
President's budget	745.1	1,006.5	925.5	–180.4
Budget resolution	750.9	1,021.4	932.1	–181.2
Actual	734.1	1,074.1	946.3	–212.2
1986				
President's budget	793.7	1,060.0	973.7	–180.0
Budget resolution	795.7	1,069.7	967.6	–171.9
Actual	769.1	1,072.8	989.8	–220.7
1987				
President's budget	850.4	1,102.0	994.0	–143.6
Budget resolution	852.4	1,093.4	995.0	–142.6
Actual	854.1	1,099.9	1,003.8	–149.7
1988				
President's budget	916.6	1,142.2	1,024.4	–107.8
Budget resolution	921.6	1,153.2	1,055.5	–133.9
Actual	909.0	1,185.5	1,064.0	–155.0
1989				
President's budget	964.7	1,222.1	1,094.2	–129.5
Budget resolution	964.3	1,232.0	1,098.2	–133.9
Actual	990.7	1,309.9	1,144.1	–153.4
1990				
President's budget	1,059.3	1,331.2	1,151.8	–92.5
Budget resolution	1,065.5	1,350.9	1,165.3	–99.8
Actual	1,031.3	1,368.5	1,251.7	–220.4
1991				
President's budget	1,170.2	1,396.5	1,233.3	–63.1
Budget resolution	1,172.9	1,485.6	1,236.9	–64.0
Actual	1,054.3	1,398.2	1,323.0	–268.7
1992				
President's budget	1,172.2	1,579.3	1,442.2	–270.0
Budget resolution	1,169.2	1,590.1	1,448.0	–278.8
Actual	1,091.7	1,469.2	1,381.9	–290.2
1993				
President's budget	1,171.2	1,516.8	1,503.0	–331.8
Budget resolution	1,173.4	1,516.4	1,500.0	–326.6
Actual	1,153.5	1,473.6	1,408.7	–255.2
1994				
President's budget	1,242.1	1,512.6	1,500.6	–258.5
Budget resolution	1,241.8	1,507.1	1,495.6	–253.8
Actual	1,257.7	1,528.4	1,460.9	–203.2
1995				
President's budget	1,353.8	1,537.0	1,518.9	–165.1[b]
Budget resolution	1,338.2	1,540.7	1,513.6	–175.4
Actual	1,351.8	1,543.3	1,515.7	–163.9
1996				
President's budget	1,415.5	1,613.8	1,612.1	–196.6
Budget resolution	1,417.2	1,591.7	1,587.5	–170.3
Actual	1,453.1	1,581.1	1,560.3	–107.2
1997				
President's budget	1,495.2	1,638.4	1,635.3	–140.1
Budget resolution	1,469.0	1,633.0	1,622.0	–153.0
Actual	1,579.3	1,642.9	1,601.2	–21.9

(continued)

Table 7-3 (continued)

Fiscal year	Revenues	Budget authority	Budget outlays	Budget deficit/surplus
1998				
President's budget	1,566.8	1,709.6	1,687.5	–120.7
Budget resolution	1,602.0	1,703.8	1,692.0	–90.0
Actual	1,721.8	1,692.3	1,652.6	69.2
1999				
President's budget[c]	1,742.7	1,751.0	1,733.2	9.5
Budget resolution[d]	1,318.0	1,408.9	1,401.0	–83.0
Actual	1,827.5	1,766.7	1,702.9	124.6
2000				
President's budget[c]	1,883.0	1,781.1	1,765.7	117.3
Budget resolution	1,408.1	1,426.7	1,408.1	0.0
Actual	2,025.2	1,825.0	1,788.8	236.4
2001				
President's budget	2,136.9	1,893.5	1,835.0	301.9
Budget resolution	1,503.2	1,467.2	1,446.0	57.2
Actual	1,991.2	1,960.0	1,863.0	128.2
2002				
President's budget	2,191.7	2,004.6	1,960.6	231.1
Budget resolution	1,638.2	1,510.9	1,476.8	161.4
Actual	1,853.2	2,090.0	2,011.0	–157.8
2003				
President's budget	1,836.0	2,154.0	2,140.0	–304.0
Budget resolution[e]				
Actual	1,782.3	2,266.1	2,159.9	–377.6
2004				
President's budget	1,922.0	2,243.0	2,229.0	–307.0
Budget Resolution	1,325.5	1,861.0	1,883.8	–558.3
Actual	1,880.3	2,293.0	2,292.2	–411.9
2005				
President's Budget	2,036.0	2,349.0	2,400.0	–364.0
Budget Resolution	1,454.6	2,005.1	1,996.0	–541.4
Actual	2,153.9	2,582.9	2,472.2	–318.3
2006				
President's Budget	2,178.0	2,547.5	2,567.0	–389.0
Budget Resolution	1,589.9	2,144.4	2,161.4	–571.5
Actual	2,407.3	2,841.7	2,655.4	–248.1
2007				
President's Budget	2,416.0	2,739.4	2,770.0	–354.0
Budget Resolution	1,780.7	2,283.0	2,326.0	–545.3
Actual[f]				

a. Larger figures for authority, outlays, and deficit assumed enactment of programs in a reserve fund.
b. This figure assumed enactment of the president's health care reforms.
c. President Clinton indicated in his FY1999 and FY2000 budget proposals that the surplus would be reserved for the Social Security trust fund, pending a legislative solution. Thus, while the budget did not call the remainder a surplus, it is treated as such in this table.
d. Although both chambers passed a FY1999 budget resolution, the two different versions were so far apart that Congress never seriously attempted to reconcile the two bills, so that FY1999 was the first year under the Congressional Budget Act that Congress did not pass a budget resolution. The figures given here are from the version of the bill resolved by the House and received in the Senate.
e. Congress did not pass a FY2003 budget resolution.
f. FY2007 ended on September 30, 2007. Figures not available at time of publication.

Sources: *Congressional Quarterly Almanac* (Washington, D.C.: Congressional Quarterly, various years); *President's Budget, Fiscal Years 2001–2008,* U.S. Government Printing Office (http://www.gpoaccess.gov).

Table 7-4 Relatively Uncontrollable Federal Outlays under Present Law, FY1967–FY2006 (billions of dollars)

Fiscal year	Social security and other retirement	Medical care	Other direct payments to individuals	Net interest	All other uncontrollables	Total uncontrollables	Total outlays	Percent budget uncontrollable
1967	26.3	6.1	10.7	10.3	37.0	90.4	157.5	57.4
1968	29.1	9.0	11.4	11.1	42.3	102.9	178.1	57.8
1969	33.1	10.9	12.9	12.7	41.9	111.5	183.6	60.7
1970	36.9	12.1	15.4	14.4	41.5	120.3	195.6	61.5
1971	44.1	13.5	22.3	14.8	40.2	134.9	210.2	64.2
1972	49.7	16.2	25.8	15.5	39.2	146.4	230.7	63.5
1973	60.6	17.4	18.3	17.3	41.4	155.0	245.7	63.1
1974	69.4	20.4	21.4	21.4	46.0	178.6	269.4	66.3
1975	82.6	25.8	34.3	23.2	53.3	219.2	332.3	66.0
1976	92.6	31.6	43.5	26.7	53.7	248.1	371.8	66.7
1977	106.4	36.6	39.6	29.9	58.8	271.3	409.2	66.3
1978	117.1	41.3	36.9	35.5	76.9	307.7	458.7	67.1
1979	131.1	47.0	46.5	42.6	85.3	352.5	504.0	69.9
1980	150.2	55.3	47.0	52.5	103.2	408.2	590.9	69.1
1981	176.3	66.0	51.5	68.8	108.6	471.2	678.2	69.5
1982	195.9	74.0	53.2	85.0	121.5	529.6	745.7	71.0
1983	212.8	81.2	61.2	89.8	128.7	573.7	808.4	71.0
1984	221.7	88.0	49.2	111.1	145.3	615.3	851.9	72.2
1985	232.9	99.4	49.7	129.5	162.2	673.7	946.4	71.2
1986	245.5	106.1	52.0	136.0	181.3	720.9	990.4	72.8
1987	256.7	115.1	52.1	138.6	185.2	747.7	1,004.1	74.5
1988	271.6	123.4	53.7	151.8	186.8	787.3	1,064.5	74.0
1989	287.4	133.4	52.3	169.0	210.4	852.5	1,143.8	74.5
1990	305.8	155.8	57.4	184.3	231.6	934.9	1,253.1	74.6
1991	330.1	175.7	69.9	194.4	233.8	1,003.9	1,324.3	75.8
1992	350.7	208.5	84.7	199.3	233.8	1,077.0	1,381.6	78.0
1993	369.0	230.0	87.8	198.7	236.7	1,122.2	1,409.5	79.6
1994	387.8	251.9	75.0	202.9	228.2	1,145.8	1,461.9	78.4
1995	406.8	275.3	77.9	232.1	233.2	1,225.3	1,515.9	80.8
1996	423.0	293.6	76.9	241.1	227.9	1,262.5	1,560.6	80.9
1997	441.5	313.9	75.9	244.0	228.8	1,304.1	1,601.3	81.4
1998	457.3	324.3	77.0	241.1	228.0	1,327.7	1,652.7	80.3
1999	467.0	331.5	79.9	229.7	240.2	1,348.3	1,702.0	79.2
2000	491.8	351.6	76.8	222.9	253.6	1,396.8	1,789.2	78.1
2001	519.7	389.7	87.4	206.2	292.6	1,495.6	1,863.2	80.3
2002	545.1	427.4	123.8	170.9	312.5	1,579.8	2,011.2	78.5
2003	566.9	469.0	139.6	153.1	345.2	1,673.8	2,160.1	77.5
2004	590.9	509.5	132.9	160.2	368.5	1,762.1	2,293.0	76.8
2005	623.6	549.3	133.0	184.0	392.3	1,882.1	2,472.2	76.1
2006	651.4	582.6	148.2	226.6	425.0	2,033.8	2,655.4	76.6

Note: Occasionally, the Office of Management and Budget reclassifies or redefines uncontrollables. Thus, the figures in this table may not be consistent with those published in some budget documents.

Source: *President's Budget, Fiscal Year 2008, Historical Tables,* U.S. Government Printing Office (http://www.gpoaccess.gov).

Table 7-5 Supplemental Appropriations, FY1970–FY2006

Fiscal year	Number of supplemental bills[a]	Amount of budget authority (millions of dollars)	Fiscal year	Number of supplemental bills[a]	Amount of budget authority (millions of dollars)
1970	2	5,993	1989	4	5,663
1971	4	9,870	1990	2	6,374
1972	7	11,599	1991	3	48,472
1973	5	11,371	1992	3	20,815
1974	5	14,796	1993	4[b]	9,519
1975	7	27,587	1994	7	13,613
1976	7	24,638	1995	0	—[c]
1977	11	49,835	1996	4	903
1978	10	16,052	1997	1	9,163
1979	3	13,845	1998	1	6,006
1980	6	19,683	1999	2	13,367
1981	2	21,217	2000	2	17,387
1982	4	27,100	2001	2	28,979
1983	2	22,732	2002	2	46,554
1984	4	16,682	2003	3	81,110
1985	3	15,545	2004	3[d]	99,858
1986	3	15,245	2005	6[e]	177,190
1987	2	9,970	2006	3	128,456
1988	3	1,322			

a. The number of supplemental bills includes all appropriations bills in which supplemental budget authority was provided.
b. Excludes $4 billion in mandatory supplemental approriations for unemployment insurance because that additional funding was offset by the same amount of mandatory offsetting receipts.
c. All FY1995 supplemental spending was offset.
d. Includes $10.275 billion from Public Law 108-324, enacted on October 13, 2004, but retroactive to FY2004.
e. Includes Public Law 108-287, enacted on August 5, 2004. The President requested the funds for FY2005.
Source: Congressional Budget Office (http://www.cbo.gov).

Table 7-6 Continuing Appropriations, FY1977–FY2007

Fiscal year	Regular appropriation bills enacted by start of fiscal year[a]	Continuing resolutions enacted for fiscal year	Fiscal year	Regular appropriation bills enacted by start of fiscal year[a]	Continuing resolutions enacted for fiscal year
1977	13	2[b]	1993	1	1
1978	9	3	1994	2	3
1979	5	1	1995	13	0
1980	3	2	1996	0	13
1981	1	2	1997	8[d]	0
1982	0	4	1998	1	6
1983	1	2	1999	1	6
1984	4	2	2000	4	7
1985	4	5	2001	2	21
1986	0	5	2002	0	8
1987	0	5	2003	0	8
1988	0	5	2004	3	5
1989	13[c]	0	2005	1	3
1990	1	3	2006	2	3
1991	0	5	2007[e]	1	4
1992	3	4			

a. There are 13 regular appropriations bills.
b. Although all 13 regular appropriations became law before the start of FY1977, the 2 CRs provided funding for activities that had not been included in the regular appropriation acts.
c. Congress cleared and sent all bills to the president by the beginning of FY1989, but he did not sign all the bills until the following day.
d. All of the appropriations bills were enacted by the beginning of FY1997, but not as 13 separate acts.
e. As of May 1, 2007.
Sources: Sandy Streeter, "Continuing Appropriations Acts: Brief Overview of Recent Practices," *Congressional Research Service*, 30 November 2004; Status of Appropriations Legislation for Fiscal Year 2005 (http://thomas.loc.gov/home/approp/app05.html); Status of Appropriations Legislation for Fiscal Year 2006 (http://thomas.loc.gov/home/approp/app06.html); Status of Appropriations Legislation for Fiscal Year 2007 (http://thomas.loc.gov/home/approp/app07.html).

Table 7-7 Budget-Related Roll Call Votes in the House, Selected Years, 1955–2006

Measure	1955	1960	1965	1970	1975	1980	1981	1983	1985	1987	1989	1990	1991	1992	1993	1994	1995	1996	1997	1998	1999	2000	2001	2002	2003	2004	2005	2006
Authorizations	27	28	78	77	147	105	70	129	95	118	68	116	83	38	94	94	57	40	82	51	39	37	44	31	47	17	48	22
Appropriations	6	16	21	39	94	111	85	112	82	86	95	110	101	129	176	121	294	146	147	119	153	165	127	61	155	127	171	49
Tax legislation	3	3	3	1	48	14	7	9	11	0	0	0	11	21	6	6	20	18	9	15	10	48	25	26	73	28	11	13
Budget resolutions	0	0	0	0	12	30	13	4	10	8	7	8	9	10	8	9	23	8	10	4	15	12	11	5	9	13	12	7
Reconciliation bills	0	0	0	0	0	6	12	2	10	6	14	5	0	0	9	0	9	8	12	0	0	0	6	0	0	0	4	13
Debt ceilings	1	2	2	2	11	7	2	3	11	7	3	6	0	0	0	1	13	10	0	0	0	0	0	2	0	3	0	0
Miscellaneous	0	1	0	2	8	4	7	3	1	2	0	8	4	16	12	34	65	11	9	23	13	16	9	2	14	8	0	47
Total budget-related roll calls	37	50	104	121	320	277	196	262	220	227	187	253	208	214	305	265	481	241	269	212	230	278	222	127	298	196	246	151
Total roll calls	147	206	383	459	828	681	371	533	482	511	379	536	444	488	615	507	885	455	640	547	611	603	512	484	677	544	671	541
Percentage budget-related	25.2	24.3	27.2	26.4	38.6	40.7	52.8	49.2	45.6	44.4	49.3	47.2	46.8	43.9	49.6	52.3	54.4	53.0	42.0	38.8	37.6	46.1	43.4	26.2	44.0	36.0	36.7	27.9

Source: *Congressional Quarterly Roll Call Vote Index.*

Table 7-8 Budget-Related Roll Call Votes in the Senate, Selected Years, 1955–2006

Measure	1955	1960	1965	1970	1975	1980	1981	1983	1985	1987	1989	1990	1991	1992	1993	1994	1995	1996	1997	1998	1999	2000	2001	2002	2003	2004	2005	2006
Authorizations	22	48	87	83	96	82	55	58	67	84	42	81	73	20	27	68	38	33	33	38	18	26	55	5	10	9	8	2
Appropriations	12	28	27	77	87	128	130	107	59	66	75	58	66	64	114	108	113	80	82	81	83	89	76	12	129	11	116	10
Tax legislation	2	10	10	6	48	10	56	13	7	0	5	0	5	41	27	3	27	10	18	37	9	47	10	8	52	24	12	10
Budget resolutions	0	0	0	0	8	50	26	34	39	17	8	1	12	14	46	15	56	42	22	34	12	31	23	1	13	11	38	11
Reconciliation bills	0	0	0	0	0	4	63	2	23	8	2	6	0	0	6	0	48	31	51	0	0	0	55	0	0	0	33	15
Debt ceilings	0	2	1	3	3	6	12	15	29	17	0	1	0	0	0	0	4	2	0	0	0	0	0	1	0	2	0	1
Miscellaneous	1	0	0	1	4	3	2	9	6	3	6	10	3	9	16	9	58	15	3	6	10	13	6	0	30	11	0	21
Total budget-related roll calls	37	88	125	170	246	283	344	238	230	195	138	157	159	148	236	203	344	213	209	196	132	206	225	27	234	68	207	70
Total roll calls	88	207	259	422	611	546	497	381	381	420	312	326	280	270	395	329	613	306	298	314	374	298	380	253	459	216	366	279
Percentage budget-related	42.0	42.5	48.3	40.3	40.3	51.8	69.2	62.5	60.4	46.4	44.2	48.2	56.8	54.8	59.7	61.7	56.1	69.6	70.1	62.4	35.3	69.1	59.2	10.7	51.0	31.5	56.6	25.1

Source: *Congressional Quarterly Roll Call Vote Index.*

8

Voting Alignments

Table 8-1 Presidential Victories on Votes in Congress, 1953–2007

President and year	House and Senate (%)	House (%)	No. of votes	Senate (%)	No. of votes
Eisenhower					
1953	89.2	91.2	34	87.8	49
1954	78.3	n.a.	n.a.	n.a.	n.a.
1955	75.3	63.4	41	84.6	52
1956	69.7	73.5	34	67.7	65
1957	68.4	58.3	60	78.9	57
1958	75.7	74.0	50	76.5	98
1959	52.0	55.5	54	50.4	121
1960	65.1	65.0	43	65.1	86
Average	71.7				
Kennedy					
1961	81.4	83.1	65	80.6	124
1962	85.4	85.0	60	85.6	125
1963	87.1	83.1	71	89.6	115
Average	84.6				
Johnson					
1964	87.9	88.5	52	87.6	97
1965	93.1	93.8	112	92.6	162
1966	78.9	91.3	103	68.8	125
1967	78.8	75.6	127	81.2	165
1968	74.5	83.5	103	68.9	164
Average	82.6				
Nixon					
1969	73.9	72.3	47	76.4	72
1970	76.9	84.6	65	71.4	91
1971	74.8	82.5	57	69.5	82
1972	66.3	81.1	37	54.3	46
1973	50.6	48.0	125	52.4	185
1974	59.6	67.9	53	54.2	83
Average	67.0				
Ford					
1974	58.2	59.3	54	57.4	68
1975	61.0	50.6	89	71.0	93
1976	53.8	43.1	51	64.2	53
Average	57.7				
Carter					
1977	75.4	74.7	79	76.1	88
1978	78.3	69.6	112	84.8	151
1979	76.8	71.7	145	81.4	161
1980	75.1	76.9	117	73.3	116
Average	76.4				

President and year	House and Senate (%)	House (%)	No. of votes	Senate (%)	No. of votes
Reagan					
1981	82.4	72.4	76	88.3	128
1982	72.4	55.8	77	83.2	119
1983	67.1	47.6	82	85.9	85
1984	65.8	52.2	113	85.7	77
1985	59.9	45.0	80	71.6	102
1986	56.1	34.1	88	81.2	80
1987	43.5	33.3	99	56.4	78
1988	47.4	32.7	104	64.8	88
Average	61.8				
Bush					
1989	62.6	50.0	86	73.3	101
1990	46.8	32.4	108	63.4	93
1991	54.2	43.0	111	69.0	81
1992	43.0	37.0	105	53.0	60
Average	51.7				
Clinton					
1993	86.4	87.2	102	85.4	89
1994	86.4	87.2	78	85.5	62
1995	36.2	26.3	133	49.0	102
1996	55.1	53.2	79	57.6	59
1997	53.6	38.7	75	71.4	63
1998	50.6	36.6	82	67.0	72
1999	37.8	35.4	82	42.2	45
2000	55.0	49.3	69	65.0	40
Average	57.6				
Bush					
2001	86.7	83.7	43	88.3	77
2002	87.8	82.5	40	91.4	58
2003	78.7	87.3	48	74.8	89
2004	72.6	70.6	24	74.0	37
2005	78.0	78.3	46	77.8	45
2006	80.9	85.0	40	78.6	70
2007	38.3	15.4	18	66.0	64
Average	74.7				

n.a. = not available

Notes: Percentages indicate the number of congressional votes supporting the president divided by the total number of votes on which the president had taken a clear position. The percentages are normalized to eliminate the effects of absences as follows: support = (votes in favor)/(votes in favor + votes against).

Source: *Congressional Quarterly Weekly Report*, various issues.

Table 8-2 Congressional Voting in Support of the President's Position, 1954–2007 (percent)

	House			Senate		
President and year	All Democrats	Southern Democrats	Republicans	All Democrats	Southern Democrats	Republicans
Eisenhower						
1954	54	n.a.	n.a.	45	n.a.	82
1955	58	n.a.	67	65	n.a.	85
1956	58	n.a.	79	44	n.a.	80
1957	54	n.a.	60	60	n.a.	80
1958	63	n.a.	65	51	n.a.	77
1959	44	n.a.	76	44	n.a.	80
1960	49	n.a.	63	52	n.a.	76
Kennedy						
1961	81	n.a.	41	73	n.a.	42
1962	83	71	47	76	63	48
1963	84	71	36	77	65	52
Johnson						
1964	84	70	42	73	63	52
1965	83	65	46	75	60	55
1966	81	64	45	71	59	53
1967	80	65	51	73	69	63
1968	77	63	59	64	50	57
Nixon						
1969	56	55	65	55	56	74
1970	64	64	79	56	62	74
1971	53	69	79	48	59	76
1972	56	59	74	52	71	77
1973	39	49	67	42	55	70
1974	52	64	71	44	60	65
Ford						
1974	48	52	59	45	55	67
1975	40	48	67	53	67	76
1976	36	52	70	47	61	73
Carter						
1977	69	58	46	77	71	58
1978	67	54	40	74	61	47
1979	70	58	37	75	66	51
1980	71	63	44	71	69	50

	House			Senate		
President and year	All Democrats	Southern Democrats	Republicans	All Democrats	Southern Democrats	Republicans
Reagan						
1981	46	60	72	52	63	84
1982	43	55	70	46	57	77
1983	30	45	74	45	46	77
1984	37	47	64	45	58	81
1985	31	43	69	36	46	80
1986	26	37	69	39	56	90
1987	26	36	64	38	42	67
1988	27	34	61	51	58	73
Bush						
1989	38	49	72	56	66	84
1990	26	35	65	39	49	72
1991	35	43	74	42	53	83
1992	27	38	75	33	41	75
Clinton						
1993	80	81	39	87	84	30
1994	78	68	49	88	88	44
1995	75	69	22	81	78	29
1996	74	70	38	83	75	37
1997	73	68	31	87	84	61
1998	78	72	27	86	84	42
1999	75	70	24	86	84	35
2000	76	68	28	92	88	47
Bush						
2001	32	38	92	67	71	96
2002	33	40	85	73	81	95
2003	27	36	92	52	60	96
2004	31	42	83	63	70	93
2005	24	33	81	38	54	86
2006	31	45	85	51	62	85
2007	7	11	72	37	43	78

n.a.= not available

Note: Percentages indicate the number of congressional votes supporting the president divided by the total number of votes on which the president had taken a clear position. The percentages are normalized to eliminate the effects of absences as follows: support = (votes in favor)/(votes in favor + votes against).

Source: *Congressional Quarterly Weekly Report,* various issues.

Table 8-3 Party Unity Votes in Congress, 1953–2007 (percentage of all votes)

Year	House	Senate	Year	House	Senate
1953	52.1	51.7	1981	37.4	47.8
1954	38.2	48.0	1982	36.4	43.4
1955	40.8	29.9	1983	55.6	43.7
1956	43.8	53.1	1984	47.1	40.0
1957	59.0	35.5	1985	61.0	49.6
1958	39.8	43.5	1986	56.5	52.3
1959	55.2	47.9	1987	63.7	40.7
1960	52.7	36.7	1988	47.0	42.5
1961	50.0	62.3	1989	56.3	35.3
1962	46.0	41.1	1990	49.1	54.3
1963	48.7	47.2	1991	55.1	49.3
1964	54.9	35.7	1992	64.5	53.0
1965	52.2	41.9	1993	65.5	67.1
1966	41.5	50.2	1994	61.8	51.7
1967	36.3	34.6	1995	73.2	68.8
1968	35.2	32.0	1996	56.4	62.4
1969	31.1	36.3	1997	50.4	50.3
1970	27.1	35.2	1998	55.5	55.7
1971	37.8	41.6	1999	47.3	62.8
1972	27.1	36.5	2000	43.2	48.7
1973	41.8	29.9	2001	40.2	55.3
1974	29.4	44.3	2002	43.3	45.5
1975	48.4	47.8	2003	51.7	66.7
1976	35.9	37.2	2004	47.0	52.3
1977	42.2	42.4	2005	49.0	62.6
1978	33.2	45.2	2006	54.5	57.3
1979	47.3	46.7	2007	62.0	60.0
1980	37.6	45.8			

Note: Data indicate the percentage of all roll call votes on which a majority of voting Democrats opposed a majority of voting Republicans.

Source: *Congressional Quarterly Weekly Report*, various issues.

Table 8-4 Party Unity Scores in Congressional Voting, 1954–2007 (percent)

	House			Senate		
Year	All Democrats	Southern Democrats	Republicans	All Democrats	Southern Democrats	Republicans
1954	80	n.a.	84	77	n.a.	89
1955	84	68	78	82	78	82
1956	80	79	78	80	75	80
1957	79	71	75	79	81	81
1958	77	67	73	82	76	74
1959	85	77	85	76	63	80
1960	75	62	77	73	60	74
1961	n.a.	n.a.	n.a.	n.a.	n.a.	n.a.
1962	81	n.a.	80	80	n.a.	81
1963	85	n.a.	84	79	n.a.	79
1964	82	n.a.	81	73	n.a.	75
1965	80	55	81	75	55	78
1966	78	55	82	73	52	78
1967	77	53	82	75	59	73
1968	73	48	76	71	57	74
1969	71	47	71	74	53	72
1970	71	52	72	71	49	71
1971	72	48	76	74	56	75
1972	70	44	76	72	43	73
1973	75	55	74	79	52	74
1974	72	51	71	72	41	68
1975	75	53	78	76	48	71
1976	75	52	75	74	46	72
1977	74	55	77	72	48	75
1978	71	53	77	75	54	66
1979	75	60	79	76	62	73
1980	78	64	79	76	64	74
1981	75	57	80	77	64	85
1982	77	62	76	76	62	80
1983	82	67	80	76	70	79
1984	81	68	77	75	61	83
1985	86	76	80	79	68	81
1986	86	76	76	74	59	80
1987	88	78	79	85	80	78
1988	88	81	80	85	78	74
1989	86	77	76	79	69	79
1990	86	78	78	82	75	77
1991	86	78	81	83	73	83
1992	86	79	84	82	70	83
1993	89	83	87	87	78	86
1994	88	83	87	86	77	81
1995	84	75	93	84	76	91
1996	84	76	90	86	75	91
1997	85	79	91	86	76	88
1998	86	79	89	90	85	88
1999	86	77	88	91	86	90
2000	86	80	90	90	80	91
2001	86	77	94	90	79	90
2002	90	82	93	85	69	88
2003	91	85	95	89	76	95
2004	91	83	93	88	76	93
2005	91	84	93	90	81	90
2006	86	77	88	86	79	86
2007	92	90	85	87	83	81

n.a. = not available

Note: Data show the percentage of members voting with a majority of their party on party unity votes. Party unity votes are those roll calls on which a majority of a party votes on one side of the issue and a majority of the other party votes on the other side. The percentages are normalized to eliminate the effects of absences as follows: party unity = (votes in support)/(votes in support + votes in opposition).

Source: *Congressional Quarterly Weekly Report*, various issues.

Table 8-5 Conservative Coalition Votes and Victories in Congress, 1957–2000 (percent)

	House		Senate	
Year	Votes	Victories	Votes	Victories
1957	16	81	11	100
1958	15	64	19	86
1959	13	91	19	65
1960	20	35	22	67
1961	30	74	32	48
1962	13	44	15	71
1963	13	67	19	44
1964	11	67	17	47
1965	25	25	24	39
1966	19	32	30	51
1967	22	73	18	54
1968	22	63	25	80
1969	25	71	28	67
1970	17	70	26	64
1971	31	79	28	86
1972	25	79	29	63
1973	25	67	21	54
1974	22	67	30	54
1975	28	52	28	48
1976	17	59	26	58
1977	22	60	29	74
1978	20	57	23	46
1979	21	73	18	65
1980	16	67	20	75
1981	21	88	21	95
1982	16	78	20	90
1983	18	71	12	89
1984	14	75	17	94
1985	13	84	16	93
1986	11	78	20	93
1987	9	88	8	100
1988	8	82	10	97
1989	11	80	12	95
1990	10	74	11	95
1991	9	86	14	95
1992	10	88	14	87
1993	7	98	10	90
1994	7	92	10	72
1995	13	100	9	95
1996	11	100	12	97
1997	9	100	8	92
1998	8	95	3	100
2000	4	41	4	31

* *Congressional Quarterly* stopped compiling these data after 2000. The ideological scores developed by Keith Poole and Howard Rosenthal (voteview.com) are used in tables 8-7, 8-8, 8-9, and 8-10.

Note: "Votes" is the percentage of all roll call votes on which a majority of voting southern Democrats and a majority of voting Republicans—the conservative coalition—opposed the stand taken by a majority of voting northern Democrats. "Victories" is the percentage of conservative coalition votes won by the coalition.

Sources: *Congressional Quarterly Almanac* (Washington, D.C.: Congressional Quarterly, various years); *Congressional Quarterly Weekly Report*, various issues.

Table 8-6 Votes in Support of the Conservative Coalition, 1959–2000 (percent)

	House			Senate		
Year	Northern Democrats	Southern Democrats	Republicans	Northern Democrats	Southern Democrats	Republicans
1959	17	85	87	23	69	80
1960	8	66	77	21	77	74
1961	15	69	83	15	74	75
1962	14	65	75	29	77	79
1963	13	70	78	20	73	76
1964	13	72	76	20	78	72
1965	10	69	81	19	71	81
1966	13	69	82	17	75	80
1967	15	75	81	24	76	72
1968	16	77	75	31	77	74
1969	21	79	75	24	77	73
1970	19	79	78	21	74	72
1971	25	76	80	38	80	79
1972	24	75	79	20	78	74
1973	22	69	77	17	74	76
1974	24	72	69	19	79	69
1975	22	69	81	19	79	69
1976	25	72	80	21	73	76
1977	25	68	82	26	75	80
1978	26	68	79	24	70	69
1979	29	70	85	29	75	74
1980	27	69	81	26	72	74
1981	30	75	82	29	76	84
1982	27	73	81	30	76	81
1983	22	68	81	30	69	81
1984	23	68	84	27	74	85
1985	23	67	84	30	72	82
1986	27	70	83	26	70	83
1987	27	71	87	30	70	79
1988	27	67	88	29	72	80
1989	27	68	87	31	69	84
1990	27	69	85	29	70	83
1991	30	69	90	33	71	84
1992	31	67	87	27	67	79
1993	31	63	87	31	70	84
1994	39	58	89	30	69	81
1995	28	57	90	24	68	87
1996	31	63	85	30	66	88
1997	34	65	90	32	73	88
1998	32	63	90	36	76	87
2000	49	45	49	31	58	70

* *Congressional Quarterly* stopped compiling this data after 2000. The ideological scores developed by Keith Poole and Howard Rosenthal (voteview.com) are used in tables 8-7, 8-8, 8-9, and 8-10.

Note: Data indicate the percentage of conservative coalition votes on which members voted in agreement with the position of the conservative coalition. Conservative coalition votes are those on which a majority of northern Democrats voted against a majority of southern Democrats and Republicans—the conservative coalition. The percentages are normalized to eliminate the effects of not voting as follows: conservative coalition support = (votes in favor)/(votes in favor + votes against).

Sources: *Congressional Quarterly Almanac* (Washington, D.C.: Congressional Quarterly, various years); *Congressional Quarterly Weekly Report*, various issues.

Table 8-7 Average Ideological Positions of House Committees, 80th–108th Congresses

Committee		80th 1947	81st 1949	82nd 1951	83rd 1953	84th 1955	85th 1957	86th 1959	87th 1961	88th 1963	89th 1965	90th 1967	91st 1969
Agriculture	All members	0.188	0.034	0.092	0.166	0.077	0.079	0.030	0.065	0.049	–0.002	0.121	0.102
	Democrats	–0.084	–0.123	–0.071	–0.031	–0.141	–0.140	–0.134	–0.124	–0.158	–0.161	–0.034	–0.060
	Republicans	0.375	0.301	0.304	0.338	0.352	0.357	0.315	0.348	0.361	0.345	0.327	0.297
Appropriations	All members	0.144	0.019	0.025	0.164	0.012	0.029	0.019	0.011	–0.004	–0.062	–0.012	–0.028
	Democrats	–0.170	–0.196	–0.206	–0.162	–0.217	–0.195	–0.201	–0.210	–0.218	–0.225	–0.211	–0.218
	Republicans	0.370	0.342	0.371	0.382	0.356	0.352	0.348	0.330	0.316	0.286	0.288	0.273
Armed Services	All members	0.131	0.019	0.050	0.098	0.020	0.014	–0.018	0.024	0.045	–0.030	0.021	0.039
	Democrats	–0.105	–0.189	–0.172	–0.132	–0.169	–0.172	–0.185	–0.153	–0.148	–0.178	–0.167	–0.145
	Republicans	0.306	0.323	0.313	0.305	0.243	0.232	0.256	0.257	0.285	0.278	0.274	0.304
Budget	All members	n.a.	n.a.	n.a.	n.a.	n.a.	n.a.	n.a.	n.a.	n.a.	n.a.	n.a.	n.a.
	Democrats	n.a.	n.a.	n.a.	n.a.	n.a.	n.a.	n.a.	n.a.	n.a.	n.a.	n.a.	n.a.
	Republicans	n.a.	n.a.	n.a.	n.a.	n.a.	n.a.	n.a.	n.a.	n.a.	n.a.	n.a.	n.a.
District of Columbia	All members	0.125	0.024	0.055	0.075	0.034	0.029	–0.005	0.010	–0.004	–0.048	–0.012	0.000
	Democrats	–0.119	–0.166	–0.129	–0.129	–0.136	–0.142	–0.158	–0.095	–0.134	–0.159	–0.161	–0.160
	Republicans	0.317	0.308	0.271	0.264	0.250	0.246	0.269	0.167	0.191	0.188	0.177	0.202
Education and the Workforce	All members	0.123	–0.088	0.016	0.014	–0.083	–0.112	–0.151	–0.066	–0.113	–0.189	–0.125	–0.126
	Democrats	–0.305	–0.345	–0.280	–0.365	–0.441	–0.440	–0.400	–0.354	–0.397	–0.415	–0.427	–0.459
	Republicans	0.408	0.369	0.393	0.365	0.386	0.317	0.348	0.390	0.338	0.285	0.285	0.318
Energy and Commerce	All members	0.065	–0.087	0.000	0.042	–0.001	0.028	–0.006	–0.003	–0.021	–0.065	–0.021	–0.043
	Democrats	–0.235	–0.321	–0.226	–0.244	–0.211	–0.179	–0.176	–0.181	–0.201	–0.224	–0.249	–0.284
	Republicans	0.271	0.253	0.260	0.261	0.254	0.277	0.292	0.270	0.255	0.284	0.288	0.272
Financial Services	All members	0.106	–0.061	–0.027	0.010	–0.051	–0.058	–0.139	–0.119	–0.124	–0.149	–0.105	–0.073
	Democrats	–0.270	–0.366	–0.325	–0.374	–0.354	–0.356	–0.366	–0.369	–0.369	–0.327	–0.354	–0.292
	Republicans	0.365	0.382	0.321	0.342	0.344	0.332	0.253	0.255	0.215	0.206	0.233	0.218
Government Reform and Oversight	All members	0.123	–0.156	–0.036	0.003	–0.035	–0.025	–0.082	–0.088	–0.129	–0.151	–0.113	–0.147
	Democrats	–0.248	–0.380	–0.310	–0.366	–0.342	–0.310	–0.296	–0.294	–0.337	–0.352	–0.338	–0.360
	Republicans	0.355	0.420	0.362	0.325	0.367	0.347	0.288	0.269	0.200	0.268	0.185	0.156
House Oversight	All members	0.172	–0.097	–0.012	0.106	0.004	0.016	–0.014	0.025	0.013	–0.042	0.048	–0.027
	Democrats	–0.062	–0.183	–0.179	–0.182	–0.196	–0.189	–0.183	–0.193	–0.170	–0.220	–0.155	–0.281
	Republicans	0.356	0.340	0.300	0.312	0.258	0.277	0.286	0.353	0.288	0.337	0.306	0.295
International Relations	All members	–0.032	–0.071	–0.053	0.019	0.015	–0.019	–0.152	–0.110	–0.066	–0.126	–0.072	–0.072
	Democrats	–0.320	–0.297	–0.279	–0.236	–0.199	–0.261	–0.353	–0.294	–0.308	–0.340	–0.346	–0.381
	Republicans	0.213	0.196	0.212	0.227	0.257	0.256	0.230	0.172	0.306	0.302	0.310	0.310
Judiciary	All members	0.080	–0.006	0.028	0.072	0.008	0.005	–0.048	–0.005	–0.038	–0.115	–0.059	–0.093
	Democrats	–0.208	–0.190	–0.176	–0.159	–0.198	–0.196	–0.222	–0.198	–0.233	–0.278	–0.277	–0.347
	Republicans	0.310	0.306	0.316	0.260	0.272	0.262	0.283	0.271	0.240	0.239	0.232	0.245
Merchant Marine and Fisheries	All members	0.039	–0.011	–0.020	0.031	–0.049	–0.008	–0.039	–0.019	–0.052	–0.105	–0.058	–0.049
	Democrats	–0.256	–0.199	–0.251	–0.194	–0.296	–0.233	–0.242	–0.236	–0.221	–0.253	–0.282	–0.259
	Republicans	0.272	0.271	0.267	0.255	0.256	0.264	0.332	0.324	0.217	0.207	0.227	0.227
Post Office and Civil Service	All members	0.135	–0.018	–0.009	0.101	0.060	0.037	–0.020	0.088	0.026	–0.086	–0.045	–0.047
	Democrats	–0.145	–0.204	–0.249	–0.111	–0.170	–0.206	–0.258	–0.143	–0.284	–0.301	–0.312	–0.331
	Republicans	0.322	0.261	0.263	0.281	0.352	0.348	0.363	0.382	0.393	0.371	0.318	0.340
Resources	All members	0.107	0.020	0.041	0.119	–0.012	–0.006	–0.060	–0.007	0.001	–0.070	–0.069	–0.060
	Democrats	–0.181	–0.172	–0.231	–0.113	–0.293	–0.281	–0.293	–0.218	–0.232	–0.253	–0.318	–0.326
	Republicans	0.300	0.289	0.381	0.317	0.334	0.328	0.290	0.285	0.318	0.295	0.269	0.301
Rules	All members	0.245	0.002	0.002	0.190	–0.028	–0.049	–0.004	–0.040	–0.023	–0.047	–0.088	–0.088
	Democrats	–0.121	–0.168	–0.176	–0.046	–0.222	–0.221	–0.220	–0.247	–0.246	–0.250	–0.308	–0.303
	Republicans	0.429	0.341	0.357	0.308	0.359	0.295	0.429	0.478	0.424	0.359	0.351	0.342

92nd 1971	93rd 1973	94th 1975	95th 1977	96th 1979	97th 1981	98th 1983	99th 1985	100th 1987	101st 1989	102nd 1991	103rd 1993	104th 1995	105th 1997	106th 1999	107th 2001	108th 2003
–0.034	0.033	–0.085	–0.065	–0.040	0.019	0.008	–0.002	0.008	0.020	0.027	0.052	0.121	0.155	0.141	0.165	0.152
–0.150	–0.190	–0.248	–0.228	–0.213	–0.211	–0.187	–0.211	–0.211	–0.196	–0.210	–0.237	–0.305	–0.251	–0.239	–0.257	–0.243
0.323	0.311	0.267	0.260	0.271	0.309	0.333	0.318	0.343	0.362	0.403	0.438	0.468	0.471	0.464	0.462	0.473
–0.048	–0.058	–0.114	–0.126	–0.145	–0.102	–0.128	–0.122	–0.113	–0.118	–0.120	–0.101	0.038	0.028	0.035	0.052	0.047
–0.255	–0.270	–0.289	–0.307	–0.337	–0.340	–0.346	–0.361	–0.360	–0.364	–0.373	–0.386	–0.404	–0.428	–0.410	–0.412	–0.395
0.277	0.274	0.247	0.247	0.238	0.254	0.247	0.258	0.279	0.275	0.306	0.344	0.365	0.388	0.389	0.403	0.403
0.040	0.064	0.005	0.010	0.024	0.068	0.081	0.064	0.035	0.022	0.003	0.025	0.137	0.168	0.119	0.114	0.144
–0.125	–0.148	–0.139	–0.129	–0.117	–0.094	–0.127	–0.153	–0.182	–0.209	–0.231	–0.229	–0.261	–0.281	–0.303	–0.324	–0.289
0.298	0.331	0.291	0.299	0.278	0.292	0.411	0.372	0.371	0.353	0.370	0.395	0.456	0.466	0.462	0.470	0.485
n.a.	–0.096	–0.105	–0.138	–0.150	–0.015	–0.077	–0.036	–0.047	–0.058	–0.074	–0.083	0.094	0.094	0.096	0.130	0.127
n.a.	–0.380	–0.322	–0.368	–0.378	–0.303	–0.339	–0.325	–0.338	–0.326	–0.316	–0.323	–0.356	–0.360	–0.375	–0.413	–0.381
n.a.	0.347	0.358	0.352	0.335	0.394	0.400	0.408	0.388	0.345	0.324	0.346	0.446	0.466	0.484	0.500	0.529
–0.012	–0.059	–0.189	–0.179	–0.164	–0.278	–0.254	–0.241	–0.237	–0.211	–0.205	–0.161	n.a.	n.a.	n.a.	n.a.	n.a.
–0.180	–0.380	–0.288	–0.295	–0.397	–0.520	–0.539	–0.540	–0.531	–0.579	–0.577	–0.553	n.a.	n.a.	n.a.	n.a.	n.a.
0.241	0.321	0.036	0.037	0.209	0.206	0.245	0.282	0.279	0.433	0.446	0.427	n.a.	n.a.	n.a.	n.a.	n.a.
–0.140	–0.112	–0.197	–0.173	–0.153	–0.101	–0.161	–0.090	–0.114	–0.155	–0.164	–0.119	0.027	0.022	0.071	0.038	0.052
–0.429	–0.436	–0.393	–0.381	–0.403	–0.405	–0.400	–0.414	–0.377	–0.437	–0.454	–0.426	–0.456	–0.447	–0.455	–0.460	–0.465
0.285	0.320	0.228	0.242	0.327	0.312	0.295	0.327	0.312	0.321	0.350	0.400	0.404	0.467	0.496	0.459	0.459
–0.028	–0.029	–0.114	–0.120	–0.069	–0.021	–0.031	–0.045	–0.019	–0.026	–0.048	–0.044	0.071	0.069	0.067	0.080	0.074
–0.289	–0.285	–0.305	–0.310	–0.300	–0.289	–0.296	–0.303	–0.303	–0.307	–0.306	–0.324	–0.344	–0.380	–0.386	–0.399	–0.396
0.335	0.294	0.270	0.273	0.331	0.323	0.360	0.373	0.399	0.402	0.418	0.402	0.419	0.432	0.442	0.447	0.452
–0.085	–0.118	–0.122	–0.128	–0.080	–0.052	–0.041	–0.058	–0.045	–0.055	–0.061	–0.110	–0.004	–0.009	0.027	0.091	0.072
–0.331	–0.401	–0.341	–0.301	–0.307	–0.324	–0.299	–0.298	–0.289	–0.321	–0.311	–0.413	–0.462	–0.477	–0.430	–0.454	–0.393
0.277	0.273	0.318	0.229	0.304	0.311	0.360	0.314	0.320	0.344	0.373	0.365	0.390	0.412	0.432	0.445	0.479
–0.142	–0.118	–0.180	–0.144	–0.105	–0.050	–0.139	–0.046	–0.084	–0.103	–0.121	–0.139	0.029	0.091	0.023	–0.019	0.036
–0.382	–0.384	–0.374	–0.349	–0.324	–0.317	–0.343	–0.366	–0.358	–0.396	–0.355	–0.423	–0.377	–0.390	–0.433	–0.470	–0.457
0.205	0.221	0.223	0.279	0.285	0.295	0.304	0.387	0.387	0.367	0.296	0.330	0.365	0.418	0.404	0.392	0.431
–0.019	–0.075	–0.123	–0.122	–0.099	–0.050	–0.075	–0.071	–0.069	–0.086	–0.098	–0.114	0.031	0.064	0.278	0.000	0.134
–0.308	–0.367	–0.345	–0.352	–0.372	–0.354	–0.342	–0.367	–0.366	–0.355	–0.369	–0.383	–0.428	–0.453	–0.342	–0.334	–0.448
0.414	0.349	0.347	0.367	0.385	0.368	0.383	0.436	0.439	0.350	0.354	0.424	0.360	0.374	0.381	0.334	0.425
–0.077	–0.062	–0.192	–0.195	–0.140	–0.102	–0.177	–0.101	–0.117	–0.137	–0.134	–0.103	0.055	0.052	0.074	0.098	0.069
–0.340	–0.326	–0.371	–0.382	–0.343	–0.351	–0.394	–0.391	–0.376	–0.415	–0.397	–0.406	–0.401	–0.415	–0.419	–0.470	–0.449
0.249	0.233	0.152	0.178	0.216	0.230	0.258	0.325	0.321	0.287	0.276	0.336	0.427	0.406	0.415	0.491	0.507
–0.121	–0.117	–0.167	–0.130	–0.112	–0.062	–0.132	–0.037	–0.072	–0.065	–0.112	–0.108	0.042	0.054	0.040	0.088	0.112
–0.408	–0.436	–0.395	–0.327	–0.351	–0.358	–0.372	–0.387	–0.403	–0.395	–0.401	–0.440	–0.486	–0.489	–0.506	–0.508	–0.506
0.257	0.278	0.308	0.281	0.323	0.332	0.348	0.429	0.424	0.429	0.356	0.389	0.437	0.461	0.477	0.542	0.582
–0.049	–0.057	–0.124	–0.128	–0.095	–0.038	–0.036	–0.024	–0.021	–0.019	–0.026	–0.037	n.a.	n.a.	n.a.	n.a.	n.a.
–0.227	–0.278	–0.283	–0.307	–0.287	–0.218	–0.248	–0.242	–0.239	–0.242	–0.255	–0.285	n.a.	n.a.	n.a.	n.a.	n.a.
0.213	0.228	0.192	0.246	0.247	0.217	0.290	0.296	0.300	0.323	0.352	0.349	n.a.	n.a.	n.a.	n.a.	n.a.
0.009	–0.032	–0.126	–0.151	–0.088	–0.129	–0.085	–0.163	–0.196	–0.185	–0.181	–0.170	n.a.	n.a.	n.a.	n.a.	n.a.
–0.279	–0.366	–0.357	–0.392	–0.335	–0.458	–0.432	–0.445	–0.451	–0.442	–0.422	–0.431	n.a.	n.a.	n.a.	n.a.	n.a.
0.442	0.427	0.361	0.360	0.350	0.363	0.400	0.296	0.219	0.214	0.212	0.237	n.a.	n.a.	n.a.	n.a.	n.a.
–0.084	–0.055	–0.089	–0.091	–0.083	–0.040	–0.052	–0.017	–0.031	–0.065	–0.025	–0.046	0.130	0.119	0.133	0.130	0.156
–0.339	–0.331	–0.314	–0.293	–0.300	–0.330	–0.289	–0.325	–0.318	–0.347	–0.333	–0.336	–0.359	–0.400	–0.381	–0.403	–0.406
0.308	0.268	0.329	0.327	0.321	0.378	0.388	0.434	0.439	0.434	0.456	0.452	0.477	0.508	0.499	0.491	0.497
–0.088	–0.122	–0.157	–0.161	–0.166	–0.168	–0.083	–0.093	–0.135	–0.130	–0.119	–0.123	0.162	0.186	0.196	0.198	0.161
–0.299	–0.359	–0.380	–0.386	–0.388	–0.398	–0.385	–0.401	–0.395	–0.370	–0.369	–0.368	–0.351	–0.374	–0.381	–0.388	–0.522
0.333	0.352	0.333	0.336	0.321	0.337	0.400	0.399	0.385	0.351	0.446	0.428	0.390	0.434	0.453	0.458	0.465

(continued)

Table 8-7 (continued)

Committee		80th 1947	81st 1949	82nd 1951	83rd 1953	84th 1955	85th 1957	86th 1959	87th 1961	88th 1963	89th 1965	90th 1967	91st 1969
Science	All members	n.a.	n.a.	n.a.	n.a.	n.a.	n.a.	−0.095	−0.075	−0.040	−0.081	−0.036	−0.040
	Democrats	n.a.	n.a.	n.a.	n.a.	n.a.	n.a.	−0.266	−0.254	−0.239	−0.233	−0.256	−0.251
	Republicans	n.a.	n.a.	n.a.	n.a.	n.a.	n.a.	0.209	0.211	0.235	0.238	0.268	0.254
Small Business	All members	n.a.	n.a.	n.a.	n.a.	n.a.	n.a.	n.a.	n.a.	n.a.	n.a.	n.a.	n.a.
	Democrats	n.a.	n.a.	n.a.	n.a.	n.a.	n.a.	n.a.	n.a.	n.a.	n.a.	n.a.	n.a.
	Republicans	n.a.	n.a.	n.a.	n.a.	n.a.	n.a.	n.a.	n.a.	n.a.	n.a.	n.a.	n.a.
Standards of Official Conduct	All members	n.a.	n.a.	n.a.	n.a.	n.a.	n.a.	n.a.	n.a.	n.a.	n.a.	0.049	0.084
	Democrats	n.a.	n.a.	n.a.	n.a.	n.a.	n.a.	n.a.	n.a.	n.a.	n.a.	−0.166	−0.131
	Republicans	n.a.	n.a.	n.a.	n.a.	n.a.	n.a.	n.a.	n.a.	n.a.	n.a.	0.263	0.298
Transportation and Infrastructure	All members	0.132	−0.002	0.018	0.057	0.027	0.011	−0.082	−0.042	−0.061	−0.087	−0.029	−0.029
	Democrats	−0.150	−0.210	−0.219	−0.285	−0.197	−0.208	−0.273	−0.272	−0.279	−0.267	−0.270	−0.279
	Republicans	0.319	0.301	0.314	0.334	0.321	0.289	0.269	0.286	0.251	0.291	0.276	0.287
Veterans Affairs	All members	0.090	−0.024	0.040	0.031	−0.019	0.001	−0.081	−0.004	−0.014	−0.060	−0.011	−0.019
	Democrats	−0.148	−0.193	−0.098	−0.127	−0.192	−0.150	−0.222	−0.137	−0.151	−0.172	−0.136	−0.191
	Republicans	0.254	0.261	0.219	0.179	0.241	0.227	0.183	0.195	0.214	0.178	0.148	0.199
Ways and Means	All members	0.174	0.001	0.017	0.107	−0.025	−0.031	−0.006	0.004	−0.016	−0.065	−0.026	−0.046
	Democrats	−0.193	−0.276	−0.251	−0.299	−0.278	−0.288	−0.293	−0.281	−0.309	−0.285	−0.297	−0.284
	Republicans	0.418	0.418	0.419	0.377	0.356	0.354	0.471	0.479	0.424	0.402	0.382	0.350
Chamber average	All members	0.100	−0.020	0.033	0.054	0.023	0.016	−0.057	−0.018	−0.026	−0.086	−0.026	−0.031
	Democrats	−0.189	−0.235	−0.211	−0.209	−0.229	−0.228	−0.250	−0.229	−0.249	−0.264	−0.255	−0.270
	Republicans	0.328	0.313	0.315	0.309	0.309	0.297	0.299	0.300	0.294	0.286	0.277	0.278

n.a. = not available

Note: In 1995, the new Republican majority abolished the District of Columbia, Merchant Marine and Fisheries, and Post Office and Civil Service Committees. It also renamed several committees. For the changes, please see chapter 4. The committee titles here reflect the current names.

Source: Keith Poole, Professor of Political Science at the University of California, San Diego, and Howard Rosenthal, Professor of Politics at Princeton University, developed ideological scores based on members' voting records. The Poole-Rosenthal scores can be viewed at voteview.com. A positive score denotes a conservative ideology, while a negative score denotes a liberal one. Scores closest to zero reflect the most centrist ideologies, while more extreme scores reflect stronger conservative or liberal ideologies. Data above represent a statistical analysis of committee members' voting records performed by Charles Stewart, Professor of Political Science at the Massachusetts Institute of Technology.

92nd 1971	93rd 1973	94th 1975	95th 1977	96th 1979	97th 1981	98th 1983	99th 1985	100th 1987	101st 1989	102nd 1991	103rd 1993	104th 1995	105th 1997	106th 1999	107th 2001	108th 2003
–0.055	0.000	–0.094	–0.060	–0.052	–0.030	–0.086	0.014	0.009	–0.032	–0.032	0.037	0.131	0.062	0.065	0.081	0.083
–0.259	–0.206	–0.257	–0.223	–0.238	–0.249	–0.310	–0.228	–0.228	–0.244	–0.248	–0.214	–0.266	–0.291	–0.344	–0.358	–0.349
0.249	0.270	0.278	0.278	0.283	0.267	0.347	0.356	0.332	0.301	0.333	0.420	0.470	0.414	0.438	0.465	0.464
n.a.	n.a.	–0.172	–0.164	–0.118	–0.050	–0.050	–0.033	–0.057	–0.047	–0.046	–0.061	0.054	0.085	0.070	0.067	0.140
n.a.	n.a.	–0.350	–0.344	–0.304	–0.296	–0.257	–0.268	–0.294	–0.302	–0.302	–0.374	–0.411	–0.322	–0.391	–0.410	–0.401
n.a.	n.a.	0.184	0.180	0.194	0.267	0.296	0.335	0.319	0.359	0.388	0.390	0.455	0.469	0.474	0.491	0.538
0.088	0.082	0.081	0.061	0.030	0.039	0.002	–0.036	–0.001	0.011	–0.034	–0.052	–0.081	–0.002	–0.329	0.150	0.058
–0.124	–0.160	–0.100	–0.085	–0.242	–0.340	–0.417	–0.374	–0.373	–0.364	–0.450	–0.445	–0.477	–0.483	–0.479	–0.409	–0.335
0.300	0.324	0.261	0.206	0.301	0.418	0.421	0.303	0.371	0.386	0.381	0.340	0.315	0.479	0.420	0.708	0.451
–0.103	–0.057	–0.096	–0.070	–0.037	–0.005	–0.074	–0.063	–0.036	–0.021	–0.016	–0.054	0.042	0.034	0.044	0.047	0.055
–0.335	–0.294	–0.281	–0.244	–0.220	–0.258	–0.335	–0.333	–0.336	–0.302	–0.266	–0.296	–0.304	–0.333	–0.328	–0.358	–0.387
0.276	0.284	0.274	0.277	0.298	0.314	0.292	0.321	0.343	0.400	0.389	0.353	0.344	0.356	0.376	0.381	0.410
–0.023	–0.002	–0.066	–0.031	0.014	0.072	–0.035	–0.011	0.012	0.031	0.015	–0.053	0.085	0.082	0.093	0.068	0.063
–0.177	–0.154	–0.202	–0.154	–0.129	–0.139	–0.199	–0.224	–0.224	–0.209	–0.212	–0.314	–0.356	–0.380	–0.362	–0.365	–0.414
0.223	0.207	0.223	0.227	0.274	0.314	0.341	0.293	0.394	0.374	0.383	0.404	0.453	0.457	0.450	0.423	0.428
–0.052	–0.024	–0.076	–0.076	–0.099	–0.062	–0.064	–0.065	–0.074	–0.083	–0.098	–0.101	0.066	0.060	0.060	0.065	0.074
–0.278	–0.263	–0.286	–0.288	–0.339	–0.304	–0.288	–0.304	–0.324	–0.327	–0.348	–0.382	–0.425	–0.455	–0.467	–0.463	–0.463
0.325	0.335	0.400	0.365	0.382	0.382	0.364	0.357	0.368	0.349	0.344	0.417	0.435	0.435	0.426	0.440	0.455
–0.050	–0.039	–0.113	–0.107	–0.079	–0.028	–0.052	–0.060	–0.073	–0.076	–0.091	–0.083	–0.071	0.039	0.033	0.034	0.054
–0.281	–0.296	–0.301	–0.293	–0.295	–0.296	–0.297	–0.313	–0.317	–0.324	–0.321	–0.329	–0.368	–0.387	–0.392	–0.399	–0.403
0.284	0.282	0.267	0.266	0.290	0.308	0.334	0.332	0.337	0.338	0.339	0.365	0.380	0.428	0.434	0.445	0.462

Table 8-8 Average Ideological Positions of Senate Committees, 80th–108th Congresses

Committee		80th 1947	81st 1949	82nd 1951	83rd 1953	84th 1955	85th 1957	86th 1959	87th 1961	88th 1963	89th 1965	90th 1967	91st 1969
Agriculture, Nutrition, and Forestry	All members	0.081	0.036	0.072	0.152	0.067	0.082	−0.006	−0.083	−0.050	−0.056	−0.040	0.089
	Democrats	−0.168	−0.103	−0.097	−0.052	−0.139	−0.114	−0.200	−0.239	−0.211	−0.177	−0.125	−0.042
	Republicans	0.294	0.258	0.268	0.331	0.302	0.306	0.350	0.201	0.245	0.160	0.129	0.243
Appropriations	All members	0.133	0.056	0.093	0.106	0.081	0.079	−0.017	0.008	−0.058	−0.048	−0.078	−0.024
	Democrats	−0.095	−0.102	−0.109	−0.098	−0.101	−0.087	−0.167	−0.164	−0.191	−0.176	−0.200	−0.183
	Republicans	0.305	0.314	0.316	0.293	0.279	0.278	0.283	0.301	0.207	0.206	0.153	0.199
Armed Services	All members	0.083	0.060	0.087	0.044	0.063	0.067	0.000	0.009	−0.051	−0.013	−0.021	0.018
	Democrats	−0.108	−0.059	−0.052	−0.095	−0.106	−0.107	−0.140	−0.130	−0.150	−0.158	−0.192	−0.173
	Republicans	0.275	0.228	0.255	0.166	0.255	0.266	0.234	0.240	0.167	0.334	0.319	0.255
Banking, Housing, and Urban Affairs	All members	0.023	−0.066	0.112	0.070	−0.057	0.011	−0.131	−0.174	−0.143	−0.143	−0.124	−0.192
	Democrats	−0.316	−0.284	−0.127	−0.206	−0.258	−0.204	−0.312	−0.353	−0.403	−0.393	−0.329	−0.380
	Republicans	0.313	0.284	0.392	0.312	0.260	0.257	0.229	0.184	0.377	0.484	0.246	0.090
Budget	All members	n.a.	n.a.	n.a.	n.a.	n.a.	n.a.	n.a.	n.a.	n.a.	n.a.	n.a.	n.a.
	Democrats	n.a.	n.a.	n.a.	n.a.	n.a.	n.a.	n.a.	n.a.	n.a.	n.a.	n.a.	n.a.
	Republicans	n.a.	n.a.	n.a.	n.a.	n.a.	n.a.	n.a.	n.a.	n.a.	n.a.	n.a.	n.a.
Commerce, Science, and Transportation	All members	0.094	−0.018	0.089	0.048	0.058	0.097	−0.095	−0.093	−0.156	−0.146	−0.115	−0.102
	Democrats	−0.206	−0.234	−0.173	−0.179	−0.149	−0.164	−0.291	−0.289	−0.320	−0.342	−0.283	−0.319
	Republicans	0.351	0.328	0.395	0.246	0.266	0.321	0.232	0.234	0.204	0.247	0.222	0.197
Energy and Natural Resources	All members	0.144	0.036	0.022	0.087	−0.004	−0.059	−0.205	−0.159	−0.127	−0.169	−0.170	−0.112
	Democrats	−0.289	−0.276	−0.294	−0.204	−0.318	−0.405	−0.448	−0.417	−0.419	−0.418	−0.416	−0.403
	Republicans	0.415	0.400	0.391	0.342	0.354	0.335	0.280	0.316	0.409	0.379	0.281	0.304
Environment and Public Works	All members	0.190	0.110	0.147	0.061	−0.026	−0.059	−0.238	−0.236	−0.259	−0.254	−0.156	−0.136
	Democrats	−0.004	−0.097	−0.086	−0.120	−0.386	−0.410	−0.444	−0.440	−0.440	−0.430	−0.384	−0.357
	Republicans	0.357	0.441	0.381	0.242	0.334	0.351	0.175	0.140	0.175	0.170	0.223	0.195
Finance	All members	0.180	0.159	0.218	0.226	0.140	0.127	0.047	0.005	−0.022	−0.031	−0.064	0.019
	Democrats	−0.100	−0.065	0.037	0.035	−0.065	−0.149	−0.182	−0.234	−0.270	−0.283	−0.336	−0.299
	Republicans	0.419	0.421	0.430	0.394	0.375	0.442	0.468	0.442	0.431	0.432	0.433	0.474
Foreign Relations	All members	−0.022	−0.089	−0.058	−0.004	−0.095	−0.110	−0.157	−0.113	−0.125	−0.161	−0.175	−0.163
	Democrats	−0.268	−0.243	−0.166	−0.221	−0.279	−0.381	−0.335	−0.339	−0.324	−0.354	−0.411	−0.355
	Republicans	0.189	0.157	0.093	0.185	0.199	0.200	0.169	0.300	0.355	0.257	0.231	0.125
Health, Education, Labor, and Pensions	All members	−0.029	−0.214	−0.211	−0.092	−0.183	−0.165	−0.245	−0.268	−0.226	−0.287	−0.235	−0.225
	Democrats	−0.347	−0.405	−0.449	−0.477	−0.514	−0.537	−0.499	−0.477	−0.492	−0.523	−0.519	−0.473
	Republicans	0.198	0.169	0.123	0.237	0.204	0.208	0.137	0.150	0.307	0.231	0.239	0.128
Homeland Security and Governmental Affairs	All members	0.074	−0.015	0.048	0.064	0.005	0.061	−0.054	−0.118	−0.125	−0.156	−0.138	−0.105
	Democrats	−0.124	−0.209	−0.162	−0.234	−0.234	−0.198	−0.288	−0.289	−0.311	−0.354	−0.355	−0.264
	Republicans	0.245	0.211	0.292	0.319	0.244	0.320	0.415	0.225	0.248	0.339	0.295	0.134
Judiciary	All members	0.041	−0.044	0.058	0.112	0.072	0.054	−0.102	−0.050	−0.110	−0.128	−0.082	−0.064
	Democrats	−0.207	−0.270	−0.139	−0.153	−0.181	−0.205	−0.274	−0.211	−0.266	−0.270	−0.256	−0.253
	Republicans	0.254	0.273	0.287	0.344	0.361	0.351	0.241	0.272	0.201	0.155	0.301	0.205

92nd 1971	93rd 1973	94th 1975	95th 1977	96th 1979	97th 1981	98th 1983	99th 1985	100th 1987	101st 1989	102nd 1991	103rd 1993	104th 1995	105th 1997	106th 1999	107th 2001	108th 2003
0.046	−0.011	−0.015	−0.020	0.022	0.081	0.100	0.059	0.038	0.024	0.042	−0.006	0.063	0.096	0.081	0.077	0.044
−0.126	−0.278	−0.244	−0.269	−0.228	−0.189	−0.193	−0.234	−0.315	−0.309	−0.313	−0.355	−0.327	−0.345	−0.339	−0.300	−0.297
0.275	0.345	0.396	0.394	0.335	0.322	0.335	0.319	0.351	0.357	0.397	0.429	0.410	0.448	0.417	0.454	0.355
−0.052	−0.123	−0.148	−0.195	−0.099	−0.014	−0.031	−0.042	−0.083	−0.080	−0.103	−0.065	−0.022	−0.001	−0.002	−0.026	−0.008
−0.224	−0.266	−0.260	−0.270	−0.298	−0.272	−0.272	−0.297	−0.302	−0.350	−0.354	−0.355	−0.373	−0.411	−0.406	−0.382	−0.383
0.151	0.071	0.032	−0.045	0.209	0.226	0.194	0.197	0.187	0.253	0.231	0.293	0.282	0.354	0.348	0.330	0.342
0.030	0.082	0.033	0.031	0.048	0.147	0.084	0.081	0.049	−0.010	−0.004	0.044	0.067	0.069	0.072	0.040	0.016
−0.227	−0.220	−0.297	−0.323	−0.263	−0.240	−0.297	−0.292	−0.263	−0.286	−0.287	−0.278	−0.319	−0.360	−0.371	−0.370	−0.392
0.299	0.463	0.494	0.525	0.416	0.431	0.389	0.416	0.431	0.370	0.386	0.437	0.418	0.412	0.435	0.449	0.392
−0.066	−0.107	−0.092	−0.089	−0.100	−0.039	−0.001	−0.005	−0.033	−0.035	−0.036	−0.056	0.049	0.063	0.080	0.054	0.041
−0.335	−0.350	−0.333	−0.354	−0.394	−0.412	−0.397	−0.387	−0.321	−0.346	−0.346	−0.376	−0.441	−0.455	−0.408	−0.371	−0.371
0.242	0.205	0.292	0.309	0.340	0.287	0.350	0.377	0.328	0.307	0.305	0.384	0.431	0.477	0.479	0.478	0.416
n.a.	−0.138	−0.107	−0.137	−0.110	0.025	0.025	0.009	−0.009	−0.005	0.013	−0.047	0.023	−0.021	−0.017	−0.019	0.042
n.a.	−0.408	−0.371	−0.381	−0.345	−0.337	−0.340	−0.348	−0.319	−0.325	−0.341	−0.395	−0.396	−0.472	−0.473	−0.426	−0.436
n.a.	0.268	0.295	0.268	0.243	0.326	0.329	0.307	0.301	0.344	0.403	0.419	0.373	0.355	0.363	0.387	0.480
−0.094	−0.105	−0.151	−0.148	−0.049	0.011	−0.002	−0.010	−0.077	−0.049	−0.046	−0.014	0.023	0.044	0.046	−0.014	−0.009
−0.306	−0.324	−0.321	−0.275	−0.251	−0.225	−0.255	−0.283	−0.327	−0.280	−0.282	−0.294	−0.300	−0.327	−0.325	−0.348	−0.378
0.172	0.208	0.120	0.232	0.239	0.221	0.223	0.232	0.229	0.269	0.278	0.296	0.314	0.347	0.350	0.320	0.330
−0.077	−0.003	−0.074	−0.098	−0.135	−0.007	−0.028	0.009	−0.011	0.013	−0.007	−0.012	0.035	0.072	0.070	0.035	0.051
−0.373	−0.384	−0.356	−0.376	−0.355	−0.352	−0.362	−0.347	−0.357	−0.323	−0.331	−0.323	−0.375	−0.341	−0.323	−0.352	−0.354
0.304	0.427	0.436	0.411	0.212	0.275	0.245	0.294	0.300	0.386	0.388	0.369	0.364	0.409	0.392	0.422	0.423
−0.080	−0.048	−0.095	−0.128	−0.142	0.004	0.006	−0.025	−0.102	−0.066	−0.145	−0.081	0.100	0.090	0.051	−0.027	0.027
−0.307	−0.355	−0.316	−0.305	−0.347	−0.327	−0.328	−0.359	−0.344	−0.318	−0.368	−0.396	−0.364	−0.378	−0.384	−0.392	−0.369
0.163	0.330	0.251	0.192	0.132	0.262	0.266	0.267	0.210	0.257	0.190	0.369	0.461	0.464	0.399	0.337	0.381
0.032	−0.004	−0.029	−0.013	−0.080	0.042	0.017	0.019	−0.088	−0.085	−0.088	−0.061	0.003	0.036	0.057	0.045	0.081
−0.341	−0.345	−0.348	−0.280	−0.272	−0.270	−0.273	−0.280	−0.342	−0.347	−0.329	−0.347	−0.343	−0.313	−0.296	−0.301	−0.300
0.436	0.404	0.388	0.342	0.138	0.245	0.254	0.263	0.223	0.234	0.205	0.257	0.286	0.322	0.347	0.390	0.430
−0.187	−0.237	−0.229	−0.239	−0.119	−0.063	−0.052	−0.040	−0.071	−0.014	−0.037	−0.105	0.034	0.032	0.018	−0.066	−0.064
−0.341	−0.394	−0.396	−0.371	−0.361	−0.380	−0.378	−0.381	−0.435	−0.405	−0.411	−0.440	−0.445	−0.489	−0.527	−0.510	−0.506
0.012	−0.012	0.010	−0.042	0.244	0.219	0.238	0.263	0.334	0.420	0.430	0.354	0.416	0.448	0.454	0.378	0.334
−0.243	−0.269	−0.234	−0.258	−0.173	−0.021	−0.032	−0.046	−0.151	−0.185	−0.209	−0.194	−0.067	−0.050	−0.032	−0.076	−0.011
−0.461	−0.458	−0.453	−0.422	−0.459	−0.449	−0.443	−0.479	−0.493	−0.497	−0.508	−0.498	−0.526	−0.506	−0.507	−0.493	−0.457
0.069	0.048	0.095	0.070	0.256	0.311	0.287	0.292	0.289	0.217	0.219	0.241	0.291	0.315	0.349	0.340	0.383
−0.075	−0.065	−0.114	−0.171	−0.151	−0.097	−0.065	−0.106	−0.143	−0.113	−0.129	−0.130	0.009	−0.006	−0.028	−0.035	−0.061
−0.243	−0.194	−0.218	−0.227	−0.299	−0.287	−0.296	−0.306	−0.306	−0.295	−0.320	−0.347	−0.353	−0.387	−0.390	−0.367	−0.433
0.135	0.149	0.072	0.141	0.015	0.072	0.121	0.066	0.074	0.129	0.126	0.217	0.326	0.291	0.253	0.297	0.270
−0.045	−0.044	−0.088	−0.156	−0.097	0.020	−0.002	−0.013	−0.064	−0.063	−0.074	−0.085	0.010	0.009	0.034	−0.047	−0.017
−0.249	−0.248	−0.339	−0.333	−0.384	−0.350	−0.350	−0.372	−0.375	−0.372	−0.376	−0.388	−0.418	−0.459	−0.450	−0.476	−0.476
0.217	0.218	0.288	0.162	0.313	0.316	0.276	0.274	0.351	0.350	0.329	0.293	0.353	0.384	0.421	0.382	0.396

(continued)

Table 8-8 (continued)

Committee		80th 1947	81st 1949	82nd 1951	83rd 1953	84th 1955	85th 1957	86th 1959	87th 1961	88th 1963	89th 1965	90th 1967	91st 1969
Rules and Administration	All members	0.092	–0.015	–0.040	0.057	0.033	–0.115	–0.113	–0.059	–0.119	–0.119	–0.119	0.046
	Democrats	–0.279	–0.183	–0.291	–0.244	–0.335	–0.252	–0.262	–0.246	–0.293	–0.296	–0.299	–0.164
	Republicans	0.324	0.256	0.252	0.297	0.493	0.114	0.186	0.315	0.229	0.235	0.242	0.308
Small Business and Entrepreneurship	All members	n.a.	n.a.	n.a.	n.a.	n.a.	n.a.	n.a.	n.a.	n.a.	n.a.	n.a.	n.a.
	Democrats	n.a.	n.a.	n.a.	n.a.	n.a.	n.a.	n.a.	n.a.	n.a.	n.a.	n.a.	n.a.
	Republicans	n.a.	n.a.	n.a.	n.a.	n.a.	n.a.	n.a.	n.a.	n.a.	n.a.	n.a.	n.a.
Veterans' Affairs	All members	n.a.	n.a.	n.a.	n.a.	n.a.	n.a.	n.a.	n.a.	n.a.	n.a.	n.a.	n.a.
	Democrats	n.a.	n.a.	n.a.	n.a.	n.a.	n.a.	n.a.	n.a.	n.a.	n.a.	n.a.	n.a.
	Republicans	n.a.	n.a.	n.a.	n.a.	n.a.	n.a.	n.a.	n.a.	n.a.	n.a.	n.a.	n.a.
Chamber average	All members	0.082	0.018	0.064	0.048	0.023	0.014	–0.100	–0.096	–0.113	–0.125	–0.110	–0.077
	Democrats	–0.173	–0.194	–0.162	–0.171	–0.226	–0.245	–0.290	–0.291	–0.310	–0.321	–0.311	–0.298
	Republicans	0.307	0.287	0.306	0.280	0.291	0.278	0.248	0.260	0.279	0.284	0.248	0.217

n.a. = not available

Source: Keith Poole, Professor of Political Science at the University of California, San Diego, and Howard Rosenthal, Professor of Politics at Princeton University, developed ideological scores based on members' voting records. The Poole-Rosenthal scores can be viewed at voteview.com. A positive score denotes a conservative ideology, while a negative score denotes a liberal one. Scores closest to zero reflect the most centrist ideologies, while more extreme scores reflect stronger conservative or liberal ideologies. Data above represent a statistical analysis of committee members' voting records performed by Charles Stewart, Professor of Political Science at the Massachusetts Institute of Technology.

92nd 1971	93rd 1973	94th 1975	95th 1977	96th 1979	97th 1981	98th 1983	99th 1985	100th 1987	101st 1989	102nd 1991	103rd 1993	104th 1995	105th 1997	106th 1999	107th 2001	108th 2003
–0.018	–0.073	–0.090	–0.104	–0.096	0.025	0.032	0.024	–0.041	–0.035	–0.075	–0.049	0.042	0.089	0.082	0.043	0.032
–0.161	–0.232	–0.227	–0.287	–0.292	–0.318	–0.304	–0.307	–0.364	–0.366	–0.368	–0.335	–0.359	–0.338	–0.363	–0.351	–0.376
0.161	0.124	0.140	0.262	0.198	0.270	0.272	0.261	0.374	0.390	0.364	0.319	0.354	0.421	0.429	0.436	0.400
n.a.	n.a.	n.a.	n.a.	n.a.	–0.062	–0.073	–0.059	–0.096	–0.037	–0.079	–0.056	0.013	0.029	0.001	–0.038	0.006
n.a.	n.a.	n.a.	n.a.	n.a.	–0.321	–0.289	–0.317	–0.330	–0.315	–0.367	–0.393	–0.395	–0.427	–0.428	–0.430	–0.372
n.a.	n.a.	n.a.	n.a.	n.a.	0.168	0.143	0.199	0.196	0.345	0.374	0.394	0.347	0.394	0.344	0.354	0.345
–0.066	–0.035	0.027	–0.052	–0.034	0.054	0.017	0.039	–0.095	–0.108	–0.131	–0.118	0.033	–0.034	–0.033	–0.021	0.059
–0.362	–0.367	–0.274	–0.272	–0.294	–0.329	–0.335	–0.367	–0.371	–0.377	–0.380	–0.332	–0.336	–0.477	–0.487	–0.341	–0.268
0.303	0.380	0.403	0.315	0.357	0.328	0.268	0.271	0.235	0.213	0.219	0.182	0.296	0.283	0.291	0.300	0.354
–0.061	–0.080	–0.097	–0.101	–0.080	0.011	0.012	0.002	–0.047	–0.045	–0.060	–0.059	–0.040	0.029	0.028	–0.005	–0.002
–0.302	–0.331	–0.323	–0.318	–0.315	–0.304	–0.309	–0.324	–0.332	–0.336	–0.340	–0.349	–0.358	–0.396	–0.394	–0.388	–0.388
0.210	0.239	0.246	0.234	0.244	0.279	0.284	0.292	0.293	0.310	0.306	0.308	0.304	0.389	0.387	0.386	0.369

Table 8-9 Average Ideological Positions of House Party Coalitions, 80th–109th Congresses, 1947–2005

Congress	Entire chamber	Democrats	Republicans	Nonsouthern Democrats	Southern Democrats
80th (1947)	0.145	–0.178	0.319	–0.327	–0.052
81st (1949)	–0.029	–0.225	0.305	–0.338	–0.045
82nd (1951)	0.069	–0.203	0.307	–0.335	–0.033
83rd (1953)	0.121	–0.197	0.303	–0.346	–0.026
84th (1955)	0.061	–0.223	0.303	–0.361	–0.032
85th (1957)	0.059	–0.222	0.291	–0.359	–0.034
86th (1959)	–0.067	–0.244	0.294	–0.354	–0.032
87th (1961)	–0.003	–0.225	0.295	–0.341	–0.034
88th (1963)	–0.005	–0.245	0.289	–0.362	–0.045
89th (1965)	–0.141	–0.258	0.279	–0.354	–0.045
90th (1967)	0.012	–0.251	0.270	–0.366	–0.025
91st (1969)	–0.003	–0.273	0.279	–0.378	–0.043
92nd (1971)	–0.035	–0.275	0.274	–0.375	–0.050
93rd (1973)	–0.033	–0.295	0.275	–0.376	–0.108
94th (1975)	–0.178	–0.296	0.259	–0.364	–0.125
95th (1977)	–0.172	–0.289	0.254	–0.351	–0.127
96th (1979)	–0.147	–0.288	0.278	–0.349	–0.130
97th (1981)	–0.056	–0.291	0.300	–0.358	–0.122
98th (1983)	–0.127	–0.297	0.323	–0.366	–0.138
99th (1985)	–0.101	–0.312	0.334	–0.370	–0.171
100th (1987)	–0.120	–0.313	0.336	–0.368	–0.184
101st (1989)	–0.124	–0.315	0.336	–0.367	–0.188
102nd (1991)	–0.142	–0.320	0.351	–0.366	–0.206
103rd (1993)	–0.158	–0.341	0.375	–0.374	–0.260
104th (1995)	0.184	–0.370	0.415	–0.407	–0.280
105th (1997)	0.186	–0.381	0.432	–0.410	–0.300
106th (1999)	0.169	–0.381	0.449	–0.412	–0.289
107th (2001)	0.206	–0.388	0.473	–0.416	–0.301
108th (2003)	0.266	–0.388	0.496	–0.428	–0.282
109th (2005)	0.302	–0.399	0.509	–0.432	–0.298

Source: Keith Poole, Professor of Political Science at the University of California, San Diego, and Howard Rosenthal, Professor of Politics at Princeton University, developed ideological scores based on members' voting records. The Poole-Rosenthal scores can be viewed at voteview.com. A positive score denotes a conservative ideology, while a negative score denotes a liberal one. Scores closest to zero reflect the most centrist ideologies, while more extreme scores reflect stronger conservative or liberal ideologies. Data above represent a statistical analysis computed by Timothy Ryan, American Enterprise Institute.

Table 8-10 Average Ideological Positions of Senate Party Coalitions, 80th–109th Congresses, 1947–2005

Congress	Entire chamber	Democrats	Republicans	Nonsouthern Democrats	Southern Democrats
80th (1947)	0.093	–0.134	0.273	–0.270	0.001
81st (1949)	0.044	–0.194	0.253	–0.272	–0.069
82nd (1951)	0.066	–0.146	0.270	–0.255	–0.007
83rd (1953)	0.094	–0.142	0.276	–0.265	0.010
84th (1955)	0.069	–0.201	0.285	–0.340	–0.033
85th (1957)	0.074	–0.221	0.276	–0.362	–0.049
86th (1959)	–0.129	–0.265	0.253	–0.375	–0.042
87th (1961)	–0.123	–0.272	0.277	–0.399	–0.018
88th (1963)	–0.192	–0.290	0.279	–0.407	–0.031
89th (1965)	–0.200	–0.301	0.282	–0.415	–0.036
90th (1967)	–0.184	–0.304	0.233	–0.395	–0.083
91st (1969)	–0.124	–0.291	0.222	–0.391	–0.070
92nd (1971)	–0.078	–0.283	0.209	–0.379	–0.068
93rd (1973)	–0.110	–0.319	0.243	–0.398	–0.076
94th (1975)	–0.185	–0.313	0.244	–0.389	–0.080
95th (1977)	–0.186	–0.308	0.227	–0.389	–0.093
96th (1979)	–0.146	–0.307	0.235	–0.356	–0.160
97th (1981)	–0.022	–0.294	0.273	–0.334	–0.167
98th (1983)	–0.029	–0.299	0.276	–0.339	–0.172
99th (1985)	–0.034	–0.315	0.289	–0.356	–0.194
100th (1987)	–0.136	–0.324	0.291	–0.372	–0.209
101st (1989)	–0.166	–0.331	0.306	–0.370	–0.225
102nd (1991)	–0.178	–0.345	0.317	–0.384	–0.231
103rd (1993)	–0.200	–0.358	0.339	–0.399	–0.216
104th (1995)	0.003	–0.378	0.362	–0.409	–0.238
105th (1997)	0.071	–0.402	0.399	–0.425	–0.274
106th (1999)	0.078	–0.393	0.399	–0.433	–0.222
107th (2001)	–0.021	–0.395	0.423	–0.434	–0.221
108th (2003)	0.075	–0.398	0.425	–0.438	–0.222
109th (2005)	0.171	–0.428	0.458	–0.445	–0.255

Source: Keith Poole, Professor of Political Science at the University of California, San Diego, and Howard Rosenthal, Professor of Politics at Princeton University, developed ideological scores based on members' voting records. The Poole-Rosenthal scores can be viewed at voteview.com. A positive score denotes a conservative ideology, while a negative score denotes a liberal one. Scores closest to zero reflect the most centrist ideologies, while more extreme scores reflect stronger conservative or liberal ideologies. Data above represent a statistical analysis computed by Timothy Ryan, American Enterprise Institute.

Figure 8-1 Presidential Victories on Votes in Congress, 1953–2006 (percentage)

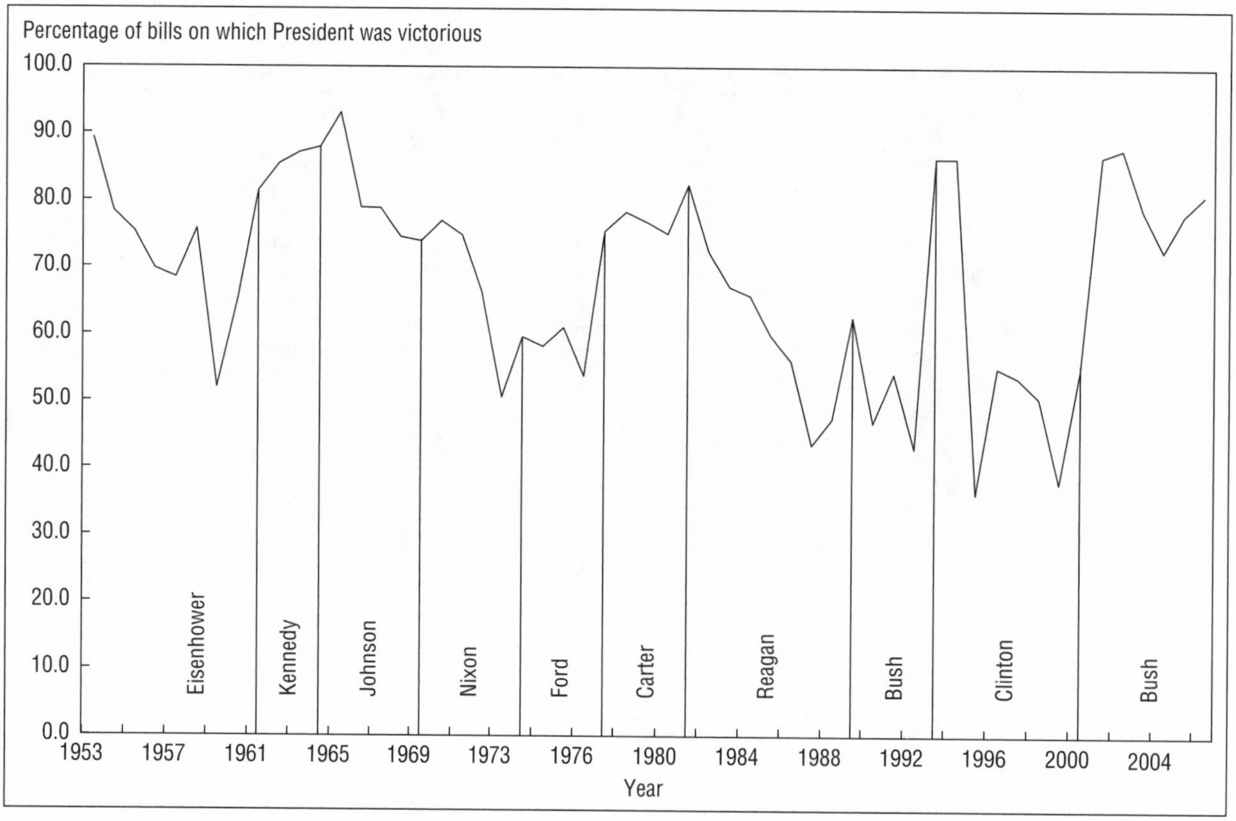

Source: Table 8-1.

Figure 8-2 Ideological Positions of House Party Coalitions, 80th–109th Congresses, 1947–2005

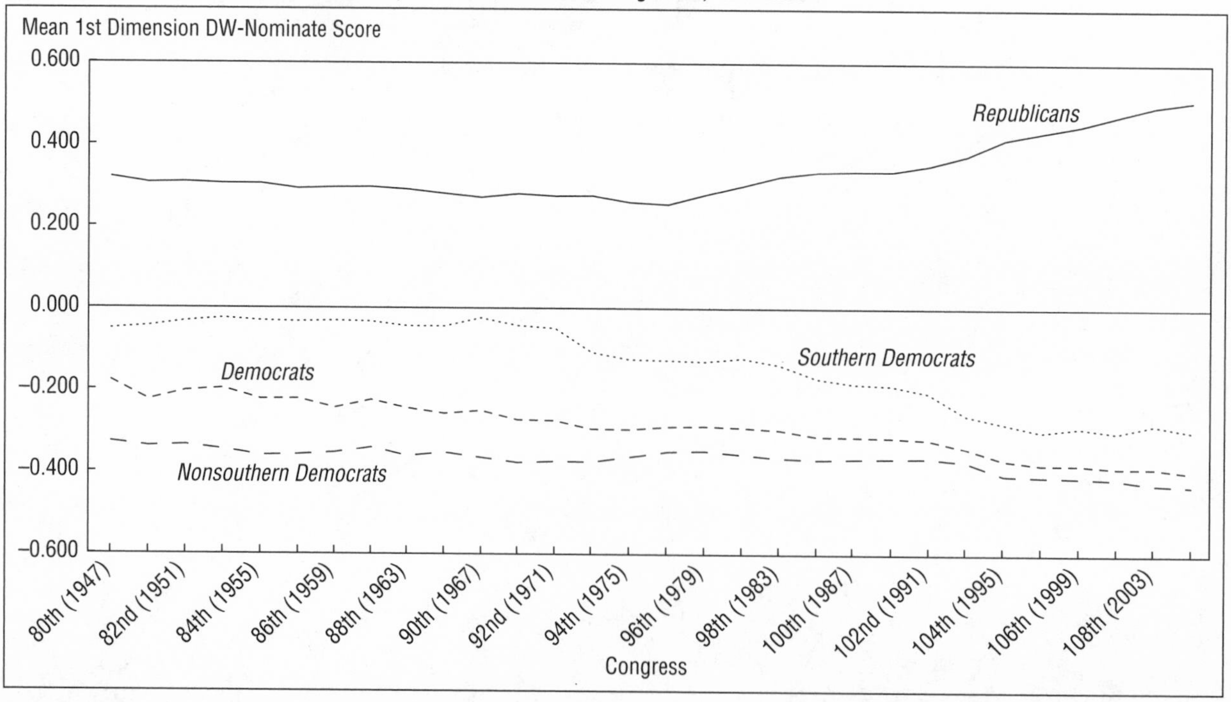

Source: Table 8-9.

Figure 8-3 Ideological Positions of Senate Party Coalitions, 80th–109th Congresses, 1947–2005

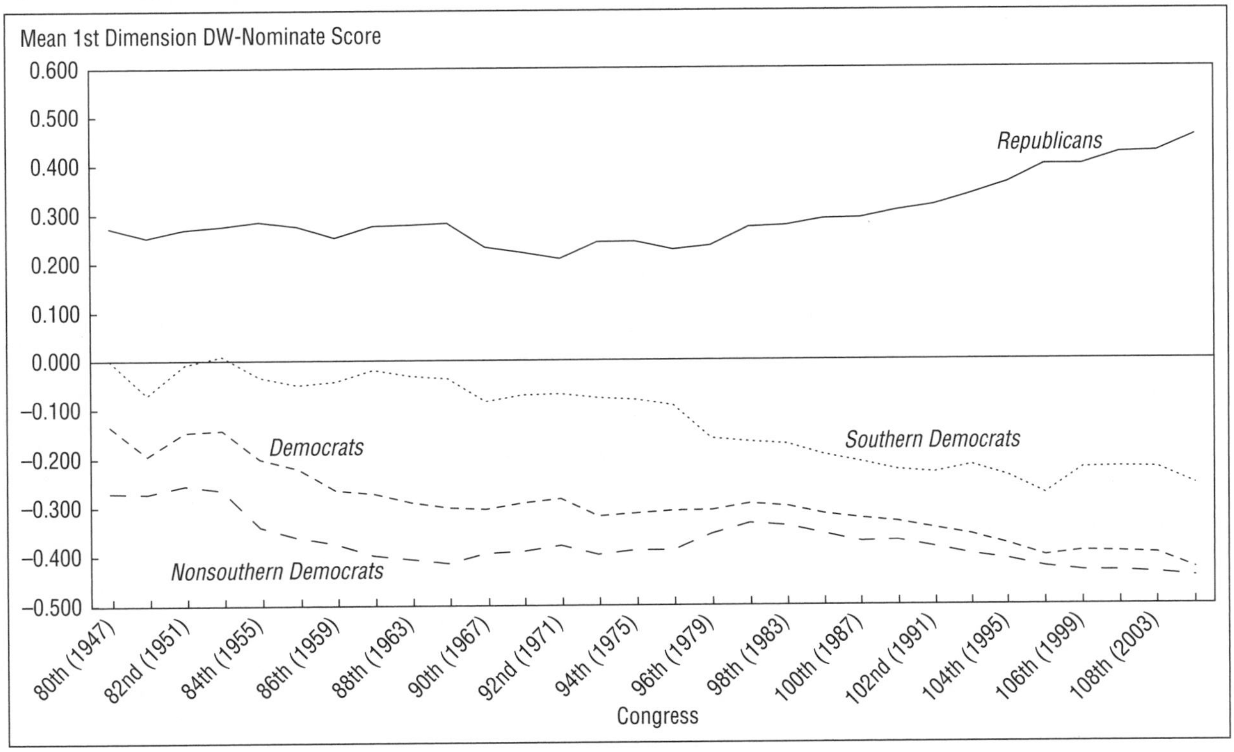

Source: Table 8-10.

Appendix

Table A-1 House of Representatives, 109th Congress

State	District	Representative	Party	Term	Birthdate	Age	% vote in 2004 Primary	% vote in 2004 General	2004 ratings[a] ADA	2004 ratings[a] ACU	109th Congress Poole-Rosenthal (party unity)[b]	109th Congress CQ Presidential Support Score[c]
Alaska	AL	Young, Don	R	16	6/9/1933	71	Unopposed	71%	0	95	91.738	90
Alabama	1	Bonner, Jo	R	2	11/19/1959	45	Unopposed	63%	0	95	95.710	93
	2	Everett, Terry	R	7	2/15/1937	67	Unopposed	71%	0	92	95.847	87
	3	Rogers, Mike	R	2	7/16/1958	46	Unopposed	61%	10	88	95.008	83
	4	Aderholt, Robert	R	5	7/22/1965	39	Unopposed	75%	0	92	95.652	87
	5	Cramer, Bud	D	8	8/22/1947	57	90%	73%	75	50	59.867	72
	6	Bachus, Spencer	R	7	12/28/1947	57	87%	99%	5	96	97.171	97
	7	Davis, Artur	D	2	10/9/1967	37	88%	75%	75	24	81.433	53
Arkansas	1	Berry, Marion	D	5	8/27/1942	62	Unopposed	67%	60	36	75.645	50
	2	Snyder, Vic	D	5	9/27/1947	57	Unopposed	58%	95	20	86.003	45
	3	Boozman, John	R	2	12/10/1950	54	Unopposed	59%	10	96	96.211	92
	4	Ross, Mike	D	3	8/2/1961	43	Unopposed	Unopposed	65	44	75.954	53
Arizona	1	Renzi, Rick	R	2	6/11/1958	46	Unopposed	59%	10	88	90.048	85
	2	Franks, Trent	R	2	6/19/1957	47	64%	59%	0	100	97.373	90
	3	Shadegg, John	R	6	10/22/1949	55	Unopposed	80%	0	100	96.817	90
	4	Pastor, Ed	D	7	6/28/1943	61	Unopposed	70%	100	4	91.586	20
	5	Hayworth, J. D.	R	6	7/12/1958	46	79%	59%	5	96	93.984	87
	6	Flake, Jeff	R	3	12/31/1962	42	59%	79%	15	96	88.364	72
	7	Grijalva, Raul	D	2	2/19/1948	56	Unopposed	62%	100	0	98.699	10
	8	Kolbe, Jim	R	11	6/28/1942	62	57%	60%	20	56	90.404	81
California	1	Thompson, Mike	D	4	1/24/1951	53	Unopposed	67%	90	13	92.419	23
	2	Herger, Wally	R	10	5/20/1945	59	Unopposed	67%	5	100	98.537	95
	3	Lungren, Dan	R	1	9/22/1946	58	39%	62%	—	—	95.652	93
	4	Doolittle, John	R	8	10/30/1950	54	Unopposed	65%	0	92	97.368	90
	5	Matsui, Doris[d]	D	1	9/25/1944	60	Unopposed	68%	—	—	97.603	25
	6	Woolsey, Lynn	D	7	11/3/1937	67	84%	73%	95	8	98.525	7
	7	Miller, George	D	16	5/17/1945	59	Unopposed	76%	100	4	98.849	13
	8	Pelosi, Nancy	D	9	3/26/1940	64	Unopposed	83%	100	8	98.525	25
	9	Lee, Barbara	D	4	7/16/1946	58	Unopposed	85%	95	0	98.856	7
	10	Tauscher, Ellen	D	5	11/15/1951	53	Unopposed	66%	100	16	94.309	25
	11	Pombo, Richard	R	7	1/8/1961	43	Unopposed	61%	0	100	94.684	92
	12	Lantos, Tom	D	13	2/1/1928	76	74%	68%	95	9	96.678	24
	13	Stark, Pete	D	17	11/11/1931	73	Unopposed	72%	90	0	98.469	5
	14	Eshoo, Anna	D	7	12/13/1942	62	Unopposed	70%	100	12	96.494	23
	15	Honda, Mike	D	3	6/27/1941	63	Unopposed	72%	95	10	98.030	23
	16	Lofgren, Zoe	D	6	12/21/1947	57	Unopposed	71%	95	12	96.602	23
	17	Farr, Sam	D	6	7/4/1941	63	91%	67%	100	4	97.087	13
	18	Cardoza, Dennis	D	2	3/31/1959	45	Unopposed	68%	85	25	79.027	50
	19	Radanovich, George	R	6	6/20/1955	49	Unopposed	66%	0	100	96.604	95
	20	Costa, Jim	D	1	4/13/1952	52	73%	53%	—	—	77.349	47
	21	Nunes, Devin	R	2	10/1/1973	31	Unopposed	73%	0	96	96.870	95
	22	Thomas, Bill	R	14	10/6/1941	63	Unopposed	Unopposed	5	88	93.174	87
	23	Capps, Lois	D	4	1/10/1938	66	Unopposed	63%	100	0	98.042	15
	24	Gallegly, Elton	R	10	3/7/1944	60	Unopposed	63%	0	96	96.296	94
	25	McKeon, Buck	R	7	9/9/1938	66	Unopposed	64%	0	88	96.885	95
	26	Dreier, David	R	13	7/5/1952	52	84%	54%	5	88	95.185	93
	27	Sherman, Brad	D	5	10/24/1954	50	Unopposed	62%	95	4	94.959	28
	28	Berman, Howard	D	12	4/15/1941	63	82%	71%	90	0	95.812	29
	29	Schiff, Adam	D	3	6/22/1960	44	Unopposed	65%	95	12	94.030	35
	30	Waxman, Henry	D	16	9/12/1939	65	Unopposed	71%	100	0	98.167	8
	31	Becerra, Xavier	D	7	1/26/1958	46	89%	80%	95	0	99.164	21
	32	Solis, Hilda	D	3	10/20/1957	47	Unopposed	85%	100	0	98.684	13
	33	Watson, Diane	D	2	11/12/1933	71	Unopposed	89%	85	0	98.438	9

State	District	Representative	Party	Term	Birthdate	Age	% vote in 2004 Primary	% vote in 2004 General	2004 ratings[a] ADA	2004 ratings[a] ACU	109th Congress Poole-Rosenthal (party unity)[b]	109th Congress CQ Presidential Support Score[c]
	34	Roybal-Allard, Lucille	D	7	6/12/1941	63	Unopposed	74%	100	0	95.447	27
	35	Waters, Maxine	D	8	8/15/1938	66	Unopposed	81%	95	4	96.194	13
	36	Harman, Jane	D	3	6/28/1945	59	Unopposed	62%	95	13	90.227	25
	37	Millender-McDonald, Juanita	D	5	9/7/1938	66	65%	75%	75	9	97.037	24
	38	Napolitano, Grace	D	4	12/4/1936	68	79%	Unopposed	95	0	98.139	21
	39	Sanchez, Linda	D	2	1/28/1969	35	Unopposed	61%	100	0	98.379	15
	40	Royce, Ed	R	7	10/12/1951	53	Unopposed	68%	15	96	95.130	93
	41	Lewis, Jerry	R	14	10/21/1934	70	Unopposed	83%	0	88	94.822	90
	42	Miller, Gary	R	4	10/16/1948	56	Unopposed	68%	0	100	97.826	95
	43	Baca, Joe	D	3	1/23/1947	57	Unopposed	66%	90	12	89.412	35
	44	Calvert, Ken	R	7	6/8/1953	51	86%	62%	0	88	96.104	95
	45	Bono, Mary	R	4	10/24/1961	43	86%	67%	35	56	89.175	81
	46	Rohrabacher, Dana	R	9	6/21/1947	57	84%	62%	15	91	92.045	90
	47	Sanchez, Loretta	D	5	1/7/1960	44	Unopposed	60%	100	12	94.030	26
	48	Cox, Christopher	R	9	10/16/1952	52	Unopposed	65%	5	100	95.413[e]	90[e]
	49	Issa, Darrell	R	3	11/1/1953	51	Unopposed	63%	0	92	94.333	95
	50	Cunningham, Randy (Duke)	R	8	12/8/1941	63	Unopposed	58%	5	92	94.643	93[f]
	51	Filner, Bob	D	7	9/4/1942	62	77%	62%	95	9	97.678	18
	52	Hunter, Duncan	R	13	5/31/1948	56	Unopposed	69%	5	87	95.645	92
	53	Davis, Susan	D	3	4/13/1944	60	Unopposed	66%	100	4	94.851	26
Colorado	1	DeGette, Diana	D	5	7/29/1957	47	Unopposed	73%	90	0	96.849	25
	2	Udall, Mark	D	4	7/18/1950	54	Unopposed	67%	100	8	91.896	30
	3	Salazar, John	D	1	7/21/1953	51	Unopposed	51%	—	—	78.583	57
	4	Musgrave, Marilyn	R	2	1/27/1949	55	78%	51%	0	100	98.336	90
	5	Hefley, Joel	R	10	4/18/1935	69	Unopposed	71%	15	92	92.131	77
	6	Tancredo, Tom	R	4	12/20/1945	59	Unopposed	59%	10	100	91.973	79
	7	Beauprez, Bob	R	2	9/22/1948	56	Unopposed	55%	5	92	96.447	97
Connecticut	1	Larson, John	D	4	7/22/1948	56	Unopposed	73%	100	16	97.326	24
	2	Simmons, Rob	R	3	2/11/1943	61	Unopposed	54%	55	40	71.287	54
	3	DeLauro, Rosa	D	8	3/2/1943	61	Unopposed	72%	100	4	98.382	13
	4	Shays, Christopher	R	9	10/18/1945	59	Unopposed	52%	70	38	62.563	53
	5	Johnson, Nancy	R	12	1/5/1935	69	Unopposed	60%	45	56	77.273	65
Delaware	AL	Castle, Michael	R	7	7/2/1939	65	Unopposed	69%	50	52	76.858	78
Florida	1	Miller, Jeff	R	2	6/27/1959	45	Unopposed	77%	5	100	96.661	92
	2	Boyd, Allen	D	5	6/6/1945	59	Unopposed	62%	70	46	71.186	62
	3	Brown, Corrine	D	7	11/11/1946	58	81%	81%	90	8	95.345	33
	4	Crenshaw, Ander	R	3	9/1/1944	60	90%	Unopposed	0	92	96.272	97
	5	Brown-Waite, Ginny	R	2	10/5/1943	61	Unopposed	66%	5	96	89.850	90
	6	Stearns, Cliff	R	9	4/16/1941	63	Unopposed	64%	0	96	93.689	85
	7	Mica, John	R	7	1/27/1943	61	Unopposed	Unopposed	0	84	97.731	95
	8	Keller, Ric	R	3	9/5/1964	40	Unopposed	61%	0	100	95.118	95
	9	Bilirakis, Michael	R	12	7/16/1930	74	84%	Unopposed	5	92	92.679	90
	10	Young, Bill	R	18	12/16/1930	74	Unopposed	69%	10	87	91.222	87
	11	Davis, Jim	D	5	10/11/1957	47	Unopposed	86%	90	4	90.215	37
	12	Putnam, Adam	R	3	7/31/1974	30	92%	65%	0	100	97.092	97
	13	Harris, Katherine	R	2	4/5/1957	47	Unopposed	55%	0	92	92.281	100
	14	Mack, Connie	R	1	8/12/1967	37	36%	68%	—	—	94.327	87
	15	Weldon, Dave	R	6	8/31/1953	51	Unopposed	65%	0	91	95.895	90
	16	Foley, Mark	R	6	9/8/1954	50	Unopposed	68%	25	68	86.780	82
	17	Meek, Kendrick	D	3	9/6/1966	38	Unopposed	Unopposed	85	9	90.854	37
	18	Ros-Lehtinen, Ileana	R	8	7/12/1952	52	Unopposed	65%	15	80	90.085	85

(continued)

Table A-1 (continued)

State	District	Representative	Party	Term	Birthdate	Age	% vote in 2004		2004 ratings[a]		109th Congress	
							Primary	General	ADA	ACU	Poole-Rosenthal (party unity)[b]	CQ Presidential Support Score[c]
	19	Wexler, Robert	D	5	1/2/1961	44	Unopposed	Unopposed	95	0	95.392	30
	20	Wasserman Schultz, Debbie	D	1	9/27/1966	38	Unopposed	70%	—	—	93.924	33
	21	Diaz-Balart, Lincoln	R	7	8/13/1954	50	Unopposed	73%	10	83	90.051	87
	22	Shaw, Clay	R	13	4/19/1939	65	Unopposed	63%	10	80	92.144	93
	23	Hastings, Alcee	D	7	9/5/1936	68	74%	Unopposed	55	0	94.876	31
	24	Feeney, Tom	R	2	5/21/1958	46	Unopposed	Unopposed	0	100	96.633	90
	25	Diaz-Balart, Mario	R	2	9/25/1961	43	Unopposed	Unopposed	5	96	92.281	90
Georgia	1	Kingston, Jack	R	7	4/24/1955	49	Unopposed	Unopposed	0	96	96.453	97
	2	Bishop, Sanford	D	7	2/4/1947	57	Unopposed	67%	55	35	74.585	63
	3	Marshall, Jim	D	2	3/31/1948	56	Unopposed	63%	55	48	66.003	65
	4	McKinney, Cynthia	D	1	3/17/1955	49	51%	64%	—	—	97.007	10
	5	Lewis, John	D	10	2/21/1940	64	Unopposed	Unopposed	100	4	99.225	15
	6	Price, Tom	R	1	10/8/1954	50	54%	Unopposed	—	—	96.272	97
	7	Linder, John	R	7	9/9/1942	62	Unopposed	Unopposed	0	100	97.500	93
	8	Westmoreland, Lynn	R	1	4/2/1950	54	55%[g]	76%	—	—	97.479	83
	9	Norwood, Charlie	R	6	7/27/1941	63	Unopposed	74%	0	100	98.103	88
	10	Deal, Nathan	R	7	8/25/1942	62	Unopposed	Unopposed	0	100	97.479	80
	11	Gingrey, Phil	R	2	7/10/1942	62	Unopposed	57%	5	96	96.248	87
	12	Barrow, John	D	1	10/31/1955	49	51%	52%	—	—	71.637	65
	13	Scott, David	D	2	6/27/1946	58	84%	Unopposed	75	30	82.072	45
Hawaii	1	Abercrombie, Neil	D	8	6/26/1938	66	Unopposed	63%	85	0	91.776	17
	2	Case, Ed	D	1	9/27/1952	52	95%	63%	90	20	80.579	53
Idaho	1	Otter, Butch	R	3	5/3/1942	62	78%	70%	5	100	90.016	72
	2	Simpson, Mike	R	4	9/8/1950	54	Unopposed	71%	0	92	94.737	89
Illinois	1	Rush, Bobby	D	7	11/23/1946	58	Unopposed	85%	100	0	94.658	32
	2	Jackson, Jesse	D	5	3/11/1965	39	89%	88%	100	0	98.074	23
	3	Lipinski, Daniel	D	1	7/15/1966	38	Unopposed	73%	—	—	86.268	49
	4	Gutierrez, Luis	D	7	12/10/1953	51	Unopposed	84%	90	0	97.312	23
	5	Emanuel, Rahm	D	2	11/29/1959	45	83%	76%	100	0	93.344	33
	6	Hyde, Henry	R	16	4/18/1924	80	Unopposed	56%	15	75	95.362	95
	7	Davis, Danny	D	5	9/6/1941	63	82%	86%	90	0	96.758	25
	8	Bean, Melissa	D	1	1/22/1962	42	78%	52%	—	—	79.260	50
	9	Schakowsky, Jan	D	4	5/26/1944	60	Unopposed	76%	100	0	99.345	15
	10	Kirk, Mark	R	3	9/15/1959	45	Unopposed	64%	45	63	79.869	80
	11	Weller, Jerry	R	6	7/7/1957	47	Unopposed	59%	15	84	91.489	95
	12	Costello, Jerry	D	9	9/25/1949	55	90%	69%	70	36	84.666	37
	13	Biggert, Judy	R	4	8/15/1937	67	100%	65%	35	64	87.138	80
	14	Hastert, Dennis	R	10	1/2/1942	63	Unopposed	69%	—	—	98.810	100
	15	Johnson, Tim	R	3	7/23/1946	58	Unopposed	53%	40	64	77.941	74
	16	Manzullo, Don	R	7	3/24/1944	60	Unopposed	69%	5	100	94.963	94
	17	Evans, Lane	D	12	8/4/1951	53	Unopposed	61%	95	4	97.399	0
	18	LaHood, Ray	R	6	12/6/1945	59	Unopposed	70%	20	71	89.130	93
	19	Shimkus, John	R	5	2/21/1958	46	Unopposed	69%	20	88	92.471	92
Indiana	1	Visclosky, Peter	D	11	8/13/1949	55	Unopposed	68%	95	4	90.499	20
	2	Chocola, Chris	R	2	2/24/1962	42	84%	54%	5	96	97.581	95
	3	Souder, Mark	R	6	7/18/1950	54	79%	69%	5	88	95.106	92
	4	Buyer, Steve	R	7	11/26/1958	46	66%	69%	5	96	97.449	90
	5	Burton, Dan	R	12	6/21/1938	66	86%	72%	0	100	96.252	91
	6	Pence, Mike	R	6	6/7/1959	45	Unopposed	67%	0	100	97.190	90
	7	Carson, Julia	D	7	7/8/1938	66	89%	54%	75	0	97.619	21
	8	Hostettler, John	R	6	7/19/1961	43	Unopposed	53%	20	88	89.789	72
	9	Sodrel, Mike	R	1	12/17/1945	59	Unopposed	49%	—	—	96.469	93

State	District	Representative	Party	Term	Birthdate	Age	% vote in 2004 Primary	% vote in 2004 General	2004 ratings[a] ADA	2004 ratings[a] ACU	109th Congress Poole-Rosenthal (party unity)[b]	109th Congress CQ Presidential Support Score[c]
Iowa	1	Nussle, Jim	R	8	6/27/1960	44	Unopposed	55%	15	80	94.513	93
	2	Leach, Jim	R	15	10/15/1942	62	Unopposed	59%	55	43	62.521	43
	3	Boswell, Leonard	D	5	1/10/1934	70	Unopposed	55%	80	20	79.931	47
	4	Latham, Tom	R	6	7/14/1948	56	Unopposed	61%	10	72	95.498	97
	5	King, Steve	R	2	5/28/1949	55	Unopposed	63%	5	96	97.106	83
Kansas	1	Moran, Jerry	R	5	5/29/1954	50	Unopposed	91%	10	92	89.431	70
	2	Ryun, Jim	R	5	4/29/1947	57	Unopposed	56%	5	96	98.546	95
	3	Moore, Dennis	D	4	11/8/1945	59	Unopposed	55%	90	20	85.526	37
	4	Tiahrt, Todd	R	6	6/15/1951	53	Unopposed	66%	5	92	96.529	87
Kentucky	1	Whitfield, Ed	R	6	5/25/1943	61	Unopposed	67%	5	88	92.270	87
	2	Lewis, Ron	R	6	9/14/1946	58	Unopposed	68%	5	84	96.272	95
	3	Northup, Anne	R	5	1/22/1948	56	Unopposed	60%	5	83	96.082	91
	4	Davis, Geoff	R	1	10/26/1958	46	58%	54%	—	—	94.959	95
	5	Rogers, Harold	R	13	12/31/1937	67	91%	Unopposed	0	88	95.955	93
	6	Chandler, Ben	D	1	9/12/1959	45	Unopposed	59%	70	—	81.190	56
Louisiana	1	Jindal, Bobby	R	1	6/10/1971	33	—	78%	—	—	92.659	90
	2	Jefferson, William	D	8	3/14/1947	57	—	79%	80	17	89.175	46
	3	Melancon, Charlie	D	1	10/3/1947	57	32%	50%	—	—	66.612	72
	4	McCrery, Jim	R	9	9/18/1949	55	—	Unopposed	5	96	97.025	100
	5	Alexander, Rodney	R	2	12/5/1946	58	—	59%	40	48	97.106	93
	6	Baker, Richard	R	10	5/22/1948	56	—	72%	5	88	97.830	95
	7	Boustany, Charles	R	1	2/21/1956	48	39%	55%	—	—	95.261	95
Massachusetts	1	Olver, John	D	7	9/3/1936	68	Unopposed	Unopposed	100	0	97.381	15
	2	Neal, Richard	D	9	2/14/1949	55	Unopposed	Unopposed	94	4	96.995	18
	3	McGovern, Jim	D	5	11/20/1959	45	Unopposed	71%	100	4	98.548	23
	4	Frank, Barney	D	13	3/31/1940	64	Unopposed	78%	100	4	95.581	15
	5	Meehan, Martin	D	7	12/30/1956	48	Unopposed	67%	100	4	98.446	22
	6	Tierney, John	D	5	9/18/1951	53	Unopposed	70%	100	0	97.101	13
	7	Markey, Edward	D	15	7/11/1946	58	Unopposed	74%	100	0	98.055	7
	8	Capuano, Michael	D	4	1/9/1952	52	Unopposed	Unopposed	90	4	95.948	25
	9	Lynch, Stephen	D	2	3/31/1955	49	Unopposed	Unopposed	85	28	91.340	30
	10	Delahunt, Bill	D	5	7/18/1941	63	Unopposed	66%	95	0	96.610	33
Maryland	1	Gilchrest, Wayne	R	8	4/15/1946	58	62%	76%	35	56	77.541	57
	2	Ruppersberger, Dutch	D	2	1/31/1946	58	Unopposed	67%	90	12	87.028	46
	3	Cardin, Ben	D	10	10/5/1943	61	90%	63%	95	0	95.025	25
	4	Wynn, Albert	D	7	9/10/1951	53	84%	75%	95	20	88.871	33
	5	Hoyer, Steny	D	12	6/14/1939	65	Unopposed	69%	100	0	92.695	27
	6	Bartlett, Roscoe	R	7	6/3/1926	78	70%	67%	10	92	87.055	77
	7	Cummings, Elijah	D	5	1/18/1951	53	91%	73%	100	0	96.557	23
	8	Van Hollen, Chris	D	2	1/10/1959	45	91%	75%	100	4	97.262	30
Maine	1	Allen, Tom	D	5	4/16/1945	59	Unopposed	60%	100	8	95.786	23
	2	Michaud, Michael	D	2	1/18/1955	49	Unopposed	58%	90	20	91.935	30
Michigan	1	Stupak, Bart	D	7	2/29/1952	52	Unopposed	66%	80	16	88.616	37
	2	Hoekstra, Pete	R	7	10/30/1953	51	Unopposed	69%	5	86	95.417	90
	3	Ehlers, Vernon	R	6	2/6/1934	70	Unopposed	67%	20	67	80.945	95
	4	Camp, Dave	R	8	7/9/1953	51	Unopposed	64%	10	88	94.868	100
	5	Kildee, Dale	D	15	9/16/1929	75	Unopposed	67%	90	16	93.419	33
	6	Upton, Fred	R	10	4/23/1953	51	Unopposed	65%	35	76	84.109	80
	7	Schwarz, Joe	R	1	11/15/1937	67	28%	58%	—	—	84.754	75
	8	Rogers, Mike	R	3	6/2/1963	41	Unopposed	61%	10	92	94.454	90
	9	Knollenberg, Joe	R	7	11/28/1933	71	Unopposed	58%	5	84	95.610	95

(continued)

Table A-1 (continued)

State	District	Representative	Party	Term	Birthdate	Age	% vote in 2004 Primary	% vote in 2004 General	2004 ratings[a] ADA	2004 ratings[a] ACU	109th Congress Poole-Rosenthal (party unity)[b]	109th Congress CQ Presidential Support Score[c]
	10	Miller, Candice	R	2	5/7/1954	50	Unopposed	69%	10	84	91.667	94
	11	McCotter, Thaddeus	R	2	8/22/1965	39	Unopposed	57%	15	88	87.987	82
	12	Levin, Sander	D	12	9/6/1931	73	Unopposed	69%	100	0	94.061	25
	13	Kilpatrick, Carolyn Cheeks	D	5	6/25/1945	59	Unopposed	78%	95	4	96.523	23
	14	Conyers, John	D	21	5/16/1929	75	Unopposed	84%	90	0	97.342	8
	15	Dingell, John	D	25	7/8/1926	78	Unopposed	71%	95	4	91.368	23
Minnesota	1	Gutknecht, Gil	R	6	3/20/1951	53	Unopposed	60%	5	92	92.857	90
	2	Kline, John	R	2	9/6/1947	57	Unopposed	56%	5	96	95.987	95
	3	Ramstad, Jim	R	8	5/6/1946	58	90%	65%	25	76	75.204	70
	4	McCollum, Betty	D	3	7/12/1954	50	Unopposed	57%	100	0	97.236	20
	5	Sabo, Martin Olav	D	14	2/28/1938	66	91%	70%	100	0	93.103	27
	6	Kennedy, Mark	R	3	4/11/1957	47	Unopposed	54%	5	92	89.836	90
	7	Peterson, Collin	D	8	6/29/1944	60	Unopposed	66%	55	52	63.725	60
	8	Oberstar, James	D	16	9/10/1934	70	86%	65%	75	12	90.646	35
Missouri	1	Clay, William Lacy	D	3	7/27/1956	48	Unopposed	75%	100	8	94.655	28
	2	Akin, Todd	R	3	7/5/1947	57	Unopposed	65%	0	100	98.532	95
	3	Carnahan, Russ	D	1	7/10/1958	46	23%	53%	—	—	92.419	40
	4	Skelton, Ike	D	15	12/20/1931	73	Unopposed	66%	64	48	75.497	60
	5	Cleaver, Emanuel	D	1	10/26/1944	60	60%	55%	—	—	94.482	32
	6	Graves, Sam	R	3	11/7/1963	41	Unopposed	64%	10	92	96.405	95
	7	Blunt, Roy	R	5	1/10/1950	54	Unopposed	70%	0	96	98.020	97
	8	Emerson, Jo Ann	R	5	9/16/1950	54	89%	72%	20	76	89.803	74
	9	Hulshof, Kenny	R	5	5/22/1958	46	Unopposed	65%	5	91	93.851	97
Mississippi	1	Wicker, Roger	R	6	7/5/1951	53	Unopposed	79%	0	87	97.360	97
	2	Thompson, Bennie	D	6	1/28/1948	56	Unopposed	58%	85	8	91.503	41
	3	Pickering, Chip	R	5	8/10/1963	41	Unopposed	80%	5	92	93.255	97
	4	Taylor, Gene	D	8	9/17/1953	51	Unopposed	64%	60	54	68.885	60
Montana	AL	Rehberg, Denny	R	3	10/5/1955	49	Unopposed	64%	5	96	95.800	95
North Carolina	1	Butterfield, G. K.	D	1	4/27/1947	57	71%	64%	35	0	91.071	37
	2	Etheridge, Bob	D	5	8/7/1941	63	Unopposed	62%	85	20	86.107	50
	3	Jones, Walter	R	6	2/10/1943	61	Unopposed	71%	30	79	72.759	53
	4	Price, David	D	5	8/17/1940	64	Unopposed	64%	95	12	94.194	33
	5	Foxx, Virginia	R	1	6/29/1943	61	55%[h]	59%	—	—	97.907	83
	6	Coble, Howard	R	11	3/18/1931	73	Unopposed	73%	5	88	93.688	73
	7	McIntyre, Mike	D	5	8/6/1956	48	Unopposed	73%	60	60	72.285	63
	8	Hayes, Robin	R	4	8/14/1945	59	Unopposed	56%	5	88	96.721	85
	9	Myrick, Sue	R	6	8/1/1941	63	Unopposed	70%	0	100	96.817	92
	10	McHenry, Patrick	R	1	10/22/1975	29	50%[i]	64%	—	—	98.527	83
	11	Taylor, Charles	R	8	1/23/1941	63	Unopposed	55%	5	88	96.500	89
	12	Watt, Melvin	D	7	8/26/1945	59	85%	67%	95	0	97.068	17
	13	Miller, Brad	D	2	5/19/1953	51	Unopposed	59%	90	8	91.787	38
North Dakota	AL	Pomeroy, Earl	D	7	9/2/1952	52	Unopposed	60%	85	28	80.524	47
Nebraska	1	Fortenberry, Jeff	R	1	12/27/1960	44	39%	54%	—	—	92.370	87
	2	Terry, Lee	R	4	1/29/1962	42	Unopposed	61%	0	92	94.992	97
	3	Osborne, Tom	R	3	2/23/1937	67	Unopposed	87%	10	84	93.144	95
New Hampshire	1	Bradley, Jeb	R	2	10/20/1952	52	90%	63%	30	76	84.887	80
	2	Bass, Charles	R	6	1/8/1952	52	71%	58%	45	56	84.441	72
New Jersey	1	Andrews, Robert	D	8	8/4/1957	47	Unopposed	75%	95	0	93.299	35
	2	LoBiondo, Frank	R	6	5/12/1946	58	Unopposed	65%	30	60	77.528	73
	3	Saxton, Jim	R	11	1/22/1943	61	Unopposed	63%	35	64	83.089	80
	4	Smith, Chris	R	13	3/4/1953	51	Unopposed	67%	40	54	75.534	67

State	District	Representative	Party	Term	Birthdate	Age	% vote in 2004 Primary	% vote in 2004 General	2004 ratings[a] ADA	2004 ratings[a] ACU	109th Congress Poole-Rosenthal (party unity)[b]	109th Congress CQ Presidential Support Score[c]
	5	Garrett, Scott	R	2	7/9/1959	45	Unopposed	58%	5	100	94.137	83
	6	Pallone, Frank	D	9	10/30/1951	53	Unopposed	67%	95	4	97.106	23
	7	Ferguson, Michael	R	3	7/22/1970	34	Unopposed	57%	30	67	83.387	87
	8	Pascrell, Bill	D	5	1/25/1937	67	Unopposed	69%	90	4	93.954	25
	9	Rothman, Steven	D	5	10/14/1952	52	Unopposed	68%	95	5	95.051	9
	10	Payne, Donald	D	9	7/16/1934	70	Unopposed	97%	95	0	99.458	5
	11	Frelinghuysen, Rodney	R	6	4/29/1946	58	Unopposed	68%	25	67	88.130	83
	12	Holt, Rush	D	4	10/15/1948	56	Unopposed	59%	95	4	96.911	15
	13	Menendez, Robert	D	7	1/1/1954	51	87%	76%	85	8	92.971	40[j]
New Mexico	1	Wilson, Heather	R	4	12/30/1960	44	Unopposed	54%	25	84	82.867	87
	2	Pearce, Steve	R	2	8/24/1947	57	Unopposed	60%	0	96	97.039	97
	3	Udall, Tom	D	4	5/18/1948	56	Unopposed	69%	100	8	96.205	10
Nevada	1	Berkley, Shelley	D	4	1/20/1951	53	83%	66%	95	8	91.122	32
	2	Gibbons, Jim	R	5	12/16/1944	60	Unopposed	67%	10	96	90.690	90
	3	Porter, Jon	R	2	5/16/1955	49	Unopposed	54%	15	76	87.299	93
New York	1	Bishop, Tim	D	2	6/1/1950	54	Unopposed	56%	100	4	95.595	31
	2	Israel, Steve	D	3	5/30/1958	46	Unopposed	67%	100	13	93.355	28
	3	King, Peter	R	7	4/5/1944	60	84%	63%	25	71	88.618	95
	4	McCarthy, Carolyn	D	5	1/5/1944	60	Unopposed	63%	100	12	92.537	30
	5	Ackerman, Gary	D	11	11/19/1942	62	Unopposed	71%	95	4	96.205	33
	6	Meeks, Gregory	D	4	9/25/1953	51	Unopposed	Unopposed	75	9	90.566	41
	7	Crowley, Joseph	D	4	3/16/1962	42	63%	81%	90	9	93.312	35
	8	Nadler, Jerrold	D	7	6/13/1947	57	Unopposed	81%	100	0	98.852	15
	9	Weiner, Anthony	D	4	9/4/1964	40	Unopposed	71%	100	4	97.368	23
	10	Towns, Edolphus	D	12	7/21/1934	70	Unopposed	91%	90	0	93.121	30
	11	Owens, Major	D	12	6/28/1936	68	45%	94%	100	0	98.673	15
	12	Velazquez, Nydia	D	7	3/28/1953	51	Unopposed	86%	100	8	98.366	10
	13	Fossella, Vito	R	4	3/9/1965	39	Unopposed	59%	20	78	88.525	93
	14	Maloney, Carolyn	D	7	2/19/1948	56	Unopposed	81%	100	4	95.942	33
	15	Rangel, Charles	D	18	6/11/1930	74	76%	91%	95	0	96.980	27
	16	Serrano, Jose	D	8	10/24/1943	61	Unopposed	95%	100	0	96.040	16
	17	Engel, Eliot	D	9	2/18/1947	57	59%	76%	90	4	93.994	34
	18	Lowey, Nita	D	9	7/5/1937	67	Unopposed	70%	100	4	97.746	23
	19	Kelly, Sue	R	6	9/26/1936	68	Unopposed	67%	40	56	81.260	75
	20	Sweeney, John	R	4	8/9/1955	49	Unopposed	66%	25	72	85.326	77
	21	McNulty, Michael	D	9	9/16/1947	57	Unopposed	71%	90	16	94.745	18
	22	Hinchey, Maurice	D	7	10/27/1938	66	Unopposed	67%	95	0	98.167	7
	23	McHugh, John	R	7	9/29/1948	56	Unopposed	71%	20	64	86.678	85
	24	Boehlert, Sherwood	R	12	9/28/1936	68	59%	57%	40	50	76.159	67
	25	Walsh, James	R	9	6/19/1947	57	Unopposed	90%	20	67	87.874	79
	26	Reynolds, Tom	R	4	9/3/1950	54	Unopposed	56%	5	92	93.559	95
	27	Higgins, Brian	D	1	10/6/1959	45	44%	51%	—	—	89.233	33
	28	Slaughter, Louise	D	10	8/14/1929	75	79%	73%	95	0	97.927	14
	29	Kuhl, Randy	R	1	4/19/1943	61	64%	51%	—	—	91.129	95
Ohio	1	Chabot, Steve	R	6	1/22/1953	51	Unopposed	60%	10	96	92.532	95
	2	Portman, Robert	R	6	12/19/1955	49	Unopposed	72%	10	88	96.011[j]	97[k]
	3	Turner, Mike	R	2	1/11/1960	44	Unopposed	62%	5	88	91.787	90
	4	Oxley, Michael	R	12	2/11/1944	60	Unopposed	59%	0	96	96.937	100
	5	Gillmor, Paul	R	9	2/1/1939	65	Unopposed	67%	5	84	93.761	91
	6	Strickland, Ted	D	5	8/4/1941	63	83%	Unopposed	95	8	90.060	34
	7	Hobson, David	R	8	10/17/1936	68	Unopposed	65%	5	88	93.984	87
	8	Boehner, John	R	8	11/17/1949	55	Unopposed	69%	0	100	96.748	100
	9	Kaptur, Marcy	D	12	6/17/1946	58	Unopposed	68%	95	8	90.759	27

(continued)

Table A-1 (continued)

							% vote in 2004		2004 ratings[a]		109th Congress	
State	District	Representative	Party	Term	Birthdate	Age	Primary	General	ADA	ACU	Poole-Rosenthal (party unity)[b]	CQ Presidential Support Score[c]
	10	Kucinich, Dennis	D	5	10/6/1946	58	86%	60%	90	0	97.231	13
	11	Jones, Stephanie Tubbs	D	4	9/10/1949	55	Unopposed	Unopposed	85	5	95.540	27
	12	Tiberi, Pat	R	3	10/21/1962	42	Unopposed	62%	10	96	93.475	87
	13	Brown, Sherrod	D	7	11/9/1952	52	Unopposed	67%	95	4	94.932	36
	14	LaTourette, Steven	R	6	7/22/1954	50	Unopposed	63%	15	71	84.053	73
	15	Pryce, Deborah	R	7	7/29/1951	53	84%	60%	15	83	91.843	90
	16	Regula, Ralph	R	17	12/3/1924	80	Unopposed	67%	0	88	90.836	85
	17	Ryan, Tim	D	2	7/16/1973	31	Unopposed	77%	80	17	90.759	37
	18	Ney, Bob	R	6	7/5/1954	50	Unopposed	66%	10	92	88.969	81
Oklahoma	1	Sullivan, John	R	2	1/1/1965	40	70%	60%	0	100	97.329	95
	2	Boren, Dan	D	1	8/2/1973	31	58%	66%	—	—	56.694	85
	3	Lucas, Frank	R	6	1/6/1960	44	Unopposed	82%	0	96	97.545	95
	4	Cole, Tom	R	2	4/28/1949	55	Unopposed	78%	0	96	97.386	95
	5	Istook, Ernest	R	7	2/11/1950	54	Unopposed	66%	0	92	97.952	92
Oregon	1	Wu, David	D	4	4/8/1955	49	Unopposed	58%	90	12	91.721	23
	2	Walden, Greg	R	4	1/10/1957	47	Unopposed	72%	15	80	92.395	87
	3	Blumenauer, Earl	D	5	8/16/1948	56	89%	71%	95	9	96.823	8
	4	DeFazio, Peter	D	10	5/27/1947	57	Unopposed	61%	95	16	91.234	17
	5	Hooley, Darlene	D	5	4/4/1939	65	86%	53%	95	16	91.830	25
Pennsylvania	1	Brady, Robert	D	4	4/7/1945	59	Unopposed	86%	95	4	92.282	30
	2	Fattah, Chaka	D	6	11/21/1956	48	Unopposed	88%	85	0	96.329	28
	3	English, Phil	R	6	6/20/1956	48	Unopposed	60%	25	68	91.503	95
	4	Hart, Melissa	R	3	4/4/1962	42	Unopposed	63%	10	92	94.855	90
	5	Peterson, John	R	5	12/25/1938	66	78%	88%	15	83	96.007	92
	6	Gerlach, Jim	R	2	2/25/1955	49	Unopposed	51%	20	68	76.639	69
	7	Weldon, Curt	R	10	7/22/1947	57	Unopposed	59%	15	79	80.880	77
	8	Fitzpatrick, Mike	R	1	6/28/1963	41	69%[l]	55%	—	—	71.026	65
	9	Shuster, Bill	R	2	1/10/1961	43	51%	69%	5	96	97.078	93
	10	Sherwood, Don	R	4	5/5/1941	63	Unopposed	93%	0	88	94.224	85
	11	Kanjorski, Paul	D	11	4/2/1937	67	Unopposed	94%	80	21	81.322	36
	12	Murtha, John	D	16	6/17/1932	72	Unopposed	Unopposed	50	30	75.828	43
	13	Schwartz, Allyson	D	1	10/3/1948	56	52%	56%	—	—	91.948	27
	14	Doyle, Mike	D	6	8/5/1953	51	Unopposed	Unopposed	80	12	90.484	35
	15	Dent, Charlie	R	1	5/24/1960	44	51%	59%	—	—	85.233	80
	16	Pitts, Joe	R	5	10/10/1939	65	Unopposed	64%	5	100	95.765	84
	17	Holden, Tim	D	7	3/5/1957	47	Unopposed	59%	70	48	76.606	56
	18	Murphy, Tim	R	2	11/11/1952	52	Unopposed	63%	20	92	91.297	87
	19	Platts, Todd	R	3	3/5/1962	42	Unopposed	91%	20	84	78.678	80
Rhode Island	1	Kennedy, Patrick	D	6	7/14/1967	37	Unopposed	64%	95	8	95.780	21
	2	Langevin, Jim	D	3	4/22/1964	40	Unopposed	75%	85	25	92.915	30
South Carolina	1	Brown, Henry	R	3	12/20/1935	69	83%	88%	0	96	96.494	95
	2	Wilson, Joe	R	2	7/31/1947	57	Unopposed	65%	0	96	97.000	92
	3	Barrett, Gresham	R	2	2/14/1961	43	Unopposed	Unopposed	0	100	97.701	90
	4	Inglis, Bob	R	1	10/11/1959	45	84%	70%	—	—	90.777	90
	5	Spratt, John	D	12	11/1/1942	62	Unopposed	63%	80	20	85.877	44
	6	Clyburn, James	D	7	7/21/1940	64	Unopposed	67%	90	13	93.257	35
South Dakota	AL	Herseth, Stephanie	D	1	12/3/1970	34	Unanimous	53%	55	31	77.430	50
Tennessee	1	Jenkins, Bill	R	5	11/29/1936	68	90%	74%	0	91	95.840	93
	2	Duncan, John	R	9	7/21/1947	57	91%	79%	5	88	91.060	74
	3	Wamp, Zach	R	6	10/28/1957	47	90%	65%	0	88	94.281	87
	4	Davis, Lincoln	D	2	9/13/1943	61	91%	55%	60	56	66.883	70
	5	Cooper, Jim	D	2	6/19/1954	50	Unopposed	69%	85	13	80.921	37

State	District	Representative	Party	Term	Birthdate	Age	% vote in 2004		2004 ratings[a]		109th Congress	
							Primary	General	ADA	ACU	Poole-Rosenthal (party unity)[b]	CQ Presidential Support Score[c]
	6	Gordon, Bart	D	11	1/24/1949	55	93%	64%	75	42	73.977	63
	7	Blackburn, Marsha	R	2	6/6/1952	52	Unopposed	Unopposed	0	100	98.701	89
	8	Tanner, John	D	9	9/22/1944	60	Unopposed	74%	60	43	73.641	66
	9	Ford, Harold	D	5	5/11/1970	34	Unopposed	82%	75	21	83.242	55
Texas	1	Gohmert, Louie	R	1	8/18/1953	51	57%[m]	61%	—	—	94.168	78
	2	Poe, Ted	R	1	9/10/1948	56	61%	56%	—	—	92.244	85
	3	Johnson, Sam	R	7	10/11/1930	74	84%	86%	0	100	97.887	82
	4	Hall, Ralph	R	13	5/3/1923	81	77%	68%	5	84	94.290	85
	5	Hensarling, Jeb	R	2	5/29/1957	47	Unopposed	64%	0	100	96.940	85
	6	Barton, Joe	R	11	9/15/1949	55	Unopposed	66%	0	96	95.690	87
	7	Culberson, John	R	3	8/24/1956	48	92%	64%	0	96	97.647	95
	8	Brady, Kevin	R	5	4/11/1955	49	Unopposed	69%	0	100	97.311	97
	9	Green, Al	D	1	9/1/1947	57	66%	72%	—	—	93.569	30
	10	McCaul, Michael	R	1	1/14/1962	42	63%[n]	79%	—	—	94.926	90
	11	Conaway, Mike	R	1	6/11/1948	56	75%	77%	—	—	96.849	93
	12	Granger, Kay	R	5	1/18/1943	61	Unopposed	72%	0	91	96.865	95
	13	Thornberry, Mac	R	6	7/15/1958	46	Unopposed	92%	0	100	97.415	95
	14	Paul, Ron	R	5	8/20/1935	69	Unopposed	Unopposed	50	78	69.707	36
	15	Hinojosa, Ruben	D	5	8/20/1940	64	Unopposed	58%	90	13	81.022	49
	16	Reyes, Silvestre	D	5	11/10/1944	60	Unopposed	68%	70	26	82.509	47
	17	Edwards, Chet	D	8	11/24/1951	53	Unopposed	51%	65	48	70.436	60
	18	Jackson-Lee, Sheila	D	6	1/12/1950	54	Unopposed	89%	95	4	92.979	34
	19	Neugebauer, Randy	R	1	12/24/1949	55	Unopposed	58%	5	96	98.390	87
	20	Gonzalez, Charles	D	4	5/5/1945	59	Unopposed	65%	95	20	87.624	33
	21	Smith, Lamar	R	10	11/19/1947	57	Unopposed	61%	0	92	97.671	97
	22	DeLay, Tom	R	11	4/8/1947	57	Unopposed	55%	0	100	98.364	89
	23	Bonilla, Henry	R	7	1/2/1954	51	Unopposed	69%	0	92	97.735	97
	24	Marchant, Kenny	R	1	2/23/1951	53	73%	64%	—	—	97.705	97
	25	Doggett, Lloyd	D	6	10/6/1946	58	64%	68%	95	4	97.020	21
	26	Burgess, Michael	R	2	12/23/1950	54	Unopposed	66%	5	96	94.943	87
	27	Ortiz, Solomon	D	12	6/3/1937	67	Unopposed	63%	55	28	76.807	57
	28	Cuellar, Henry	D	1	9/19/1955	49	50%	59%	—	—	66.998	85
	29	Green, Gene	D	7	10/17/1947	57	Unopposed	94%	85	20	82.724	43
	30	Johnson, Eddie Bernice	D	7	12/3/1935	69	Unopposed	93%	100	17	95.082	35
	31	Carter, John	R	2	11/6/1941	63	70%	65%	0	96	97.830	95
	32	Sessions, Pete	R	5	3/22/1955	49	Unopposed	54%	0	100	98.750	100
Utah	1	Bishop, Rob	R	2	7/13/1951	53	Unopposed	68%	5	100	97.152	89
	2	Matheson, Jim	D	3	3/21/1960	44	Unopposed	55%	70	48	67.903	67
	3	Cannon, Chris	R	5	10/20/1950	54	58%	63%	0	100	96.661	92
Virginia	1	Davis, Jo Ann	R	3	6/29/1950	54	Unopposed	79%	10	88	89.964	87
	2	Drake, Thelma	R	1	11/20/1949	55	Unopposed[o]	55%	—	—	97.271	95
	3	Scott, Bobby	D	7	4/30/1947	57	Unopposed	69%	100	4	95.285	27
	4	Forbes, Randy	R	2	2/17/1952	52	Unopposed	64%	5	100	94.290	93
	5	Goode, Virgil	R	5	10/17/1946	58	Unopposed	64%	10	96	93.148	82
	6	Goodlatte, Bob	R	7	9/22/1952	52	Unopposed	97%	0	100	97.432	95
	7	Cantor, Eric	R	3	6/6/1963	41	Unopposed	75%	0	100	98.061	95
	8	Moran, Jim	D	8	5/16/1945	59	59%	60%	95	24	91.457	33
	9	Boucher, Rick	D	12	8/1/1946	58	Unopposed	59%	75	32	80.952	33
	10	Wolf, Frank	R	13	1/30/1939	65	Unopposed	64%	25	76	87.642	80
	11	Davis, Tom	R	6	1/5/1949	55	Unopposed	60%	10	80	86.847	85
Vermont	AL	Sanders, Bernie	I	8	9/8/1941	63	Unopposed	67%	95	4	96.661	15

(continued)

Table A-1 (continued)

State	District	Representative	Party	Term	Birthdate	Age	% vote in 2004		2004 ratings[a]		109th Congress	
							Primary	General	ADA	ACU	Poole-Rosenthal (party unity)[b]	CQ Presidential Support Score[c]
Washington	1	Inslee, Jay	D	4	2/9/1951	53	Unopposed	62%	100	4	95.153	28
	2	Larsen, Rick	D	3	6/15/1965	39	Unopposed	64%	90	8	91.220	35
	3	Baird, Brian	D	4	3/7/1956	48	85%	62%	90	17	90.404	37
	4	Hastings, Doc	R	6	2/7/1941	63	Unopposed	63%	0	100	96.488	95
	5	McMorris, Cathy	R	1	5/22/1969	35	50%	60%	—	—	97.541	92
	6	Dicks, Norm	D	15	12/16/1940	64	Unopposed	69%	85	13	89.216	33
	7	McDermott, Jim	D	9	12/28/1936	68	Unopposed	81%	95	0	97.848	15
	8	Reichert, Dave	R	1	8/29/1950	54	43%	52%	—	—	84.150	82
	9	Smith, Adam	D	5	6/15/1965	39	Unopposed	63%	90	17	89.344	45
Wisconsin	1	Ryan, Paul	R	4	1/29/1970	34	Unopposed	65%	20	92	94.013	93
	2	Baldwin, Tammy	D	4	2/11/1962	42	Unopposed	63%	100	4	99.037	13
	3	Kind, Ron	D	5	2/16/1963	41	Unopposed	56%	90	24	88.322	34
	4	Moore, Gwen	D	1	4/18/1951	53	64%	70%	—	—	97.862	13
	5	Sensenbrenner, Jim	R	14	6/14/1943	61	Unopposed	67%	20	92	92.434	84
	6	Petri, Tom	R	13	5/28/1940	64	Unopposed	67%	20	80	88.853	85
	7	Obey, David	D	18	10/3/1938	66	Unopposed	86%	90	4	94.649	22
	8	Green, Mark	R	4	6/1/1960	44	Unopposed	70%	20	88	86.120	87
West Virginia	1	Mollohan, Alan	D	12	5/14/1943	61	Unopposed	68%	65	24	77.554	54
	2	Capito, Shelley Moore	R	3	11/26/1953	51	Unopposed	57%	30	72	88.871	87
	3	Rahall, Nick	D	15	5/20/1949	55	Unopposed	65%	75	28	84.578	47
Wyoming	AL	Cubin, Barbara	R	6	11/30/1946	58	55%	55%	0	91	96.092	94

Note: Figures represent the makeup of the House of Representatives on the first day of the 109th Congress.

a. ADA ratings, compiled by Americans for Democratic Action, indicate members' support of generally liberal positions on a set of key votes; ACU ratings, compiled by the American Conservative Union, indicate members' support of generally conservative positions on a different set of key votes. Members with no scores were serving their first terms in the 109th Congress.

b. The Poole-Rosenthal data represent an analysis of how often senators voted with their parties during the roll call votes of the 109th Congress. A full, detailed explantation can be found at http://voteview.com/.

c. Presidential Support Scores were reported in *Congressional Quarterly Weekly Report,* January 1, 2007. They represent the percentage of votes on which a representative voted with the President's position in the second session of the 109th Congress.

d. Rep. Robert Matsui was reelected in 2004, but died before taking his seat in the 109th Congress. Rep. Doris Matsui was elected in a special election and filled the seat on March 8, 2005.

e. Rep. Christopher Cox resigned from Congress on August 2, 2005. The Poole-Rosenthal data and CQ Presidential Support Score are for his replacement, Rep. John Campbell.

f. Rep. Randy "Duke" Cunningham resigned from Congress on November 28, 2005. The CQ Presidential Support Score is for his replacement, Rep. Brian Bilbray.

g. Rep. Lynn Westmoreland won a plurality of votes in his party's primary and won the runoff primary election with 55.5% of the vote.

h. Rep. Virginia Foxx placed second in her party's primary, but won the runoff primary election with 55% of the vote.

i. Rep. Patrick McHenry placed second in his party's primary, but won the runoff primary election with 50.1% of the vote.

j. Sen. Robert Menendez was appointed to the Senate by Gov. Jon Corzine. Rep. Albio Sires won a special election and filled the seat on November 13, 2006. The CQ Presidential Support Score is that of Rep. Sires.

k. Rep. Rob Portman resigned from Congress on May 2, 2005. The Poole-Rosenthal data and CQ Presidential Support Score are for his replacement, Rep. Jean Schmidt.

l. Rep. Jim Greenwood won his party's primary, but dropped out before the general election. Rep. Michael Fitzpatrick was picked by the local party to be the Republican nominee in the general election.

m. Rep. Louie Gohmert won a plurality of votes in his party's primary and won the runoff primary election with 57% of the vote.

n. Rep. Michael McCaul placed second in his party's primary, but won the runoff primary election with 63% of the vote.

o. Rep. Ed Schrock was unopposed in his party's primary, but dropped out before the general election. Rep. Thelma Drake was picked by the local party to be the Republican nominee in the general election.

Table A-2 House of Representatives, 110th Congress

							% vote in 2006	
State	District	Representative	Party	Term	Birthdate	Age	Primary	General
Alaska	AL	Young, Don	R	17	6/9/1933	73	Unopposed	57%
Alabama	1	Bonner, Jo	R	3	11/19/1959	47	Unopposed	68%
	2	Everett, Terry	R	8	2/15/1937	69	Unopposed	70%
	3	Rogers, Mike	R	3	7/16/1958	48	Unopposed	60%
	4	Aderholt, Robert	R	6	7/22/1965	41	Unopposed	70%
	5	Cramer, Bud	D	9	8/22/1947	59	Unopposed	Unopposed
	6	Bachus, Spencer	R	8	12/28/1947	59	Unopposed	Unopposed
	7	Davis, Artur	D	3	10/9/1967	39	91%	Unopposed
Arkansas	1	Berry, Marion	D	6	8/27/1942	64	Unopposed	69%
	2	Snyder, Vic	D	6	9/27/1947	59	Unopposed	61%
	3	Boozman, John	R	3	12/10/1950	56	Unopposed	62%
	4	Ross, Mike	D	4	8/2/1961	45	Unopposed	75%
Arizona	1	Renzi, Rick	R	3	6/11/1958	48	Unopposed	52%
	2	Franks, Trent	R	3	6/19/1957	49	Unopposed	59%
	3	Shadegg, John	R	7	10/22/1949	57	Unopposed	59%
	4	Pastor, Ed	D	8	6/28/1943	63	Unopposed	73%
	5	Mitchell, Harry	D	1	7/18/1940	66	Unopposed	50%
	6	Flake, Jeff	R	4	12/31/1962	44	Unopposed	75%
	7	Grijalva, Raul	D	3	2/19/1948	58	Unopposed	61%
	8	Giffords, Gabrielle	D	1	6/8/1970	36	54%	54%
California	1	Thompson, Mike	D	5	1/24/1951	55	Unopposed	66%
	2	Herger, Wally	R	11	5/20/1945	61	Unopposed	64%
	3	Lungren, Dan	R	2	9/22/1946	60	Unopposed	60%
	4	Doolittle, John	R	9	10/30/1950	56	67%	49%
	5	Matsui, Doris	D	2	9/25/1944	62	Unopposed	71%
	6	Woolsey, Lynn	D	8	11/3/1937	69	66%	70%
	7	Miller, George	D	17	5/17/1945	61	Unopposed	84%
	8	Pelosi, Nancy	D	10	3/26/1940	66	Unopposed	80%
	9	Lee, Barbara	D	5	7/16/1946	60	Unopposed	86%
	10	Tauscher, Ellen	D	6	11/15/1951	55	Unopposed	66%
	11	McNerney, Jerry	D	1	6/18/1951	55	53%	53%
	12	Lantos, Tom	D	14	2/1/1928	78	83%	76%
	13	Stark, Pete	D	18	11/11/1931	75	Unopposed	75%
	14	Eshoo, Anna	D	8	12/13/1942	64	Unopposed	71%
	15	Honda, Mike	D	4	6/27/1941	65	Unopposed	72%
	16	Lofgren, Zoe	D	7	12/21/1947	59	Unopposed	73%
	17	Farr, Sam	D	7	7/4/1941	65	Unopposed	76%
	18	Cardoza, Dennis	D	3	3/31/1959	47	Unopposed	66%
	19	Radanovich, George	R	7	6/20/1955	51	Unopposed	61%
	20	Costa, Jim	D	2	4/13/1952	54	Unopposed	Unopposed
	21	Nunes, Devin	R	3	10/1/1973	33	Unopposed	67%
	22	McCarthy, Kevin	R	1	1/26/1965	41	85%	71%
	23	Capps, Lois	D	5	1/10/1938	68	Unopposed	65%
	24	Gallegly, Elton	R	10	3/7/1944	62	80%	62%
	25	McKeon, Buck	R	8	9/9/1938	68	Unopposed	60%
	26	Dreier, David	R	13	7/5/1952	54	65%	57%
	27	Sherman, Brad	D	6	10/24/1954	52	Unopposed	69%
	28	Berman, Howard	D	13	4/15/1941	65	80%	74%
	29	Schiff, Adam	D	4	6/22/1960	46	82%	64%
	30	Waxman, Henry	D	17	9/12/1939	67	Unopposed	72%
	31	Becerra, Xavier	D	8	1/26/1958	48	90%	Unopposed
	32	Solis, Hilda	D	4	10/20/1957	49	Unopposed	83%
	33	Watson, Diane	D	3	11/12/1933	73	91%	Unopposed
	34	Roybal-Allard, Lucille	D	8	6/12/1941	65	Unopposed	77%
	35	Waters, Maxine	D	9	8/15/1938	68	86%	84%

(continued)

Table A-2 (continued)

State	District	Representative	Party	Term	Birthdate	Age	% vote in 2006 Primary	% vote in 2006 General
	36	Harman, Jane	D	4	6/28/1945	61	62%	63%
	37	Millender-McDonald, Juanita	D	6	9/7/1938	68	76%	82%
	38	Napolitano, Grace	D	5	12/4/1936	70	Unopposed	75%
	39	Sanchez, Linda	D	3	1/28/1969	37	78%	66%
	40	Royce, Ed	R	8	10/12/1951	55	Unopposed	67%
	41	Lewis, Jerry	R	15	10/21/1934	72	Unopposed	67%
	42	Miller, Gary	R	5	10/16/1948	58	Unopposed	Unopposed
	43	Baca, Joe	D	4	1/23/1947	59	Unopposed	65%
	44	Calvert, Ken	R	8	6/8/1953	53	Unopposed	60%
	45	Bono, Mary	R	5	10/24/1961	45	Unopposed	61%
	46	Rohrabacher, Dana	R	10	6/21/1947	59	Unopposed	60%
	47	Sanchez, Loretta	D	6	1/7/1960	46	Unopposed	62%
	48	Campbell, John	R	1	7/19/1955	51	Unopposed	60%
	49	Issa, Darrell	R	4	11/1/1953	53	Unopposed	63%
	50	Bilbray, Brian	R	1	1/28/1951	55	Unopposed	54%
	51	Filner, Bob	D	8	9/4/1942	64	52%	68%
	52	Hunter, Duncan	R	15	5/31/1948	58	Unopposed	65%
	53	Davis, Susan	D	4	4/13/1944	62	Unopposed	68%
Colorado	1	DeGette, Diana	D	6	7/29/1957	49	Unopposed	80%
	2	Udall, Mark	D	5	7/18/1950	56	Unopposed	68%
	3	Salazar, John	D	2	7/21/1953	53	Unopposed	62%
	4	Musgrave, Marilyn	R	3	1/27/1949	57	Unopposed	46%
	5	Lamborn, Doug	R	1	5/24/1954	52	27%	60%
	6	Tancredo, Tom	R	5	12/20/1945	61	Unopposed	59%
	7	Perlmutter, Ed	D	1	5/1/1953	53	53%	55%
Connecticut	1	Larson, John	D	5	7/22/1948	58	Unopposed	74%
	2	Courtney, Joe	D	1	4/6/1953	53	Unopposed	50%
	3	DeLauro, Rosa	D	9	3/2/1943	63	Unopposed	76%
	4	Shays, Christopher	R	10	10/18/1945	61	Unopposed	51%
	5	Murphy, Chris	D	1	8/3/1973	33	Unopposed	54%
Delaware	AL	Castle, Michael	R	8	7/2/1939	67	Unopposed	57%
Florida	1	Miller, Jeff	R	3	6/27/1959	47	Unopposed	69%
	2	Boyd, Allen	D	6	6/6/1945	61	Unopposed	Unopposed
	3	Brown, Corrine	D	8	11/11/1946	60	Unopposed	Unopposed
	4	Crenshaw, Ander	R	4	9/1/1944	62	Unopposed	70%
	5	Brown-Waite, Ginny	R	3	10/5/1943	63	Unopposed	60%
	6	Stearns, Cliff	R	10	4/16/1941	65	Unopposed	60%
	7	Mica, John	R	8	1/27/1943	63	Unopposed	63%
	8	Keller, Ric	R	4	9/5/1964	42	73%	53%
	9	Billirakis, Gus	R	1	2/8/1963	43	82%	56%
	10	Young, Bill	R	19	12/16/1930	76	Unopposed	66%
	11	Castor, Kathy	D	1	8/20/1966	40	54%	70%
	12	Putnam, Adam	R	4	7/31/1974	32	Unopposed	69%
	13	Buchanan, Vern	R	1	5/8/1951	55	32%	50%
	14	Mack, Connie	R	2	8/12/1967	39	Unopposed	64%
	15	Weldon, Dave	R	7	8/31/1953	53	Unopposed	56%
	16	Mahoney, Tim	D	1	8/15/1956	50	Unopposed	50%
	17	Meek, Kendrick	D	3	9/6/1966	40	89%	Unopposed
	18	Ros-Lehtinen, Ileana	R	9	7/12/1952	54	Unopposed	62%
	19	Wexler, Robert	D	6	1/2/1961	46	Unopposed	Unopposed
	20	Wasserman Schultz, Debbie	D	2	9/27/1966	40	Unopposed	Unopposed
	21	Diaz-Balart, Lincoln	R	8	8/13/1954	52	Unopposed	59%
	22	Klein, Ron	D	1	7/10/1957	49	Unopposed	51%
	23	Hastings, Alcee	D	8	9/5/1936	70	Unopposed	Unopposed
	24	Feeney, Tom	R	3	5/21/1958	48	Unopposed	58%
	25	Diaz-Balart, Mario	R	3	9/25/1961	45	Unopposed	58%

State	District	Representative	Party	Term	Birthdate	Age	% vote in 2006 Primary	% vote in 2006 General
Georgia	1	Kingston, Jack	R	8	4/24/1955	51	Unopposed	68%
	2	Bishop, Sanford	D	8	2/4/1947	59	Unopposed	68%
	3	Westmoreland, Lynn	R	2	4/2/1950	56	Unopposed	68%
	4	Johnson, Hank	D	1	10/2/1954	52	59%	75%
	5	Lewis, John	D	11	2/21/1940	66	Unopposed	Unopposed
	6	Price, Tom	R	2	10/8/1954	52	82%	72%
	7	Linder, John	R	8	9/9/1942	64	Unopposed	71%
	8	Marshall, Jim	D	3	3/31/1948	58	Unopposed	51%
	9	Norwood, Charlie	R	8	7/27/1941	65	Unopposed	77%
	10	Deal, Nathan	R	7	8/25/1942	64	Unopposed	67%
	11	Gingrey, Phil	R	3	7/10/1942	64	Unopposed	71%
	12	Barrow, John	D	2	10/31/1955	51	Unopposed	50%
	13	Scott, David	D	3	6/27/1946	60	67%	69%
Hawaii	1	Abercrombie, Neil	D	9	6/26/1938	68	79%	66%
	2	Hirono, Mazie	D	1	11/3/1947	59	22%	60%
Iowa	1	Braley, Bruce	D	1	10/30/1957	49	37%	55%
	2	Loebsack, David	D	1	12/23/1952	54	Unopposed	51%
	3	Boswell, Leonard	D	6	1/10/1934	72	Unopposed	52%
	4	Latham, Tom	R	7	7/14/1948	58	Unopposed	57%
	5	King, Steve	R	3	5/28/1949	57	Unopposed	59%
Idaho	1	Sali, William	R	1	2/17/1954	52	25%	50%
	2	Simpson, Mike	R	5	9/8/1950	56	Unopposed	62%
Illinois	1	Rush, Bobby	D	8	11/23/1946	60	81%	84%
	2	Jackson, Jesse	D	6	3/11/1965	41	Unopposed	85%
	3	Lipinski, Daniel	D	2	7/15/1966	40	55%	77%
	4	Gutierrez, Luis	D	8	12/10/1953	53	Unopposed	86%
	5	Emanuel, Rahm	D	3	11/29/1959	47	83%	78%
	6	Roskam, Peter	R	1	9/13/1961	45	Unopposed	51%
	7	Davis, Danny	D	6	9/6/1941	65	88%	87%
	8	Bean, Melissa	D	2	1/22/1962	44	Unopposed	51%
	9	Schakowsky, Jan	D	5	5/26/1944	62	Unopposed	75%
	10	Kirk, Mark	R	4	9/15/1959	47	Unopposed	53%
	11	Weller, Jerry	R	6	7/7/1957	49	Unopposed	55%
	12	Costello, Jerry	D	10	9/25/1949	57	90%	Unopposed
	13	Biggert, Judy	R	5	8/15/1937	69	79%	58%
	14	Hastert, Dennis	R	11	1/2/1942	65	Unopposed	60%
	15	Johnson, Tim	R	4	7/23/1946	60	Unopposed	58%
	16	Manzullo, Don	R	8	3/24/1944	62	Unopposed	67%
	17	Hare, Philip	D	1	2/21/1949	57	Unopposed	57%
	18	LaHood, Ray	R	7	12/6/1945	61	Unopposed	67%
	19	Shimkus, John	R	6	2/21/1958	48	Unopposed	61%
Indiana	1	Visclosky, Peter	D	12	8/13/1949	57	Unopposed	70%
	2	Donnelly, Joe	D	1	9/29/1955	51	83%	54%
	3	Souder, Mark	R	7	7/18/1950	56	71%	54%
	4	Buyer, Steve	R	8	11/26/1958	48	73%	62%
	5	Burton, Dan	R	13	6/21/1938	68	84%	65%
	6	Pence, Mike	R	3	6/7/1959	47	86%	60%
	7	Carson, Julia	D	8	7/8/1938	68	81%	54%
	8	Ellsworth, Brad	D	1	9/11/1958	48	Unopposed	61%
	9	Hill, Baron	D	1	6/20/1953	53	79%	50%
Kansas	1	Moran, Jerry	R	6	5/29/1954	52	Unopposed	79%
	2	Boyda, Nancy	D	1	8/2/1955	51	Unopposed	51%
	3	Moore, Dennis	D	5	11/8/1945	61	Unopposed	65%
	4	Tiahrt, Todd	R	7	6/15/1951	55	Unopposed	64%

(continued)

Table A-2 (continued)

State	District	Representative	Party	Term	Birthdate	Age	% vote in 2006 Primary	% vote in 2006 General
Kentucky	1	Whitfield, Ed	R	7	5/25/1943	63	Unopposed	60%
	2	Lewis, Ron	R	7	9/14/1946	60	Unopposed	55%
	3	Yarmuth, John	D	1	11/4/1947	59	54%	51%
	4	Davis, Geoff	R	2	10/26/1958	48	Unopposed	52%
	5	Rogers, Harold	R	14	12/31/1937	69	Unopposed	74%
	6	Chandler, Ben	D	2	9/12/1959	47	Unopposed	85%
Louisiana	1	Jindal, Bobby	R	2	6/10/1971	35	—	88%
	2	Jefferson, William	D	9	3/14/1947	59	30%	57%
	3	Melancon, Charlie	D	1	10/3/1947	59	—	55%
	4	McCrery, Jim	R	10	9/18/1949	57	—	57%
	5	Alexander, Rodney	R	3	12/5/1946	60	—	68%
	6	Baker, Richard	R	11	5/22/1948	58	—	83%
	7	Boustany, Charles	R	2	2/21/1956	50	—	71%
Massachusetts	1	Olver, John	D	8	9/3/1936	70	Unopposed	72%
	2	Neal, Richard	D	10	2/14/1949	57	Unopposed	Unopposed
	3	McGovern, Jim	D	6	11/20/1959	47	Unopposed	Unopposed
	4	Frank, Barney	D	14	3/31/1940	66	Unopposed	Unopposed
	5	Meehan, Martin	D	8	12/30/1956	50	Unopposed	Unopposed
	6	Tierney, John	D	6	9/18/1951	55	Unopposed	66%
	7	Markey, Edward	D	16	7/11/1946	60	Unopposed	Unopposed
	8	Capuano, Michael	D	5	1/9/1952	54	Unopposed	91%
	9	Lynch, Stephen	D	3	3/31/1955	51	77%	78%
	10	Delahunt, Bill	D	6	7/18/1941	65	Unopposed	65%
Maryland	1	Gilchrest, Wayne	R	9	4/15/1946	60	Unopposed	69%
	2	Ruppersberger, Dutch	D	3	1/31/1946	60	82%	69%
	3	Sarbanes, John	D	1	5/22/1962	44	32%	64%
	4	Wynn, Albert	D	8	9/10/1951	55	50%	81%
	5	Hoyer, Steny	D	13	6/14/1939	67	Unopposed	83%
	6	Bartlett, Roscoe	R	8	6/3/1926	80	79%	59%
	7	Cummings, Elijah	D	6	1/18/1951	55	Unopposed	Unopposed
	8	Van Hollen, Chris	D	3	1/10/1959	47	92%	77%
Maine	1	Allen, Tom	D	6	4/16/1945	61	Unopposed	61%
	2	Michaud, Michael	D	3	1/18/1955	51	Unopposed	71%
Michigan	1	Stupak, Bart	D	8	2/29/1952	54	Unopposed	69%
	2	Hoekstra, Pete	R	8	10/30/1953	53	Unopposed	66%
	3	Ehlers, Vernon	R	7	2/6/1934	72	Unopposed	63%
	4	Camp, Dave	R	9	7/9/1953	53	Unopposed	61%
	5	Kildee, Dale	D	16	9/16/1929	77	Unopposed	73%
	6	Upton, Fred	R	11	4/23/1953	53	Unopposed	61%
	7	Walberg, Tim	R	1	4/12/1951	55	53%	50%
	8	Rogers, Mike	R	4	6/2/1963	43	84%	55%
	9	Knollenberg, Joe	R	8	11/28/1933	73	70%	52%
	10	Miller, Candice	R	3	5/7/1954	52	Unopposed	66%
	11	McCotter, Thaddeus	R	3	8/22/1965	41	Unopposed	54%
	12	Levin, Sander	D	13	9/6/1931	75	Unopposed	70%
	13	Kilpatrick, Carolyn Cheeks	D	6	6/25/1945	61	Unopposed	Unopposed
	14	Conyers, John	D	22	5/16/1929	77	Unopposed	85%
	15	Dingell, John	D	26	7/8/1926	80	Unopposed	88%
Minnesota	1	Walz, Tim	D	1	4/6/1964	42	Unopposed	53%
	2	Kline, John	R	3	9/6/1947	59	Unopposed	56%
	3	Ramstad, Jim	R	9	5/6/1946	60	Unopposed	65%
	4	McCollum, Betty	D	4	7/12/1954	52	Unopposed	70%
	5	Ellison, Keith	D	1	8/4/1963	43	41%	56%
	6	Bachmann, Michele	R	1	4/6/1956	50	Unopposed	50%
	7	Peterson, Collin	D	9	6/29/1944	62	86%	70%
	8	Oberstar, James	D	17	9/10/1934	72	Unopposed	64%

State	District	Representative	Party	Term	Birthdate	Age	% vote in 2006 Primary	General
Missouri	1	Clay, William Lacy	D	4	7/27/1956	50	Unopposed	73%
	2	Akin, Todd	R	4	7/5/1947	59	88%	61%
	3	Carnahan, Russ	D	2	7/10/1958	48	76%	66%
	4	Skelton, Ike	D	16	12/20/1931	75	Unopposed	68%
	5	Cleaver, Emanuel	D	2	10/26/1944	62	Unopposed	64%
	6	Graves, Sam	R	4	11/7/1963	43	Unopposed	62%
	7	Blunt, Roy	R	6	1/10/1950	56	80%	67%
	8	Emerson, Jo Ann	R	6	9/16/1950	56	Unopposed	72%
	9	Hulshof, Kenny	R	6	5/22/1958	48	Unopposed	61%
Mississippi	1	Wicker, Roger	R	7	7/5/1951	55	Unopposed	66%
	2	Thompson, Bennie	D	7	1/28/1948	58	64%	64%
	3	Pickering, Chip	R	6	8/10/1963	43	Unopposed	78%
	4	Taylor, Gene	D	9	9/17/1953	53	Unopposed	80%
Montana	AL	Rehberg, Denny	R	4	10/5/1955	51	Unopposed	59%
North Carolina	1	Butterfield, G. K.	D	2	4/27/1947	59	Unopposed	Unopposed
	2	Etheridge, Bob	D	6	8/7/1941	65	Unopposed	67%
	3	Jones, Walter	R	7	2/10/1943	63	Unopposed	69%
	4	Price, David	D	6	8/17/1940	66	90%	65%
	5	Foxx, Virginia	R	2	6/29/1943	63	Unopposed	57%
	6	Coble, Howard	R	12	3/18/1931	75	Unopposed	71%
	7	McIntyre, Mike	D	6	8/6/1956	50	Unopposed	73%
	8	Hayes, Robin	R	5	8/14/1945	61	Unopposed	50%
	9	Myrick, Sue	R	7	8/1/1941	65	Unopposed	67%
	10	McHenry, Patrick	R	2	10/22/1975	31	Unopposed	62%
	11	Schuler, Heath	D	1	12/31/1971	35	75%	54%
	12	Watt, Melvin	D	8	8/26/1945	61	Unopposed	67%
	13	Miller, Brad	D	3	5/19/1953	53	Unopposed	64%
North Dakota	AL	Pomeroy, Earl	D	8	9/2/1952	54	59%	66%
Nebraska	1	Fortenberry, Jeff	R	2	12/27/1960	46	Unopposed	58%
	2	Terry, Lee	R	5	1/29/1962	44	84%	55%
	3	Smith, Adrian	R	1	12/19/1970	36	39%	55%
New Hampshire	1	Shea-Porter, Carol	D	1	12/2/1954	52	54%	51%
	2	Hodes, Paul	D	1	3/21/1951	55	Unopposed	53%
New Jersey	1	Andrews, Robert	D	9	8/4/1957	49	Unopposed	Unopposed
	2	LoBiondo, Frank	R	7	5/12/1946	60	Unopposed	62%
	3	Saxton, Jim	R	12	1/22/1943	63	Unopposed	58%
	4	Smith, Chris	R	14	3/4/1953	53	Unopposed	66%
	5	Garrett, Scott	R	3	7/9/1959	47	86%	55%
	6	Pallone, Frank	D	10	10/30/1951	55	Unopposed	68%
	7	Ferguson, Michael	R	4	7/22/1970	36	Unopposed	49%
	8	Pascrell, Bill	D	6	1/25/1937	69	Unopposed	71%
	9	Rothman, Steven	D	6	10/14/1952	54	Unopposed	71%
	10	Payne, Donald	D	10	7/16/1934	72	Unopposed	Unopposed
	11	Frelinghuysen, Rodney	R	7	4/29/1946	60	Unopposed	62%
	12	Holt, Rush	D	5	10/15/1948	58	Unopposed	66%
	13	Sires, Albiro	D	1	1/26/1951	55	74%	78%
New Mexico	1	Wilson, Heather	R	5	12/30/1960	46	Unopposed	50%
	2	Pearce, Steve	R	3	8/24/1947	59	Unopposed	59%
	3	Udall, Tom	D	5	5/18/1948	58	Unopposed	75%
Nevada	1	Berkley, Shelley	D	5	1/20/1951	55	87%	65%
	2	Heller, Dean	R	1	5/10/1960	46	35%	50%
	3	Porter, Jon	R	3	5/16/1955	51	Unopposed	48%

(continued)

Table A-2 (continued)

State	District	Representative	Party	Term	Birthdate	Age	% vote in 2006	
							Primary	General
New York	1	Bishop, Tim	D	3	6/1/1950	56	Unopposed	61%
	2	Israel, Steve	D	4	5/30/1958	48	Unopposed	70%
	3	King, Peter	R	8	4/5/1944	62	83%	56%
	4	McCarthy, Carolyn	D	6	1/5/1944	62	Unopposed	65%
	5	Ackerman, Gary	D	12	11/19/1942	64	Unopposed	Unopposed
	6	Meeks, Gregory	D	5	9/25/1953	53	Unopposed	Unopposed
	7	Crowley, Joseph	D	5	3/16/1962	44	Unopposed	84%
	8	Nadler, Jerrold	D	8	6/13/1947	59	Unopposed	83%
	9	Weiner, Anthony	D	5	9/4/1964	42	Unopposed	Unopposed
	10	Towns, Edolphus	D	13	7/21/1934	72	47%	92%
	11	Clarke, Yvette D.	D	1	11/21/1964	42	31%	89%
	12	Velazquez, Nydia	D	8	3/28/1953	53	Unopposed	89%
	13	Fossella, Vito	R	5	3/9/1965	41	Unopposed	57%
	14	Maloney, Carolyn	D	8	2/19/1948	58	Unopposed	84%
	15	Rangel, Charles	D	19	6/11/1930	76	Unopposed	94%
	16	Serrano, Jose	D	9	10/24/1943	63	Unopposed	96%
	17	Engel, Eliot	D	10	2/18/1947	59	82%	76%
	18	Lowey, Nita	D	10	7/5/1937	69	Unopposed	70%
	19	Hall, John	D	1	7/23/1948	58	49%	51%
	20	Gillibrand, Kristen	D	1	12/9/1966	40	Unopposed	53%
	21	McNulty, Michael	D	10	9/16/1947	59	86%	78%
	22	Hinchey, Maurice	D	8	10/27/1938	68	Unopposed	Unopposed
	23	McHugh, John	R	8	9/29/1948	58	Unopposed	63%
	24	Arcuri, Michael	D	1	6/11/1959	47	Unopposed	54%
	25	Walsh, James	R	10	6/19/1947	59	Unopposed	51%
	26	Reynolds, Tom	R	5	9/3/1950	56	Unopposed	52%
	27	Higgins, Brian	D	2	10/6/1959	47	Unopposed	79%
	28	Slaughter, Louise	D	11	8/14/1929	77	Unopposed	73%
	29	Kuhl, Randy	R	2	4/19/1943	63	Unopposed	52%
Ohio	1	Chabot, Steve	R	7	1/22/1953	53	Unopposed	52%
	2	Schmidt, Jean	R	1	11/29/1951	55	48%	50%
	3	Turner, Mike	R	3	1/11/1960	46	Unopposed	59%
	4	Jordan, Jim	R	1	2/17/1964	42	51%	60%
	5	Gillmor, Paul	R	10	2/1/1939	67	Unopposed	53%
	6	Wilson, Charlie	D	1	1/18/1943	63	66%	62%
	7	Hobson, David	R	9	10/17/1936	70	Unopposed	61%
	8	Boehner, John	R	9	11/17/1949	57	Unopposed	64%
	9	Kaptur, Marcy	D	13	6/17/1946	60	Unopposed	74%
	10	Kucinich, Dennis	D	6	10/6/1946	60	76%	66%
	11	Jones, Stephanie Tubbs	D	5	9/10/1949	57	Unopposed	83%
	12	Tiberi, Pat	R	4	10/21/1962	44	Unopposed	57%
	13	Sutton, Betty	D	1	7/31/1963	43	31%	61%
	14	LaTourette, Steven	R	7	7/22/1954	52	Unopposed	58%
	15	Pryce, Deborah	R	8	7/29/1951	55	Unopposed	50%
	16	Regula, Ralph	R	18	12/3/1924	82	58%	58%
	17	Ryan, Tim	D	3	7/16/1973	33	Unopposed	80%
	18	Space, Zach	D	1	1/27/1961	45	39%	62%
Oklahoma	1	Sullivan, John	R	4	1/1/1965	42	83%	64%
	2	Boren, Dan	D	2	8/2/1973	33	Unopposed	73%
	3	Lucas, Frank	R	7	1/6/1960	46	Unopposed	67%
	4	Cole, Tom	R	3	4/28/1949	57	Unopposed	65%
	5	Fallin, Mary	R	1	12/9/1954	52	63%[a]	60%
Oregon	1	Wu, David	D	5	4/8/1955	51	87%	63%
	2	Walden, Greg	R	5	1/10/1957	49	90%	67%
	3	Blumenauer, Earl	D	6	8/16/1948	58	90%	73%
	4	DeFazio, Peter	D	11	5/27/1947	59	Unopposed	62%
	5	Hooley, Darlene	D	6	4/4/1939	67	Unopposed	54%

State	District	Representative	Party	Term	Birthdate	Age	% vote in 2006 Primary	General
Pennsylvania	1	Brady, Robert	D	5	4/7/1945	61	Unopposed	Unopposed
	2	Fattah, Chaka	D	7	11/21/1956	50	Unopposed	89%
	3	English, Phil	R	7	6/20/1956	50	Unopposed	54%
	4	Altmire, Jason	D	1	3/7/1968	38	55%	52%
	5	Peterson, John	R	6	12/25/1938	68	Unopposed	60%
	6	Gerlach, Jim	R	3	2/25/1955	51	Unopposed	51%
	7	Sestak, Joe	D	1	12/12/1951	55	Unopposed	56%
	8	Murphy, Patrick	D	1	10/19/1973	33	65%	50%
	9	Shuster, Bill	R	3	1/10/1961	45	Unopposed	60%
	10	Carney, Chris	D	1	3/2/1959	47	Unopposed	53%
	11	Kanjorski, Paul	D	12	4/2/1937	69	Unopposed	72%
	12	Murtha, John	D	17	6/17/1932	74	Unopposed	61%
	13	Schwartz, Allyson	D	2	10/3/1948	58	Unopposed	66%
	14	Doyle, Mike	D	7	8/5/1953	53	76%	90%
	15	Dent, Charlie	R	2	5/24/1960	46	Unopposed	54%
	16	Pitts, Joe	R	6	10/10/1939	67	Unopposed	57%
	17	Holden, Tim	D	8	3/5/1957	49	Unopposed	64%
	18	Murphy, Tim	R	3	11/11/1952	54	Unopposed	58%
	19	Platts, Todd	R	4	3/5/1962	44	Unopposed	64%
Rhode Island	1	Kennedy, Patrick	D	7	7/14/1967	39	Unopposed	69%
	2	Langevin, Jim	D	4	4/22/1964	42	62%	73%
South Carolina	1	Brown, Henry	R	4	12/20/1935	71	Unopposed	60%
	2	Wilson, Joe	R	2	7/31/1947	59	Unopposed	63%
	3	Barrett, Gresham	R	2	2/14/1961	45	Unopposed	63%
	4	Inglis, Bob	R	2	10/11/1959	47	Unopposed	64%
	5	Spratt, John	D	13	11/1/1942	64	Unopposed	57%
	6	Clyburn, James	D	8	7/21/1940	66	Unopposed	64%
South Dakota	AL	Herseth Sandlin, Stephanie	D	2	12/3/1970	36	Unopposed	69%
Tennessee	1	Davis, David	R	1	11/6/1959	47	22%	61%
	2	Duncan, John	R	10	7/21/1947	59	87%	78%
	3	Wamp, Zach	R	7	10/28/1957	49	87%	66%
	4	Davis, Lincoln	D	3	9/13/1943	63	86%	66%
	5	Cooper, Jim	D	3	6/19/1954	52	92%	69%
	6	Gordon, Bart	D	12	1/24/1949	57	92%	67%
	7	Blackburn. Marsha	R	3	6/6/1952	54	Unopposed	66%
	8	Tanner, John	D	10	9/22/1944	62	Unopposed	73%
	9	Cohen, Steve	D	1	5/24/1949	57	31%	60%
Texas	1	Gohmert, Louie	R	2	8/18/1953	53	Unopposed	68%
	2	Poe, Ted	R	2	9/10/1948	58	Unopposed	66%
	3	Johnson, Sam	R	8	10/11/1930	76	85%	63%
	4	Hall, Ralph	R	14	5/3/1923	83	Unopposed	64%
	5	Hensarling, Jeb	R	3	5/29/1957	49	Unopposed	62%
	6	Barton, Joe	R	12	9/15/1949	57	Unopposed	60%
	7	Culberson, John	R	4	8/24/1956	50	Unopposed	59%
	8	Brady, Kevin	R	6	4/11/1955	51	Unopposed	67%
	9	Green, Al	D	2	9/1/1947	59	Unopposed	Unopposed
	10	McCaul, Michael	R	2	1/14/1962	44	Unopposed	55%
	11	Conaway, Mike	R	2	6/11/1948	58	Unopposed	Unopposed
	12	Granger, Kay	R	6	1/18/1943	63	Unopposed	67%
	13	Thornberry, Mac	R	7	7/15/1958	48	Unopposed	74%
	14	Paul, Ron	R	6	8/20/1935	71	78%	60%
	15	Hinojosa, Ruben	D	6	8/20/1940	66	Unopposed	62%
	16	Reyes, Silvestre	D	6	11/10/1944	62	100%	79%
	17	Edwards, Chet	D	9	11/24/1951	55	Unopposed	58%
	18	Lee, Sheila Jackson	D	7	1/12/1950	56	Unopposed	77%

(continued)

Table A-2 (continued)

State	District	Representative	Party	Term	Birthdate	Age	% vote in 2006 Primary	% vote in 2006 General
	19	Neugebauer, Randy	R	2	12/24/1949	57	Unopposed	68%
	20	Gonzalez, Charles	D	5	5/5/1945	61	Unopposed	87%
	21	Smith, Lamar	R	11	11/19/1947	59	Unopposed	60%
	22	Lampson, Nick	D	5	2/14/1945	61	Unopposed	52%
	23	Ciro Rodriguez	D	5	12/9/1946	60	20%[b]	54%[b]
	24	Marchant, Kenny	R	2	2/23/1951	55	Unopposed	60%
	25	Doggett, Lloyd	D	7	10/6/1946	60	Unopposed	67%
	26	Burgess, Michael	R	3	12/23/1950	56	Unopposed	60%
	27	Ortiz, Solomon	D	13	6/3/1937	69	Unopposed	57%
	28	Cuellar, Henry	D	2	9/19/1955	51	53%	68%
	29	Green, Gene	D	8	10/17/1947	59	Unopposed	74%
	30	Johnson, Eddie Bernice	D	8	12/3/1935	71	Unopposed	80%
	31	Carter, John	R	3	11/6/1941	65	Unopposed	58%
	32	Sessions, Pete	R	6	3/22/1955	51	Unopposed	56%
Utah	1	Bishop, Rob	R	3	7/13/1951	55	Unopposed	63%
	2	Matheson, Jim	D	4	3/21/1960	46	Unopposed	59%
	3	Cannon, Chris	R	6	10/20/1950	56	56%	58%
Virginia	1	Davis, Jo Ann	R	4	6/29/1950	56	Unopposed	63%
	2	Drake, Thelma	R	2	11/20/1949	57	Unopposed	51%
	3	Scott, Bobby	D	8	4/30/1947	59	Unopposed	Unopposed
	4	Forbes, Randy	R	2	2/17/1952	54	Unopposed	76%
	5	Goode, Virgil	R	6	10/17/1946	60	Unopposed	59%
	6	Goodlatte, Bob	R	8	9/22/1952	54	Unopposed	75%
	7	Cantor, Eric	R	4	6/6/1963	43	Unopposed	64%
	8	Moran, Jim	D	9	5/16/1945	61	Unopposed	66%
	9	Boucher, Rick	D	13	8/1/1946	60	Unopposed	68%
	10	Wolf, Frank	R	14	1/30/1939	67	Unopposed	57%
	11	Davis, Tom	R	7	1/5/1949	57	Unopposed	55%
Vermont	AL	Welch, Peter	D	1	5/2/1947	59	Unopposed	53%
Washington	1	Inslee, Jay	D	5	2/9/1951	55	Unopposed	68%
	2	Larsen, Rick	D	4	6/15/1965	41	Unopposed	64%
	3	Baird, Brian	D	5	3/7/1956	50	Unopposed	63%
	4	Hastings, Doc	R	7	2/7/1941	65	77%	60%
	5	McMorris Rodgers, Cathy	R	2	5/22/1969	37	Unopposed	56%
	6	Dicks, Norm	D	16	12/16/1940	66	Unopposed	71%
	7	McDermott, Jim	D	10	12/28/1936	70	92%	79%
	8	Reichert, Dave	R	2	8/29/1950	56	Unopposed	51%
	9	Smith, Adam	D	6	6/15/1965	41	Unopposed	66%
Wisconsin	1	Ryan, Paul	R	5	1/29/1970	36	Unopposed	63%
	2	Baldwin, Tammy	D	5	2/11/1962	44	Unopposed	63%
	3	Kind, Ron	D	5	2/16/1963	43	25%	56%
	4	Moore, Gwen	D	2	4/18/1951	55	Unopposed	71%
	5	Sensenbrenner, Jim	R	15	6/14/1943	63	Unopposed	62%
	6	Petri, Tom	R	14	5/28/1940	66	Unopposed	Unopposed
	7	Obey, David	D	19	10/3/1938	68	Unopposed	62%
	8	Kagen, Steve	D	1	12/12/1949	57	48%	51%
West Virginia	1	Mollohan, Alan	D	12	5/14/1943	63	Unopposed	64%
	2	Capito, Shelley Moore	R	4	11/26/1953	53	Unopposed	57%
	3	Rahall, Nick	D	16	5/20/1949	57	Unopposed	69%
Wyoming	AL	Cubin, Barbara	R	7	11/30/1946	60	60%	50%

Note: Figures represent the makeup of the House of Representatives on the first day of the 110th Congress.

a. Rep. Mary Fallin won a plurality of votes in her party's primary and won the runoff primary election with 63% of the vote.

b. Rep. Ciro Rodriguez entered the race for the Texas 23rd District after the U.S. Supreme Court ruled that the district boundaries be redrawn. There was no time to run primaries, so an open election was held on Election Day and Rep. Rodriguez received 20% of the vote to 49.9% of the vote for incumbent Rep. Henry Bonilla. In the runoff election, Rep. Rodriguez defeated Rep. Bonilla with 54% of the vote.

Table A-3 Senate, 109th Congress

State	Senator	Party	Term	Birthdate	Age	% vote in previous election		2004 ratings[a]		109th Congress	
						Primary	General	ADA	ACU	Poole-Rosenthal (party unity)[b]	CQ Presidential Support Score[c]
Alaska	Stevens, Ted	R	6	11/18/1923	81	89%	78%	20	92	88.571	93
	Murkowski, Lisa	R	1	5/22/1957	47	58%	49%	35	74	88.372	89
Alabama	Shelby, Richard	R	4	5/6/1934	70	Unopposed	68%	20	84	91.927	86
	Sessions, Jeff	R	2	12/24/1946	58	Unopposed	59%	10	96	96.401	91
Arkansas	Lincoln, Blanche	D	2	9/30/1960	44	83%	56%	95	20	80.977	59
	Pryor, Mark	D	1	1/10/1963	41	Unopposed	54%	85	20	78.406	64
Arizona	McCain, John	R	4	8/29/1936	68	Unopposed	77%	35	72	80.593	89
	Kyl, Jon	R	2	4/25/1942	62	Unopposed	79%	5	100	96.401	90
California	Boxer, Barbara	D	3	11/11/1940	71	Unopposed	58%	95	4	98.143	47
	Feinstein, Dianne	D	2	6/22/1933	64	52%	56%	100	4	91.384	54
Colorado	Allard, Wayne	R	2	12/2/1943	61	Unopposed	51%	5	96	96.144	91
	Salazar, Ken	D	1	3/2/1955	49	73%	51%	—	—	86.162	58
Connecticut	Dodd, Christopher	D	5	5/27/1944	62	Unopposed	66%	100	4	94.211	49
	Lieberman, Joe	D	3	2/24/1942	60	Unopposed	63%	75	0	88.011	62
Delaware	Biden, Joseph	D	6	11/20/1942	62	Unopposed	58%	95	0	90.027	55
	Carper, Thomas	D	1	1/23/1947	57	Unopposed	56%	95	12	77.577	64
Florida	Nelson, Bill	D	1	9/29/1942	62	78%	51%	80	4	81.234	60
	Martinez, Mel	R	1	10/23/1946	58	45%	49%	—	—	90.551	92
Georgia	Chambliss, Saxby	R	1	11/10/1943	61	61%	53%	5	96	94.531	93
	Isakson, Johnny	R	1	12/28/1944	60	53%	58%	5	95	95.337	93
Hawaii	Inouye, Daniel	D	8	9/7/1924	80	94%	76%	100	8	89.714	56
	Akaka, Daniel	D	2	9/11/1924	80	91%	73%	95	5	95.833	48
Idaho	Craig, Larry	R	3	7/20/1945	59	Unopposed	65%	5	96	92.228	94
	Crapo, Mike	R	2	5/20/1951	53	Unopposed	99%	10	92	94.859	88
Illinois	Durbin, Richard	D	2	11/21/1944	60	Unopposed	60%	95	4	98.187	47
	Obama, Barack	D	1	8/4/1961	43	53%	70%	—	—	96.373	49
Indiana	Lugar, Richard	R	5	4/4/1932	72	Unopposed	67%	20	84	83.161	91
	Bayh, Evan	D	2	12/26/1955	49	Unopposed	62%	90	20	89.406	58
Iowa	Grassley, Charles	R	5	9/17/1933	71	Unopposed	70%	20	96	94.615	57
	Harkin, Tom	D	4	11/19/1939	65	Unopposed	54%	100	8	96.373	46
Kansas	Brownback, Sam	R	2	9/12/1956	48	87%	69%	15	96	90.909	92
	Roberts, Pat	R	2	4/20/1936	68	84%	83%	15	92	94.01	88
Kentucky	McConnell, Mitch	R	4	2/20/1942	62	Unopposed	65%	15	96	97.686	91
	Bunning, Jim	R	2	10/23/1931	73	84%	51%	15	100	97.895	90
Louisiana	Landrieu, Mary	D	2	11/23/1955	49	46%	52%	85	32	75.526	71
	Vitter, David	R	1	5/3/1961	43	—	51%	5	96	93.734	87
Massachusetts	Kennedy, Edward	D	7	2/22/1932	72	Unopposed	73%	100	0	99.215	48
	Kerry, John	D	4	12/11/1943	61	Unopposed	80%	25	0	96.042	51
Maryland	Sarbanes, Paul	D	5	2/3/1933	71	83%	63%	100	0	97.423	54
	Mikulski, Barbara	D	4	7/20/1936	68	90%	65%	100	8	97.035	49
Maine	Snowe, Olympia	R	2	2/21/1947	57	Unopposed	69%	65	60	56.136	75
	Collins, Susan	R	2	12/7/1952	52	Unopposed	58%	45	68	62.051	79
Michigan	Levin, Carl	D	5	6/28/1934	70	Unopposed	61%	100	0	95.876	56
	Stabenow, Debbie	D	1	4/29/1950	54	Unopposed	49%	100	8	91.969	51

(continued)

Table A-3 (continued)

State	Senator	Party	Term	Birthdate	Age	% vote in previous election		2004 ratings[a]		109th Congress	
						Primary	General	ADA	ACU	Poole-Rosenthal (party unity)[b]	CQ Presidential Support Score[c]
Minnesota	Dayton, Mark	D	1	1/26/1947	57	41%	49%	95	12	95.135	48
	Coleman, Norm	R	1	8/17/1949	55	94%	50%	30	84	77.151	88
Missouri	Bond, Christopher	R	4	3/6/1939	65	88%	56%	20	96	93.059	89
	Talent, Jim	R	1	10/18/1956	48	90%	50%	20	96	83.846	82
Mississippi	Cochran, Thad	R	5	12/7/1937	67	Unopposed	85%	15	92	93.041	89
	Lott, Trent	R	3	10/9/1941	63	Unopposed	66%	5	96	94.663	88
Montana	Baucus, Max	D	5	12/11/1941	63	Unopposed	63%	85	29	76.178	61
	Burns, Conrad	R	3	1/25/1935	69	Unopposed	51%	5	100	92.126	85
North Carolina	Dole, Elizabeth	R	1	7/29/1936	68	80%	54%	25	92	93.557	90
	Burr, Richard	R	1	11/30/1955	49	88%	52%	10	87	94.574	88
North Dakota	Dorgan, Byron	D	3	5/14/1942	62	Unopposed	68%	95	20	84.514	46
	Conrad, Kent	D	2	3/12/1948	56	Unopposed	62%	90	20	76.923	52
Nebraska	Hagel, Chuck	R	2	10/4/1946	58	Unopposed	83%	20	87	90.181	96
	Nelson, Ben	D	1	5/17/1941	63	92%	51%	65	52	41.388	76
New Hampshire	Gregg, Judd	R	3	2/14/1947	57	92%	66%	15	88	90.390	93
	Sununu, John	R	1	9/10/1964	40	53%	51%	10	100	88.391	90
New Jersey	Corzine, John	D	1	1/1/1947	58	58%	50%	100	4	96.644	50[d]
	Lautenberg, Frank	D	4	1/23/1924	80	Unopposed[e]	54%	100	0	97.416	46
New Mexico	Domenici, Pete	R	6	5/7/1932	72	Unopposed	65%	15	95	89.488	91
	Bingaman, Jeff	D	4	10/3/1943	61	Unopposed	62%	90	12	88.947	51
Nevada	Reid, Harry	D	4	12/2/1939	65	Unopposed	61%	90	21	92.308	57
	Ensign, John	R	1	3/25/1958	46	88%	55%	15	92	92.487	90
New York	Schumer, Charles	D	2	11/23/1950	54	Unopposed	71%	100	12	93.282	52
	Clinton, Hillary Rodham	D	1	10/26/1947	57	82%	55%	95	0	94.488	50
Ohio	DeWine, Mike	R	2	1/5/1947	57	80%	60%	35	68	68.123	86
	Voinovich, George	R	2	7/15/1936	68	77%	64%	30	76	81.395	89
Oklahoma	Inhofe, James	R	2	11/17/1934	70	Unopposed	57%	10	100	94.010	88
	Coburn, Tom	R	1	3/14/1948	56	61%	53%	—	—	92.746	88
Oregon	Wyden, Ron	D	2	5/3/1949	55	Unopposed	63%	100	4	94.013	51
	Smith, Gordon	R	2	5/25/1952	52	Unopposed	56%	40	76	81.606	83
Pennsylvania	Specter, Arlen	R	5	2/12/1930	74	51%	53%	45	75	65.354	76
	Santorum, Rick	R	2	5/10/1958	46	Unopposed	52%	15	96	92.348	86
Rhode Island	Reed, Jack	D	2	11/12/1949	55	Unopposed	78%	100	0	96.915	53
	Chafee, Lincoln	R	1	3/26/1953	51	Unopposed	57%	55	40	44.357	71
South Carolina	Graham, Lindsey	R	1	7/9/1955	49	Unopposed	54%	25	92	88.189	91
	DeMint, Jim	R	1	9/2/1951	53	59%[f]	54%	—	—	96.632	90
South Dakota	Johnson, Tim	D	2	12/28/1946	58	95%	50%	85	11	82.857	57
	Thune, John	R	1	1/7/1961	43	Unopposed	51%	—	—	90.314	87
Tennessee	Frist, Bill	R	2	2/22/1952	52	Unopposed	65%	20	92	95.128	93
	Alexander, Lamar	R	1	7/3/1940	64	54%	54%	15	92	92.487	93
Texas	Hutchison, Kay Bailey	R	2	7/22/1943	61	Unopposed	65%	25	84	90.231	84
	Cornyn, John	R	1	2/2/1952	52	77%	55%	5	100	95.855	91
Utah	Hatch, Orrin	R	5	3/22/1934	70	Unopposed	66%	10	96	94.517	88
	Bennett, Robert	R	3	9/18/1933	71	Unopposed	69%	20	88	92.689	90
Virginia	Warner, John	R	5	2/18/1927	77	Unopposed	83%	25	72	84.238	91
	Allen, George	R	1	3/8/1952	52	Unopposed	52%	15	92	94.859	91

State	Senator	Party	Term	Birthdate	Age	% vote in previous election: Primary	% vote in previous election: General	2004 ratings[a]: ADA	2004 ratings[a]: ACU	109th Congress: Poole-Rosenthal (party unity)[b]	109th Congress: CQ Presidential Support Score[c]
Vermont	Leahy, Patrick	D	6	3/31/1940	64	95%	71%	100	8	96.649	46
	Jeffords, James	I	3	5/11/1934	70	78%	66%	85	4	94.517	49
Washington	Murray, Patty	D	3	10/11/1950	54	92%	55%	90	8	93.523	59
	Cantwell, Maria	D	1	10/13/1958	46	37%	49%	95	8	91.753	54
Wisconsin	Kohl, Herb	D	3	2/7/1935	69	90%	62%	100	4	89.406	57
	Feingold, Russell	D	3	3/2/1953	51	Unopposed	55%	100	8	93.979	47
West Virginia	Byrd, Robert	D	8	11/20/1917	87	Unopposed	78%	90	8	79.896	49
	Rockefeller, Jay	D	4	6/18/1937	67	90%	63%	90	12	89.873	55
Wyoming	Thomas, Craig	R	2	2/17/1933	71	Unopposed	74%	5	100	94.920	91
	Enzi, Michael	R	2	2/1/1944	60	86%	73%	5	96	95.699	91

Note: Figures represent the makeup of the Senate on the first day of the 109th Congress.

a. ADA ratings, compiled by Americans for Democratic Action, indicate senators' support of generally liberal positions on a set of key votes; ACU ratings, compiled by the American Conservative Union, indicate senators' support of generally conservative positions on a different set of key votes. Senators with no scores were serving their first terms in the 109th Congress.

b. The Poole-Rosenthal data represent an analysis of how often senators voted with their parties during the roll call votes of the 109th Congress. A full, detailed explantation can be found at http://voteview.com/.

c. Presidential Support Scores were reported in *Congressional Quarterly Weekly Report,* January 1, 2007. They represent the percentage of votes on which a senator voted with the president's position in the second session of the 109th Congress.

d. Sen. Jon Corzine was replaced by Sen. Robert Menendez. The Presidential Support Score is that of Sen. Menendez.

e. Sen. Robert Torricelli was unopposed in his party's primary, but dropped out before the general election. Sen. Frank Lautenberg was picked by the state party to be the Democratic nominee in the general election.

f. Sen. Jim DeMint placed second in his party's primary, but won the runoff primary election with 59% of the vote.

Table A-4 Senate, 110th Congress

State	Senator	Party	Term	Birthdate	Age	% vote in previous election: Primary	% vote in previous election: General
Alaska	Stevens, Ted	R	6	11/18/1923	83	89%	78%
	Murkowski, Lisa	R	1	5/22/1957	49	58%	49%
Alabama	Shelby, Richard	R	4	5/6/1934	72	Unopposed	68%
	Sessions, Jeff	R	2	12/24/1946	60	Unopposed	59%
Arkansas	Lincoln, Blanche	D	2	9/30/1960	46	83%	56%
	Pryor, Mark	D	1	1/10/1963	43	Unopposed	54%
Arizona	McCain, John	R	4	8/29/1936	70	Unopposed	77%
	Kyl, Jon	R	3	4/25/1942	64	Unopposed	53%
California	Feinstein, Dianne	D	3	6/22/1933	73	87%	60%
	Boxer, Barbara	D	3	11/11/1940	66	Unopposed	58%
Colorado	Allard, Wayne	R	2	12/2/1943	63	Unopposed	51%
	Salazar, Ken	D	1	3/2/1955	51	73%	51%
Connecticut	Dodd, Christopher	D	5	5/27/1944	62	Unopposed	66%
	Lieberman, Joe	I	4	2/24/1942	64	48%[a]	50%
Delaware	Biden, Joseph	D	6	11/20/1942	64	Unopposed	58%
	Carper, Thomas	D	2	1/23/1947	59	Unopposed	70%
Florida	Nelson, Bill	D	2	9/29/1942	64	Unopposed	60%
	Martinez, Mel	R	1	10/23/1946	60	45%	49%
Georgia	Chambliss, Saxby	R	1	11/10/1943	63	61%	53%
	Isakson, Johnny	R	1	12/28/1944	62	53%	58%
Hawaii	Inouye, Daniel	D	8	9/7/1924	81	94%	76%
	Akaka, Daniel	D	3	9/11/1924	80	54%	61%
Iowa	Grassley, Charles	R	5	9/17/1933	73	Unopposed	70%
	Harkin, Tom	D	4	11/19/1939	67	Unopposed	54%
Idaho	Craig, Larry	R	3	7/20/1945	61	Unopposed	65%
	Crapo, Mike	R	2	5/20/1951	55	Unopposed	99%
Illinois	Durbin, Richard	D	2	11/21/1944	62	Unopposed	60%
	Obama, Barack	D	1	8/4/1961	45	53%	70%
Indiana	Lugar, Richard	R	6	4/4/1932	74	Unopposed	87%
	Bayh, Evan	D	2	12/26/1955	51	Unopposed	62%
Kansas	Brownback, Sam	R	2	9/12/1956	50	87%	69%
	Roberts, Pat	R	2	4/20/1936	70	84%	83%
Kentucky	McConnell, Mitch	R	4	2/20/1942	64	Unopposed	65%
	Bunning, Jim	R	2	10/23/1931	75	84%	51%
Louisiana	Landrieu, Mary	D	2	11/23/1955	51	46%	52%
	Vitter, David	R	1	5/3/1961	45	—	51%
Massachusetts	Kennedy, Edward	D	8	2/22/1932	74	Unopposed	69%
	Kerry, John	D	4	12/11/1943	63	Unopposed	80%
Maryland	Mikulski, Barbara	D	4	7/20/1936	70	90%	65%
	Cardin, Ben	D	1	10/5/1943	63	44%	54%
Maine	Snowe, Olympia	R	3	2/21/1947	59	Unopposed	74%
	Collins, Susan	R	2	12/7/1952	54	Unopposed	58%
Michigan	Levin, Carl	D	5	6/28/1934	72	Unopposed	61%
	Stabenow, Debbie	D	2	4/29/1950	56	Unopposed	57%
Minnesota	Coleman, Norm	R	1	8/17/1949	57	94%	50%
	Klobuchar, Amy	D	1	5/25/1960	46	93%	58%

State	Senator	Party	Term	Birthdate	Age	% vote in previous election Primary	General
Missouri	Bond, Christopher	R	4	3/6/1939	67	88%	56%
	McCaskill, Claire	D	1	7/24/1953	53	80%	50%
Mississippi	Cochran, Thad	R	5	12/7/1937	69	Unopposed	85%
	Lott, Trent	R	4	10/9/1941	65	Unopposed	64%
Montana	Baucus, Max	D	5	12/11/1941	65	Unopposed	63%
	Tester, Jon	D	1	8/21/1956	50	61%	49%
North Carolina	Dole, Elizabeth	R	1	7/29/1936	70	80%	54%
	Burr, Richard	R	1	11/30/1955	51	88%	52%
North Dakota	Conrad, Kent	D	4	3/12/1948	58	Unopposed	69%
	Dorgan, Byron	D	3	5/14/1942	64	Unopposed	68%
Nebraska	Hagel, Chuck	R	2	10/4/1946	60	Unopposed	83%
	Nelson, Ben	D	2	5/17/1941	65	Unopposed	64%
New Hampshire	Gregg, Judd	R	3	2/14/1947	59	92%	66%
	Sununu, John	R	1	9/10/1964	42	53%	51%
New Jersey	Lautenberg, Frank	D	1	1/23/1924	82	Unopposed[b]	54%
	Menendez, Robert	D	1	1/1/1954	53	84%	53%
New Mexico	Domenici, Pete	R	6	5/7/1932	74	Unopposed	65%
	Bingaman, Jeff	D	5	10/3/1943	63	Unopposed	70%
Nevada	Reid, Harry	D	4	12/2/1939	67	Unopposed	61%
	Ensign, John	R	2	3/25/1958	48	90%	55%
New York	Schumer, Charles	D	2	11/23/1950	56	Unopposed	71%
	Clinton, Hillary Rodham	D	2	10/26/1947	59	83%	67%
Ohio	Voinovich, George	R	2	7/15/1936	70	77%	64%
	Brown, Sherrod	D	1	11/9/1952	54	77%	56%
Oklahoma	Inhofe, James	R	2	11/17/1934	72	Unopposed	57%
	Coburn, Tom	R	1	3/14/1948	58	61%	53%
Oregon	Wyden, Ron	D	2	5/3/1949	57	Unopposed	63%
	Smith, Gordon	R	2	5/25/1952	54	Unopposed	56%
Pennsylvania	Specter, Arlen	R	5	2/12/1930	76	51%	53%
	Casey, Robert, Jr.	D	1	4/13/1960	46	85%	59%
Rhode Island	Reed, Jack	D	2	11/12/1949	57	Unopposed	78%
	Whitehouse, Sheldon	D	1	10/20/1955	51	82%	53%
South Carolina	Graham, Lindsey	R	1	7/9/1955	51	Unopposed	54%
	DeMint, Jim	R	1	9/2/1951	55	59%[c]	54%
South Dakota	Johnson, Tim	D	2	12/28/1946	60	95%	50%
	Thune, John	R	1	1/7/1961	45	Unopposed	51%
Tennessee	Alexander, Lamar	R	1	7/3/1940	66	54%	54%
	Corker, Bob	R	1	8/24/1952	54	48%	51%
Texas	Hutchison, Kay Bailey	R	3	7/22/1943	63	Unopposed	62%
	Cornyn, John	R	1	2/2/1952	54	77%	55%
Utah	Hatch, Orrin	R	6	3/22/1934	72	Unopposed	63%
	Bennett, Robert	R	3	9/18/1933	73	Unopposed	69%
Virginia	Warner, John	R	5	2/18/1927	79	Unopposed	83%
	Webb, Jim	D	1	2/9/1946	60	53%	50%
Vermont	Leahy, Patrick	D	6	3/31/1940	66	95%	71%
	Sanders, Bernard	I	1	5/11/1934	72	95%[d]	65%

(continued)

Table A-4 (continued)

						% vote in previous election	
State	**Senator**	**Party**	**Term**	**Birthdate**	**Age**	**Primary**	**General**
Washington	Murray, Patty	D	3	10/11/1950	56	92%	55%
	Cantwell, Maria	D	2	10/13/1958	48	91%	57%
Wisconsin	Kohl, Herb	D	4	2/7/1935	71	85%	67%
	Feingold, Russell	D	3	3/2/1953	53	Unopposed	55%
West Virginia	Byrd, Robert	D	9	11/20/1917	89	86%	64%
	Rockefeller, Jay	D	4	6/18/1937	69	90%	63%
Wyoming	Thomas, Craig	R	3	2/17/1933	73	Unopposed	70%
	Enzi, Michael	R	2	2/1/1944	62	86%	73%

Note: Figures represent the makeup of the Senate on the first day of the 110th Congress.

a. Sen. Joe Lieberman lost his party's primary to Ned Lamont. He ran as an Independent in the general election.

b. Sen. Robert Torricelli was unopposed in his party's primary, but dropped out before the general election. Sen. Frank Lautenberg was picked by the state party to be the Democratic nominee in the general election.

c. Sen. Jim DeMint placed second in his party's primary, but won the runoff primary election with 59% of the vote.

d. Sen. Bernard Sanders was nominated by the Democratic Party with 95% of the vote in its primary, but he declined the nomination to run as an Independent.

Index